في ذكرى

مارك لينز

Pagan Christmas

Winter Feasts of the Kalasha of the Hindu Kush

Augusto S. Cacopardo

GINGKO
LIBRARY

First published in Italian by Sellerio editore as *Natale Pagano*
Copyright © 2010 Sellerio editore, Palermo

Revised and updated by the author for its publication in the United Kingdom, published by
Gingko Library
70 Cadogan Place
London SW1X 9AH

Copyright © Augusto S. Cacopardo 2016
Translation copyright © Augusto S. Cacopardo 2016

A CIP catalogue record for this book is available from the British Library.

ISBN 978 1 909942 84 4
eISBN 978 1 909942 85 1

Typeset in Times by MacGuru Ltd

Printed in Spain

www.gingkolibrary.com
@gingkolibrary

To little Martin who was born just as this book saw the light

To Amina, his mother
To the memory of my mother, Gianna

Contents

List of Maps

Map I – Peristan and surrounding countries.

Map II – The Chitral valley (south-western section) and the Nuristani valley of Bashgal. The thicker line in the middle indicates the border between Afghanistan and Pakistan.

Map III – The three Kalasha valleys and the upper part of the Bashgal valley, separated by the state border.

Map IV – The valley of Birir.

Maps I, II and III are portions of larger maps prepared by Alberto M. Cacopardo and drawn by Giovanni Mattioli in 2001. The physical features on the maps are based on the US Air Force Tactical Pilotage charts, 1:500.000 (St. Louis 1981), but several other sources have been used (see Cacopardo & Cacopardo 2001: 317). Map IV was prepared by Augusto S. Cacopardo and drawn by Giovanni Mattioli. It is based, for the physical part, on aerial photos available at the site http://www.bing.com/maps/; toponyms are mostly derived from direct observation.

II

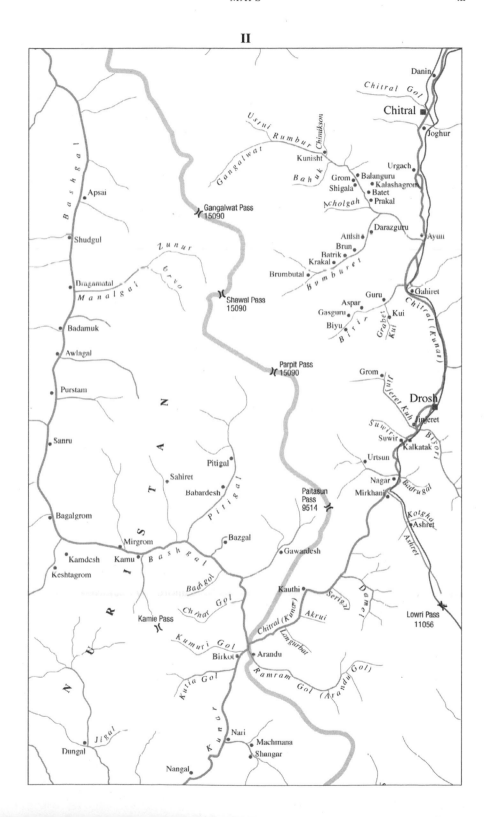

III

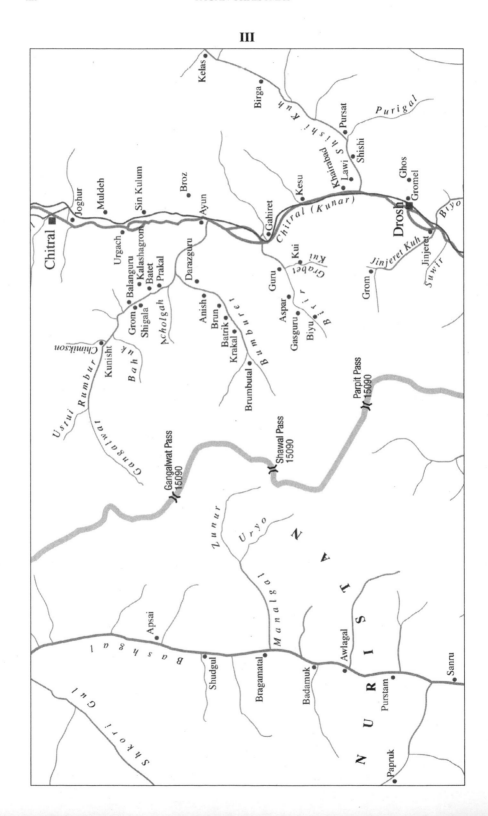

IV

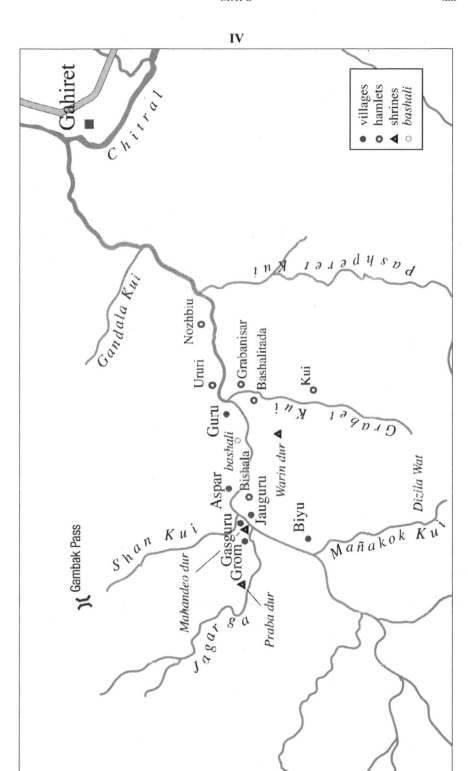

villages ●
hamlets ○
shrines ▲
bashali ○

Gahiret ■

Chitral

Gandala Kui

Pashperet Kui

Nozhbiu ○
Ururi ○
Guru ●
Grabanisar ○
Bashalitada
Kui ○

Grabet Kui

Aspar ●
bashali ○
Bishala ○
Jauguru ●
Warin dur ▲
Biyu ●
Dizila Wat

Gasguru ●
Grom ▲

Shan Kui

Mahandeo dur

)(Gambak Pass

Jagarga

Praba dur

Mañakok Kui

Acknowledgements

Many people have contributed in different ways to the research on which this work is based, both in Pakistan and in Italy.

In Pakistan I must thank first of all my hosts and my friends in Birir. Without their cooperation this work would not have been possible. I am especially grateful to my host Erfan and to his wife, to Baras Khan, my main assistant, to Danok and Gulistan who cooperated with me with dedication for the whole time of my research, to Ala-ud-din and Gulfurus, who helped me in various ways, and to *kaz'i* Saidan Shah, a true expert in Kalasha tradition. My thought goes also to old Sherbek, he too a guardian of tradition, always available for long conversations, who is no longer with us. I must thank also the women of Guru Village who, in the most sacred night of the Lagaur festival, implored on my behalf the White Crow to give me soon a son (a prayer that was fulfilled). Apart from my hosts and friends in Birir, several other people offered me assistance in the Kalasha valleys. I want to remember the late Shah Juwan, my first host and assistant in Rumbur, and Lader Khan, my fraternal friend, who led me into the world of the high summer pastures. The complete list would be too long. I heartily thank everybody.

In Italy I owe gratitude to Antonino Buttitta, anthropologist at the University of Palermo, who gave both friendly encouragement and vital support to my research, as well as to Lucio Melazzo, linguist in that same university, who was also very helpful. I must recall the late Gherardo Gnoli, former President of the Istituto Italiano per l'Africa e l'Oriente (IsIAO) which partially funded my project, covering my travel expenses with money made available by the Italian Ministry of Foreign Affairs. For precious assistance in the reading of works in German I am grateful to my old friend Mario Gulli and to Alberto M. Cacopardo, my brother, himself a scholar of the Hindu Kush, who also commented on a former version of this work (the responsibility for any shortcomings is, of course, my own) and prepared most of the maps. I want to recall also the support of Silvia Lelli, friend and colleague, who assisted me in one of my field trips. I am grateful to Pierpaolo

Di Carlo, the linguist in our research team, for his generous assistance with questions concerning linguistics and Indo-European studies. The cooperation of my colleague ethnographer and friend Martino Nicoletti was also important; while in Pakistan on a project of his own, he joined me in Birir to film the events of the four central days of the winter solstice festival. For the realization of this English edition I owe a lot to the support of my dear old student Edoardo Braschi. A final expression of gratitude goes to my wife, Amina De Napoli, who personally took care of various tasks concerning my research – including the ordering of the bibliographic references – and supported me enormously in all possible ways.

Note on Transliteration

Capital letters are used in Kalasha words to express a retroflex articulation, which in the Kalasha language occurs not only in consonants but also in vowels. < sh > represents the voiceless palatal-alveolar fricative (< S > in its retroflex version), < zh > its voiced counterpart, but all other consonants followed by an < h > are to be considered aspirated; < y > represents the palatal approximant and < w > the voiced labiovelar approximant. All the other phones are transcribed according to Masica's (1991: XV–XVI) Standard Orientalist Transcription, including the voiceless palatal-alveolar affricate expressed with < c >. Nasalization is expressed with ~ following the nasal letter. Since thorough studies of Kalasha syllabification are still lacking, stress is marked by the symbol < ' > in front of the stressed vowel and not, as in the International Phonetic Alphabet, in front of the stressed syllable.

Glossary of Kalasha Words Used in the Text

'aya: mother
ajh'ona: guest
aLaS'in~g: marriage by elopement
'an~ak: short-legged stool
arw'a: sprits of the dead
at'aLaka: plateau
a'u: bread
b'aba: sister
b'aya: brother
balima'in: Visitor god of Chaumos (in Bumburet/Rumbur)
bash'ali: menstruation and birthing house
b'aira: member of impure servant caste
bal'a: down-valley evil spirits
baSzhu'aw: eaters of a share (epithet of gods)
b'asun: spring
baz'a: hand
b'eu: willow
bi: seed
hidrakal'en: name given in a chant to the Visitor god of Chaumos
bih'ik: to be afraid
biram'or: the main merit feast
biT'Oik: the shrugging of the sacrificial victim signalling its assent
bonj: evergreen oak (*quercus balut*)
bhut: spirits living near torrents and mills
bhut: trousers
bhumk'i: autoctonous

buD'aLak: fecundating shepherd of the Prun (*pU~*) festival (only in Birir)

ca~: the most lively type of dance

c'Ahaka: thick bread cake

c'ay: tea

caman'i: cheese

Can~J'a: long ceremonial torch

cap'an: coat of honour

caum'os: winter solstice festival.

ceL'ik: woollen white dress, female style, worn by male children at the first stage of their initiation

cik: funeral

chu: daughter

d'ada: father

Da: wine

daran'O~: roofed shelter located on the terraced roof of goat sheds

d'ashak bhut: ceremonial trousers

dah'u: drum

daSg'oraLa: a god of Bumburet

dast'ur: tradition

dA'u: beans

deh'ar: shaman

desh: country

d'ewa dur: altar (lit. 'house of the god')

dewal'ok: god

dewasam'E~a: Chaumos celebration

diC: period of sexual abstinence and seclusion from the external world (in Bumburet/Rumbur during Chaumos)

D'izila D'izaw: Creator god

don: bull

dr'ay: large open-ended basket for drying maize

drazha'ilak: a style of dance

dram'i: terraced roof

dup'uri: two-storied

d'ushak: a style of dance

ghaC: secret prayer

ganD'aw: wooden ancestor statue

ganD'alik: little wooden statue

gad'erak: elder

gand'uriak: fragrance

ghul: game with bats and ball (only on snow)

gher'ek: rotate

ghO~: song, chant

gh'ona: big, large

goST: goat-shed

goSTj'uzhi: large bread cake to be brought to the goat sheds for Lagaur

granz'uliak: chain-dance

gren: knot

gri: open-air dancing ground

grom: village

g'Uak: boy

gum: wheat

gund'ik. walking stick

han: house (in Birir), temple (in Bumburet/Rumbur)

hansar'ik: celebration for the completion of a new house

h'arik: to take or take away something (inanimate)

h'Iia: heart

ishtik'ek: eulogy

idrO~: rainbow

idrO~zh: intestine

indr: god of Chaumos

indr'eyn: holy place dedicated to Balimain in Bumburet

ishper'i: ritual meal with bread and cheese

ishp'on~ak: ceremonial food (flour cooked in meat broth)

ist'on~gas: male initiation and purification rite

JaC: name of a divinity

ja~: walnut mush

jA~'u: bread-cake filled with walnut mush

jam'ili: term designating the married women of an exogamous patrilineal lineage

jhan'i: winter celebration for little girls

jhes: feast celebrating the delivery of dowry goods

j'ita!: hail!

kam: lineage

kaS'on~g: woollen hat

k'aw: year

khaltab'ar: affines

kh'aw: threshing floor
kw'erik: pine tree
kot: fortress, castle
krom: work
kumbAp'ur: intercrossing roof
kumbA'uchak: doll
kup'as: female ceremonial headdress
k'ushala: clever, ingenious
kush'un: family group composed of all those who eat together
kush'urik: small ceremonial loaves
kutaw'ati: woollen leggings
kwat: energy
La~ST: level
Law'ak: fox
laga'ur: winter feast following Chaumos (only in Birir)
L'udrum gaD'ulai: special ceremonial necklace
mad'ir: shelf running along the back wall of houses
magl'is: circle of singers
mahand'eo: god with altars in all the three valleys
m'Aka: married men, as such considered impure
mal: bride price
manDawj'aw: graveyard
mar'at: animal sacrifice
mastr'uk: moon, month
m'oa: maternal uncle
mraCw'aki: spring celebration
namus'i moc: marvellous man (title of rank)
nash'a: drunk
nat: dance
naw'au: grandchild
nish'an: sign, mark
nom nom'ek: sung eulogy (lit. 'to name the names')
non~g: monstrous serpent spirit
nog'or: fortress, castle
'onjiSTa: pure
'onjiSTa mar'at: holocaust
pac'ek: to cook
paC'ew: bat for *ghal* game

pakt'i: cooked rice

par'ik: to go

pishm'otray: homosexuality

pr'aba: god of Birir

prac'ona: clarified butter

pr'agata: impure (Bumburet/Rumbur dialect)

pr'EA: spleen

prec'esh: type of sacrifice, a type of merit feast

pr'enaw: down-valley

prinz: wooden ball for playing *ghal*

pU~: autumn feast (only in Birir)

p'ushaw: divinity accompanying Balimain

putr: son

ra'istam: end-of-winter feast (only in Birir)

r'ela: impure (Birir dialect)

rikh'ini: village temple (Birir dialect)

r'oy: yearly-appointed functionaries guarding the crops (in Birir)

ruzh'i: witch

S'abaS!: bravo!

sad'ar: mantle

sambar'i: cheese and walnut mush dish

sat'ar: main roof-beam of a house

sajig'or: god of Rumbur

salgher'ek: New Year celebration

sambi'ek: to dress

samb'iik: to wear

s'araz: juniper

sari'ek: feast for the delivery of the dowry in grandiose form

sh'ara b'ira: markhor (*capra falconeri*)

sharabir'ayak: bread animal figurines

sharacat'aki nat: markhor dance

shish'oyak: beautiful

SaT'ek: to light a fire, to set on fire

she~he~: so

shish a'u: female initiation and purification rite

sho~g: bough

sh'ura: brave

sh'ura moc: valiant man (title of rank)

soh'olyak: flower-covered conical headdress worn by girls for a ritual of Prun festival (Birir)

s'uda: boy

s'uci: mountain spirits

suc'ek: ritually purify, sanctify

s'uri: sun

suw'al: prayer

tas'iLi: thin bread-cake

tsip'ana: meat and walnut mush dish

uc'aw: end-of-summer feast marking the return of the herds from the transhumance

ucund'ik: to descend, to come down

uk: water

un~gush'ek: to excite, to anger

up'hor: ritual dance of the victorious warrior

'ushak: ritually pure flour

war'in: god of Birir

w'enaw: up-valley

zar'ori: mistletoe

zh'An~gu: liver

zh'awik: to have sexual intercourse

zh'ew: transhumance

zh'oshi: main spring celebration

Introduction

The Kalasha and the objectives of the present research

The topic of this book is a great ritual cycle celebrated by the Kalasha people of Chitral in north-western Pakistan, a small population of mountain dwellers of special interest not only for anthropology but also for religious studies and Indo-European studies, because it offers the only living example of Indo-European 'paganism' or, we may say, of a 'tribal' Indo-European religion.[1] It is indeed the only religion practised by speakers of an Indo-European language that was never absorbed by any of the great historical religious traditions – Buddhism, Hinduism, Zoroastrianism, Christianity, Islam – that have moulded the thought and the social organizations of all other peoples belonging to that large linguistic family.[2]

The Kalasha are the last polytheistic[3] people of the Hindu Kush, the Paropamisos of the ancient Greeks, i.e. the westernmost end of the great Asian mountain chain rising from the Iranian Plateau and stretching eastward across Afghanistan and northern Pakistan, finally joining the Karakoram range in the heights of the Pamir massif on the borders of Kashmir. The sole non-Islamized island in the vast Muslim ocean extending from Turkey to India, the Kalasha are the last shred

---

1 The statement that the Kalasha are the last example of Indo-European 'paganism' or polytheism, is actually not quite correct because Hinduism is also a polytheistic religion practiced by speakers of Indo-European languages seen as 'infidels' (and therefore 'pagans') by Muslims. The expression 'tribal Indo-European religion', in spite of the well known objections to the use of terms like 'tribe' or 'tribal' seems to better convey the gist of the phenomenon we are dealing with.

2 As it is well known, the concept of 'Indo-European' is strictly linguistic and not racial. The concept itself of race, on the other hand, is seen today as highly problematic by geneticists (Cavalli-Sforza 1996: 50–8).

3 However, as it will be explained in detail further on the Kalasha of today do not see themselves as polytheistic, due to a not-so-recent reinterpretation of their religion in monotheistic terms.

of a vast and multifarious polytheistic world, predominantly of Indo-European language, that occupied a large part of the Hindu Kush/Karakoram chain until two centuries ago, when it gradually started to convert to Islam. They are only a few thousand in number, settled in three small valleys wedged in among the mountains of north-western Pakistan along the Afghan border at altitudes just below 6,000 feet. They speak Kalashamon, an eastern Indo-European language of the Indo-Aryan branch belonging to the Dardic group, and they practice a religion with roots harking back to pre-Vedic times, i.e., to the earliest stages of the Indo-European world.

The knowledge of Kalasha culture, therefore, can on the one hand, like that of all traditional cultures, reveal manifestations of human potentials that differ from those developed historically in the urban-centred civilizations to which we ourselves belong. But on the other hand, at a more specific level, it can also give a precious contribution to the understanding of those Indo-European cultural and religious forms that preceded the advent of the great religions and that are at the roots of our civilization: from Greek, Celtic and Germanic polytheism to ancient Iranian or Vedic religion. Furthermore, Kalasha rituality can also help us to better understand the enduring influences of those religious systems on the folklore and the popular religiosity of Eurasia.

The core of Kalasha religion is a symbolic system that contains a fully-fledged cosmology finely expressed in the language of ritual. The system is orthopraxic rather than orthodoxic, based, that is, more on the respect of a code of behaviour – mainly ritualistic – than on the adherence to a set of beliefs.[4] The present work is, therefore, in the first place a study in the anthropology of ritual. Field research was concentrated especially on the winter ritual cycle, focussed on the solstice celebrations. The grand festal complex of the winter solstice – the Chaumos (*caum'os*) – is the fulcrum of the Kalasha ritual system and it enshrines the ideal values inspiring the whole culture. It is one of those 'great cultural representations' in which the ethos and spiritual consciousness of a community is expressed (Geertz [1973] 1987: 167–8).

The analysis of Chaumos represents, therefore, in the first place a privileged key for the interpretation of Kalasha culture. In the second place – a perspective expressed in the oxymoron we have chosen for a title – it may help us to better understand the pre-Christian roots of our December feasts, because it is a widely-shared opinion[5] that the Christian festivities focused on Christmas are

---

4 For a detailed discussion of this distinction see Bell 1997: 191–7.
5 Miles ([1912] 1976: 23–4 and Part II; Frazer ([1922] 1987: 358–609; Propp 1963: 32; Motz 1984:

superimposed on pagan ritual cycles – Celtic, Germanic, Slavic, Italic – of the winter season. Finally, in the third place, the analysis of Chaumos can enrich with new data the study of the 'great feast' (Lanternari [1976] 1983a), the New Year festival that plays a central role in the ritual systems of many people world-wide, and may help to formulate some generalizations about it. In addition, it could perhaps provide as well some useful elements to evaluate whether it may be possible, or not, to detect the contours, blurry as they may be, of a specifically Indo-European form of this great celebration.

The background: early research on Chaumos

The origins of the present research date back to over forty years ago, precisely to September 1973, when, in my early twenties, I travelled overland to north-western Pakistan for my first field research among the Kalasha of Chitral.

A journey of this kind, from Europe to India overland by public transport, was not something exceptional then: in those years, when in the eyes of a traveller nothing seemed to predict the wars that were to upset the region in the following decades, many young people from Western Europe and America followed that itinerary across Turkey, Iran, Afghanistan and Pakistan, attracted by the exotic fascination of India. I was a member of a small, self-funded research team. My companions were Manuela Borriello and my brother Alberto M. Cacopardo, both students, like myself, at the University of Florence, Italy. Ethnographic research among the Kalasha, in those days, was still taking its first steps: although their valleys had already been visited by a linguistic mission in 1929 and by four ethno-graphic expeditions between 1948 and 1960,[6] scientific literature on the Kalasha amounted to only a few articles, at that point several years old;[7] no researcher had visited them for over a decade. For all we knew at the moment of our departure, the last polytheists of the Hindu Kush could very well have all converted.

In those days the Kalasha valleys – Birir, Bumburet and Rumbur[8] – could be

---

159; Cattabiani 1988: 69–71; Cardini 1995: 47, 107; Hutton 1996: 1–8; Bell 1997: 216; Rappaport 1999: 338–9.

6 A Danish one in 1948, a German one in 1955–6, and two Italian ones, in 1955 and 1960.

7 Morgenstierne 1947a, 1965; Siiger 1956, 1963, 1967; Snoy 1959, 1960, 1965; Graziosi 1961, 1964.

8 These are the names of the valleys in Khowar, the main language of Chitral District, which have long become established in the literature. The Kalasha names are *bir'iu, mumur'et, rukm'u*. We prefer as a rule to stick to the established names because, otherwise, the names of all

reached only on foot following rugged mountain trails branching west from the main valley of the Chitral/Kunar river, a tributary of the Kabul river. But they were certainly not inaccessible. From Chitral town, the capital of the District, the mouths of the valleys could be reached in less than two hours by jeep and from there after a march of five or six hours the first villages would come into sight.

Adopting a new (for the Hindu Kush) style of research (also more in keeping with our meagre budgets), as compared to that of the official expeditions that had preceded us – which normally included a cook, an interpreter/guide and some porters carrying provisions so that the group could manage its own lodging – we entered the Kalasha valleys with no guide or interpreter, our backpacks on our shoulders, counting on the hospitality of the people. We had the plan to concentrate all our efforts at first on learning the language. Nobody in the valleys spoke English then, and the study of the Kalasha language had only just begun; we could count only on the help of a single pioneering linguistic publication (Morgenstierne 1965).

We started our tour from the southernmost valley of Birir, the very same one to which the present research is dedicated. We toured the three valleys on foot, always welcomed in the most hospitable way. When we came in sight of a village, a band of children would usually gather around to greet us and lead us to the one house that was often the only home that had room to accommodate us. Victims for centuries of the contempt of their Muslim neighbours, the Kalasha people seemed happy to meet non-Muslim foreigners who appeared to value their way of living.

With no roads in the valleys, there was no electricity in the villages or any form of running water. Pine-torches or some rare kerosene lanterns were used to light up the night, and there were no fountains or toilets. The women used to carry water to the villages from the stream, and for bodily functions there were the fields. There were no hotels, and money, though certainly not unknown, was rarely used. In each of the three valleys there was a little primary school, but the pupils were few; in total, no more than a dozen Kalasha children attended the classes.

We settled at last in the valley of Rumbur, which was considered the strongest bastion of polytheism for the reason that it had the lowest number of converts. We were just beginning to get acquainted with our surroundings and to make our first steps in the practice of the language when, at the beginning of November, we were suddenly caught up in a whirlpool of ritual activities of a social character – two important merit feasts connected to the marriage system – that opened the way to Chaumos, the great winter solstice festival, which started in early December.

---

places mentioned should be expressed in the local language, which could generate confusion or perplexity in the reader.

Between preparations and celebrations, the festival continued for the whole month of December and culminated, at the time of the solstice, in a massive sacrifice of billy goats at the shrine of one of the main local divinities, followed, the next night, by singing and dancing around a huge bonfire, at the centre of a clearing where the shaman led a phallic dance holding a huge torch between his legs until he went into a trance to communicate with the solar deity believed to visit the valleys in the course of that most holy night.

The reader can perhaps imagine the impression made by that great celebration on young people in their twenties, born and raised in a Western city, as we were. No scientific description existed yet of Chaumos. The only available writing was a brief and imprecise account of an adventurous journalist – Tchecov Mirne – who had taken part in the festival the year before.[9] We were the first (would-be) ethnographers to participate in that great ritual event in the valley of Rumbur.

The very first ethnographers, and most likely also the first Westerners, to witness a Kalasha winter solstice festival were the German anthropologists Adolf Friedrich and Peter Snoy, who spent the fall and winter of 1955–6 in the Bumburet valley, as members of the Deutsche Hindukusch Expedition. The conclusion of their mission was unfortunate. In winter, the entire District of Chitral remains isolated from the rest of the country due to the closure of the high mountain passes,[10] and the Kalasha valleys were only connected then (as was still the case in the 1970s) to the main valley by rugged mountain paths. Seriously ill, Friedrich had to leave the valleys and met his death in a Rawalpindi hospital after being carried on a stretcher over the 10,000-foot high Lowari pass still covered in snow (Buddruss and Snoy 2008: 11–14). For the locals his tragic end was due to a serious ritual violation: according to a story still told today,[11] he had surreptitiously approached – without having undergone the necessary rite of purification – the main sanctuary of the valley while the most sacred ritual of the winter solstice festival was being performed.

In spite of Friedrich's and Snoy's work, however, the Chaumos festival remained completely unknown to researchers for twenty more years, for the

---

9 *L'Europeo*, summer 1973.

10 There was no air connection with Peshawar in those times, as there is today (subject as it is to weather conditions).

11 It was told in 2006 to Alberto M. Cacopardo by Abdul Khalik of Krakar village, Bumburet valley, who had heard it from his father Sumal Beg, a prominent elder at the time of Friedrich and Snoy's visit (Cacopardo A.M. 2006: 479). The same story, in a slightly different version, is related by Snoy in a recent article (Buddruss and Snoy 2008: 14).

materials collected by the two German ethnographers were only published in 1975 when they were (in part) included in Karl Jettmar's[12] comprehensive work on the religions of the Hindu Kush (Jettmar 1975), while a first-hand account by Snoy appeared only in 2008, more then fifty years after the conclusion of the German expedition. After 1955, no other ethnographer participated in a Chaumos until 1973, when, in addition to our little research group settled in Rumbur, the Kalasha were visited by the Austrian Karl Wutt who, like Friedrich and Snoy, participated in the Bumburet festival.

In the course of the 1970s and 1980s other ethnographers visited the valleys. Just about all researchers focussed their fieldwork on the valley of Rumbur, which appeared to everyone, as it had appeared to us, as the most solid bastion of the polytheistic religion that gave Kalasha culture its special fascination. The Chaumos festivals of Rumbur and Bumburet – which, as we shall see, differ only slightly – were gradually documented,[13] and in the course of the years the general ethnographies of the Rumbur and Bumburet communities were investigated at length.[14]

The valley of Birir and the present research

Though the Kalasha number no more than 4,000 souls, we are not dealing with a homogenous cultural universe, tiny as it may be. There are, in fact, two distinct varieties of Kalasha culture: that of the two northern valleys of Rumbur and Bumburet, and that of the southern valley of Birir. Even if in the general frame of a clearly recognizable common model, the cultural differences between the two are quite remarkable. They concern in the first place the ritual system, and particularly the cycle of seasonal festivals; in Birir there are festivals unknown in the other two valleys, and even those that correspond in name and time of the year often display a very different morphology; especially noteworthy are the differences in the morphology of Chaumos. The Kalasha world, small as it is, offers, therefore,

---

12 Karl Jettmar, who later became a leading scholar in Hindu Kush studies, was also a member of the German Hindu Kush Expedition but worked in other areas of Northern Pakistan. See Buddruss & Snoy 2008.

13 See especially Loude & Lièvre 1984; but also Cacopardo A.S. 1974, 1985; Wutt 1983; Cacopardo & Cacopardo 1989.

14 In addition to the works on Chaumos indicated in the preceding footnote, see Cacopardo A.M. 1974, 1985; Wutt 1976; Cacopardo & Cacopardo 1977; Darling 1979; Loude 1980, 1982; Loude & Lièvre 1987; Lièvre & Loude 1990, 1991; Lièvre 1996; Parkes 1983, 1987, 1991, 1992, 1994, 1996, 1997, 2008; Glavind Sperber 1995, 1996, 2008; Maggi 2001, 2008; Cacopardo A.S. 2006; Klimburg 2008a, 2008b; Fentz 2010.

two quite distinct examples of the non-Muslim cultures of the Hindu Kush, and not just one as was initially thought. To this cultural distinction corresponds also a quite neat linguistic distinction: though the two dialects are mutually intelligible, they present clearly perceptible phonological and lexical differences.[15] While the northern communities are by now fairly well known, research in the southern one has only recently made some progress.

If the valley of Birir was overlooked by researchers this is probably due to the fact that its culture was seen as a secondary variant of the main model – which was considered to be that of Bumburet/Rumbur – more exposed also to Islamic influences, with its high percentage of converts in the total population. Both reasons were, in fact, quite unfounded. In spite of the high number of converts, Birir is actually the more conservative of the three communities. Moreover, research conducted in the 1990s in the neighbouring valleys of south Chitral among Kalasha communities that had long been converted to Islam,[16] has shown that in the past the typical model of the area was that of Birir, and that possibly it was the northern model that can be seen as a marginal variant.

In spite of this renewed perspective, however, the southern valley continued to be neglected with the awkward result that, at almost a century from the first ethnographic investigations, a cultural universe as small as that of the Kalasha was still not completely known. Even the winter solstice festival of Birir had not been documented until 2006–7, when the present research was conducted.

The winter feasts of Birir are carried out in a long ritual sequence focussed on the winter solstice festival, formed by a series of ritual events that take place at intervals of one or two weeks from December to February. My field research has covered this whole span of time, lasting, therefore, almost four months, from November 2006 to February 2007; but the project could not have been carried out without the knowledge of the Kalasha language and culture I had acquired in the course of a number of former visits to the valleys.[17]

---

15 On Kalasha dialects see Morgenstierne 1932: 52–3, 1965: 187–8; Cacopardo A.M. 1991: 281–4; Decker 1992: 104–6; Mørch 2000; Di Carlo 2010b: 12–13.
16 Cacopardo A.M. 1991, 1996; Cacopardo & Cacopardo 1992, 1996; Cacopardo A.S. 1991, 1996.
17 Before 2006, field trips to the Kalasha valleys and surrounding areas, lasting from one month to seven months, were taken by the author in 1973, 1977, 1989, 1990, 1993 and 1995; Alberto M. Cacopardo accompanied the author on all of these trips apart from the one in 1977. Starting from 1990 the two researchers worked under the aegis of the Istituto Italiano per l'Africa e l'Oriente of Rome (Is.I.A.O. ex-Is.M.E.O.) with funds provided by the Italian National Council of Research (C.N.R.) and by the Ministry for Foreign Affairs.

The present volume is divided in three parts that differ stylistically, on account of the different functions they play in the overall plan of the work. The focal one is the second section, devoted to the description and analysis of Chaumos and of the other feasts that compose the winter sequence (Part II, Chapters 4 and 5). Here the style adopted is that of chronological narration in the first person based on the field journal, so as to give a representation of the events as close as possible to the concrete experience lived by the author, and to allow the reader to follow the itinerary of the research. The chronological narration is accompanied by interpretations of the rites based on data collected through participant observation, as well as on the texts recorded in the field, which are interspersed in the narrative as the various ritual events occur. Since a rite is not a mere succession of acts, but a complex event in which acts and words are indissolubly intertwined in the production of meanings, participant observation was coupled with systematic linguistic documentation work concerning the words of the rituals.[18] Due to the length and complexity of the ritual cycle analyzed, the reader may find it difficult to visualize in a single picture the whole series of events. An obvious need for ethnographic accuracy has prevented us from simplifying our account, but to help the reader to find his/her way through the labyrinth of the ritual events, we offer in an appendix a table in which the entire sequence of the Birir winter feasts is summed up in a schematic way (see Appendix). One more chapter (Chapter 6), in which the narrative style is set aside, completes this second section of the volume by tracing the relations between the Chaumos of Birir and that of the two northern valleys and proposing an overall interpretation of the Kalasha symbolic system.

As for the first section (Part I) of the book, it has an introductory function. It is written in a descriptive rather than narrative style because it has the purpose of outlining the broader historical and cultural context of the ritual system under study.[19] It is composed of three chapters in which the general context is outlined by

---

18 A large part of the chants and prayers accompanying the rituals were recorded. The texts were transcribed in the Kalasha language in the field and subsequently translated in an interlinear form (parsing) with the support of the software *Toolbox for Linguists*. The materials included in this work are only a part of the transcribed material, which, in its turn, is only a part of the material recorded, which amounts to a total of 28 hours and 29 minutes. Only English translations are presented in this volume, but the Kalasha originals in an interlinear form are published in Cacopardo A.S. 2008 and 2010.

19 Following a recently rediscovered practice, which is certainly not an invention of modern (or postmodern) ethnography (Pratt 1986: 33), we have combined both description and narration in our account. It is a practice that has also an important precedent in the literature on our area because it was adopted by Col. George Scott Robertson in his seminal book *The Kafirs of the Hindu Kush* (Robertson 1896).

gradually narrowing the field of attention. The first chapter (Chapter 1) describes the broader historical, political and socio-cultural context of the Hindu Kush/ Karakoram region and of Chitral in particular. The second one (Chapter 2) synthetically outlines traditional Kalasha culture focussing in succession on the economic, the symbolic and the religious systems. In the third one (Chapter 3) the social structure of the Birir community is described and a synthetic outline is given of the annual ritual cycle of which the Chaumos festival is the focal point.

The third and last section of the volume (Part III) is dedicated to intercultural connections and is composed of three chapters that deal – certainly with no claim to exhaustiveness – with the Indian world (Chapter 7), with archaic Europe (Chapter 8) and with the Proto-Indo-Europeans (Chapter 9). The reader is thus offered a broad comparative overview that takes, however, only a few steps on paths still almost untrodden (apart from the Indian world) by Hindu Kush scholars, and which has the main objective of suggesting new directions for future research. But before directly broaching our subject we must make explicit the perspective we adopted. A cultural analysis in general, and the interpretation of a ritual event in particular – especially as rich and complex as the one this work deals with – pose indeed a number of theoretical problems that cannot be overlooked and that need to be pre-emptively examined.[20]

Theoretical approaches

First of all I must acknowledge that this research is not quite in line with the current dominant trends in anthropology. The study of traditional societies, the peculiarity of anthropology at its beginning and for a long time afterwards, has recently lost appeal in favour of an interest for the 'contemporary'. Though peoples like the Kalasha are obviously recognized as our chronological contemporaries, their worlds now tend to be seen as survivors from a distant past that, apparently, is no longer considered to have much to say to our post-industrial world. Hence a flourishing of ethnographies of the contemporary, aiming at gaining new insights into arenas of contemporary life, such as corporations, the military, the media, video games and virtual reality, science or public administration – looking, in other words, at places closer to home. Francesco Remotti, a senior Italian anthropologist, has recently argued in favour of what he has called an 'in-actual anthropology' (Remotti 2013: 43–6), contrasting it with this recent 'contemporaneist' trend

---

20 Readers anxious to plunge themselves into the world of the Hindu Kush may skip the following three paragraphs, to go back to them whenever they will feel the need to do so.

that, in his view, though undoubtedly useful and legitimate, is discarding the precious heritage of classical anthropological studies. He believes, in contrast, that
there is still scope, not as an alternative to, but alongside this attraction for con-
temporaneousness, for the classical endeavour of anthropology, i.e. that of looking
afar in search of the Other, in space and in time. Even salvage ethnography, an
obsolete genre, he remarks, still makes sense (ibid.: 39–40). I agree. Indeed, at
a time when traditional societies are changing more rapidly than ever and non-
literate societies are quickly becoming literate – a process I have witnessed with
my own eyes among the Kalasha – the wealth of disappearing cultural data to
be recorded is only increasing. As an evolutionary biologist like Jared Diamond
has argued in a book (Diamond 2012) that draws a lot from anthropology and is
based on an idea that, Remotti (ibid.: 102–4) remarks, should maybe have come
first to an anthropologist, there is in general a lot we can still learn from traditional
societies – both for what they were and, we may acknowledge, for what they are
becoming. Indeed, fortunately the world is not turning into a homogenous block.
Cultural responses to the impact of modernity are extremely varied. New forms
of cultural *métissages* are arising. These have rightfully attracted the interest of
anthropologists. But enticing as the new may in some cases be, this does not
imply that the old is no longer worth investigating. The contribution it can give
to cultural critique, to the critical appraisal of our own world – an old ambition of
anthropology (Marcus & Fischer 1986: 111–68) – is in many respects irreplace-
able. *Le regard eloigné* is still precious. Among the Kalasha, great changes are
occurring today. I hear from my friends that computers and mobile phones are
now entering the valleys.[21] A study of the attitude of the younger generations faced
with the impact of modernity could be, of course, of great interest, and should be
carried out, but it is just as interesting, and maybe more crucial, to look backwards
to capture the last flash of an ancient cultural model that, as we shall see, has still
much to say to us.

From another aspect, this work departs from an established trend, dating from
the 1980s. Since then, it has become an imperative for ethnographers to delve
into the question of their interaction with the subjects of their research, to the
point of making it, at times, the main topic of their work. Epistemologically it
is an important theme, because it sheds light on the circumstances at the source
of the anthropologist's knowledge. Therefore, it is not absent from this research,

---

21 Just last week the son of one of them called me with his mobile from the dancing ground
during the Joshi spring festival, something neither he nor I would have imagined ever being
possible in the 1970s.

but is mostly referred to only indirectly. It will emerge essentially in the second, central, section of the volume, where my fieldwork experience is related in the first person, the role of my collaborators is described and my relations with the people become manifest. However, even there, by not focussing specifically on the ethnographer/actors interaction, the subjective dimension of the ethnographic experience remains somewhat in the backstage. It is a choice. Given the objectives indicated at the beginning, it seemed to me that the confessional mode often adopted in ethnographic writings in the wake of the epistemological debate triggered by postmodernism would have been out of place.

While adopting a rather different approach I do not mean, however, to underestimate the import of that debate. I believe that, though somewhat paradoxically, the postmodern critique of the neo-positivist stand in anthropology has produced some worthy contributions to the scientific quality of ethnographic research, especially with regard to the validity of ethnographic representations, the grounded quality of an ethnographic work.[22] We have, for example, the work of Roger Sanjek, a distinguished US anthropologist, who has argued in an important essay that if in ethnography you cannot evaluate the reliability of an account – as you can with the results of an experiment, which, if repeated by different researchers, gives the same outcome – you can, however, evaluate its validity, i.e. the extent to which the argument presented is supported by the evidence displayed. Indeed for him validity, rather than reliability, 'lies at the core of evaluating ethnography' (Sanjek 1990: 392–5).

The history of ethnographic research among the Kalasha, actually, appears to contradict the idea that reliability cannot be assessed, because, at least for what concerns the ideology underlying their symbolic system – the traditional vision described in Chapter 2 – separate researchers of different nationalities who were not in contact with each other, issued from different schools, described it in quite similar terms (compare Parkes 1987 and Cacopardo A.M. 1985), something not altogether surprising if we consider – as historians say of their discipline – that if there may not be an ethnographic truth, there are ethnographic facts.[23]

Nevertheless, Sanjek's reflection is meaningful: even if it can be argued, as just seen, that reliability may not be un verifiable in absolute terms, it certainly can be assessed only rarely, while validity can much more easily (for Sanjek even

---

22 Sanjek 1990: 395–404; Olivier de Sardan 1995; Fabietti 1999: 84–5.
23 Here my position coincides with that of the British-Czech philosopher and social anthropologist Ernest Gellner (1995: 6) who has argued that truth is unique though nobody possesses it and though it is never available with finality.

more aptly) be referred to for the evaluation of an ethnographic account. Let us see how.

Sanjek (1990: 395–404) indicates three canons on which such an evaluation should be based: (a) theoretical candour; (b) portrayal of the ethnographer's path; (c) fieldnote evidence. If the reader is informed about the theoretical stand of the ethnographer, about the processes through which the data presented were collected, and if he/she will find these data quoted in the crucial points of the text, he/she will no doubt be in a better position to judge to what extent the representation offered by the author is actually supported by the materials he/she presents. To apply the first canon I shall try to illustrate in this introduction my theoretical perspective and its rationale (and to some extent I have already begun to do so). The network of social relations I was involved in, the informants I worked with, and the conditions I worked in, are described at the beginning of Part II, while the use of the first person in the narration, will hopefully give an idea of how the research was conducted, and therefore of the ethnographer's path. Finally, the texts recorded in the field and the excerpts from my field journal will put the reader in contact with the most immediate data, the ones closer to the event. I hope he/she will be thus in the condition to assess the ethnographic validity of my account.

Hence, to apply Sanjek's first canon let us now examine the question of the interpretation of ritual and, more generally, of a symbolic system, so that the theoretical approach adopted may be clear to the reader.

Problems of interpretation

The issue of the interpretation of ritual is certainly not new, since it has been widely discussed from the very beginnings of anthropology. If we reject positions like that of Frits Staal who believes that ritual has no meaning or aim outside of itself (Staal 1979: 9), the question arises of where should the meaning of ritual be sought: in the interpretations of the actors or in the ritual acts themselves? In broader terms it is the question of the relation between the interpretations of the subjects, the so-called 'native interpretations', and the interpretations of the anthropologist. Should the latter adhere to the former? Or can they be completely detached from them? The second option appears already in the writings of Robertson Smith, who observes that the 'real' purpose and meaning of ritual may at times differ from what believed by the actors (in Bell 1997: 12),[24] and in the works

---

24 Beidelman, W. *Robertson Smith*, p. 65, in Bell 1997: 12.

of Dumézil (1949: 37) or of Evans-Pritchard when he remarks that 'there is a deeper symbolism which is so embedded in ritual action that its meaning is neither obvious nor explicit. The performer may be only partly aware or even unaware that it has one' (Evans-Pritchard 1956: 232), as well as in those of Edmund Leach ([1976] 1981: 60), who states that it is one of the tasks of social anthropology to decipher the implicit code of a symbolic system, whether or not it is understood by its practitioners. More recently, in the general frame of his ecological approach to ritual, Roy Rappaport also seeks its meaning at a level that does not coincide with that of the interpretations of the actors when he writes that 'never do the basic assumptions of any society simply stand naked to the view of its members' (Rappaport 1999: 172);[25] and Philippe Descola (2005: 136) appears to agree when he remarks that only very rarely in non-literate societies (at least) have some individuals been able to propose partial synthesis – surely not common knowledge – of the foundations of their cultures. But it was structuralism, of course, the trend of thought that postulated most sternly the need for the anthropologist to articulate his explanations on a level that goes beyond native interpretations (Lévi-Strauss [1964] 1992: 313–15).

The opposite option – according to which the analysis must proceed from the interpretations of the actors and should remain close to them – already followed by Monica Wilson in the 1950s (in Turner [1969] 1990: 18) and subsequently by the neo-intellectualists (Scarduelli 2007: 32–3), has been reformulated in the frame of Clifford Geertz's ([1973] 1987) interpretive anthropology and later resumed and developed by postmodern ethnography (e.g. Crapanzano in Bell 1997: 56).

In an intermediate position, though, in fact, closer to this second option, we may place the approach of Victor Turner, whose work represents a major contribution to the study of ritual. Turner on the one hand considers informants' interpretations to be the indispensable point of departure (Turner 1967: 47, [1969] 1990: 19), but, on the other hand, recognizes that the overall meaning of a symbol includes behavioural aspects that escape the understanding, and even the awareness, of the actors. The ability to bring to the surface the meanings of such behaviours justifies, in Turner's view (1967: 26–7), the anthropologist's claim that he is able to interpret the ritual symbols of a community in a deeper and more complete way than its members can. To illustrate how the analysis of Kalasha winter feasts has been carried out, it is worthwhile considering briefly some aspects of his thought.

According to Victor Turner ritual symbols can be analyzed on the basis of three classes of data: '(1) external form and observable characteristics; (2)

---

25 See also Rappaport [1968] 1984, 1971: 60–1; cf. Scarduelli 2007: 37.

interpretations offered by specialists and by laymen; (3) significant contexts largely worked out by the anthropologist' (Turner 1967: 20). In a ritual symbol it will be possible therefore to detect an operational meaning, which derives from its social and ritual context, an exegetic meaning, the one transmitted by the actors to the anthropologist; and a positional meaning that depends on the position it occupies in the symbolic system, and hence on the relations connecting it to other symbols (cf. Scarduelli 2007: 28). In the course of his research among the Ndembu of Zambia, Turner ([1969] 1990: 18–19) found some people who were able to offer interpretations of the rituals, from whom he collected some interpretive texts. He subsequently realized, however, that such exegetic meanings often contrasted with the meanings that emerged at the operational and positional levels. Hence his statement that in his/her search for meanings, the anthropologist must go beyond native interpretations.

In our case the option of native interpretations has to be ruled out because among the Kalasha interpretations of the kind Turner considered 'reliable' – representing, that is, a shared standard hermeneutics of Ndembu culture (ibid.: 18) – are not available. Though some individuals, confronted with a question about the meaning of a rite, may at times improvise a personal interpretation, among the Kalasha, only the form of ritual is transmitted, not its meanings; there is no shared, standard interpretation. The most common answer to questions concerning the sense of a rite, as it has been found in many other contexts,[26] is that it is done because it is prescribed by tradition. In the perspective of Lévi-Straussian structuralism we would be in the most favourable condition for ethnological research, for the absence of an 'apparent structure' that could obscure the 'deep structure' (Lévi-Strauss [1964] 1992: 314).

The fact that no interpretations of ritual are available does not mean, however, that the Kalasha do not discuss rites. Similarly to what was observed for example by Pierre Smith ([1979] 1988: 140) among the Bedik of Senegal, the Kalasha discuss them intensely, and even argue about them, but solely for what concerns their practical enactment – where, how, when and by whom must they be performed – but they do not interpret them.

The analysis of the Birir Chaumos, and of the Kalasha ritual and symbolic system as a whole, presented here, will therefore be based only on the other two classes of data indicated by Turner: on their 'external form and observable characteristics'

---

26 For example, Lévi-Strauss [1964] 1992: 31; Staal 1979: 4; Bausinger 1982: 89; Buttitta I.E. 1999: 20, 39, 44, 201; Scarduelli 2007: 165; cf. also Miles ([1912] 1976: 164) who makes the same general point quoting Robertson Smith in support.

and on the relations between the symbols. In other words, it will only be possible to investigate the operational and positional meaning of the ritual symbols, not the exegetic one. The voice of the actors will nevertheless enter the analysis, through the texts of the songs, chants and prayers, but it will mostly be a voice within the rituals and not, apart from a few instances, a comment on the rituals.

To adhere to the canon of 'theoretical candor' proposed by Sanjek (1990: 395–8), I must acknowledge, on the other hand, that, at least for the ends of the present research, between the two 'fundamental meta-theoretical options', the 'interpretive' and the 'explicative' one, under which have been grouped by Scarduelli (2007: 47–54) the main theoretical models of ritual, I am closer to the second one. By adopting the explicative approach the anthropologist is ready to go beyond the interpretations of the actors and takes upon himself the impervious task of explaining ritual.

Apart from Turner I shall refer also to structuralism; but more than Lévi-Strauss I shall follow those pupils of his, like Izard and Smith ([1979] 1988), who have applied to ritual the method he applied first to kinship and then to myth. My main interest is not, however, the form of the logic structure underpinning the symbolic system expressed in Chaumos, but rather the web of meanings it conveys. In this, I feel closer to Edmund Leach, who remarks that the structuralist method applied to the ritual system of a certain society does not bring to the light, as Lévi-Strauss believed, universal mental functions – an idea that he rejects – but brings rather to the surface the cultural ideals of that particular community.[27]

Such cultural ideals are indeed the focus of this research. From the analysis of the Birir Chaumos a true cosmology will emerge that, though present in many of its traits to the consciousness of the actors, is not ordinarily understood by them in all its implications. The unitary character of this cosmology is expressed in the Chaumos festival, which I shall analyze as an enacted text in which meanings are conveyed through a special form of language where actions and words are deeply intertwined: the language of ritual.

Ritual as a language

In the theory of ritual the idea that ritual is a form of communication, and therefore, obviously, a language, is found already in Radcliff-Brown and in Mircea Eliade, the prominent historian of religions (Bell 1997: 62), as well as in Gregory Bateson's ([1958] 1988) pioneer study on the Naven ritual of New Guinea. In

---

27 Bell 1997: 64; Lévi-Strauss 1992: 314.

the wake of Lévi-Strauss's reflection, the same idea was subsequently investigated especially by Edmund Leach ([1976]) 1981). More recently, it was taken up,
among others, by Stanley Tambiah ([1985] 1995: 131), who sees ritual as a cul-
turally-constructed system of symbolic communication, as well as by Roy Rappaport in his rich last work (1999).[28] Leach – following Lévi-Strauss for whom, in
ritual, words are replaced by gestures and objects – carries the linguistic analogy
maybe further than anybody else, stating that ritual, as a non-verbal language,
is organized in clusters structured so as to incorporate information encoded just
like sounds, words and sentences of a natural language (Leach [1976] 1981: 25).
Ritual behaviour, in his view, is to be seen as a system of signs and therefore as a
linguistic system, endowed therefore with a grammar that can be enucleated. As
a system of signs it could therefore be seen as belonging to the field of semiotics.
In this perspective, as in any structuralist approach, the single units do not convey
a full meaning in themselves, but can only be understood in the broader frame of
the system they belong to (Leach [1976] 1981: 70).

Along this line of thought, my analysis of Kalasha Chaumos proceeds from
Radcliff-Brown's and Eliade's intuition, who saw an analogy between the small-
est units of meaning in a language, the morphemes, and the elementary structural
units of ritual. We shall examine, that is, in the first place these elementary units,
to be seen as knots, as ritual themes, that we may call 'ritemes' in analogy
with morphemes or 'mythemes'. These are the individual rites composing the
various festive clusters that will come under scrutiny. It will appear that though
these units do contain a nucleus of meaning, their full meaning will only be
understood in the broader context of the whole system, to the point that it will
be quite clear – following Saussure and Lévi-Strauss – that the constituent units
of the system, rather than the single elements, are, in fact, the relations between
the elements. This will appear as the most structuralist part of the analysis,
because it presents a model aimed at bringing to the surface the cultural ideals
underlying the system by investigating the relations between the elements that
compose it.

Structural approaches, as noted by Descola (2005: 135–6), have been hit in the
last two or three decades by a wave of discredit; yet, as he adds, how can it be
denied that there are regularities in the practices of a community that can hardly
be attributed by the actors to a system of institutionalized rules? In contrast to

---

28 Rappaport warns however also against the risk of obliterating the differences between ritual
and language. See also Leach ([1976] 1981: 62–3, 128).

Geertz's ([1973] 1987: 64, 69) stance – and as advocated by Remotti[29] – I believe that anthropology must be seen as a cumulative science. Past achievements should not be discarded, and theoretical tools that have given important results are not to be dismissed just because they were at times used too ambitiously or because they turned out to be one-sided. If structural analysis may not do justice to individual representations, a structural approach can still be effective if our aim is, as in this case, to reveal the cultural ideals that shape a symbolic system and the cosmology underpinning it.

However, what is proposed here is, as mentioned, a modified structural approach. My main interest, as made clear above, is not so much the form or the characteristics of such a structure, but rather the ideology it expresses. Moreover, in contrast to what is generally the case in structuralist explanations, I have tried to highlight the verbal dimension of ritual, the words of the rituals: the prayers, the songs, the chants, the panegyrics, the invocations. These texts, apart from a few instances, were not solicited and are presented, as mentioned, in the chronological narration as they were uttered, and recorded; they are specimens, so to say, of 'speech in action'.[30] Their contents on the one hand can better elucidate the nature of the relations in which the language of ritual is articulated, and can thus contribute to the semantic analysis; while, on the other, they can help us to understand the performative character of ritual, in the innovative sense proposed by Stanley Tambiah. In the standard sense of the term, as defined by philosophers of language, a performative sentence is one that changes a given social reality, rather than just describing it; it is an action performed with words. For sure we can observe this in ritual; by performing certain acts and by pronouncing certain words the social status of a person may be changed, as is the case in baptism or marriage, whether celebrated in a church or in a municipal building.[31] But Tambiah goes beyond this most familiar sense of the term, for he does not focus directly on the actors, but directs his attention on the performative character of ritual as such.[32] He highlights two more meanings that can be given to the term. On one side, he

---

29 He specifies that this does not necessarily mean to confirm, but also to criticize and reformulate 'categories, theories, and theoretical perspectives' (Remotti 2014: 44).

30 The 'original dialogue' (in this case the original circumstances) through which they were acquired, therefore, is not obliterated, as for Tedlock ([1983] 2002: 294) is generally the case in what he calls 'analogical anthropology'.

31 Turner [1969] 1990: 103; Connerton [1989] 1999: 67–9.

32 The perspective he adopts is apparently shared by Rappaport who states that performativity does not depend only on the effects that words and actions may have on the participants in a rite (Rappaport 1999: 114)

shows how ritual may be endowed with characteristics that can confirm or enact aspects of social order (cf. Rappaport 1999: 131); rituals of royalty may be one of the most familiar examples of this type of performativity. Further, for Tambiah ritual may be seen as a performative act in the sense that it is a dramatic enactment that has to do with the production of an intensified, elevated, feeling of communication (Tambiah [1985] 1995: 159); an experience at times described as a switch to a state of consciousness termed 'numinous', 'transcendental', 'altered'; or as a euphoric communion with other fellow beings, or as a deep involvement in a collective performance (ibid.). We shall see that a performative approach such as this one can be applied to some extent in the analysis of the Kalasha Chaumos. We shall encounter rites that can be said to be performative in the classical sense of the term, rituals that confirm and actuate the standing social order, and rituals of a Dionysian flavour that provoke, often through the stimulus of wine, a euphoric sense of communion with all fellow beings. This type of investigation, though it remains outside the sphere of subjective individual experience, shall help us to connect the ritual complex of Chaumos to its broader social context.

Among scholars who believe that ritual is a language that speaks of structural relations, two main approaches have been singled out by Catherine Bell (1997: 68–9) in her comprehensive study on ritual: a 'symbolic', semantic or semiotic one, focussed on the meanings of acts, events and utterances; and a 'syntactic' one which, rather than meanings, investigates the grammatical rules on which ritual as a form of communication is based. Bell indicates Turner and Geertz as subscribers to the first approach, and Leach and Tambiah as supporters of the second one. For the first one, ritual communicates concepts; for the second one, in contrast, ritual leads through experience to an implicit comprehension of a cultural system. Under this aspect, our analysis will perhaps appear to be closer to the first approach, because ritual communication is investigated in its contents and meanings, rather than in its grammar. The approach chosen here, however, remains quite distinct from that of Turner and, especially, of Geertz, because, for the reasons mentioned above, it is not based on those native interpretations that both authors take as a point of departure; and it may recall that of Leach and Tambiah for its recognition of the role of experience in ritual action.

It should be quite clear at this point that this work moves on a systemic, structural plane, that of the *langue* – to use a distinction dear to structuralism – rather than that of the *parole*, the plane of individual perceptions and representations, following a trend that has an established tradition especially in folk studies. Chaumos is seen, therefore, as a super-individual corpus that, due to its ritual character, is more impenetrable to individual innovation than is the case with other super-individual products of folk culture, like for example oral literature (cf. Bogatyrev [1975] 1982: 70–1). It seems to me that it is this systemic, structural, approach that, in the case of Kalasha rituality, can give a peculiarly significant contribution not only to ethnography and religious studies, but also to cultural critique, i.e. to the reflection on our own society. But to proceed from the level of the *langue* does not mean proceeding as if the sphere of the *parole* did not exist. As a language is spoken by individuals, so is a ritual enacted by individuals – who have their own representations of it, inspired by the social environment and by the historical circumstances they experience. This plane of individuality will therefore emerge in our analysis of Chaumos and of the Kalasha ritual system. It will emerge, as mentioned, mainly in the narration written in the first person of the ritual and social events that took place in the valley of Birir from December 2006 to February 2007, where the interaction of the ethnographer with the people comes to the surface. Yet, it is not to individual representations that this work is dedicated, but rather to the models and values that in ritual take form. Individual representations tend to change in time, at times even rapidly, as is starting to happen today among the Kalasha; while ritual seems to be aimed at keeping in check this movement with its invariability (Connerton [1989] 1999: 67), to the point that it could appear as a mechanism devised exactly for the purpose of pre-serving the cultural ideals it expresses from the passing of time.

For Tambiah ([1985] 1995: 132–3) those ideals are expressed in cosmologies, found in all societies, that refer to the relations between human beings, between humans and the environment, and between humans and gods and demons, or other non-human entities (ibid.: 132; cf. Izard e Smith [1979] 1988: 14); these cosmo-logical constructions, he remarks, are incorporated in ritual and are enacted in rites. To enucleate those ideals through the analysis of the cosmological construc-tion incorporated in Chaumos is, as already stated, the main objective of this work.

It is my wish and hope that such research may not only enrich – even if just to a very limited extent – anthropological, historical and religious knowledge, but may also increase the self-awareness of the people among whom it has been conducted. The numerous young Kalasha who have by now attained good levels of education through the school system, though they represent the sector of the population that has departed the most from the traditional way of life, are often among the sterner supporters of traditional Kalasha culture and they frequently affirm their Kalasha identity with pride. They are living a contradictory predicament. While on the one hand they declare their loyalty to the traditional model, they cannot help raising questions about the meanings of the symbolic and ritual system on which that model is based, in the light of the new conceptual tools they have acquired.

'Do you believe our religion is true?' I was once asked by a young attorney from Bumburet valley. I do not think that this work can answer such a question, which goes beyond the scope of anthropology. But I do hope that our investigation into the symbolic meanings of Chaumos, and our discussion of the cosmology that emerges from them, can help that new Kalasha generation to understand what sense can be attributed to that ancient system in the world of today.

We can now start from the beginning by taking a look at the historical, social and cultural context of which the Kalasha are a part.

PART I

The Context

1

The Kalasha: Historical and Cultural Context

Peristan

The Kalasha, as non-Muslims, are disparagingly called 'kafirs', Arabic for infidel, by their Islamic neighbours. Today their customs and way of life – at least in their most macroscopic aspects – appear to be so different from those of the peoples surrounding them that legends have recently proliferated, particularly in publications for the tourist market, assigning them an external origin, and especially a Greek-Macedonian descent. According to such stories, they would be the descendants of stray groups of Alexander the Great's soldiers or, in some more sophisticated hypothesis, of the Greeks of Asia. Such legends have indeed no historical foundation[1] and it is quite certain, in contrast, that the Kalasha are not outsiders in the Hindu Kush. Their culture represents, rather, the very last example of a complex that, until the eighteenth century, was spread throughout the Hindu Kush/Karakorum, from the valleys of Afghan Nuristan to the north-east of Kabul, to the borders of Kashmir and the Tibetan Plateau (Map I). Just a bit smaller than Northern Italy, this vast kafir area (Peristan in the map), was delimited to the north by the main range of the Hindu Kush/Karakorum separating the Indian subcontinent from Central Asia, and extended to the south as far as the lowest ramparts of the chain that finally give way to the plains where we find today the Pakistani cities of Peshawar and Rawalpindi. Proceeding from west to east it included the mountains of Nuristan with their many valleys, the entire basin of the Chitral/Kunar River almost all the way to Jalalabad, and the whole mountain fastness extending to the upper Indus valley and to the Gilgit valley that flows into it.

---

1 For a detailed reconstruction of the genesis of such legends see Cacopardo A.S. 2011.

Though never united in a single political entity, in pre-Islamic times this impervious mountain region formed what may be seen as a basically homogeneous 'culture area', because the people inhabiting it practiced a variety of polytheistic religions that, though differing in many respects – such as the names of divinities, the mythology or the morphology of rituals – had at the core of their symbolic systems a common fundamental ideology. This was a 'pastoral ideology'[2] based – in extreme synthesis – on an all-encompassing pure/impure polarity associating positive values such as social solidarity and harmony with the spirits of nature to a male pastoral sphere of the mountain wilderness, opposed to a female agricultural sphere connected to the domestic environment of the villages and the low valley-bottom, where individual interests supposedly prevail and the natural environment is moulded to satisfy the needs of humans.[3] A series of common cultural traits were grafted onto this ideology, ranging from the division of labour between genders, to the exogamic rule, the segmentary social structure, the role of shamans, merit feasting, wine drinking, the ritual use of juniper, and the belief in mountain spirits resembling the fairies of European folklore.[4] The general model was that of societies based on patrilineal exogamous lineages, lacking a priestly class, with a stateless political organization, a system of rank in which prestige could be acquired by distributing wealth in codified feasts and by killing enemies, and a division of labour assigning herding strictly to men and agricultural chores largely to women.

Since no single name is available to refer to this area as a whole, for the sake of convenience in a former work (Cacopardo & Cacopardo 2001: 15–16) we resorted to a name of pure fantasy, 'Peristan', with reference to the belief in the mountain spirits, called with a Persian term *peri* or *pari*, that still in recent times – and to some extent even today – was shared by all the inhabitants of the Hindu Kush, whether Muslims or not.[5] It is a name of pure fantasy that may be literally trans-

---

2 For detailed illustrations of this ideology see Jettmar 1975: 215–20, Cacopardo A.M. 1985, and especially Parkes 1987.

3 There are indications that the reach of this fundamental pastoral ideology once extended even beyond the geographical limits indicated above and to the northern slopes of the Hindu Kush chain (Munphool 1869: 132; Wood 1872: 187, 193, 198; Bellew 1891: 143; Robertson 1896: 406; Scarcia 1965: CX) and, as we shall see in detail in Chapter 8, at least to the western Himalayas. That we are dealing with a single cultural area here is an idea expressed also by Claus Peter Zoller (in Bhatt, Wessler & Zoller 2015: 115–21).

4 Cf. Fussman 1983: 195; Bhatt, Wessler & Zoller 2015: 84.

5 Lorimer 1929: 518–22; Schomberg 1938: 235–9; Hussam-ul-Mulk 1974b: 96–7; Jettmar 1975: 220–2.

lated as 'Land of the Fairies', and refers to an entity that belongs to the pre-Islamic past and not to the present. A name we shall use again in this work, for the self-same sake of convenience.

Among the many points of interest of this area there is one circumstance that makes it absolutely unique: if on one side it has traits as the ones we indicated, considered typical of societies once termed 'primitive', on the other it is geographically located in the very heart of Asia, in a region adjoining areas that, from the remotest times – when the Indo-Aryan world had not yet taken form – had become centres of some of the most ancient civilizations on Earth.

Recent archaeological research has shown that the great literate civilization of the Indus valley had an outpost in Shortugai at the northern border of our area and that in the Oxus valley – in ancient Bactria – already in the third millennium BCE, another important civilization flourished, considered to be one of the most brilliant in Asia,[6] a civilization linked to yet another, just as ancient, that had developed in south-eastern Turkmenistan, in Margiana. Together with the one represented by the Indus valley, these two great centres of urban culture formed a network – fuelled by commercial exchanges – that according to several scholars was connected to the Mesopotamian civilizations. The prehistorical site of Tepe Fullol, belonging to the ancient Bronze Age complex known as Bactrian civilization, is located right at the foot of the mountains enclosing Peristan to the north-west.[7] For the Harvard Indologist Michael Witzel (2004: 597) the ancient speakers of Indo-Iranian – the proto-language from which derive the Iranian and the Indic, or Indo-Aryan, branches forming the two subdivisions of the eastern Indo-European languages – must surely have come in contact with this great cultural complex, and for the Finnish Indologist Asko Parpola (2015: 76) an early wave of proto-Indo-Aryan speakers, around 2000 BCE, even acquired a dominant position in it.

In historical times, moreover, some of the most refined civilizations of the world developed in succession right at the borders of our area: from the Tibetan to the Chinese one, from the Graeco-Bactrian to the Iranian and Indian ones. To this contiguity are maybe due some not-exactly 'primitive' features of Peristani cultures, such as the high levels achieved by the technique of wood carving, the ingenuity of the irrigation systems and the knowledge of metallurgy. Polytheism itself as a religious form, as we shall see, is considered by historians of religions typical of societies that have attained a certain level of complexity.

Though the first attested Muslim incursions into Peristan date back to the times

---

6 Sergent 1997: 151–61; Parpola 2015: 69–83.
7 La Cecla & Tosi 2000: 34–5; Jarrige 2007: 25–32.

of Mahmud of Ghazni (Raverty 1888: 134–5) who in the eleventh century was the first Muslim invader of India, our area was fully Islamized only in the second half of the nineteenth century – a very late conversion if we consider that the regions of Kabul and Jalalabad, immediately to the south, and of Kashgar and Yarkand in the Tarim basin to the north, were Muslim respectively since the tenth (Scarcìa 1965: CXXXII–CXXXV) and the fourteenth (Hambly 1970: 132–3) centuries.

Islam started to erode the borders of Peristan, and to establish some outposts there, only after the appearance of firearms in the sixteenth century, but two more centuries had to elapse before it gained firm footholds in the mountains with the conversion of the Indus Kohistan – the upper Indus valley – and of the 'kafir' communities of the southern valleys of Dir and Swat in the late eighteenth century.[8] The last impenetrable polytheistic stronghold of the Hindu Kush – present-day Afghan Nuristan – which had resisted to the attacks of Mahmud of Ghazni, of Tamerlane, and of the Moghul Emperor Akbar,[9] was subdued and forcibly converted to Islam by the Amir of Kabul Abdur Rahman Khan only in 1895–6, immediately after the border with British India was defined through the Durand Agreement of 1893. The country, called until then by Muslims Kafiristan, 'Land of the Infidels', was re-baptized Nuristan, the 'Land of Light'.[10] It was a territory populated by communities much more numerous than the Kalasha one, numbering many thousands of people, and where five distinct languages were spoken. A precious book by a British envoy, Colonel George Scott Robertson (1896) who had managed in 1890–1 to spend one whole year in that unknown world – which had inspired one of Kipling's most famous novels[11] – is the only first-hand account by a Westerner of those now extinct cultures.[12] Left by the Durand Agreement on the British side of the border, the Kalasha escaped the Amir's crusade and, as mentioned above, represent today the only surviving shred of the vast pre-Islamic world of the Hindu Kush/Karakoram.

This century-long resistance by the people of Peristan was no doubt due to their determination, but also to the fact that their territory, though surrounded by ancient civilizations, was historically one of the most remote and secluded areas

---

8 Holzwarth 1998: 313–15; Frembgen 1999: 83–5; Cacopardo & Cacopardo 2001: 31–8.

9 Rennell 1792: 164–5; Raverty 1888: 135–8, 141.

10 Alder 1963: 287–99, 330–3; Jones 1974: 1–20; Kakar 1981; Cacopardo & Cacopardo 2001: 182–5; Buddruss 2008.

11 *The Man Who Would Be King*. Original edition A.H. Wheeler & Co. Allahabad 1888.

12 Recently, an important native account has been published, derived from a manuscript bought by Georg Morgenstierne in Chitral in 1929 (Cacopardo A.M. & R. L. Schmidt 2006).

of the entire Eurasian continent. Locked in its mountain fastness, for centuries it received only distant echoes of the historical events involving the literate civilizations of the Asian plains, where kingdoms and empires rose and fell, and where the great historical religions competed for influence. Indeed, the astounding circumstance is not only that Peristani cultures resisted the pressures of Islam for so long, but that, still before the rise of Muslim power, they had been touched only marginally by the influxes of the great religions of Asia, Hinduism and Buddhism, which had managed to reach, and at times even penetrate, the mountains, but without ever putting roots there.

The Graeco-Buddhist civilization of Gandhara, which reached its highest peak in the Peshawar plain in the wake of the collapse of Alexander's empire between the first century BCE and the third century CE, expanded as far as the lower Swat valley (Uddiyana, the homeland of Padmasambhava, who brought Buddhism to Tibet),[13] at the southern borders of Peristan, but no further (Tucci 1963: 155; 1978: 56). Only in the eastern part of our area some Buddhist principalities were established in the early centuries of the Christian Era, which controlled the Indus valley trail that was then an important, though very impervious, route for trade and pilgrimage connecting Gandhara and the Indian subcontinent to Central Asia along the itinerary followed today by the Karakoram Highway;[14] but there too Buddhism never spread among the local population. The rest of the area, with its myriads of communities linguistically and politically distinct, remained beyond the sway of the empires and the kingdoms that surrounded the mountains, and preserved for many centuries its polytheisms and its political independence.[15] Though relations with the outside world were then probably more open and less conflictual than was later the case after the Muslim conquest of the plains,[16] the cultures of Peristan maintained throughout that period of time a very distinct identity. The central part of the area especially – where the Kalasha valleys are located – remained almost completely outside any substantial Brahmanic or Buddhist influence.[17]

---

13 Tucci 1977: 56ff., 1978: 69–73; Olivieri 2009: 43–6.

14 Jettmar 1982; Fussman 1988; Neelis 2006.

15 This is how it was found by Marco Polo in the middle of the 1200s. Marco Polo's route kept to the north of the great Asian chain and he travelled therefore along the northern border of Peristan. On hearsay he describes the country – the region he calls Belor – as a vast mountain fastness, naturally avoided by caravans because no lodging or hospitality was available there, inhabited by wild people – 'salvatica gente' – worshippers of idols living on very high mountains (Polo 2005: 40).

16 Masson 1842: 196; Jettmar 1974: 39, 1986: 132; Fussman 1977: 23–4.

17 Fussman 1977: 25; Cacopardo & Cacopardo 2001: 26–8.

Such influences could have easily generated syncretisms such as those found among some Himalayan populations, in the Indian states of Himachal and Uttar Pradesh, or in Ladakh, where ancient beliefs and local practices are mixed with Lamaistic or Hinduistic rituals.[18] This is not, however, the case in Peristan where, until the advent of Islam, a cultural universe with archaic roots had been preserved that, though obviously not to be seen as left aside by history, had followed its own lines of development.

This circumstance acquires a very special interest if we consider that the peoples of the Hindu Kush/Karakorum – with one single exception[19] – are speakers of Indo-European languages; moreover, they speak languages considered the most conservative[20] of the Asiatic branch[21] of this linguistic family: the North-West-Indo-Aryan or Dardic languages,[22] believed to be very ancient offshoots of the Indic (or Indo-Aryan) branch; and the Nuristani languages, which may even derive from the undivided Indo-Iranian speech, forming a third offshoot of it, distinct from the Iranian and the Indic branches.[23] For Georg Morgenstierne, the great Norwegian linguist who dedicated his whole life to the study of the languages of our area, it is very likely that the Nuristani languages derive from the tongue spoken by a vanguard of the proto-Indo-Iranian speaking migrants (Morgenstierne 1974: 9), and for the French linguist and Indologist Gérard Fussman (1977: 25) it may very well be that the ancestors of the speakers of these languages formed an ancient migratory wave that halted in the mountains, without ever reaching the plains of the Punjab and of the Ganges valley.

---

18 For example, see Berreman 1963, 1972; Dolfus 1987; Chandra 1992.

19 Represented by Burushaski, a rare example of a language that – as in the better-known case of Basque – linguists have not been able so far to assign to any known linguistic family (Lorimer 1935; van Skyhawk 2003; Berger 2008: 149; Tikkanen 2008: 257–8).

20 In the sense that they retain some traits that have disappeared from the Indo-Aryan languages of the plains.

21 The European one, as is well known, is formed by almost all the languages spoken in Europe, with the exception of Basque and the languages of the Finno-Ugric group.

22 For a reconstruction of the history of the linguistic use of the term see Mock 1977.

23 Morgenstierne 1932, 1974; Fussman 1972; Strand 1973, 2001, 1997–2008; Edelman 1983; Masica 1991: 21–2, 461–2; Backstrom & Radloff 1992; Rensch, Decker & Hallberg 1992; Bashir 2003. The linguistic geography of Peristan is extremely complex. Strand (2001: 258–9) divides Nuristani languages in a northern and a southern group, for a total of five languages, and the Dardic one in six groups, including seventeen idioms in total. The highest concentration of different languages is found exactly where the Kalasha valleys are located, in south Chitral, a tiny corner of Peristan that Morgenstierne (1942: 115) described as 'the most polyglot corner of the Hindu Kush'.

We are confronted therefore with a rare coincidence between cultural and linguistic phenomena that deserves consideration. We have in Peristan a constellation of cultures with archaic roots, which have developed historically outside the sphere of influence of the great world religions, the bearers of which show parallel 'archaisms' in the linguistic field. There are strong indications that the pre-Islamic cultures of Peristan had their roots in the Indian world, once reaching as far as Nuristan,[24] but of that world they were only the remotest periphery. Everything seems to indicate that we are dealing here with an independent development of an ancient Indo-Iranian or Indo-Aryan substratum harking back to pre-Vedic times (cf. Buddruss 2002: 120) – a development, not a frozen reproduction of a long-lost world (cf. Fussman 1977: 47). As rightfully stressed by Fussman we certainly do not expect to find '… in the Kafiristan of the end of the XIX century a happy valley where the inhabitants would speak (pre-Vedic) Sanskrit and would have preserved intact the cults and myths of the Arian tribes on the road to India';[25] yet there are '… some irrefutable clues, some linguistic and cultural fossils that justify the statement that the Kafir religions and the ancient Indo-Aryan religions have a common origin' (Fussman 1977: 26).[26]

The knowledge we have of several of these now extinct cultures is limited to what has been possible to gather before their final (though recent) disappearance, but in the case of the Kalasha we can observe one of these systems in function even today.

The Islamization of Chitral and the establishment of the Muslim kingdom

While the Chitral basin, where the Kalasha are settled, was, with Nuristan, the area of Peristan that remained more untouched by Brahmanic and Buddhist influences, it was one of the first to be reached by Islam. The religion of Muhammad, however, did not arrive from the south where Muslim rulers had held the throne of Delhi since the thirteenth century (Thapar 1966: 238), but from the north. On the

---

24 Fussman 1977: 25, cf. Buddruss 1973: 39, 2002: 117. However, Tucci (1963: 158), Jettmar (1974) and Gnoli (1980: 70–4) highlight connections with the Iranian world.

25 Unless otherwise stated, the translations of all textual quotations from works in French, German and Italian are my own.

26 Fussman's 1977 statement refers, in particular, to the religions of pre-Islamic Nuristan, but in the light of the subsequent advances made by research, in our view it can be extended to those of Peristan in general.

basis of a comparative analysis of local written sources, coming from the literate civilizations that surrounded our area, the German historian Wolfgang Holzwarth (1994, 1996, 1998, 2006) was able to reconstruct to a significant extent the early phases of the Muslim conquest of Chitral.

The territory of the present-day Chitral District – in the Khyber Pakhtunkhwa Province – is formed by the northern section of the basin of the Chitral/Kunar River, which originates in the main Hindu Kush range, enters Afghan territory some fifty miles south of Chitral town, and flows near Jalalabad into the Kabul River, a tributary in its turn of the Indus (Map II). In pre-Islamic times the population of the region was formed mainly by the Kho and the Kalasha, who speak closely related[27] Dardic languages.[28] In those days the Kho, who subsequently became the dominant group, were settled only in the northernmost tip of the long valley, while the Kalasha occupied a territory much larger than the one they hold at present, including also the ample plain where the town of Chitral, the true centre of the region, is located.

The first Muslim incursions into Peristan from the north were carried out by troops from Yarkand, an important urban centre of the Tarim basin, along the Silk Route, on the impulse of an expansionist wave of the Chagatai Khanate, one of the political entities which rose from the collapse of the Mongol Empire at the death of Genghis Khan. The first documented expedition was carried out in 1527–8 CE by Mirza Muhammad Haidar Dughlat – author of the *Tarikh-i-Rashidi* and cousin of Babur, the first Moghul emperor of India – who in all likelihood penetrated the mountains exactly through the passes leading to Chitral, and found it inhabited by infidel mountaineers (Dughlat 1895: 384). From then on, the Turkish lords from the north gradually established a military presence south of the main Hindu Kush range, from which the Muslim kingdom of Chitral originates (Holzwarth 1996: 121–3, 1998: 303–5). Formerly, the local population had a stateless political organization that could allow, at the most, for the emerging of influential leaders, but not of a power structure based on the centralized monopoly of force.

The creation of a Muslim state, however, did not bring about the immediate conversion of the people, who continued practicing their local, polytheistic religions. Of the pre-Islamic religion of the Kho we have little information; oral

---

27 Morgenstierne 1965: 188; see also Morgenstierne 1947b; Bashir 1988: 139–47, 249.
28 After Morgenstierne's (1965, 1973a) the most extensive works on the Kalasha language are: Bashir 1988, Trail & Cooper 1999, Heegård 2006, Di Carlo 2010b, Heegård 2015. But see also Decker 1992: 96–114, 1996; Trail 1996; Heegård 1998; Mørch 2000; Heegård & Mørch 2004; Mørch & Heegård 2008, Di Carlo 2010a, 2011, Mela-Athanasopoulou 2011.

traditions, not unexpectedly, are silent on this point. The little we know seems to indicate that their religion was probably quite similar to that of the Kalasha.[29] Their conversion to Islam must have taken place gradually, starting from the following century, initially through the influence (or pressure) of a wave of Ismaili refugees from Badakhshan, in the north-west of present day Afghanistan, led by a sovereign called Shah Babur, who had been forced to flee his reign by the Sunni Uzbeks who in 1584 had occupied his land, annexing it under the rule of Bokhara.[30]

Shah Babur is the first ruler of Chitral mentioned by name in the sources and he is the founder of the first independent[31] Islamic dynasty of Chitral, that of the Rais rulers. The Ismaili faith he brought to Chitral remained the prevalent one among the Kho population for a long time. As a more flexible version of Islam, it possibly accommodated non-Islamic practices for a considerable period. From the earliest British sources[32] we can deduce that, in fact, still at the beginning of the nineteenth century there were many 'idolaters' among the subjects of the Chitral state – not only Kalasha, but possibly Kho as well.

The Kingdom of Chitral was most probably the first Islamic state of Peristan. Its control extended initially only to the upper part of the long valley of the Chitral river, inhabited by the Kho, and only very gradually did it reach its central and lower parts. As mentioned, that was then the territory of the Kalasha, who in those times occupied the main valley of the Chitral River from the southern end of the present-day district, where we find today the Afghan border, to the area of Chitral town and further north still (Map II). Of these times of glory, when the Kalasha were their own masters, oral traditions have only saved vague memories: it is told that for the spring festival thousands and thousands of people gathered in the main valley in the vast plain near Nagar, and that the Kalasha herds were so numerous that they filled up, when out grazing, a long stretch of the broad valley of the Chitral river. Of those ancient times we can possibly see a concrete trace in the headgear of Kalasha women (Fig. 1) which, adorned as it is with cowrie shells coming from India where they were once used as currency, appears as a symbol of prosperity not quite in tune with the condition of subjection under which the Kalasha lived for centuries.

---

29 Hasrat 1996: 187; Shah 1974: 69.

30 Leitner 1895, App. 2: 23, Holzwarth 1994: 19, 1996:123–5, 1998: 306–7.

31 The preceding Muslim rulers, established in Chitral after Mirza Haidar's incursion, were military governors of the Chagatai Khanate (Raverty 1888: 171; Holzwarth 1998: 8).

32 Rennel 1792: 165–6; Thornton 1844: 142.

Soon the Kalasha came into conflict with the rulers of the Muslim kingdom. Of this clash oral traditions have preserved, in contrast, a vivid memory as the founding event of Kalasha history. It is depicted as a tragic event marked by continuous persecutions that forced the Kalasha to flee to the side valleys, where they were again hunted down by the armed men of the Muslim king who massacred entire families and forced them again to flee elsewhere. Everything began with the defeat of the Kalasha 'kings'[33] and their expulsion from the ample basin of Chitral, which became then the centre of the Muslim kingdom. Presumably the final attack on the Kalasha strongholds of the south was launched from there.

To conquer them the Rais rulers conducted a fully-fledged military campaign which, on the basis of written documents, can be situated around the end of the seventeenth century.[34] Defeated by the power of the new state, the Kalasha were also overcome by groups of refugees coming from surrounding areas, who occupied parts of their former territory. In those times they lived mostly in tower-houses – of which some rare examples has survived[35] – where they took refuge at night, and they built their villages on high ridges and inaccessible crests where their ruins are still visible today.

Submission did not, however, bring about the immediate conversion of the population, nor was the territory abandoned (Israr-ud-Din 1969). If on one side the Muslim conquest forced many groups of Kalasha to seek refuge in the side valleys, others remained in the main valley and continued to practise their polytheistic religion for a long time yet. They were, however, obliged to pay heavy tributes in kind and to provide forced labour for the Muslim rulers. Shortly after the defeat of the Kalasha, around the middle of the eighteenth century, the Rais dynasty inaugurated by Shah Babur, and connected to Yarkand, was ousted by the ancestors of the last rulers of Chitral, the Kator, who had the support of the Moghul emperor of India and of the Pashtun tribes to the south. The new dynasty took the Chitral throne only after a long and harsh conflict, but it managed in the end to permanently expel its adversaries. The ties with Yarkand, however, were not severed. As late as the end of the eighteenth century the rulers of Chitral were still paying tribute to the Manchu emperor of China, who had taken control of

---

33 Oral traditions speak of defeated 'kings', but it is quite certain that the Kalasha never had
a state-like political organization; in those times they may, however, have been organized in
chiefdoms, led by powerful chiefs.

34 For an appraisal of the documentary evidence see Cacopardo & Cacopardo 2001: 50.

35 Only in the Jinjeret Kuh valley, immediately to the south of Birir. See Cacopardo & Cacopardo
1992, 1996 (especially 1992 for more detailed data and photographs).

Yarkand after the decline of the Chagatai Khanate and of the Oirate confederation that had briefly replaced it.

The Chitral kingdom was, in fact, a constellation of quasi-independent state-lets, ruled by members of the royal family, which only rarely were united under a single sovereign. The last ruler to accomplish such a unity was the great Mehtar[36] Aman-ul-Mulk, who in the second half of the nineteenth century led his kingdom to achieve its maximum territorial extension. In 1873 the kingdom finally became tributary of the Maharaja of Kashmir, a vassal of the British, to enter at last the orbit of the British Empire at the end of the century, after a military campaign that remained famous in British colonial history. British interest in Chitral was strictly of a strategic nature in the light of the expansionist policy adopted at that time by Russia in Central Asia (Keay 1990: 98–102). For its geographical position Chitral was for the British an important – in spite of its small size – pawn in that 'Great Game' we can consider as the ancestor of the more recent 'Cold War'.

On the death of Aman ul-Mulk in 1892, one of those dynastic wars erupted between his closest relatives that, following a custom widespread in Central-Asian kingdoms, were usually won through the outright physical elimination of all adversaries. The war of succession lasted three years. In 1895 the Pashtun chief Umrà Khan of Jandul invaded Chitral at the head of a tribal militia several thousand strong in support of a candidate hostile to the British. The small British garrison, besieged in the fort of the Mehtar, was only saved thanks to the remark-able feat of a relief contingent dispatched from Gilgit which, at forced marches, managed to cross the Shandur pass (12,500ft), still covered in snow, and to reach Chitral with stunning speed, catching the enemy by surprise. Umra Khan, defeated, sought refuge in Kabul, and the British established themselves perma-nently in Chitral, according to the provisions of the Durand Agreement they had signed with the Amir of Afghanistan in 1893.[37]

The British government modernized the administration of the kingdom but, following the classic policy of 'indirect rule', left its internal structure basically unchanged. Far from being the herald of any form of democracy, British rule

---

36 A Turkish title, in line with the Central-Asian origins of the kingdom.

37 Younghusband & Younghusband 1976 [1895]; Robertson 1898. The event was of central importance in the recent history of Chitral. Even today the local political world is split between pro-British and independentists in the evaluation of the event. At the Third International Hindu Kush Cultural Conference, held in Chitral in 1995, on the centennial of the siege, several local scholars presented contributions that analyzed that crucial period: Karim Baig 2008; Faizi 2008a; Khan Mir 2008; Nawaz Khan 2008.

strengthened, instead, the power of the Mehtar who, thanks to the support of such a powerful ally, could placidly dispense even with the limited consensus his predecessors had to seek at least among the members of the nobility. With the advent of the new overlords the condition of subjection endured by the Kalasha remained therefore basically unchanged, apart from one point, far from secondary, which we shall now consider at length.

The Kingdom of Chitral

The Kalasha therefore remained subject to the Kingdom of Chitral for two and a half centuries, until its final dissolution after the birth of Pakistan. The kingdom had the structure of a true state with a complex administrative machinery bent mainly on the exaction of tribute, which, before the arrival of the British, amazingly functioned without the aid of writing or the use of money. Money was just about unknown in Chitral and even the ruling class, ruler included, was almost totally illiterate. The Mehtar wielded an absolute power only slightly tempered by the necessity of ensuring at least the passive support of the aristocracy, and he personally administered justice in all cases of any importance.

Chitral society was quite complex as well, because social strata, linguistic groups, kinship groups and caste-like trade subdivisions were inextricably intertwined in its structure. To put it simply, we may say that the population was basically divided in two strata kept separate by the prohibition of intermarriage. The upper stratum was formed by a landed aristocracy connected to the royal house by ties of kinship or affinity; its members always belonged therefore to the Khowar-speaking majority and were virtually exempt from all tribute. The lower one included the whole peasant population and bore on itself the whole weight of taxation, in kind and in services in the form of forced labour. Although this lower class was internally quite differentiated and the patrimonial and personal obligations imposed were extremely varied, all its members were the victims of very heavy exactions that confined them to a life often below subsistence level. Furthermore, all were potential victims of the slave trade. Such a practice had been widespread for centuries in the principalities of central Asia, where the rulers considered their subjects as personal property which they could dispose of as they pleased. The Mehtar of Chitral was actively engaged in this trade and he considered the sale of his subjects on the Central-Asian slave markets as a legitimate source of entry for his state.[38] The most likely victims were, of course, all those

---

38 Cf. Biddulph 1880: 67–8; Drew 1875: 461; Forsyth 1875: 76–7; Karinm Baig 1994: 16–17, 1997:

who fell foul of the ruler and in general the members of the weakest groups. Any excuse could be used to punish someone with slavery. But, more often than not, little girls and young women were just taken by force from their homes by the thugs of the Mehtar with no excuse whatsoever. Since the only form of resistance, in this lower social stratum, could come from large and united kinship groups, the Mehtar did his best to fragment them with frequent deportations of groups of peasants.[39]

If, in this context, the Kalasha could possibly have enjoyed a safer position than that of the landless peasants of the main valley thanks to the solid kinship systems of their communities, their status, as infidels, marked them as particularly low. Like all members of the lower class, they had to endure heavy exactions in kind, they had to host and feed the emissaries of the state (*ashim'at*) who visited frequently their villages, staying for several days, and they were obliged to provide annually a certain number of men for forced public labour (*beg'ar*). In addition, as 'infidels', they were the first victims of the slave trade.[40] Although Muslim peasants were also often sold off without any scruple, for the sale of an infidel, scruples were just out of the question. For this very reason the Kalasha, though subject to all sorts of pressures by their Muslim neighbours, were never the target of organized 'crusades' aimed at converting them on the part of the Mehtar of Chitral.

Violent pressures to convert them to Islam came from the south, rather than from the rulers of Chitral. Around the middle of the nineteenth century, a Sunni wave that had its propelling centre among the Pashtun tribes of the frontier reached southern Chitral replacing the more tolerant Shia and Ismaili confessions, and causing the conversion of many Kalasha communities of the main Chitral valley and of its eastern tributary valleys, as well as those of other linguistic minorities – like the Damcli and the Palula[41] – which were still mostly polytheistic at that time. Under Sunni pressure, exerted with outright violence in some cases, and with the weapons of derision and contempt in others, the process of conversion gradually progressed in the following decades. Soon only a few families of the

---

81; Montgomerie 1872: 187; Muller-Stellrecht 1981: 399–401, 415 17; Murtaza 1982: 233, Stein 1921: 26.

39 See Cacopardo & Cacopardo 2001: 54–9 for a detailed description of the political and social structure of Chitral with the indication of the sources; among the main ones are Karim Baig 1994: 1–44; Eggert 1990.

40 Hayward & Mahomed Amin 1869: 130; Munphool Mir 1869: 131–2.

41 The ethnography and the oral traditions of these two tiny linguistic communities are treated at length in Cacopardo & Cacopardo 2001: 79–171.

villages on the western bank of the Chitral river and the five communities of its western tributaries – Urtsun, Jinjeret Kuh, Birir, Bumburet and Rumbur (Map II) – remained unconverted; the proximity of the still kafir Nuristan probably played its role in this resistance.[42]

In contrast to what happened later in Nuristan, where conversion did not bring about a change in language, in the course of a few generations Kalasha converts completely abandoned not only the religion and the customs, but also the language of their ancestors. Some communities, on the basis of a collective agreement, even went as far as imposing a fine on anyone who dared to continue speaking the Kalasha language. The majority language of Chitral, Khowar, was adopted and a process was initiated – certainly painful for many – aimed at erasing from collective memory all traces of the pagan past. Such a radical change of identity is due to the fact that the contempt of which the Kalasha were victims was not only due to their 'infidel' status, but even more to their subjection to the Chitral Mehtar and to the fact that they carried the brand of a defeated people (Cacopardo A.M. 1991). The Kafirs of pre-Islamic Nuristan, who maintained their independence until the end, even today rank at the top of the social hierarchy of the ethnic groups of the area and have not felt the need to undergo a similar change of identity; together with their language they have kept all those cultural traits that were not in open contrast with Islam.[43]

In the course of the second decade of the twentieth century the southernmost western valleys – Urtsun and Jinjeret Kuh[44] – also began to convert, until Birir, Bumburet and Rumbur (Map III) were finally left as the last polytheistic communities of the Hindu Kush. As we shall see, the process of conversion had already then begun in Birir as well, while in the two northern valleys at that time there were almost no converts at all.

---

42 For the sources – mostly nineteenth-century British envoys – of this synthetic reconstruction see Cacopardo & Cacopardo 2001: 53–4.

43 For an anthropological linguistic approach, highlighting the role of ritual and verbal art as loci of the reproduction of Kalasha culture see Di Carlo 2010a. On the relations between language and ethnic identity in general see Dorian 1999 (but the whole volume, edited by J.A. Fishman, which includes Dorian's essay, is dedicated to this topic). See also Matera 2004: 93–103.

44 For oral traditions and process of conversion in Jinjeret Kuh see Cacopardo & Cacopardo 1992, 1996; in Urtsun see Cacopardo A.S. 1991, 1996, 2001: 261–77.

An encapsulated society: the Kalasha political organization

For the almost three centuries of their subjection to the Chitral kingdom, the Kalasha communities that remained polytheists managed to preserve their traditional social and political organization basically intact, which remained, so to say, encapsulated in the Muslim princely state. Such a situation, from an analytical point of view, is rather anomalous, because it puts the Kalasha society of those times in an intermediate position between so-called 'peasant' and 'tribal' communities. Peasant communities, being part of a social order defined on the basis of relations with a centre of power, generally have a quite amorphous and unstable internal organization, while independent tribal societies, lacking an external point of reference, must find within themselves the principles on which a social order can be founded. The Kalasha were close to the former for their condition of subjection to a dominant power, and to the latter for the fact that they had an internal organization independent of that power. In practice, an essentially egalitarian system was encapsulated in an extremely hierarchical social structure. In the internal organization of Kalasha society – and this still applies fully today – the hierarchical principle, apart from gender relations, is applied only within the family group, generally an extended family, where the leadership for social and ceremonial activities, is entrusted to a respected elder considered its chief. At the other levels of social structure prevails instead a strongly egalitarian ideology, based on the explicit principle that 'all Kalasha are poor and all Kalasha are equal'.[45] Every family-head is potentially an influential elder and has, at any rate, the right to participate in the meetings where decisions on issues of collective interest are taken. Such decisions are not taken by formal organs composed by representatives of the community, but in the course of assemblies basically open to all people concerned. We can say that Kalasha internal political organization is a direct democracy. Assemblies are generally informal meetings of influential elders. Otherwise, in exceptional circumstances, when an issue concerning the whole community must be discussed – as for example the building of a road or the distribution of the revenues of forest rights – participation in the assembly becomes compulsory and each family must send a representative. In short, Kalasha society lacks a locus of power, because the only role that can institutionally exert a precise form of authority is that of r'oy, an annually-nominated officer who basically has the duty to ensure that the rule that forbids reaping the crops before the established time is respected. The influence acquired by some elders is not connected, in contrast, to any role and derives mainly from personal qualities

---

45 Parkes 1992; Saifullah Jan 1996.

that come to the fore especially in the resolution of disputes and in the ability to protect the interests of the community in the face of external threats, as well as – still in very recent times – from personal success in the traditional way of *nam'us* – prestige or glory – based on a series of prescribed merit feasts requiring meticulously regulated distributions of alimentary goods. It must be noted, however, that mere prestige, so acquired, is not directly connected to political influence, even if it is no doubt a useful precondition for it.[46]

The British anthropologist Peter Parkes, who was among the very first ethnographers to study the Kalasha, has remarked that the political ethos of the Kalasha communities has many elements typical of what Mary Douglas has termed 'enclave culture'. According to Douglas, encapsulated societies mould their social institutions to achieve internal solidarity in the face of the dominant system that contains them, so as to discourage defections in its favour, as it happens indeed, in the Kalasha case, when a conversion takes place. The egalitarian political institutions typical of societies of this type would have taken form, in this light, in reaction to the hierarchical models of the systems encapsulating them. In this perspective, the egalitarian ideology is represented as a product of a historical contingence and, rather than as a value in itself, is seen as a device to contain defections (Parkes 1994: 158–60).

Parkes himself shows the extent to which in his view Mary Douglas's model does not fit Kalasha communities. But what is worth stressing here is that the egalitarian ethos, in their case, has certainly nothing to do with their condition of encapsulation. An egalitarian ideology that produced political organizations of the type the Kalasha have preserved for their internal affairs was deeply rooted throughout pre-Islamic Peristan in a myriad of independent communities that were not in a condition of encapsulation. Since such an ideology is not foreign to the Islamic world either, it is found to this day in many Islamized Peristani communities.[47]

In this condition of encapsulation, the Kalasha, after their defeat at the hands of the first Muslim dynasty of the Rais, reached a forced compromise with their successors, the Kator (see Parkes 2008), which, while it did not spare them the heavy exactions in kind or the forced labour, or the ever pending threat of slavery, guaranteed them at least a partial protection from the raids of the Kati of Bashgal, their warlike cross-frontier neighbours.

British domination, we have seen, did not change the despotic character of the Mehtar's rule in any way. But if the lower stratum of the population of Chitral

---

46 For an in-depth analysis of Kalasha political organization see Cacopardo A.M. 2009: 173–213.
47 Cacopardo & Cacopardo 2001: 39–42; Cacopardo A.M. 2009: 118–45.

remained under the yoke of heavy taxation in British times – forced labour included – it was freed at least from the threat of the slave trade. The generous allowance assigned by the British to the royal house amply made up for the abolition of slavery. From what we can gather from the local sources, it seems that this was the greatest concrete benefit that British rule brought to the bulk of the Chitrali population; for the Kalasha who, as we have seen, were the main victims of that trade, it was not a change of little import.

But it was only with the advent of Pakistan in 1947 that the living conditions of the peasant class began to improve. While the movement created by Jinnah was struggling for the creation of Pakistan, in Chitral an open rebellion, inspired by Islamic leaders, broke out against the Mehtar and his corrupt administrative system. In November 1947 the Mehtar applied for accession to Pakistan. In 1949 the first Political Agent of the Pakistani government was sent to Chitral, and in the same year the hated *beg'ar* was finally abolished. Tensions between peasants and landowners erupted again in the fifties together with the deepening of the fracture between the supporters of the Mehtar, who were modernists and pro-British but tied to the interests of the landed aristocracy, and his adversaries supported by the Islamist movement, who were giving voice instead to those of the peasant population. However, it was only in 1969 that the princely state of Chitral was finally abolished, while three more years had to elapse before all the privileges of the last Mehtar were cancelled by a 1972 decree of President Zulfikar Ali Bhutto.[48] For the Kalasha, who, as a protected minority, were freed from having to give tribute, there then began an era of unprecedented affluence, as witnessed by a steady increase in the population. Though still the target of contempt and pressure from their neighbours, they started to enjoy effective protection from the central government who included them among the minorities represented in parliament. Today they also elect their representatives in the local administrations and if their communities still form an enclave, they, however, are encapsulated in a system with the form, at least, of a representative democracy. A system within which their traditional political organization is still in place and with which their egalitarian ethos, at least in terms of law, is no longer in contrast.

A brief note on Chitral and the Afghan conflict

In the last decades Chitral has been, even if to a lesser extent as compared to the Federally Administered Tribal Areas (FATA) immediately to the south, a

---

48 Faizi 2008b.

backstage of the Afghan conflict. In the years of the Soviet occupation the district hosted tens of thousands of refugees who today have mostly returned to their homeland. Russian bombs occasionally hit Chitral territory by mistake, and some also hit the Kalasha valleys, but always in uninhabited mountain areas.[49] After the retreat of the Red Army, in the last phase of the civil war that followed, before U.S. intervention after 9/11, through Chitral passed the main connections with the territory controlled by the Northern Alliance of Ahmad Shah Masud, the legendary commander, hero of the resistance against the USSR and irreducible adversary of the Taliban, who was killed in a suicide attack in the wake of 9/11. After that Chitral was involved only marginally in the anti-US guerrilla warfare.

In the autumn and winter of 2006–7 the situation in the district was quite peaceful, though there was news of fighting going on just on the other side of the border, along the lower valley of the Chitral river, which takes the name of Kunar after entering Afghanistan past the mouths of the Kalasha valleys. In the bazaar of Chitral normal activities went on as usual, as if the conflict was taking place thousands of miles away. Yet, when I went to the police station for registration, a compulsory procedure for all foreigners, the policeman in the office offered me (probably just as a formality) an armed escort – which I refused – and urged me not to approach the border because, he said, al-Qaeda was there. In the years that followed tensions increased, but the Chitralis have been quite determined to stay out of the conflict: in 2008 a 'peace committee' of local representatives openly opposed the visit of a fundamentalist leader from the nearby Swat valley, a stronghold of the Pakistani Taliban, claiming that the event would threaten public safety and the peace of the district.[50] In 2009 the situation became even more tense. The Kalasha spring festival took place under police protection and, in October, a band of militia-men from across the border kidnapped in the Bumburet valley a Greek volunteer – Athanasios Lerounis – working on a project aimed at reinforcing Kalasha identity and improving the conditions of life in the valleys. He was finally released in April 2010. Indeed, an advance of the Islamist wave into Chitral would put at risk not only the very survival of Kalasha culture, but also the peace of the whole district.

---

49 I saw one of these bombs ingeniously transformed into a water heater in the home of a Birir family.

50 For an in-depth analysis and discussion of the multifarious ways in which Chitral Muslims responded to Islamizing pressures in the crucial period between 1995 and 2003, see Marsden 2005.

2

The Kalasha: the Traditional Model

Kalasha tradition

Before beginning our analysis of the winter ritual sequence centred around Chaumos, it is necessary to illustrate the socio-cultural context of these rites, which is based on a system called *dast'ur* by the Kalasha, a term of Persian origin used in the sense of 'traditional order'. It is an orally transmitted system of rules, concerning the religious as well the economic and social spheres. In addition to strictly ritual practices, *dast'ur* regulates for example the division of labour between genders, the form of kinship and affinal relations, the rules of hereditary transmission, the harvesting of agricultural products, the transhumance of the herds, decision-making processes, the resolution of conflicts and even the way people dress. A code not made of abstract and general moral norms, but of concrete and detailed prescriptions concerning the totality of social life and based on a specific vision of the world and of the place human beings have in it.

This totalizing dimension of *dast'ur* could prompt us to identify it with Kalasha culture *tout court*, which would not be an unfounded or unreasonable identification. However, we must keep in mind in the first place that *dast'ur* is an ideal model to which the actual practice of social life may not fully correspond. The gap between a rule and its enactment, as is well known, can be quite large. In the second place, the identification of *dast'ur* with culture would imply a notion of Kalasha culture as a perfectly homogenous system, shared in equal measure by all members of society, obliterating the plurality of perspectives and individual representations of cultural models found in any society that is at the root of the tension between conservation and change and therefore of cultural innovation – an issue felt as quite crucial by the Kalasha of today, who are involved in an uninterrupted process of reinterpretation of *dast'ur* in the light of the new conditions determined by schooling, by the greater accessibility of their valleys and by the intensification of relations with the external world in general. In spite of its totalizing character, therefore, *dast'ur* represents only the ideological dimension of culture, that of how things should be. In other terms, by describing Kalasha *dast'ur* we shall focus our attention on structure and not on process, on the system, the rules, the norms, and not on their enactment or on the way individuals perceive them today. The system itself, however, although it has in its DNA, so to speak, the idea of permanence and resistance to change, cannot obviously escape the grip of history. Structures too undergo a process that, though at a slow pace, gradually transforms them. In the case of the Kalasha, as in many oral cultures, the lack of documentation means we have little knowledge of the past history of this process. Comparison with the other pre-Islamic cultures of the Hindu Kush indicates, as we have seen, that we are dealing with a very ancient complex, but we must keep in mind that the description we are about to give of it can only depict it in the form it had assumed at the end of the twentieth century, the time when our research was conducted. It is reasonable to believe, however, that this form had probably undergone for centuries only limited changes, due to the permanence of the conditions of material production, and it is quite clear that, since the building of the roads and the ensuing impact of modernity, the Kalasha traditional system is now faced with an unprecedented challenge.

It is important to recall here that Kalasha *dast'ur* is not only of one type. We remarked earlier that the *dast'ur* of Birir differs quite markedly from that of the other two valleys, especially regarding the ritual cycle.[1] We are faced no doubt with two variants of the same model, but the marked differences they present can give us an idea of how multifarious the pre-Islamic world of the Hindu Kush must have been. Before concentrating specifically on Birir in the chapters dedicated to the winter celebrations, we shall briefly illustrate here the common cultural traits, those found in all three valleys.

The system of production

The traditional Kalasha economy is based on a model closely resembling that of the *Alpwirtschaft*, formulated by the Swedish geographer John Frödin, which has been successfully applied to mountain environments as far apart as the Alps, the Andes and the Himalayas (Viazzo [1989] 1990: 38–44). The model contemplates

---

1 But there are also differences in birth rituals, in the functions of the village temples, in the morphology of the main rite, the goat sacrifice; and in the past there were differences also in the system of rank.

a combination of cultivation and herding, made necessary on the one hand by the fact that in mountain areas agriculture alone can rarely satisfy the needs of a human community; and made possible, on the other, by the availability of land unsuitable for agriculture but rich in resources, which herding can, in contrast, transform into foodstuffs. It is a system based therefore on two separate spheres of production occupying also two distinct spaces, that of fields and that of pastures, requiring two types of settlements, the village and the *Alp* (the structures hosting the herds and their guardians during the summer months), and which permits the full exploitation of the resources available at the various altitudes. The herds move along a vertical transhumance itinerary, articulated in several stations, that follows the ripening of the pastures with the advance of the good season and culminates in a prolonged summer halt in the highest mountain areas. The same itinerary is followed slowly at the end of the summer, exploiting the pastures regenerated in the meantime, to reach the valley bottom again at the beginning of autumn. Just like the pastures, the fields too are located at different altitudes, meaning that agriculture as well, requires a high degree of mobility on the part of those engaged in it.

This is indeed what happens in the Kalasha valleys and in the Hindu Kush at large.[2] The transhumance begins in late spring, in the month of May, and gradually brings the herds from the altitude of 4,000ft of the valley bottom to the 13,000ft of the mountain heights. It generally includes three stations: the first one at the level of the highest fields, and the last one, where the herds spend about two months, far above the timberline at the foot of the rocky peaks. The descent starts at the end of summer and the cycle is completed with the return to the winter sheds in November, a few weeks before the beginning of Chaumos. The 'verticality' of the environment also plays an important role in the sphere of agriculture. As the snow retreats and transhumance begins, the fields located at the various altitudes are gradually put under cultivation. The lower fields yield two crops, one of wheat or barley and one of maize, with a biannual system of rotation that leaves the fields fallow at regular intervals. The highest ones give instead only one crop, of maize or, now more rarely, of millet. These fields are generally located at too great a distance from the villages to allow a return trip in one day. In addition to the winter villages, there are therefore many small summer settlements scattered near the fields located in the various side valleys, where a part of the population moves for the whole period of agricultural work. So it happens that the community, following the thaw, disperses across the whole territory in summer, while it concentrates in the lower villages in winter.

---

2 Cf. Barth 1956; Snoy 1993; Clemens & Nüsser 2008.

A key point in which the Kalasha system differs from the one outlined in Frödin's classical model concerns the winter feeding of the animals. In the *Alp-wirtschaft* they are kept in stables in winter and are therefore fed with hay. This means, on the one hand, that the animals using the summer pastures cannot be more numerous than the ones that can be fed in winter; and, on the other, that the production of hay is the cornerstone of the whole system, for it connects animal husbandry and agricultural production. Indeed, the amount of hay produced deter-mines the size of the herds as well as the amount of land devoted to the alimentary needs of the human communities, because the best fields for the production of grain are also the best fields for producing hay (Viazzo [1989] 1990: 44). In the case of the Kalasha, however, the pastoral sector remains quite separate from the agricultural one, because the natural environment of the Hindu Kush offers a winter pasture – the *bonj* (*quercus balut*) forest – that can be used by at least one domestic animal: the goat. The Kalasha are indeed, in the first place, goat herders, and we shall see that, correspondingly, goats play a central role in the ritual sphere. The availability of this precious winter pasture therefore frees herding and agri-culture from all reciprocal constraints, for the production of hay can be reduced to a minimum, since it must only satisfy the needs of a small number of cattle, raised almost exclusively for animal traction. Such a resource, however, does not free animal husbandry from the constraints imposed by the relation between summer and winter pastures. Though the former are usually more extensive than the latter, it may not be possible to exploit them in full, precisely due to the limits imposed by the winter pastures. Among the Kalasha as well, the rule remains valid that the size of a herd depends on the number of animals that can be fed in winter. Under this respect, as we shall see, an important role is played by the ritual system, because the November and December celebrations entail the slaughtering of large numbers of male animals right at the beginning of winter, lifting therefore, to some extent, the pressure on available resources (cf. Biddulph 1880: 100).[3]

One of the problems of an agro-pastoral mountain economy is the fact that both agriculture and animal husbandry require the maximum effort on the part of the labour force at exactly the same time of the year. To this environmental constraint, Kalasha society responds in the first place with a division of labour between genders that fully involves women in activities outside the home. To women are entrusted especially the daily care of the crops, which means the irriga-tion of the fields, a task that forces them to spend, in the farming season, virtually

---

3 A dynamics that recalls, even if only vaguely, the one analyzed in detail in the classical study by Roy Rappaport ([1968] 1984) on the Maring of New Guinea.

the whole day away from home; young mothers take their children with them. Hence the need for living quarters close to the fields, which has brought about the formation of the small summer settlements mentioned above.

As for the men, their main occupation is the care of the goats, from which women are ritually excluded. All activities connected to herding, cheese-making included, are strictly the task of men, to the point that even access to the goat-sheds and the pastures is banned for women. But if women are excluded from herding, men are not excluded in the same way from agriculture because they take care of the ploughing and the harvesting.

In a mountain environment, a widespread solution to the problem of the pressure exerted on the labour force by the contemporaneous needs of the two productive sectors is the collective management of the summer pastures, which not only saves manpower but offers also an answer to the problem of the distance between fields and pastures. Among the Kalasha collective management is indeed the rule for the summer pastures, while family management is the rule for agricultural activities. To these different systems of management of resources in the two spheres corresponds – exactly as predicted by the *Alpwirtschaft* model (cf. Viazzo [1989] 1990: 40–1) – also a distinction in the regime of property: while the ownership of fields is divided at the family level, that of the mountain pastures remains undivided at the level of the community or, at least, of the lineages.

If reduced to its strictly productive dimension, the Kalasha system seems therefore quite similar to those of mountain communities in many parts of the world. But if we consider it in its broadest context, highlighting the cultural dimension, its peculiarities immediately emerge. The physical space of the valley is perceived by the Kalasha through the prism of a symbolic system which designs a 'sacred geography' that regulates the way in which people relate to the natural as well as to the social environment, depending on their gender, their age, their ritual status. We shall now consider this aspect.

The Kalasha symbolic system and its social projections

The Kalasha symbolic system is based on a fundamental opposition between two poles. *'onjiSTa* and *pr'agata*, or *r'ela* in the language of Birir. In the literature, these Kalasha words have usually been rendered with the terms 'pure' and 'impure', a polarity with semantic connotations that have actually little in common with those of the Kalasha one. If *'onjiSTa* does have a positive connotation that its opposite lacks, it has nothing to do with a joyous life in the world of beyond, nor does *pr'agata* have anything to do with sin or the devil (cf. Augé [1982] 2002: 69).

Furthermore, the two poles are in no way connected to sexual morals, cleanliness or devotion, as is the case with our 'pure/impure' contraposition (cf. Augé 1980: 444). Today Kalasha people, because of their prolonged contact with Islam, speak of paradise and hell and sometimes relate the myth of Adam and Eve. But the traditional vision embedded in their religious system appears to have little interest in the world beyond, and seems to lack completely the idea of a prize or a punishment in the afterlife[4] – an attitude found also in the Veda (Dumézil [1959] 1974: 94) and in early Rome (Dumézil [1974] 1977: 320) as well as, according to the Italian linguist Enrico Campanile ([1993] 1997: 27, 1990: 93), in the ancient Indo-European religion. Ritual violations must be ritually atoned at once, and the reward for meritorious acts is bestowed here on Earth, with the prestige they give and the everlasting memory posterity will keep of he who performed them. The idea of immortality does not seem to be connected to some entity that survives death, like the Christian/Islamic soul, and it does not concern another world. Rather, it has to do with being remembered in this world, with remembrance; which is kept alive through the chants and panegyrics celebrating the feats of the ancestors, constantly repeated at every festival, and through the wooden effigies[5] carved for those who in their lives have accomplished meritorious deeds. It seems that we are dealing here with a cultural ideal of 'heroism' that, according Campanile ([1993] 1997: 33–8), is broadly attested in the Indo-European world, and that concerns not only valour in fighting enemies, but also generosity towards one's community as well as the ability to foster consensus (Campanile 1990: 112), the most appreciated talents of a Kalasha great man.

Although, as we shall see in a moment, the two poles are in a hierarchical relation, because the former is deemed superior to the latter, they cannot be opposed as celestial and chthonian, or divine and diabolic. The *'onjiSTa/pr'agata* polarity is rather the fulcrum of a system of classification of the world that, as such, concerns humans as well as animals, plants, the spaces of the valleys and the invisible beings inhabiting them. The polarity operates perhaps in the most perceptible way in the conceptualization of the spaces of the valleys, where it is reproduced at all levels: from the 'macro' dimension of the valley to the 'micro' dimension of the home. There are *'onjiSTa* and *pr'agata* places, distributed so as to indicate a clear connection between 'purity' and altitude.

---

4 Loude & Lièvre 1984: 162–3. One of the last Kafirs of Nuristan used to say to new converts among the young: 'You console yourself with beholding God in the life to come, but we prefer to see him in this life' (Edelberg 1972: 73).

5 Loude 1982; Klimburg 2008.

At the first level, the largest, the prototypical *'onjiSTa* territory is the high mountain wilderness, where agriculture cannot be practised and where the herds of goats graze in summer; the most *'onjiSTa* places are the mountain peaks where, according to traditional lore, are found the golden homes of the *pari'an* (or *s'uchi*, to use the proper Kalasha term), the nature spirits – who recall, as previously mentioned, the fairies of European folklore – deemed to be the rightful owners of all the resources of the mountains. At the opposite pole lays the Muslim world at the mouth of the valley, the prototypical *pr'agata* space. In the symbolic language of the system, the former, the mountain wilderness, is seen as a source of life, the latter, in contrast, as a threat to life, at the cultural level at least.

In the Kalasha worldview there is an ideal representation of space in which the valley is crowned at one end by the mountain peaks encircling a sacred lake inhabited by the *pari'an*, surrounded by the high mountain pastures where goats are brought to graze in the height of summer. The 'purity' of the physical space diminishes as altitude decreases thanks to the contamination due to human presence, until it dissolves into its opposite, past the gorges at the mouth of the valley, where for centuries Islam has been advancing. In this ideal representation, the valley is closed at its lower end and it opens up at its upper end – an image that reflects the peculiar physical structure of the Hindu Kush valleys which are always closed at their lower ends by narrow rocky gorges and, in contrast, open up like a fan just below the mountain peaks at the opposite end. In the landscape, it seems, is embedded a vision of the relations between Kalasha communities and the outside world, in its double capacity of potential ally, in the case of the fairy world of the mountains, and of potential enemy, in the case of Islam. The community therefore occupies an intermediate space between these two extremes, suspended between the *'onjiSTa* world of the fairies and the *pr'agata* world of the Muslims. But the physical border between the two spaces is not rigid. In winter the *'onjiSTa* sphere of the wild extends downstream to the borders of the human area and women do not have access to the higher parts of the valleys, where, in contrast, they go freely in summer to tend the highest fields. At the beginning of spring, when the community starts to disperse over the whole territory of the valley, the borders of the *'onjiSTa* sphere shrink, after permission has been obtained from the *pari'an* – with the rites of Joshi, the spring festival that marks the beginning of the transhumance – to enter their realm of mountain wilderness.

The second level is that of the human space within the valley. The dichotomy is reproduced in this intermediate zone. *'onjiSTa* places are first of all the shrines of the male divinities, as well as the goat sheds and the forest surrounding them. The fields and the villages, located on the valley bottom, are neither *'onjiSTa*

nor *pr'agata*. Only two places are permanently *pr'agata*. These are the cemetery (*manDawj'aw*) and the *bash'ali*, the house where women retire during their
monthly period and at the moment of childbirth; both are generally located in
low places, below the villages or downstream from them. The ideal image of the
permanently-inhabited space reproduces on a smaller scale that of the valley as a
whole. But while the latter develops along a longitudinal axis following the course
of the stream, the former follows instead a vertical axis running along the slope
of the mountains. At the top, in the midst of the holly-oak forest or on the ridges
above the villages, are located the shrines of the male gods. Just below them are
found the goat sheds, small clusters of stone buildings separated from the human
settlements by the irrigation channels running horizontally across the flank of the
mountains. The villages hang also on the slopes of the mountains, to save any precious tract of quasi-level land for cultivation. The fields are located just below the
villages – small patches of land often supported by terraces. Further down, close
to the stream, as just seen, are ideally situated the *bash'ali* and the cemetery, the
only two inherently *pr'agata* places.

The last level is the level of the home. The dichotomy is reproduced within it.
The traditional Kalasha home has only one living room used both for sleeping and
eating. It is square in shape with an open fireplace in the centre. The night area is
separated from the day area by four wooden pillars supporting the roof that delimit
the space around the fire. Between these and the open fire there is room for a few
low chairs (*'an~ak*). The beds are located behind the pillars, along the walls of the
house – children seldom have a bed all to themselves. A trapdoor leads at times to an
underground storeroom. The house has no windows. Traditionally, the only sources
of light during the day were the open door and the smoke hole above the fire; at
night, the flames of the fire. The *'onjiSTa/pr'agata* polarity is reproduced here along
an axis running from the threshold of the entrance door to the opposite wall. Within
the house the *'onjiSTa* space (*'onjiSTa wah*) is the area between the fireplace and
the back wall, the most removed from the exterior. In the houses of Birir, this is the
place where the emblem of the goddess Jeshtak, tutelary deity of the home and the
family – a wooden board with two protruding horse heads – is located.

The *'onjiSTa/pr'agata* polarity does not classify only the spaces of the valleys,
but human beings and animals as well. Goats, that graze in the mountain altitudes,
are the most *'onjiSTa* of domestic animals, while chicken and their eggs are the
most *pr'agata* and are therefore banned by *dast'ur*. An intermediate position is
that of sheep and cows, animals of secondary importance in Kalasha herding.
They do not follow the goats to the mountain pastures and are often entrusted to
the care of women.

Among human beings, men are *'onjiSTa* and women are *pr'agata*. Women are therefore denied access to all *'onjiSTa* places: the goat sheds, the summer pastures and the shrines of the male deities. They do not participate in the rituals celebrated there, and they are excluded also from consumption of the meat of the sacrificial victims. This gendered connotation of the *'onjiSTa/pr'agata* polarity, also determines the division of labour: herding, the quintessential *'onjiSTa* activity, is reserved, as has been mentioned, to men, while agriculture is essentially – even if not really exclusively – the duty of women. This does not mean, however, that Kalasha women live a condition of particularly severe submission, in comparison to other traditional societies. The opposite is, in fact, the case. Although we cannot obviously speak of gender equality, Kalasha society leaves ample space for female initiative. Spaces of autonomous decision-making that have to do – as noted by Wynne Maggi (2001: 8, 79), author of a valuable study on the Kalasha female world significantly titled 'Our Women are Free' – with the essential contribution women give to material production by taking responsibility for agricultural activities, and with the freedom of movement they necessarily must have to pursue their tasks.

The logic of the system may possibly be best understood if we consider that between the two poles lays a vast intermediate sphere. If the entire mountain wilderness is *'onjiSTa*, the permanently and irredeemably *pr'agata* places are, as we have seen, just two: the cemetery and the *bash'ali*. The living space of humans, made of fields and villages, is not *'onjiSTa*, but neither is it *pr'agata*. It belongs to the intermediate sphere where agriculture and its products also belong, as well as sheep and cows, which are also neither *'onjiSTa* nor *pr'agata*. The space of social and family life, shared by men and women alike, does not belong to any of the two poles, but is rather the stage of their daily interaction.

In the light of the 'fuzzy set theory' formulated by the mathematician and computer scientist Lotfi A. Zadeh (Lakoff 1987: 21–2) we may observe that *'onjiSTa* and *pr'agata* are 'graded categories', that admit various degrees of belonging. One can be more or less *'onjiSTa* (or *pr'agata*) in relation to other persons or groups (cf. Augé 1980: 443). The gods and the *pari'an* are *'onjiSTa* to the highest degree. Among men the highest grade of 'purity' is that of virgin boys (*'onjiSTa s'uda*), while married men are *'onjiSTa* to a lower degree. In the same way women are not all *pr'agata* to the same degree, nor are women *pr'agata* to the same extent throughout their life. The highest degree of 'impurity' is that of a delivering woman, who is deemed to be more *pr'agata* than menstruating women (Maggi 2001: 147) who, in their turn, are more *pr'agata* than non-menstruating women, while prepubescent girls are the least *pr'agata* of all. The only more *pr'agata* persons than delivering women are those who violate the exogamic rule, which forbids marriage between two persons who have a common ancestor in the male line until the seventh ascending generation, and until the fifth in the female line. In the past those who violated this rule became irredeemably *pr'agata*, to the point of being virtually excluded from the community: they could no longer participate in rituals, they were denied commensality and became part of a group of untouchables called *b'aira* who were treated as serfs, to which their descendants would also belong.[6] Today, whoever violates this rule usually converts to Islam.

It must be specified, however, that the presence of asymmetries within the two categories does not mean that the *'onjiSTa* and *pr'agata* categories do not have rigid confines, like that, for example, of 'tall man', which has blurred borders (because it is not possible to set an objective threshold passed which a man becomes tall) and is properly fuzzy. In fact, we are not dealing here with fuzzy categories, but rather with categories with precisely delimited borders – like is for example that of 'bird' in contrast to that of 'tall man' – within which we may observe prototypical effects like those detected experimentally by the US cognitive psychologist Eleanor Rosch, which cause certain members of a category to be seen as 'better examples' of it in comparison to others that are, however, also considered members of it in full right.[7] Let us now consider the 'best examples', the prototypes of the two categories. The prototype of the *'onjiSTa* sphere actually would not be human, because the beings that possess to the maximum degree the *'onjiSTa* quality are the gods and the mountain spirits. The prototype of the *pr'agata* sphere as well, for opposite reasons, would resist inclusion in the category of humanity, for it is the Other, the enemy that threatens the existence of the group, who for the Kalasha, in the last four centuries, can be identified with Islam. In the first case we are dealing with an Other, the divinity, with whom an alliance is sought; in the second one with an Other from which the community must defend itself at all costs, to whom the ethics internal to the community are not applied. In the past, homicide, anathema if committed within the group, became a glorious deed if committed outside of it. One of the titles of the system of rank was acquired indeed through the killing of enemies.

If we look within the community, the prototype of the *'onjiSTa* sphere is the *'onjiSTa s'uda*, the initiated virgin boy who, by the fact of never having had intercourse with a woman, is the only one who is allowed to come in physical contact

---

6 It is likely that in the past this caste of untouchables also included survivors of former autochthonous populations.

7 Prototypical effects, in other words, are not due to differences in the degree of belonging, as it may happen in the case of fuzzy categories (Lakoff 1987: 45).

with the divinity and is therefore the preferred performer of rites.[8] In the Kalasha *'onjiSTa s'uda*, Witzel (2004: 608, 615) has seen a possible antecedent of the *brahmac'arin*, the man who chooses chastity, as described in the *Atharva Veda*, because in this figure are joined the purity of the high mountains, where he takes the goats to graze, and a pre-sexual behaviour. From the point of view of the degree of purity, close to him is only the *deh'ar*, the shaman,[9] who strictly follows the prescriptions of separation from women to come in contact with the deities.

Within the *pr'agata* sphere the prototype is maybe the corpse, which lays in one of the two most 'impure' places, or, paradoxically, a woman at childbirth (Maggi 2001: 147), an event that takes place in the *bash'ali*, the other most *pr'agata* place; both birth and death are included in the *pr'agata* sphere. Later on we shall see how this apparent paradox may be interpreted.

The ideal representation of the *'onjiSTa* sphere at the human level is in the end the masculine world of the high pastures: a community of men only engaged in the *onjiSTa* activity of herding in the quintessential *onjiSTa* space, the high mountain wilderness (Parkes 1987: 645–7). This is the world where the cultural ideal of solidarity is enacted through the collective management of the summer grazing grounds. An ideal that, until very recently, had its fullest expression in the merit feasts that gave access to the title of *namusi much*, 'marvellous man', or 'great man'.[10] The goods distributed in the course of these feasts, to which the whole community was invited, were indeed mostly meat and cheese, i.e. the products of herding. We have therefore an extraordinary sphere of exchange connected to herding in which goods are shared, as opposed to an ordinary sphere in which families consume their own food in their homes, and the food is mainly bread, beans and agricultural products in general. While the amount of these goods available to each household depends more or less on the number of fields it possesses, the amount of meat and cheese it consumes depends, in the first place, on the feasts in which its members participate.[11]

---

8 In Birir only *'onjiSTa s'uda* perform rites, but in the other two valleys adult men are also often allowed to do it.

9 For Kalasha shamanism see the volume by Lièvre & Loude (1990); but also Siiger 1963, 1967; Cacopardo A.S. 1999.

10 The last proper merit feasts (*biram'or*) were held in the 1980s (Darling 1979; Loude & Lièvre 1984), but still today imposing distributions take place for funerals (*cik*) and dowry feasts (*sari'ek*). In 2006 two small distributive feasts (*prec'esh*) and several funeral celebrations were held in Birir.

11 For a more detailed analysis of these two spheres of exchange see Cacopardo & Cacopardo 1977.

This 'pastoral ideology' inspiring the Kalasha system – common, as we saw in Chapter 1, to the whole of Peristan – is, however, an essentially masculine representation. It is certainly an essential part of the Kalasha cognitive context and, as we shall see in detail, it manifests itself in the ceremonial system, but, as remarked by Wynne Maggi (2001: 49), it is a representation that remains, by its very nature, largely outside the experience of women. Women are not involved in herding, they have never seen the summer pastures, they cannot visit the shrines of the gods, and they do not give merit feasts. For the fact that they are tied to the *pr'agata* in their very bodies, they have instead the complex responsibility of guarding the borders between the two spheres in their daily lives. According to Maggi women do not perceive their being *pr'agata* as a 'construct of denigration imposed upon them' (ibid.: 8), but as something they themselves control and manage (ibid.: 8, 49–50). Yet, in spite of this, and although women, as mentioned, do not live a condition of particular subordination, the hierarchical principle implicit in the fundamental polarity (cf. Dumont [1966] 1979) confines the female gender to a position of ritual inferiority. Indeed, we are not dealing with two poles opposed but of equal level. As prototypes of the two categories, we have on one side the gods and on the other the Muslims; *'onjiSTa* is superior to *pr'agata*. We shall see that from the set of relations connecting the fundamental polarity to the other opposed poles in the system, a true cosmology emerges, a body of notions that puts humans in relation with the natural environment, with the gods, and with other human beings, a cosmological construction that, as mentioned, remains partially outside the conscious appreciation of the actors. This should not surprise us because, as remarked by Tambiah ([1985] 1995: 132), cosmologies are not to be seen as beliefs affirmed by the subjects, they are rather found embedded in myths, in rituals and other collective representations. Among the Kalasha, as we know, it is in Chaumos that this cosmological construction is expressed to the full.

What we have just outlined, however, is only the conceptual structure on which Kalasha religion and culture are based. But a religious system moves simultaneously on several planes on which the fundamental conceptual relations articulated in that system are displayed: among them that of ritual, that of myth and that of social organization (Dumézil 1949: 36). Before analysing the social structure of Birir, to subsequently enter the dimension of ritual with the description of Chaumos, we shall examine in the following paragraph the world of myth and the morphology of the Kalasha pantheon.

Kalasha polytheism

The religion of the Kalasha, as we have said, is a form of polytheism, one of many that were practised in Peristan until a couple of centuries ago. Among some historians of religions – especially those of the well-known Roman school of Raffaele Pettazzoni (in Sabatucci 1998: 16) and his pupil Angelo Brelich who began studying polytheism in the 1950s – the idea has been prevalent that polytheism belonged with the so-called 'superior civilizations', i.e. those that knew writing, metallurgy, agriculture, social complexity etc., and not with the so-called 'primitive' societies. It was therefore regarded as a religious form typical of ancient civilizations, i.e. the classical ones of Europe and the Middle East, rather than of the 'exotic' ones traditionally studied by anthropologists – apart from a few very rare exceptions (Brelich 2007: 31, 115–17)

The case of the pre-Islamic cultures of Peristan appears to contradict this view, at least in part. Peristani societies had indeed only some of the traits considered typical of 'superior civilizations', like an agriculture based on cereal crops, metallurgy, a refined form of wood-carving art and a caste of specialized artisans.[12] But, as we have seen, they did not know writing, money or the state, while they had many traits quite typical of 'primitive' societies, like kinship-based social structures, stateless political organizations, merit feasts and shamans. A 'tribal' island in the heart of the continent that saw the rise of the first civilizations of the planet, pre-Islamic Peristan may be placed exactly at the joint of the two models.

In contrast to what is the case with Greek polytheism – which in the West has played the role of prototype of this religious form (Sabatucci 1998: 11) – in the Kalasha system there is a creator god. At the apex of the pantheon there is a supreme Creator Being called Dizala Dizaw (*D'izaLa Diz'aw*), from the root *D'iz*, connected to ancient Indo-Aryan *dehati*, 'makes, builds' (T-14621).[13] He is a typical *deus otiosus* (Morgenstierne 1973a: 155), an idle divinity, as historians of religions have defined a creator god who, after creation, enters a state of permanent inactivity and does not interfere in human affairs. Accordingly, the place of

---

12 The Kalasha, at least in recent times, lacked some of these traits, like metallurgy or specialized artisans.

13 The monumental *Comparative Dictionary of Indo-Aryan Languages* by Ralph Turner (1966) contains 14,845 'headwords' that have 'the phonetic structure proper to the earliest recorded forms of the language which, while still comparatively uniform, was brought into India by the Aryan invaders'. The reconstructed, and therefore hypothetical 'headwords' are marked with an asterisk (*). The work will be quoted from now on with the abbreviation T- followed by the number of the *headword*.

his cult in the Kalasha ritual cycle is reduced to a few rare offerings and, unlike the other deities, he has no sanctuaries or shrines. The etymology of his name does not qualify him as a god connected to the sacredness of the sky like the main gods of many peoples of Indo-European language, who have names containing the Indo-European root word *deiwos*, 'luminous', 'celestial',[14] however, lack of a cult and virtual absence from the ritual cycle are considered typical characteristics of sky gods (Eliade [1948] 1976: 51). If we were to resume a distinction outlined by Pettazzoni (1957: 91) over half a century ago, between a type of supreme being with the prevailing characteristic of omniscience and another one in which creative power prevails, Dizala Dizaw would belong to the latter one. Rather than with humans and their activities, he has to do with the world and its origins. He does not control or sanction human behaviour; his role is to ensure the permanence of creation. A supreme being of this kind should not really be considered a god, if this notion implied the idea, as believed by Brelich (2007: 29), of a 'non-human personal being...permanently efficient in a broad sphere of action...'

The other gods of the Kalasha pantheon are instead deities of this kind. They form a rather small pantheon composed of no more than ten divinities, only half of which receive a regular cult. Like the Vedic one (Eliade [1975] 1979: 218), it is a pantheon made mostly of male gods, but it includes also a few important female divinities. The term *d'ewa* (T-6523) or *dewal'ok* (T-6540) used to refer collectively to these deities derives from the ancient Indo-European root word *deiwos*. They are local gods, who are believed to manifest their presence in specific places, dedicated to their cult. While the Supreme Being has the characteristic of transcendence, these are immanent deities, who inhabit Kalasha territory and exert an active influence on the lives of humans.

As was apparently the case with the ancient speakers of Proto-Indo-European[15] and, as related by Tacitus about the ancient Germanic peoples,[16] the sanctuaries of these gods are open-air shrines; no temples are ever erected for them. As mentioned, they are usually found in commanding positions along the slopes of the mountains above the villages. In some cases these are 'consecrated holy places' chosen in primordial times through processes of divination, in others they are 'natural holy places'[17] where the presence of a divinity is signalled by some

14 Pettazzoni 1957: 28; Devoto 1962: 309; Benveniste [1969] 2001: 420; Eliade [1975] 1979: 209.
15 Eliade [1975] 1979: 211; Brelich 2007: 87.
16 Tacitus in Canali 1983: 43; see also Turville-Petre 1964: 236.
17 Brelich (2007: 86–7) traces this distinction in discussing the question of the choice of cult places in polytheistic religions.

peculiar trait of the natural environment like a tree strangely clinging to a rock, a huge boulder or unusual marks on the rocks.

The Kalasha approach these open-air shrines with respect and, in the case of some gods, even with fear. The gods invoked there are represented anthropomorphically. They have wholly human traits and are completely devoid of theriomorphic elements as those found, for example, in Egyptian divinities or, in the anthropomorphic Greek system, in the case of the god Pan. In pre-Islamic Nuristan there were many wooden statues of the various gods of the local pantheons.[18] Today the Kalasha do not have effigies of their gods, but it is quite certain that in the past they did; their removal is due in all likelihood to increasing Muslim pressure.[19]

If there are no temples in the holy places dedicated to the male gods, there are some small stone constructions (which cannot be entered) called *d'ewa dur*, literally 'house of the god', seen as the place where the god lives: if a god is represented as a human being then he needs a home. These are small quadrangular buildings made of rough stones, usually no more than three or four feet tall, with a thick wooden plank surmounted by two or four wooden horse heads fixed on its front side (Photo 2). Today the Kalasha do not keep horses, but they do know the horse as a precious animal; in their mythology they associate it with the gods who are often represented mounting a steed. Like for the Indians of Vedic times, who used horses only in war or in their rituals of royalty,[20] for the Kalasha the horse does not belong to the sphere of ordinary everyday life, and is therefore the appropriate animal to associate with the male gods. The structure of these shrines brings to the mind the image of a chariot.[21] It is a fascinating hypothesis that we may be faced with a frontal representation of the Divine Chariot, a motif widely spread since remote times throughout Eurasia, from Italy to the borders of China (Bussagli 1955). It is well known, on the other hand, that the horse-drawn chariot had an important role in the expansion of the Indo-Aryans,[22] and for Parpola (2015: 59,

---

18 Robertson 1896: 389–411, 491–2, 496; Edelberg 1960; Palwal 1970; Klimburg 1999: 141–55, 167–73.

19 For a detailed discussion of this issue see Cacopardo A.S. 2006.

20 Eliade [1975] 1979: 217, 240–1; Mallory 1989: 135–6.

21 No informant proposed this interpretation, but we found support for it in the notes of Paolo Graziosi – published posthumously in Italian fifty years after his travels – where it is stated (unfortunately without quoting any source) that the horses of the altars represent the horses of the chariot of the god (2004: 56). It seems significant also that the horse heads on the altars, as the horses of a chariot, can be two or four, but never three.

22 Renfrew 1987: 194; Mallory 1989: 35–48. It is interesting to note, in this regard, that the

68) they were actually its inventors. The use of the chariot, it is ascertained, long preceded horse riding. It was the vehicle of prestige in much of the ancient world throughout the second millennium BCE, the only one appropriate for chieftains and kings (ibid.: 109, 111) – the only one therefore worthy of a god. Once its memory faded away in the mountains a remembrance of it was apparently perpetuated across the millennia in these religious buildings.

In front of these small stone constructions rituals in honour of the gods are celebrated. The morphology of these rites is quite uniform; what varies is the type of offering. The space of the sanctuary is first sanctified by waving along its limits a burning juniper branch, which releases a fragrance believed to be dear to the gods. The Kalasha do not have priests or other kinds of religious functionaries, apart from the *deh'ar*, the shaman who is able to enter a trance to communicate the will of gods and spirits to humans.[23] In 1973, the government of Zulfiqar Alì Bhutto created the office of *kaz'i* – a title of Arab origin designating an expert in Islamic law – with a few posts endowed with a small pension in each valley, to which were assigned some elders renowned for their knowledge of *dast'ur*. It is their duty to proclaim the beginning of festivals and to ensure the correct execution of rituals. However, they are not the ones who materially perform ritual acts, as priests usually do. As mentioned above, this is a task ideally reserved to initiated virgin boys, *'onjiSTa s'uda*, the most *'onjiSTa* of all human beings. But they also have to purify themselves before the rite by washing their arms up to their elbow. In front of the 'house of the god' a fire is then lit on which are placed some boughs of juniper. After an invocation to the god guided by one of the elders present, the offering is thrown by the *'onjiSTa s'uda* first on the fire and then towards the shrine – formerly towards the effigy – in the direction of the square opening that is seen as the entrance to the 'house of the god'. According to the occasion, and the season, offerings may include dried fruits, grapes, wine, milk, cheese or the blood of a sacrificial victim, usually a he-goat or, more rarely, an ox. We can see here at work the principle of sanctification that Hubert and Mauss, in their famous study (Hubert & Mauss [1899] 1909: 23), identified as the most characteristic trait of sacrifice: juniper smoke sanctifies the space, the water used for washing sanctifies the performer of sacrifice, while the victim is sanctified through the invocation. The rite is therefore accomplished 'dans un milieux religieux et par l'intermédiaire d'agents essentiellement religieux' (ibid.: 23), in a religious environment and by essentially religious agents.

Kalasha word for yoke, *ju*, is connected to Sanskrit *yug'a* (T-10482), which is used in reference to draught horses rather than oxen, their only draught animals.

23 For bibliographic references on Kalasha shamanism, see Chapter 2 fn.9.

The fact that, as just remarked, the forms of the cult are essentially uniform for all the various divinities is due to the limited inclination for the diversification of deities that characterizes Kalasha polytheism. This is a somewhat anomalous trait, because such an inclination is deemed to be one of the most typical elements of polytheistic religions, because it is directly connected to the fundamental notion of a plurality of gods (Brelich 2007: 51). The male gods of the Kalasha pantheon, in contrast, are almost devoid of any specialized function, and appear to have quite blurred personalities, with scarce individual differentiation. There is little difference, also, in the prayers with which they are invoked; all divinities are asked to bestow fertility, abundance of goods and to protect the community from danger. The forms of ritual, in contrast to what is often found in polytheistic religions (ibid.: 84), do not fulfil the function of determining and defining the specific traits of the various deities. Consequently, as we shall see in detail in the comparative section, it seems difficult to detect in the Kalasha pantheon the imprint of the famous tri-functional ideology – sovereignty/sacredness, strength/war, prosperity/productivity – that, for George Dumézil (1958: 16–19) is typical of the speakers of Indo-European languages: the pantheon lacks a true sovereign god standing above all others like Zeus in the Greek Olympus, and the third function can be attributed just about to all deities. Only the second one appears to be represented somewhat precisely, for there are two divinities whose names – as we shall see in a moment – are etymologically connected to that of the Vedic Indra, a warrior god; but their personalities as well, like those of the other gods, lack the trait of functional specialization. We shall see that only in a couple of myths can *perhaps* be detected some faded trace of the tripartite ideology.

A true form of functional specialization exists only for female deities. The main one of these is Jeshtak (*j'eSTak*), goddess of the home and the family, who presides over kinship relations and is invoked in rites of passage; she is the only divinity to whom a true temple (*j'eSTak han*) is dedicated.[24] She is not a mother goddess[25] like the Mediterranean and Middle Eastern goddesses (Buttita, A. 1989), nor does she resemble the great goddess of popular Hindu tradition (Scialpi 1989), because she does not hold a pre-eminent position in the pantheon and her cult is

---

24 This is true for the two northern valleys. In Birir the village temples called *rihk'ini* are not dedicated to her nor to any other deity; her emblem, a small wooden board with two protruding horse heads, is instead kept in the houses.

25 This corresponds to what is normally found in the Indo-European world, where the figure of a mother goddess either has no relevance or is of external origin (Devoto 1962: 220; Witzel 2004: 601).

not specifically connected to the earth and agriculture. Another goddess is Dizalik (*Diz'alik*), who, though again not a mother goddess, is, however, the goddess of mothers, because she is the protector of delivering women. In a certain way, she too has a temple, since she is venerated in the *bash'ali*, the house where births take place. That is where is located – well hidden from Muslim eyes – her wooden effigy, the only anthropomorphic representation of a divinity to be found today among the Kalasha.[26]

The male divinities, even if not so differentiated, are, however, true gods of a polytheistic pantheon, not spirits of some other kind, like those of the dead or those of nature. In contrast to what is the case for similar categories of spirits, who are always referred to collectively – like for example the Kalasha *s'uci* – gods have a personal name, which is the most elementary instrument of differentiation (Brelich 2007: 70). Some of these names are directly connected to that of Indra, the tutelary divinity and chief god of the Indo-Aryans, frequently invoked in the hymns of the Rig Veda (Stutley & Stutley [1977] 1980: 170–2). This is case of the two main gods of Birir, Warin (*war'in*) and Praba (*pr'aba*). For Ralph Turner (T-444) the name Warin – *war'indras* in the genitive case – is etymologically connected to *a-parendra 'unrivalled Indra',[27] and the name Praba to *pravabhra*, another name for Indra, used in the Maitrayani Samhita (T-8782). It is also the case of the main divinity of the Chaumos of Bumburet and Rumbur, the Visitor god who descends in the valleys in the most sacred days of the festival. He can actually be squarely identified with Indra, because, as we shall see further on in detail, his name, Balimain (*balima'in*), is actually a compound made of an adjective taken from the neighbouring Kati language, *bal'ima*, meaning 'very powerful', and the name *in*, which stands for Indr, used also on its own in chants and invocations. Another figure of the Vedic pantheon, which appears during the winter solstice festival of Bumburet and Rumbur, is Pushaw (*p'ushaw*), who immediately recalls the Vedic Pushan, bringer of fertility and divine protector of wayfarers;[28] quite appropriately he escorts the Visitor god, taking care of his horse, on his yearly journey to the valleys. A further trace of the Vedic pantheon may be seen in the name of the goddess Jeshtak, which, according to Ralph Turner, can

---

26 Graziosi 1961; Maggi 2001: 139–41; According to one of my main informants, Dizalik is not venerated in Birir. The same was told to Graziosi in 1960 (Graziosi 2007: 108).

27 See also Morgenstierne (1973a: 158) who specifies that his informant actually identified Warin with In, Indra.

28 Stutley & Stutley [1977] 1980: 35; cf. Sergent 1997: 318.

possibly be derived from *deSTri* (T-6556), a female divinity of the Rig Veda.[29] Vedic connections surface also in the names of other spirit beings, different from the gods: the collective name for the mountain spirits, the *s'uci*, for Turner can perhaps be derived from *sucikā*, the name of one of the Apsara, the seductive celestial nymphs of Indra's paradise (Stutley & Stutley [1977] 1980: 24) or, in alternative, from **suvatsikā*, the name of a goddess (T-13514). There is also a category of spirits connected to the fertility of fields and herds, called Jac (*JaC*), whose name derives from Sanskrit *yaksha* (Morgenstierne 1973a: 156; T-10395), a term designating a class of spirit beings, who, according to Stutley & Stutley ([1977] 1980: 502), were probably vegetation spirits of rural communities venerated since pre-Vedic times.

In all likelihood this is the most archaic, ostensibly pre-Vedic layer, of the Kalasha pantheon. The names of other gods, like Sajigor (*sajig'or*) or Dajgorala (*daSg'orala*) – divinities of the two northern valleys – were instead probably formed locally, seemingly in later times. The only name of a god that shows some connection to the later Indian world, is that of Mahandeo (*mahand'eo*) – the only god with a shrine in all three Kalasha valleys[30] – that we find in the Hindu religion as an epithet first of Vishnu and then of Shiva.[31] His name is also the only one for which some correspondences may be found in the popular Hinduism of north-western India.[32]

Apart from a personal name, Kalasha gods often have an epithet, another possible instrument of differentiation (Brelich 2007: 77). Warin, for example, is called *sh'ura*, 'valiant'. This is a title – *sh'ura moc*, 'valiant man' – of the Kalasha system of rank that could be earned by killing an enemy. The epithet would therefore appear to indicate a warrior deity. Warin is not a god of war, however; he is a warrior god in the sense that he protects his people, as the *sh'ura moc* does by defending them from their enemies. Mahandeo, in his turn, is referred to with the epithet *k'ushala* – 'ingenious, clever' – because it is told that he taught men how to make cheese and gather honey. But not all gods have a differentiating epithet.

---

29 As an alternative Turner proposes a derivation from *jyeSTha*, meaning 'first, chief' or 'eldest' (T-5286).

30 His name is mentioned also in one of the of the earliest sources we have on the area, the account of the Jesuit Gregorio Roiz, posted in Agra, sent from there on a mission to Kafiristan in 1670 (MacLaghan in Jones 1966: 68).

31 Stutley & Stutley [1977] 1980: 249; Gonda in Jettmar 1986: 60.

32 Crooke 1894: 45; Berreman 1963: 385–6. According to Witzel (2004: 602), however, the cult of Indra also survives in various villages of northern India and in the New Year festivals of Nepal.

Some, like Sajigor, the main deity of Rumbur, are simply called *gh'ona*, great. In fact, all in all, epithets do not contribute much to differentiation.

Thus only myth remains as an instrument of individualization. It is through myth, indeed, that the personality of the gods is outlined. But in this case as well the instrument is used rather weakly. Kalasha mythology is poor. There are myths only about the main gods, and generally only one for each, telling the story of the installation of his shrine. These few myths perform therefore only the standard function of myth, i.e. that of 'founding' an institution, in this case the cults of the various deities, but not that – usually quite pronounced in polytheistic religions in comparison to animistic ones (Brelich 2007: 78–9) – of characterizing the divine figures whose feats it relates. Kalasha religion is, in fact, almost devoid of mythology, again an anomaly in the field of polytheism (ibid.). It lacks in the first place a true cosmogony and a cosmology in the classical sense, one embracing also the world beyond the borders of the valleys. Parkes (1991: 87–8) has found traces, in Rumbur, of a three-layered cosmological system composed of the sky (*di, asman*), the earth (*chom-th'ara duny'a*), and the subterranean world (*pariloi* < Sanskrit *paral'oka*), with a central pillar going through the three worlds, represented as three disks; a pillar believed to be resting on the belly button of a giant called Mir or Min Mara – a construction seemingly inspired by the scheme of the horizontal watermill, typical of the area. Quite correctly, Parkes connects this system to the one attested in pre-Islamic Nuristan, as well as to a model widespread in Central and Southern Asia, also considered typical, we may add, of the ancient Indo-European world, according to some scholars.[33] He specifies, however, that it is a knowledge made up of fragments of which the majority of the people have only very vague notions, often enriched by idiosyncratic traits derived from supposed revelations obtained in dreams, fragments that only few experts can connect in quasi-cosmologies, often incorporating, in addition, Islamic elements.[34] Poverty of myths, however, does not mean poverty of oral traditions. As we shall see, the Kalasha have indeed very rich oral traditions, which consist however – in contrast to what was the case in pre-Islamic Nuristan where a complex mythology existed[35] – mainly of narrations of a 'historical' rather than a 'mythological' character, and concern the feats of ancestors rather than of gods.

---

33 See: for Nuristan Robertson 1896: 380; for Asia Jettmar 1986: 36–8; for the ancient Indo-European world see Eliade [1948] 1976: 386–90; Mallory & Adams 1997: 131.

34 Parkes 1991: 88; cf. Loude 1980: 43–5.

35 See Robertson 1896; Morgenstierne 1951, 1968; Buddruss 1960, 1974, 2002, 2005, 2015; Jettmar 1986.

For Brelich (2007: 79), since myths belong to the most ancient forms of religion, their absence can only be explained by a conscious will to dispense with them. In the case of the Kalasha, such a choice may be attributed to the circumstance that for well over two centuries their territory has been encapsulated, as we have seen, in an Islamic political entity. Just like the effigies of gods were eliminated to avert the danger of being accused of idolatry, for the same reason, we can reasonably suppose, the myths narrating the feats of the gods were gradually allowed to sink into oblivion, with the result of turning Kalasha deities into the blurred and meagrely differentiated figures that we have today (cf. Parkes 1991: 91). Otherwise, we could hypothesize that their scarce differentiation may be due instead to the fact that they were originally lineage gods, rather than collective divinities (Di Carlo 2008). Indeed Pettazzoni has argued that the formation of a polytheistic pantheon is often due to the political unification of different communities (in Sabatucci 1998; 16). In the case of Birir, oral traditions do tell, as we shall see, of different places of origin of the various descent groups, which are supposed to have each a special relation with a particular god whom the apical ancestor is believed to have 'brought' into the valley.

The impoverishment of the sphere of myth did not, however, bring with it the impoverishment of the sphere of ritual. Kalasha religion, indeed, lives much more in the practice of ritual than in the fading myths of the gods. This work will show quite clearly that the Kalasha ritual system is complex and quite articulated, and that ritual activities are so intense that virtually not a single day goes by without a rite of some kind being carried out. Myth, entrusted as it is mainly to words, fell in all likelihood a victim to the long-term contacts with Islam, whilst ritual has possibly been maintained for its performative nature, i.e. for the fact of being, rather than a mere description of an action, an action in itself that is accomplished in the moment when the prescribed acts are performed and the prescribed words pronounced (Connerton [1989] 1999: 67–8). It is, on the other hand, a widely-shared opinion, as mentioned in the Introduction, that ritual activities tend to resist change and that they do it very effectively (Bell 1997: 211), fixing in a permanent way the meanings and the postulates at the heart of a religious system, protecting them thus from the dissolving action of time.

Among the Kalasha, however, the conservative power of ritual has not prevented a profound reinterpretation of the traditional religious system aimed at blunting its sharpest contrasts with Islamic tenets (Cacopardo A.S. 2006: 148–51), to which is probably due also the dissolution of the mythology. The model we have just described is indeed the one inscribed in the morphology of the system, but it must be recognized that nowadays it only partially corresponds to the perception

of the people. No Kalasha, in the first place, considers his religion a form of polytheism. Everybody professes a faith in a single God. The ancient Supreme Creator
Being, the idle God Dizala Dizaw, has been identified, now for a long time, with
the very active God of the Quran, who oversees and sanctions the actions of men.
The Supreme Being characterized by the single trait of creativity has thus been
replaced with the God of monotheistic religions, characterized rather by omniscience and by his relation to humans, rather than to the cosmos alone. The name
itself of Dizala Dizaw has now become obsolete and, as the transcribed texts of
prayers will show, the supreme God is at times even invoked with the name Allah.
More frequently, however, the name used to invoke him is Khoda (*khod'a*), a term
of Persian origin commonly used by Muslims from Iran to India. By virtue of their
profession of faith in one God, identified with the God of the Quran, the Kalasha
now reject the derogatory epithet of 'kafirs' with which they are still at times
referred to by surrounding Muslims (see Saifullah Jan 1996).

This identification of the ancient Supreme Being with the God of a strictly
monotheistic religion like Islam, has not caused, however, the elimination of the
other divine figures. Yet, as is understandable, they had to undergo a transformation to be fitted in the new model generated by the adoption of an active and
omniscient God. So it is that the gods of the traditional pantheon are no longer
considered fully fledged deities, but they are seen rather as intermediaries, as
'messengers' who deliver the prayers of men to God. The traditional system has
therefore been transformed by this reinterpretation, if not in its external forms,
certainly in the internal perception of the actors. The result is thus an original form
of syncretism in which the relation between Khoda and the other divine beings
recalls to some extent the one found in popular Catholicism between God and the
saints, but within the frame of a ritual morphology still virtually intact.

Now that the traditional Kalasha model has been synthetically outlined, we can
focus our attention on the community of the Birir valley.

3

The Community of Birir Valley

Polytheists and Muslims in Birir

In 2007, at the time of my last field trip, Birir had a population of about 1500 people, half of whom were Muslims. Of the three Kalasha communities of today,[1] it has always been the most fragile in the face of Islamic pressures and the one where the first conversions took place. But though Birir has the highest number of Muslims, it is the most Kalasha of the three valleys. In Rumbur and Bumburet there are many Muslim immigrants of non-Kalasha origin: in both valleys there are populous villages of Nuristani refugees who settled there at the time of the religious war waged by the Amir of Kabul at the end of the last century, as well as groups of Kho immigrants from the main Chitral valley, especially in Bumburet.[2] In Birir, in contrast, there are only a few recent immigrants – five Kho families in 2007 – and the Muslim inhabitants of the valley are therefore largely of Kalasha origin. We can say roughly that polytheists prevail in the lower part of the valley, while in the upper part the majority of the population is Muslim.[3]

---

1 As mentioned in Chapter 1, still in the second decade of the twentieth century there were two more unconverted Kalasha communities on the right bank of the Chitral river, in the Jinjeret Kuh and Urtsun valleys, while many more existed throughout southern Chitral until the middle of the nineteenth century.

2 We do not have numerical data for Bumburet, but in Rumbur, in addition to the Nuristani refugees, in 1995 there were eight Kho and four Gujur (a pastoral ethnic group from southern Pakistan) families. The percentage of Kalasha converts was about 10 per cent (84 people out of 848) (Maggi 2001: 24–5).

3 Of the six main villages of Birir – Grom, Jauguru, Gasguru, Biyou, Aspar, Guru (Map IV) – the first two are entirely converted, the third one had only two unconverted families in 2007, the fourth and fifth had a mixed population, while the last one, Guru, was almost entirely polytheist. Various hamlets in the surroundings of Guru had also a mostly polytheistic population.

The process of conversion has really gained momentum, it seems, starting from the 1940s (cf. Schomberg 1938: 195). The first Muslims were the ancestors of the Mirbaasé lineage, to which all the inhabitants of Jauguru village belong. According to a detailed genealogy, collected and written down by the son – a schoolteacher – of one of the elders of the lineage, their apical ancestor came from a village in the main valley and sought refuge in Birir seven generations ago. His conversion can perhaps be dated around the beginning of the twentieth century. That the Mirbaasé were truly the first Muslims of the valley seems to be confirmed by the fact that the mosque that everyone considers the oldest of the valley is to be found in Jauguru, which was built, according to the villagers, five generations ago. It is the only mosque in the three valleys built in Kalasha style; the other mosques are all in the very distinct Chitrali style. It is told that the wood for its carpentry was brought from Dizala Wat (literally: 'the stone of creation'), the most *'onjiSTa* place in the whole valley, situated in the forest upstream, where on some boulders figures of animals have been engraved (Snoy 1974). Its pagan sacredness, it seems, was seen as the appropriate chrism for the new Islamic sanctuary. As the Christian churches of antiquity drew on the sacredness of the ancient pagan temples, so did the first Muslims of Birir feel the need to connect the new *sacrum* with the pre-existing one. This tradition about the construction of the mosque is also an indication of the special relationship that this early Islamized group entertains with its Kalasha past. In their case, conversion has not brought about that radical change of identity that took place, as we have seen, in the communities of the main valley; to this day the Mirbaasé speak the Kalasha language and, as shown by the genealogy recorded by the teacher, they have kept the memory of their ancestors. His father, the teacher told me, prohibited the use of Khowar in his home, and it was on his order that he had recorded the genealogy of the lineage.

In contrast, the case of the first groups who followed the Mirbaasè on the path of conversion is quite different. These were the members of the servile caste, the *b'aira*, which, as we have seen, could not participate in rites and had in effect the status of untouchables. There were in Birir three lineages of *b'aira*, two in the village of Grom and one in Gasguru. On the basis of the memories of the elderly, their conversion can be dated between the 1920s and the 1930s. These groups are undergoing a change of identity very similar to the one that took place among the converted Kalasha of the main valley. This is easily understandable if we consider that, for them, Kalasha identity is indissolubly connected to memories of servitude. In the following decades the process of Islamization began gradually to expand. By 2007, as we have seen, about half the population of Birir was Muslim.

The relations between polytheists and Muslims are complex and cannot be reduced to mere relations of hostility due to the difference in religion. No individual, anywhere and in general, has only one identity (Sen 2006) and, in the case of Birir, religious identity often takes a back seat in favour of social and ethnic identity. Indeed relations between Kalasha polytheists and Kalasha converts are quite different from those between polytheists and Kho Muslims. Unconverted and converted Kalasha are connected by kinship ties, at times extremely close. In many villages they live side by side. Furthermore, the case of a family where some members are Muslims and others are polytheists is not at all unusual. My host Erfan, son of an elder particularly respected for his knowledge of *dast'ur*, had, for example, two Muslim brothers. In such circumstances it is not surprising to see social identity often prevailing over religious identity. Polytheists and Muslims often exchange visits. For the Eid festival,[4] our Muslim neighbours sent portions of their special dinner, and my host Erfan did the same for them during Chaumos. Several Kalasha Muslims participated in the three non-Islamic funerals celebrated during my stay, and I saw some polytheists travelling even to Bumburet to participate in the funeral of an elderly Kalasha convert.

Things are indeed quite different concerning the relations between unconverted Kalasha and Kho Muslims of the main valley, which are often hostile. But in this case as well, religious identity does not always play the front role. The quality of these relations depends much more on economic and political factors, than on the difference in religion. In 2007 there were several on-going controversies over the ownership of fields and forests, but the fracture line between the opposed groups did not follow that of religious differences. Converted and unconverted Kalasha were united in opposing some main-valley Muslims who were laying claims over portions of Birir territory.[5] Just as all the Kalasha of Birir, whether Muslims or polytheists, were united in opposing similar claims made by the Kalasha of Bumburet.

But if in everyday intra-valley relations religious identity does not appear to play a paramount role, this does not mean that no pressure is exerted to induce the non-Muslims to convert. The opposite is indeed the case. Conversions are seldom the result of free choice, whilst it is quite common to hear of changes of religion due to threats or deceit.[6] According to several of my acquaintances, heavy

---

4 In full: *Eid-ul Fitr*, the feast marking the end of the fast of Ramadan.

5 The same occurred in Rumbur, under similar circumstances (cf. Maggi 2001: 1).

6 There is not much data about Birir, but it is a common notion that in Rumbur several youngsters were converted practically by force while they were away from their valleys in search of work,

pressure was exerted especially in schools by Muslim teachers; in the course of 2006, six boys had converted in Birir, some of them still almost children. Such conversions cause great worry in the polytheistic community, which has managed, thanks to a small European NGO, to set up a school for unconverted Kalasha with strictly non-Muslim teachers.

Nevertheless, though kinship relations are a source of identity that can overshadow the religious one, a conversion to Islam opens a deep cleft in the community, because marriage will no longer be possible between converts and polytheists. Nor is the decision considered reversible. Once the step has been made – with the mere recitation of the *kalimah* (the profession of Islamic faith) – it cannot be retracted; Muslim reprisals could go as far as homicide. In time, converts leave their village, create a new settlement and the two groups move gradually further apart. In many cases, we have seen, conversion brings with it, in the long run, a complete change of identity.

Kinship and society in Birir

Kinship and affinal relations play a central role in Kalasha social life. In contrast to Rumbur, where the whole population is believed to descend from one common ancestor, in Birir we have three main lines of descent, in addition to various isolated lineages, maybe a residue of more numerous groups. The oral traditions transmitted as lineage histories indicate that in the past the valley has been a haven for various groups of refugees from other parts of southern Chitral, possibly already since the times of the Rais conquest. The eponymous ancestors of two of these lines of descent, according to these narratives, were immigrants to the valley, and the stories of the early ancestors take place in the main Chitral valley or in Shishi Kuh, an eastern tributary valley of the Chitral River, once an important centre of Kalasha culture.

Kalasha society is based on a classic segmentary system of exogamous patrilineal lineages that tend to segment when the genealogical depth of seven generations, prescribed by the exogamic rule, is reached, and marriages are allowed between its members. These lineages, called *kam*, take the name of their apical ancestor with the addition of the suffix *dari* (T-6294) or the term *nawau*, which means 'grandchildren, descendants'. We have thus the Razhuk-nawau, the Lataruk-nawau, and so on. The descent units formed through this process

---

and several elderly people have been induced to accept Islam on their deathbeds under the threat of hell.

of segmentation, remain, however, joined in macro-lineages, or maximal lineages that, though devoid of any real function, preserve the memory of common descent. The three main lines of descent of Birir are composed of a couple of these macro-lineages. For the sake of clarity we shall call the main lines of descent 'clans', even if the term is not applied in the canonical way because genealogical connections with the apical ancestors do exist, mythical as the narratives attached to the highest levels of the genealogies may be.[7] Above the clans, the next level of integration is represented by two territorial units, formed by the two sections in which the community is divided – upstream and downstream – which, as we shall see, emerge as corporate groups only in certain focal moments of the ritual cycle. The next level still, is that of the valley community, the basic social and political unit. Kalasha valley communities are corporate entities active in external relations and ruled, as we have seen in Chapter 1, by an informal group of elders who rise to positions of influence mainly through their ability to solve disputes, to attract supporters, and to deal with local authorities in the interest of the community.

The more numerous of Birir's clans is that of the descendants of Shurasì, who are settled in the lower part of the valley, in Aspar village, where the apical ancestor is believed to have built his first house, and in the village of Guru, with the many hamlets surrounding it.[8] The clan of the Bangulé-dari, who live in the village of Biyou, the main settlement in the upper part of the valley, is of similar size. The third clan, in size, is settled in the village of Gasguru, right in the middle of the valley. Of these three clans, only this last one is considered indigenous (*bhumk'i*) to the valley. Its apical ancestor, Gordimìu, is the earliest Kalasha forefather mentioned in oral tradition. It is told that to protect himself and his family from enemy attacks, he had built a *dup'uri koT*, a two-storey tower house, on the top of a rocky crest right at the centre of the valley, called *koTT'on*. To ensure a supply of water on that stony ridge, Gordimìu dug an underground pipe made of markhor horns connected to a sacred spring nearby. In a singular, mythical, battle – the story further relates – he repulsed his aggressors by dumping enormous quantities of ash on their heads.

Apart from the descendants of Gordimìu, there are a few other small lineages, probably fragments of formerly larger groups, who are considered indigenous. This division between indigenous and immigrant lineages, though seemingly

---

7 To facilitate the distinction we shall use the suffix *dari* for these 'clans" and the suffix *nawau* for the exogamous lineages.

8 In Aspar we have the Aliksher-nawau and the Sharuta-nawau, and in Guru and surrounding settlements the Lataruk-nawau, the Babura-nawau and the Ghilasur-nawau.

irrelevant from the point of view of social relations, appears to have deep roots because it is reflected in the position of the cemeteries; unconverted members of indigenous lineages have their own burial place, while there is only one cemetery for the members of the two main clans formed by the descendants of Shurasì and Bangulè.

There are in total nineteen minimal lineages in Birir, twelve of which are included in the three main clans, whilst the other seven have no genealogical connection to these or between themselves. Of these nineteen lineages, eight are entirely Muslim; converted families, in varying percentages, are found in all the remaining ones.

The oral traditions and the genealogies on which the identity of clan and lineages is founded, are transmitted mainly through the chants sung and the panegyrics recited during all the main celebrations. Genealogical memory is keenly preserved among the Kalasha, as is the case also with the other populations of Peristan (see Morgenstierne 1973b). Many adults can generally recite their own genealogy at least as far back as the apical ancestor of their minimal lineage, while the memory of some elders can reach as far back as the founders of the clans. In the Rumbur valley, where eight minimal lineages are grouped into two macro-lineages and one single clan about fifteen generations deep, our main informant Shahjuwan was able to provide the genealogy of the whole community, which, though smaller than the Birir one, still included roughly 500 people.

Since these genealogies serve first of all the purpose of guaranteeing the respect of the exogamic rule, they are surely historic until the eighth ascending generation and they can maintain a good degree of historicity even past the tenth generation. Beyond these limits they tend to acquire a mythological character. This is obviously the sphere more subject to manipulations that have to do with identity and with the image of itself the group wants to project into the present.[9] While we can therefore consider the genealogies of the minimal exogamous lineages quite historical, and practically also those of the macro-lineages, the same does not hold true for the genealogical links connecting the latter to the semi-mythical ancestors of the clans. These ancient forefathers, according to the oral traditions, had generally a special relation with the supernatural world. Suwashai (*sU~ash'ai*) for example, the father of Shurasì, apical ancestor of the clan to which the lineages of Aspar and Guru villages belong, had been saved by the god Praba from a terrible catastrophe that had destroyed his native village in a distant land where he was living with his old aunt, because he was the only one who correctly offered

---

9 Cf. Vansina 1985: 100–8; Fabietti & Matera 1999: 10–20, 153–7.

him goats in sacrifice, while the rest of the people sacrificed dogs; the god guided them, the only survivors,[10] to Birir and indicated to Suwashai the place where his shrine had to be built. Binga Bangi, apical ancestor of the clan of the Bangulè-dari, was himself a semi-divine being to whom a specific cult place is now dedicated. And Gordimìu too, the ancestor of the reputedly autochthonous clan, was not born of a woman, but was the offspring of a fairy.

The kinship system has fairly clear-cut reflections at the territorial level. Since the marriage system is patrilocal, members of a minimal lineage tend to reside in the same village and those of a maximal lineage at least in neighbouring ones; the clans, consequently, tend to concentrate in one of the two territorial halves. Due to the gemmating process of families, physical and genealogical distance tends to overlap.

The basic social unit is the *kush'un*, which is formed by those who have their meals around the same fire and, therefore, share everyday food. This is the basic subsistence unit within which production is organized. As such, it requires a precise distribution of authority and responsibilities between its members.[11] Authority is conceived by the Kalasha as ability to make decisions (*cit*) and to entrust them to others (*cit dek*, to give decisions). Usually it is the oldest male who exerts such authority, and therefore has the recognized status of representative of the family (*d'urai gad'erak*) in lineage meetings or in community gatherings. But there are cases of families in which it is the woman, thanks to her superior abilities, who in practice takes on the direction of the family. The forms that the nucleus can take are quite varied, since it can correspond to a nuclear family as well as to an extended family, depending on the stage of development the family unit is going through. As long as the parents are still alive, their married sons generally continue to live with them even after the birth of their own children. In this case the *kush'un* will have the form of a paternal extended family. If a group of brothers, as sometimes happens, continue to live together after the death of their parents, then it will be a fraternal extended family. As the elder sons begin gradually to separate, the new *kush'un* will be made just of plain nuclear families. The new houses will usually be built just to the side of the parental one, forming thus little settlements, which are the constituent nuclei of the villages.

---

10 The story of a virtuous old woman saved from a flood sent as retribution for the sins of the villagers is the theme of a widespread Hindu Kush/Karakorum narrative. See Mock (2011: 141–2) who recorded it in Wakhan.

11 For an in-depth analysis of Kalasha domestic society, see Parkes (1997), on which this brief account is based.

The functions exerted by the social units just described are limited to the ceremonial context of cyclical festivals as far as the larger ones are concerned, i.e. the two territorial sections (upstream and downstream), the clans, and the maximal lineages. Minimal lineages, in contrast, emerge as corporate units not only in the ceremonial context of festivals, but also in the networks of solidarity activated for rites of passage like funerals and, especially, in conflicts caused by the *aLaS'in~g* institution, which, as we shall see, allows women to abandon the man chosen for them by their fathers for one of their own choice. Yet, they are almost devoid of all functions for what concerns property rights. As we have seen, fields and houses are the object of private ownership at the family level, while the summer pastures belong, at least in principle, to the whole valley community.

The principles of social organization we have just outlined hold true for the entire Kalasha community. It is rather in the field of ritual that the differences between the two types of Kalasha culture become more manifest. We shall therefore examine now the ritual cycle of Birir, to shed light on its peculiarities and to place Chaumos and the other winter feasts in their broader ritual context.

The annual ritual cycle in Birir

Pierre Smith observed that one of the essential aspects of the organization of rites is the fact that every rite is connected to a circumstance that commands its occurrence, and these circumstances are organized in series. The series of circumstances on which a ritual system can be based are essentially of two types: periodical or occasional. Since these can in both cases concern the whole community or a single individual, the types become four. Annual cyclical festivals, for example, are connected to periodical circumstances concerning a whole community; while rites of passage are linked to periodical circumstances concerning single individuals. Rituals connected to occasional circumstances concerning a community have to do for example with natural catastrophes or pending dangers of human origin; while those concerning individual life have to do with disease or other threats to personal health.[12]

Among the Kalasha we find all four types of ritual systems described by Smith. In Kalasha religion, however, there is a penchant for periodical rites, which have attained a degree of complexity unparalleled by rites connected to occasional circumstances. It is the opposite of the famous case of the Ndembu, studied by Victor Turner (1966), where we find, in contrast, a complex ritual system based on the

---

12 Smith [1979] 1988: 136–8; cf. Rappaport 1999: 196.

accidents of individual life. Given their role among the Kalasha, we shall concentrate on periodical rites concerning the whole community, and especially on the winter feasts of Birir. We shall deal, however, to some extent also with periodical rites concerning the individual because, as we shall see, the ritual fulcrum of the winter solstice festival of Birir is the celebration of initiations.

As many scholars have stressed,[13] it must be kept in mind that a ritual sequence can only be correctly interpreted if it is considered within the framework of the whole system to which it belongs. This means that it must be analyzed not only internally by highlighting the relations between the elements that compose it, but also in an external perspective to reveal the relations connecting it to the other sequences forming the system. In the case of cyclical festivals, as remarked by Smith ([1979] 1988: 141), the various ritual procedures acquire meaning only as they respond to each other from one part of the year to the other. A periodical system of this kind is inevitably tied to the natural order, just as it is reflected in the productive system. On the one side, the sequence must therefore be considered in the frame of the annual ritual cycle, and on the other in the context of the economic activities taking place in the course of the year (cf. Buttitta I.E. 2006: 47).

Among the Kalasha, the system of periodical rites concerning the whole community is articulated in three great sequences: (a) a spring sequence connected to the beginning of the transhumance to the summer pastures and to the first sowings; (b) an end of summer sequence connected to the reaping of the fruits of pastoral and agricultural activities; (c) a winter sequence connected to the consumption of the goods accumulated and to the regeneration of the society and the cosmos. Such a partition of the ritual cycle corresponds quite closely to that of the Vedic year, which was divided into three seasons of four months each, marked by three festivals called *cāturmāsya*, 'quadrimestrals', celebrated in spring, in summer during the rainy season, and in autumn (Sergent [1995] 2005: 388). Due to the differences in climate between the plains and the mountains, their distribution along the year cannot coincide exactly with that of the Kalasha model; but that the connection does exist is clearly indicated by the name itself of the winter solstice festival: according to Ralph Turner (T-4742), the etymology of the term *caum'os* leads undoubtedly to *cāturmāsya*.

In Birir, the winter sequence lasts two months and is by far the more complex and articulated of the three. The solstice festival is its fulcrum, but a series of other celebrations follow it until mid-February at intervals of a week or two. Yet

---

13 Van Gennep [1909] 1981: 77; Propp [1963] 1978: 42; Leach 1971: 134; Smith [1979] 1988: 141; Bell 1997: 173–7.

the other two sequences are also very rich. They each last more than a month and both are composed of various feasts. It must be kept in mind, however, that these three great sequences are only a part of the ritual system of Birir. There are in addition a variety of other rites connected to productive activities celebrated at the family level at the moment of the autumn sowings, at the budding of wheat in late spring, at the time of the departure of the herds for the summer pastures. If we further consider that the late-autumn span of time separating the end-of-summer sequence from the winter one, is dedicated to social celebrations like those for rites of passage or merit feasts, and if we consider that there are also occasional rites, it will be quite clear that ritual activities accompany the life of the community almost without interruption for the whole course of the year. We are dealing, that is, with a community characterised by a high level of 'ritual density' (Bell 1997: 173). Ritual periodicity is linked to natural periodicity through the relation between the latter and the cycles of production (cf. Buttita I.E. 2006: 35). On the whole, the Kalasha ritual calendar seems to be moulded more by the cycle of pastoral than agricultural production. Each sequence naturally includes rites related to agriculture, but the position of the three festive nuclei in the span of the year corresponds more closely to the crucial moments of the cycle of animal husbandry. The spring sequence is explicitly connected to the transhumance, just as that of the end of summer is connected to the storage of the dairy products of the summer and to the mating of the animals. The prevalence of herding in forging the shape of the ritual calendar is also indicated by the absence of any celebration for the summer solstice, which has generally an important place in the ritual calendar of agrarian societies. As for the winter sequence, it lacks a direct connection to productive activities, because it takes place when these are at pause, leaving the community the time to concentrate on the intense ritual activity typical of the winter period.

The spring sequence includes rites for the fecundity of women (*pushg'ak*) and for the protection of crops from parasites (*p'ali d'ewaka*), but its main focus, the Joshi (*zh'oshi*) festival,[14] is a pastoral feast during which the first dairy products of the year are consumed and offered to the gods. Its main theme is the placation of the mountain spirits, the *s'uci*, when humans are about to enter their territory at the beginning of transhumance. The women, about to move to the summer settlements to tend the fields upstream, get ready as well with a purification rite.

---

14 The Joshi festival of Birir is not described in any publication, but several accounts have been published of the Rumbur Joshi: Schomberg 1938: 53–67; Morgenstierne 1947a; Siiger 1956: 24–6; 1974: 87–92; Loude 1980: 79–90; Fentz 2010: 353–77.

In the traditional Kalasha worldview, humans are not the owners of nature. The resources of the mountains do not belong to them but to the mountain spirits. Only with their consent can they be used. The rite concluding the festival is a dance ending with a sudden escape of the bearer of the *sacrum* – a composition of many different flowers – towards the goat sheds, symbolizing, perhaps, the imminent separation between the men who will follow the herds up the mountains and the women who will stay behind. A second focal point of the spring sequence, the Mrachwaki nat (*mraCw'aki nat*) takes place about two weeks after Joshi and marks the beginning of a week of night time dances, a last opportunity for the young to meet, before the imminent separation. The next day the summer migration (*zh'eu*) begins.

Though the number of the ritual sequences and their position in the ritual cycle are the same in the three Kalasha valleys, there are significant differences in their morphology between Birir and the two northern valleys. While the differences in the spring sequence – which we just briefly summed up in the Birir form – are limited, the end-of-summer sequence has a characteristic form that is one of the main traits distinguishing the culture of Birir from that of the other two valleys. It is a bifocal sequence, like the spring one. The first festival, the Uchaw (*uc'aw*) – celebrated at the end of August – consists in Birir of a simple rite[15] celebrated at the shrine of the god Mahandeo, to whom prayers are addressed for abundance of fruits and cheese, in the presence of no more than twenty men and boys, one or two per lineage. The event celebrated is the arrival of the shepherds carrying the cheese made at the high pastures, which will be consumed in all houses for the first time on that day. During the ritual the *r'oy* functionaries are appointed, who have the duty of ensuring that grapes and nuts are not picked before the appointed time. Once the grape harvest and the wine making are completed – some time in October – the Prun (*pU~*) festival begins.

The Prun is peculiar to Birir.[16] It is not celebrated in Rumbur and Bumburet. Before their Islamization it was celebrated in the Jinjeret Kuh and Urtsun valleys, and in all likelihood in the other Kalasha communities of southern Chitral, which were culturally akin to Birir, rather than to the two northern valleys. It has often

---

15 I participated in this rite in 1989. In the two northern valleys Uchaw is a much bigger festival with singing and dancing lasting three days. For the Rumbur Uchaw see Loude & Lièvre 1987: 193–203.

16 Several descriptions of the Prun festival have been published. See: Staley 1964, 1982: 71–5; Palwal 1974; Loude & Lièvre 1987; Lines 1988: 224–32; Lièvre & Loude 1991; Di Carlo 2007; Fentz 2010: 385–403.

been described as a wine festival. But, in fact, the central event – now apparently obsolete – of the celebration has to do with reproduction, of both people and animals, rather than with wine (Di Carlo 2007: 83–4). This was a ritual dance during which the Budalak (*buD'alak*) appeared,[17] young shepherds who had spent the whole summer in the mountain pastures absorbing the energy of that *'onjiSTa* environment and consuming dairy products at will. During that night these youngsters could mate with any woman they fancied, and it was believed that the chosen ones would receive the gift of fecundity. Because of the disparaging judgements Muslims make of this custom, even its past existence is now often denied but, according to Di Carlo (2007: 62 fn. 29), it cannot be excluded that it may still be practised in secret to this very day. The essentially pastoral character of this festival is indicated by the fact that its central rite was exactly the dance of the 'fecundating shepherds'. This was a rite in which humans and goats were almost fused, because the Budalak would mime, with movements and sounds, the behaviour of a he-goat in heat. The relation between the mating of humans and the mating of goats typical of the feast, is further confirmed by the circumstance that precisely during Prun, the billy goats, ornate with garlands of juniper, are released in the enclosures of the goats from which they had been kept separate for the whole summer, just like the Budalak had been kept separate from women (ibid.: 84). The central theme of Prun is therefore reproduction, as indicated also by another rite of the festival (*soh'olyak sambi'ek*) in which a band of boys, with a quite explicit symbology, snatches the richly decorated conical headgear from a group of dancing girls (ibid.: 77–80).[18] These are then carried away to a place high up on the slope of the mountain with a ritual act that seems to symbolize the acquisition by the *'onjiSTa* sphere of the female reproductive energy. The rite is clearly connected to the dance of the Budalak with which it probably formed in the past a 'complete' reproductive ritual, involving both male and female members of the community (ibid.: 84). The Prun, therefore, anticipates, and develops, a theme – that of fertility and reproduction – which plays an important role in the winter sequence as well. But while in Chaumos the theme of fertility is intertwined, as we shall see, with other themes, in Prun it seems to dominate unrivalled the symbolism of the festival.

If we consider the annual cycle as a whole, we find that the winter sequence focused on Chaumos is juxtaposed in a symmetrical and inverse way to the spring

---

17 For a description of the Budalak dancing see Staley (1964: 201), who is the only author who had the opportunity to personally observe this dance.

18 Similar conical headgear appears in some European Carnivals (see Kezich 2015: 481). Fertility and reproduction are a main theme in Carnival as well.

one centred on Joshi. The former is situated at the end of the productive cycle, the latter at the beginning of it. Joshi, we have seen, is a first-fruits celebration during which the first milk and cheese are consumed. Shortly afterwards the transhumance begins which will take the herds close to the rocky summits in mid-summer, while at the same time the women will start moving to the higher summer settlements to tend the fields situated at the various altitudes. As the snows retreat, the community expands and scatters throughout the valley. The winter villages remain partially deserted while the altitudes are re-colonized. The women, whilst moving upstream, remain within the agricultural space, which in summer expands as far as altitude allows it. The men, in contrast, penetrate with the herds deep into the heart of the mountain wilderness where agriculture cannot be practised: the territory of the *s'uci* spirits, the quintessentially *'onjiSTa* space. Humans ascend the mountains, entering the space of the spirits. The *r'ela*[19] sphere, represented by the human species, expands at the expense of the *'onjiSTa* one.

The opposite happens in the case of the winter sequence. At the beginning of Chaumos the return from the summer settlements is completed. The high-altitude fields are covered in snow and the herds are back in the sheds just above the villages. The community is reunited again in its winter quarters. If in spring humans have, physically, accomplished an ascent to the world of the spirits, now the inverse takes place: the divine descends in the valleys and mixes with humans. As we shall see, it is not the *s'uci* spirits who descend among humans but a divine bringer of fertility and abundance. If Joshi signals the beginning of the contraction of the *'onjiSTa* sphere, Chaumos is, in contrast, the time of its expansion and penetration in the territory of humans, in the intermediate sphere of everyday village life. The borders between the two spheres are not fixed, they move with the seasons. If we consider the oscillatory character of this movement we may agree with Leach (1971: 126-7) when he remarks that societies that do not have a linear perception of time must not necessarily have a circular one;[20] the passing of time can also be conceptualized as an oscillation between two poles.

The end-of-summer sequence provides the link between the other two. It starts with Uchaw, which is connected to Joshi because it marks a crucial moment of the cycle begun in spring; it signals the time when the production of milk starts to decrease and the pastoral cycle begins its declining phase; and, in Birir,

---

19 The term corresponds, in the language of Birir, to the better known term *p'agni* of Rumbur and Bumburet.

20 For A. Buttitta (1996: 262) the two conceptions have, in fact, always been present in all societies.

continues with Prun. The Uchaw festival starts just before the grape harvest and the collection of the other fruit crops, and Prun is celebrated once the process is completed and the must stored to become wine. Prun falls in its turn in another crucial moment of the pastoral cycle – the fecundation of the females – and at the same time is a prelude to Chaumos, of which it anticipates, as we have seen, one of the main themes, that of fecundity. The three sequences, though well distinct, are linked together (cf. Bell 1997: 174).

The winter sequence is articulated on a series of circumstances concerning the end of a cycle of human activities and the beginning of a new one. A cycle connected to the seasons and therefore to the course of the sun. The natural event at the centre of the Chaumos festival, the focus of the sequence, is therefore the winter solstice. The Chaumos of Birir lasts seven consecutive days, preceded, a few days before its beginning, by a day dedicated to ritual activities of preparation. To the regeneration of nature, announced by the movement of the sun, is linked the regeneration of society and of the individual. With the celebration of initiations, the ritual core of the festival, the life cycle is linked to the year cycle in a fashion typical of New Year Festivals.[21] In the structure of the feast, we shall see, the three stages of the rites of passage outlined in Van Gennep's ([1909] 1981) classical study, can be easily detected. The first four days represent the pre-*liminal* stage, in which the separation from ordinary time and space is ritually enacted. The night of the fourth day is the vigil of the *liminal* stage of margin, during which the novices are physically isolated from the rest of the community. Their isolation lasts until the seventh, and last, day, when the post-*liminal* stage is finally entered with the reintegration of the neophytes in the community.

As rich as the other two sequences may be, the winter one surpasses them by far in length and complexity with an extraordinary phantasmagoria of rites. The complete sequence lasts, as mentioned, more than two months – from 10 December 2006 to 15 February 2007, the year of our last fieldwork – and, apart from the solstice festival, the Chaumos, it includes four other festive nuclei, each of several days, separated by intervals regulated by the course of the moon.[22] The first one, Lagaur (*laga'ur*), is a remake of the main events of Chaumos with children as protagonists, in the frame of a series of rites again centred on fertility of men, animals and crops. In the second one, Jhanì (*jhan'i*), little girls are the main actresses and the dominant theme is again fertility. The third nucleus (*salgher'ek*) is the true New Year celebration, which signals also the time when

---

21 Van Gennep [1909] 1981: 6; Eliade [1948] 1976: 93; Smith [1979] 1988: 139.
22 For a schematic chart of the whole sequence see the Appendix.

it is allowed to start consuming the products of the previous year's harvests. The fourth one, (*ra'istam*), is the last stage of the initiation ceremonies celebrated during Chaumos; it includes also a propitiatory rite for the spring sowings, connecting thus the winter sequence to the spring one.

Now that we have given a complete, though synthetic, outline of Kalasha culture and history and of the society and the annual rituals of Birir, we can proceed with our account of the winter feasts of 2006–7.

PART II

Winter Feasts in Birir

4

The Narrative: the Chaumos Festival

Arrival in Birir: everyday life in the valley

On my arrival in Birir at the beginning of November 2006, I found lodgings in Guru, the only village in the valley that was almost entirely non-Muslim. My host Erfan had built a tiny guest house in a space adjoining his house, consisting of two small rooms opening on a wooden veranda that joined with that of his house. Erfan, a young man in his late thirties, had attended high school in Bumburet and was involved in local politics. He had run in the last local elections, I was told, and had missed his target just by a handful of votes. He had never had anything to do with herding and saw his future in tourism. He was modernity-oriented though his father Saidan Shah was a *kaz'i*, a custodian of tradition, highly respected for his knowledge of *dast'ur*. Erfan's family was rather small by Kalasha standards: the couple had just two children and only Erfan's mother-in-law lived with them. His *kaz'i* father, Saidan Shah, lived in another hamlet downstream with his second wife.

At the time of my first visits to the Kalasha valleys, after dark the only source of light in the houses was the fire burning in the central hearth; the hole in the roof over it was not sufficient in letting out the smoke, which stagnated in the one-room house causing widespread eye infections. Today a central open fire has become rare. In Erfan's house, the place of the open hearth was occupied by a low short-legged iron stove on the flat top of which Erfan's wife cooked bread; illumination, instead of by the flames of the fire, was provided by a dim electric bulb hanging from a nail. Since the middle of the 1990s the three Kalasha valleys have been equipped with three small hydroelectric powerplants, built with foreign funds, that provide, though rather intermittently, electricity to all the villages by harnessing the energy of the mountain torrent to drive a small generator. With electricity, the first televisions and video recorders have appeared. However, in 2006 there were only two or three of them in the whole Birir valley. Erfan was the owner of one of them. When it was turned on, all the neighbours would come and the house was immediately filled with a small crowd of all ages. The device could not be tuned to any TV station, but it could be used to watch films on VHS cassettes. Here is a brief account of a TV evening:

> Arif Ali Shah turns on the TV and puts in a cassette. Gulbahad's daughter is there with her baby, apart from Erfan's family and the *ducand'ar* (shopkeeper) who arrived shortly afterwards. The scene appears of a ridiculous fight between a man and a black and white cow, of the Dutch type, that does kung fu, jumps and somersaults, and is defeated in the end. Gulbahad's daughter asks 'What are they showing us? Cows cannot do things like that!', 'It is just for a laugh' I reply. Then they put on an Indian film. The hero mounts a white steed and challenges the British with astounding feats like holding down with a lasso an aeroplane about to take off. At every triumph of his, the *ducand'ar* exults, jumping on his stool, and yells 'Gud! Gud!' probably the only English word he knows. The children are spellbound. The enemies are the British; the Union Jack appears several times. But the palaces of power are American. The Capitol and the White House appear on the screen. The only British monument seen is Westminster Abbey. I watch it for a long while, having no alternative, but I retire to my room before the end. I could follow the film with no difficulty, even without understanding one word of what was being said. (*From my field journal – Guru 1 January 2007*).

I also happened to witness the arrival of the very first telephone in the valley, which was installed right in the home of my host. It was a wireless phone that functioned on and off, but for weeks attracted a crowd of people from all the neighbouring villages hoping to be able to speak to relatives residing in distant Pakistani cities. Initially Erfan put his own card at everybody's disposal, but when his wife realized that nobody was paying for the calls, she soon started to say that the card had run out.

Guru village is maybe the best existing example of traditional Kalasha architecture. A typical cluster village, it is built on a ridge overhanging the river, and is made of houses literally piled up together leaving space for just one little path between them (Photo 3). The terrace roofs of the houses offer the only level spaces where children can play and adults can sit, work, and chat. On the eastern side of the village a precipitous ravine opens directly onto the raging torrent below. The settlement is divided in two sections, each corresponding to a lineage. In the lower one the houses of the Lataruk-nawau, the most numerous lineage, are grouped; in the upper one are those of the Ghilasur-nawau. Rather than by their proper names, in everyday speech members of the two lineages refer to each other respectively by the appellatives 'the ones below' (nOari'ek) and 'the ones above' (tharari'ek). My hosts belonged to the Lataruk-nawau, the lineage with the least converts in the whole valley. I was in the heart of the polytheist stronghold.

Since the times of my last visit to Birir, the distribution of the settlements had changed. In 1989 Guru numbered thirty families, while in 2006 there were ten less. Due to the growth in population, the space available on the ridge had been filled up and several families had left the village to settle in surrounding sites where various new hamlets had sprung up: Grabanisar, Bashalitada and Ururi (Map IV). But these were not the only changes in seventeen years. The whole valley had undergone, to some extent, a process of modernization. By the initiative of the Kalash Valleys Development Project, a public agency under the District Coordination Officer (DCO), the administrative head of the district, as many as five stone and concrete bridges had been built. Permanent bridges, that is, to replace the traditional ones of stones and logs, which, rising only a few metres above the watercourse, were regularly washed away by the yearly floods and therefore had to be continually rebuilt. The jeep road that formerly ended just short of Guru, the lowest village, now continued upstream, reaching the uppermost village of Biyou. There was now a primary and a middle government school, in addition to two private schools funded by a European NGO and by the Aga Khan Foundation, an important Ismaili institution involved in many development projects in northern Pakistan (as well as in many other countries). In the middle of the valley, a sort of embryonic bazaar had also developed, with a couple of shops selling items like soap, cigarettes, combs, sugar, candies and the like, a very essential tea house and two small guest houses. Furthermore, the women no longer had to fetch water from the river because all villages were now provided with fountains made of a pipe and a tap, as well as with latrines located outside the houses. Together with the arrival of electricity, these were momentous innovations with a significant impact on everyday life.

Despite these changes, when the first snows settled in at the beginning of December, life in the valley took on a rhythm that did not seem to differ much from what I had experienced not seventeen, but thirty years earlier, at the time of my first visit to the Kalasha valleys, when in Birir there was just one primary school with twenty-five pupils in total, only five of whom were non-Muslims. The Kalasha attitude towards schooling, in those times, is well expressed by the comment – related by the French researchers Jean-Yves Loude and Viviane Lièvre (1984) – of a woman of Rumbur who, informed that in Europe children start school when they are five, exclaimed: 'What a pity! Right at that age when they have so much to learn!'

Once the schools – now attended by almost all children – shut down for the winter holidays, the terraced roofs of the houses filled up with boys and girls playing, while the two guest houses remained closed in their turn for the whole winter, for the complete lack of visitors. The outside world seemed far away: the only piece of news of international relevance that reached me during my stay was that of the execution of Saddam Hussein ('Bush killed him', was the main comment I heard). With the road often blocked by snow, the community, locked in its winter isolation, was starting to prepare for the great solstice festival.

Already on my arrival at the beginning of November, in the evening the village resounded with the verses of *ajh'ona b'ayak*, the most popular song of Chaumos. It is sung at contrast, with male and female groups teasingly addressing each other with semi-improvised verses. There were groups of girls singing on the terraced roofs, and groups of boys around the *bash'ali* teasing with their verses the girls inside, who replied among much laughter. Still at the beginning of December, however, nobody could say when the festival was going to begin. In Rumbur and Bumburet, for a few years now, an exact date has been fixed, the 6th and 9th of December respectively (to make it easier for the tourists who visit at that time, I was told) but in Birir the beginning of the festival is still decided in the traditional way: the *kaz'is* observe the position of the sun at sunset along the ridge closing the valley to the west, and when it reaches the place where it halts its apparent course, to start retracing it, the beginning of the festival is announced – a task traditionally entrusted to a member of the Lataruk-nawau lineage. Indeed Birir is not only the most Kalasha of the three valleys, but in several respects is also, being the least visited by outsiders, the most conservative of the three.

My assistants and the winter 'ritual logjam'

As soon as I settled in Guru village, I began to organize my research work. My Kalashamon was at first a bit rusty after an absence of eleven years, but I quickly started to recover it. To make people understand the aims of my work was not a difficult task. Even if no researcher had focussed specifically on Birir,[1] among the

---

1 Just that same September and October I had been preceded by Pierpaolo Di Carlo, the linguist in our team, who worked particularly on the Prun festival and was supposed to stay through

Kalasha the work of an ethnographer was by then well known. My intention of documenting Chaumos was appreciated, on the one hand because finally someone was giving Birir some attention, and on the other because I had the plan of recording the words of the rituals, the songs, the chants, the prayers and the panegyrics. Prayers and chants are addressed to the gods, while songs and panegyrics contain the collective memory, the stories of the ancestors and their feats, of the goods they distributed, of the enemies they killed, of the honours they received. The Kalasha attach therefore great importance to them and at times even among them there is someone who records them to play them again in the evenings. My project of transcribing them and translating them seemed to be generally approved of.

The choice of the right people to recruit as assistants was clearly of crucial importance. In the first place I needed a person with some knowledge of English to help me in the work of transcribing and translating the oral texts, who would also, during the festival, keep me well informed about the events coming up. I reached an agreement, which included also an hourly salary, with a young schoolmaster in his early thirties, by the name of Baras Khan, who was in charge of the small school for non-Muslim pupils funded by a European NGO and assisted didactically by the Aga Khan Foundation. In addition to high school, he had also attended two years of college in Chitral and was just about the only one in the valley who had a proper knowledge of English. Since his school had just closed down for the winter holidays, he was available to work with me full time.

Baras Khan did not have much interest in *dast'ur* because his choices had brought him to look elsewhere, to the world of schooling and education. Like Erfan he appeared to be a modernist. I was quite surprised therefore when once he fell ill, he decided to resort to traditional healing methods. These, however, were not the Kalasha ones: he consulted a Muslim healer who prescribed him a therapy consisting in inhaling a certain number of times per day the smoke of the combustion of some paper slips he himself had prepared, on which were written the names of Allah, Muhammad and Ali, as well as a sentence from the Quran. In addition he had to hang on his chest an amulet, consisting in a slip of paper with some words from the Quran wrapped up in a piece of material, and he was not to go out alone after dark. The diagnosis was that he had been the victim of an assault by the *bal'a*, malignant spirits of the valley bottom in which both Muslims and kafirs believe. Baras Khan explained to me that on the back of each of us there

---

Chaumos but had to leave at the beginning of November for family reasons. A third member of our group, my brother Alberto M. Cacopardo, had been doing fieldwork since the summer in other areas of Chitral.

is an invisible flame that starts to weaken when we are caught by fear. The *bal'a* see it weakening and attack right in those moments. He had had a narrow escape because he had managed to reach his home just in time, but the inflow of blood to his heart had decreased and that is why he got ill. The therapy appeared to be effective because after a couple of days he had completely recovered. But for quite a while he avoided going out on his own after dark.

In the beginning Baras Khan did not seem to have a specific interest in the topics of my research, but in time, as the work of transcription advanced, he became more and more interested in the lyrics of the songs to the point that, using a pad of his own, he started transcribing for his own use the ones he considered particularly important. His work with me, I thought, had possibly triggered a process of self-reflection, perhaps something like an embryonic auto-ethnography.[2]

Precisely because Baras Khan was not an expert in questions of *dast'ur*, I also needed another, more knowledgeable person to be sure I fully understood the lyrics of the songs and chants. Several men offered to assist me to this end. Among them my host Erfan. Apart from him, one of the most available was Gulistan, a man in his forties – also a Lataruk-nawau – who, like the majority of people his age, had not been to school. Confirming the remark I once heard from one of the most respected elders of Guru – 'when children go to school, they forget *dast'ur*' – Gulistan had a very good knowledge of tradition. Furthermore, he was also playing a self-appointed role of custodian and guardian of it with regard to younger men and women, whom, when need be, he did not hesitate to scold or encourage. Apart for his knowledge of *dast'ur*, he enjoyed special consideration for a peculiar orthopaedic talent acquired, he used to say, without any training or teaching: he could fix and bind dislocations and fractures, as long as they were not extremely serious, he specified. He lived in Guru with his old mother, his wife and his children, in an old house, blackened by the smoke of the traditional open fire, which he planned to renovate. Another quite faithful assistant was Danok, his age-mate and member of the same lineage. Like Gulistan, he had not attended school and did not speak English. He was a singer and a composer of songs, and had therefore a precise knowledge of the language and formal structure of Kalasha verbal art. Since the contents of songs and chants, including the new ones created at each festival, always refer to collective memory, Danok had also a keen interest in oral traditions, to which, unsurprisingly, he gave a historical value. When I once told him that I had found some discrepancies in the lineage stories I had been recording from different people, he appeared to be at a loss. He declared he would

---

2 On this point see Fabietti 1999: 26.

go over the issue with the other Lataruk-nawau to reach an agreement on a single version to offer me. Perhaps somewhat rashly, I asked him then how would they determine which version was the true one; the agreed-upon version never arrived. He too was living in Guru with his elderly mother, his wife and four children, one of whom was to be initiated in the upcoming Chaumos.

These were my main assistants, and they all belonged to the same Lataruk-nawau lineage. As a guest specifically of that lineage, I had no other choice. I was running the risk of remaining confined in a narrow set of relations, the risk called by some ethnographers 'enclicage',[3] i.e. the condition of being assimilated to a local clique or faction and to become, unwittingly, a transmitter of their point of view. Indeed – as observed by many anthropologists in the epistemological debate triggered by postmodernism – in the interactions that take place during ethnographic research, the actors are far from being pawns in the hands of the researcher. If he is not vigilant, in fact, the opposite may be the case,[4] as it happened when the first British envoys to Gilgit, and the first ethnographers after them, were led to believe that the region had been Muslim for centuries while it had really converted to Islam only fifty years earlier.[5] In the same way, my assistants in the course of our conversations, or of the translation of the chants, followed their own strategies, which, in their more obvious manifestations, tended to glorify the Lataruk-nawau with respect to other lineages, or to exalt the community of Birir in comparison to the other Kalasha communities. A heated discussion broke out once with Danok about the word 'kafir', which appeared in the lyrics of a traditional song I had recorded. It was used for Kalasha country referred to by the singer as 'my beautiful kafir land' (mai shish'oiak kafer'i). Danok strongly objected and insisted that in the transcription the term should be replaced with kalash'i, 'Kalasha land'. For the Muslims the word 'kafir', 'infidel', as we know, has a strong negative connotation, but apparently it was not so for the anonymous composer of the song. Possibly the text echoed a time – maybe not so remote – when the polytheistic, 'kafir', identity was stronger and took greater pride in its difference to the point of prompting a positive use of a term employed by the Muslims only in a derogatory sense. But, as noted in Chapter 1, today a reinterpretation of Kalasha religion has taken shape

---

3 Olivier de Sardan 1995; cf. Piasere 2002: 162–4,
4 There is now a vast literature on the ethnographer/informant interaction, and on the subjective experience of fieldwork in general. Some 'classic' writings are Rabinow 1977; Crapanzano [1980] 1995; Clifford & Marcus 1986; Marcus & Fischer 1986: 67–73; Clifford 1988: 44–54; cf. Herzfeld [2001] 2006: 11–12. See also Fabietti 1998.
5 For a detailed argument where evidence is presented see Cacopardo & Cacopardo 2001: 39.

that denies its polytheistic character and identifies the Supreme God of tradition with that of Islam. Since in force of this reinterpretation, as mentioned, the Kalasha reject the accusation of infidelity, the word 'kafir' has been virtually banned from use; for Danok, traditional chants had to be adapted to this new perception. I took note, of course, of the original word recorded, and of his objections.

Despite the unavoidable risk of 'enclicage', however, I managed to extend the circle of my collaborators beyond the limits of the more assiduous group of my Lataruk-nawau hosts. I interviewed various elders about oral traditions and various aspects of *dast'ur*, consulting them as experts, while on individual attitudes, life histories and personal vicissitudes, I collected data informally, mainly during the spontaneous conversations I happened to have with the many people who came to see me in the evenings in my room, or that I met elsewhere. Both the partners of my interviews and my evening visitors were always men, but I conversed habitually with women during the day, and some came also to pay me brief visits in daylight, if there were no men sitting with me. Therefore, if my social relations were by necessity mostly with men, I had a permanent contact also with the female world.

To my more assiduous assistants – Erfan, Gulistan, Danok and Baras Khan – I had promised a payment in money that was to correspond more or less to the time they would devote to my work. The practice of paying informants has been discussed at length, and criticized, in ethnography. The Italian anthropologist Carla Bianco (1988: 185–6, 210), for example, while recognizing that it is not possible to set rules valid in all circumstances, and that factors like a habit to receive payments created by previous researchers, or the amount of working time subtracted to other activities, should be considered, is not in favour of this practice; there is the risk, she believes, of introducing the habit of treating cultural information as a commodity, and of spreading wrong ideas about the objectives of a research, for example, that of being profit oriented.

In the field trips our minuscule research team[6] took in the 1990s among the Muslim populations of southern Chitral, the mere offer of a reward in cash for the information we received would have been considered offensive, for its acceptance would have amounted to a rejection of the rules of hospitality. Our hosts therefore not only lodged and fed us with the best food at their disposal, but also dedicated many hours of their time to us, only accepting, possibly, the gift of some object we had brought for that purpose from Italy. Due to the survey form of that research, however, our stay in each village never lasted more than three or four days.

---

6 Formed by my brother Alberto M. Cacopardo and myself.

Among the Kalasha, in fact, the same rules of hospitality were in force, but because of preceding research activities it had become the norm to pay informants. Moreover my stay in Birir was not going to last only a few days but several months, and the commitment of my assistants was to be a long-term one. I felt obliged, therefore, to offer something in exchange for the time they would dedicate to my work. With Baras Khan, who was going to assist me on a daily basis, I even fixed, as mentioned, an hourly salary. Neither he, however, nor anyone else, ever kept track of the hours or days they had worked with me, and the final payment was left solely to my calculations without any request being made. Our relationship did have a commercial aspect, but it could not be reduced to that aspect. The form of our exchange had to remain that of the gift, and the reward was therefore left entirely to my appreciation.

Certainly, at any rate, I never had to fear strategies like that of providing imaginary information to increase the working time and thus the reward. The texts to transcribe, translate and explain were so many that there was always work for whoever was available. However, apart from Baras Khan (thanks to the winter school holidays), my other assistants were often too busy to work with me during the day. Although the prospect of making some money – so difficult to procure in Birir – certainly attracted them, they all had daily tasks to carry out, like fetching wood for their families, taking care of their animals, or participating in ritual and social activities, which, as we shall see, happened to be very intense for the whole time of my stay. It was up to me to remind them I needed their help.

* * *

With winter approaching, the population was now concentrated in the main villages. At my arrival in Guru in early November the women, freed from agricultural labours, were mainly busy washing clothes in the river, taking flour to the mills and making bread, while the men grazed the goats in the oak forest above the village, or were busy fetching wood. This was a strenuous everyday task, because with temperatures staying below zero, the iron stoves had to stay lit all day. The wood, during the summer, had been stacked up at the goat sheds, from where it was now time to bring it down. Those who had not stacked up enough, were now forced to search for dry trees often far up the snow-covered mountain slopes. Several men left the village every day early in the morning, axe in hand and a rope coiled across their back, to return only just before dark.

But the activities that absorbed the people of Birir during my stay were mostly of a ritual nature. The month of November (*can~C'ori mastr'uk*) is traditionally devoted to social celebrations like those for the delivering of the dowry to a daughter (*jhes*), for finishing the construction of a new house (*hansar'ik*), or the merit feasts, all of which immediately precede, therefore, the beginning of the winter sequence, filling up the gap after the end-of-summer one, which lasts, we have seen, well into October. The result is an almost uninterrupted chain of ritual activities for the whole autumn and winter period, a perfect example of what Dumézil (1929: 6) called 'exaltation hivernale', 'winter frenzy', remarking that it was a phenomenon found not only among Indo-European people but among all peoples living in similar climates, due to all evidence to the summer dispersal, which makes it impossible to hold community celebrations in the good season. The time when productive activities are halted and the community is again reunited, is certainly the most favourable for religious and social celebrations.

In autumn 2006, in Birir, in addition to the social and religious events normally taking place in the autumn, an unusual number of funerals (*cik*) had to be celebrated, with the result that the rhythm of ritual activities became almost paroxysmal. During my stay from November 2006 to February 2007, as many as five funerals were held in Birir, and one had just been celebrated in October. The addition of these rites to the ones already in store produced a true ritual bottleneck in the wake of Chaumos. In November two *prec'esh* were celebrated – merit and thanksgiving feasts held at the return of the herds to their winter stables at the end of the pastoral cycle – as well as two funerals, while in the first half of December were concentrated two feasts for the delivering of the dowry and one for the completion of a new house, in the days immediately preceding the solstice festival. The latter was immediately followed by another funeral that overlapped with Lagaur – the second festive nucleus of the winter sequence – the beginning of which had to be delayed. One more funeral fell, finally, in between the ritual events of February.

If a *prec'esh* only takes one day, a *jhes* takes two, and a funeral at least three and as many as five in its most magnificent form. A death ceremony is indeed an outstanding event to which hundreds of people from all three valleys may participate, if the defunct was a man of prestige. In all cases the groups involved must undergo a strenuous effort: an economic one because of the distribution of food that the celebration requires, as well as a physical one for the enormous quantity of work needed to entertain so may guests. Furthermore, all these events greatly increased the consumption of wood, forcing on many men additional hard work to procure it. Apart from Baras Khan, often no one was available to work with me.

Acharik and gandalikan – 10 December 2006

In this frantic atmosphere of communal effort, following almost six weeks of uninterrupted ritual activity, on 10 December 2006 the winter ritual sequence began in Birir with a day of collective preparations for Chaumos. Groups of little girls, I was told, would have exceptionally crossed the border into the *'onjiSTa* area of the goat sheds to go into the oak forest to collect firewood for the central day (*koT Sat'ek*, the lighting of the castle) of the festival, when the famous race was going to take place between the two sections (upstream and downstream) into which the population of the valley is divided. In the forest they were going to meet the shepherds, grazing their goats, who were going to give them some pieces of carved wood (*ganD'aLikan*) receiving in exchange gifts of dried fruit. The girls were then going to collect wood for the bonfires to be lit on the dancing place on the main day of the feast. At the same time a group of virgin boys (*'onjiSTa s'uda*) from each of the two sections, were to go to the shrine of the god Praba to collect in the forest surrounding it bundles of dried branches to be used in the central rite of that same day. In brief, the scene was going to be prepared for the great event. I could follow, as we shall see, the activities of the boys, while I could not accompany the girls.[7] The idea was, it seems, that the girls had to prepare the bonfire on the dancing place around which the women were going to sing and dance while the men went to Praba's shrine for the ritual of the race, for which the preparations were to be made by the boys.

On the morning of the appointed day, 10 December, I started off for the holy place accompanied by Gulistan. Praba's shrine is situated on the bottom of a small lateral valley. Although it is not in a high place, its position fits perfectly the Kalasha symbolic construction of space because it is located in a site upstream from the villages in a secluded little valley hemmed in among the rocky slopes of majestic mountains. The shrine is at the centre of an ample enclosure surrounded by a stone wall. To its side, a thicket of oak trees and two groups of four poles stuck vertically in the ground, more than ten metres tall. Each group of poles formed a square with sides about half a yard long: filled up with brushwood they would become the *koT*, the fortresses to be set on fire at the end of the race. On the spot we found two bands of boys, from the upstream and the downstream sections respectively, each standing by their *koT*. As mentioned, the ritual of *koT Sat'ek* is a running race between young men of the two sections. The winner is the runner

---

7 I do not therefore know how the ritual was performed. Since *ganD'aLikan* means 'little statues' it seems likely however – though my informants did not mention it – that the girls received (traditionally at least) some roughly sculpted pieces of wood, maybe rough dolls of some sort.

who first reaches the *koT* of his section and sets it on fire; his community will be blessed with abundant crops for the following year. We found some brushwood already piled up while some boys were returning from the forest carrying dried branches. They were children, by and large; only a couple looked like young adolescents. To carry out their sacred duty they had to be *'onjiSTa*, virgin.

At the centre of the enclosure, barely visible under a thick cover of snow, was 'the house of the god', the *d'ewa dur*. With some surprise I noticed that Gulistan did not seem to worry about the contamination our presence – that of two non-virgin adults – could have brought to the sacred place. In 1973, at the time of our first visit, we were forbidden to enter the enclosure and had to stand by the stone wall. The same had happened in 1935 to the British Colonel Reginald Schomberg (1938: 192–4), author of one of the earliest descriptions of the Kalasha valleys, to whom was explained that only virgin boys could enter the sacred space and that any violation would have required the sacrifice of several billy goats to appease the anger of the god. Maybe the prohibition had been slackened or maybe Gulistan felt that our presence was allowed because it had to do with a ritual duty. But when the altar had to be cleared of snow so that I could take a picture of it, he did not do it himself but ordered a boy to brush off the snow. Only *'onjiSTa* hands could touch it.

The 'house of the god' is a small square-based construction of dry stone masonry, about a yard tall, with a thick wooden plank on the front side, on which two circles of the same size are carved side by side. Just on the top edge of the plank two little protruding horse heads are fixed. The construction is toppled by a large oblong stone set vertically; a feature not found in any other Birir shrine. Could it be that the two circles carved on a plank and the upright oblong stone represent the male sexual organ? We have seen that the name Praba, according to Turner (T-8782) may be derived from *pravabhra*, another name for Indra who had among his main attributes that of the power to generate, to the point that in Tantrism his *vajra* (lightning bolt) was identified with the penis.[8] I did not ask Gulistan for an explanation of the meaning of these features of the shrine, nor is such an interpretation reported by any other researcher, but it could be that we are faced with a very early manifestation of what became in Hinduism the Shivaitic cult of the *lingam*.[9]

---

8 Stutley & Stutley [1977] 1980: 170, 172.

9 Though not all scholars agree that it should be identified with the phallus, there is general consensus that the *lingam* is (at least also) a representation of the power to generate (Stutley & Stutley [1977] 1980: 237). It is interesting to note, in this connection, that a 'natural stone of white colour' is one of the common representations of Shiva (ibid.: 238).

Inside the enclosure the boys, with great glee, were hurling snowballs at each other just by the shrine of the god. After comforting a little rascal who had been hit right in the face and was bleeding from his nose, Gulistan decided the work had been completed and we could all leave.

Not all Kalasha gods inspire a 'holy terror'. In Rumbur people approach shrines without any caution; and also in Birir the atmosphere surrounding the shrine of Mahandeo is not of fear. But Praba, despite the rather irreverent attitude of the kids, was, and probably still is, a feared deity.

Certainly the only myth concerning him represents him as a terrible god, with traits recalling those of the God of the Bible. According to the myth, we have seen, Praba annihilated an entire population with a great flood because of their impiety. We mentioned that the myth tells of a ritual violation in a former homeland and a subsequent catastrophe from which only an old woman and her grandson, the ancestor Suwashai, were saved by the god, who guided them to Birir.[10] Once in the valley, the mythical forefather installed the Praba shrine in the place where it is found today and erected his first house where the village of Aspar now stands. That ancient house is no longer in existence, but tradition has preserved the memory of the place where it once stood. Exactly at that site, in that first day of preparations for Chaumos, as we shall now see, the settling of that first forefather was going to be commemorated with a ritual held by the descendants of Shurasì, son of Suwashai, apical ancestor of the lineages of Guru and Aspar. The common origin was to be revived.

When we reached Aspar village, about an hour's walk from Praba's shrine, we found several men waiting around on the terraced roofs of the houses, near the village temple, the *rikh'ini*: the place where Suwashai had built his first house. A small bonfire was already burning. Soon the girls appeared, seven or eight in number, draped in their mantels against the cold. They were in their early teens, judging from their looks. Wearing their cowrie-shell headdresses (*kup'as*) and displaying their most beautiful ornaments, they stood in a circle in front of the entrance to the temple and started singing *ajh'ona b'ayak*, the most typical song of Chaumos. It is, we have seen, a type of singing in which two opposed groups – typically a masculine and a feminine one – exchange improvised verses replying to each other in turn.[11] Depending on the circumstances, the groups may be formed

---

10 Various versions of the myth have been published: Hussam-ul-mulk 1974a: 82–3; Shah 1974: 80; Loude & Lièvre 1984: 324; Lièvre & Loude 1991: 190–1.

11 Witzel (2004: 613) remarks that examples of this type of verbal exchange are found in the Rig Veda (10.86).

only by a few people or by entire crowds rivalling in a gleeful competition that may last even for hours. It is a song tied to a specific time of the year, because it can only be sung from the Prun autumn festival until the end of Chaumos.

Soon two groups formed, the girls of Guru and the girls of Aspar, and they started joking and teasing each other, while the children were running around like mad. We were waiting for the *'onjiSTa s'uda*, the virgin boys we had seen earlier at Praba's shrine; they were going to bring, I was told, a big basket (*dr'ay*) to be burnt in the fire. The girls were the main singers, but some boys occasionally joined for a while one of the two groups. Here is a brief example of the verses I recorded that afternoon:

Guru girls:
The village of Aspar is known for being 'onjiSTa
And now I see that you are making it pr'agata
Ahi ahi my dear sister, my precious little sister

Aspar girls:
Why are you so stiff and haughty?
Why do you yell? Why are you so worried?
Ahi ahi my dear sister, my precious little sister

The singing went on for a while with groups of children at times joining in improvising childish verses of their own, amid general laughter. At dusk, the *'onjiSTa s'uda* finally appeared with a large basket that set the fire ablaze while the girls continued singing. Once the flames died out, the boys ran off in the dark in the direction of Guru carrying with them a second big basket, and the girls followed swiftly in their footsteps. The trail passed above the *bash'ali* from where came the voices of the women confined there, who were singing *'ajh'ona b'ayak*. When we reached Guru, in a half hour or so, a bonfire was already lit on the flat roof of the village temple and a mostly female crowd was standing around it. There too the song was *'ajh'ona b'ayak*, but every so often it was alternated with a chant called *sh'ai*, which was, in contrast, slow, drawn-out and melancholy. Two groups exchanging verses amidst claps of hands were continuously formed, dissolved and re-formed; two girls occasionally tried a dancing step. Children were running around yelling wildly while mothers seemed not at all worried by the fact that we were standing on a roof with unprotected edges. When the big basket brought by the *'onjiSTa s'uda* was thrown into the bonfire, huge flames soared up, lighting up the scene and forcing the circle to step back. Around the fire a merry-go-round of women and girls of all ages was formed, and the terraced roof of the temple became the scene of a game. A girl was left alone in the middle; she was holding a piece of wood with which she threatened another little girl who was standing outside the circle and was protected by the women from the blows of her pursuer. The girl brandishing the piece of wood, it was later explained to me, imperson-ated an angry husband and the other one a fugitive wife. The standard cause of the quarrel was an adultery committed by the woman,[12] not a rare occurrence among the Kalasha (Maggi 2001: 187). During the game, amid bursts of laughter and shrills of glee, the women were singing these verses:

> Fox, fox; fox penetrator of the vagina
> Vagina, penis; your penis went off for a little rub

The song caused great hilarity, and all women, old ladies or baby girls, were singing it full voice. Words never to be pronounced by a woman in public in ordi-nary times were being shouted out without any shame: as is typical of ritual,[13] that extraordinary behaviour was not only allowed, but mandatory. It did not depend therefore on personal choice, but was required by *dast'ur* itself. Much embar-rassment was shown instead by my male assistants when we set out to translate the recorded text. Extracted from their ritual context, the words of the song were embarrassing also for men. Baras Khan declared that those were archaic terms and that he did not know their meaning: I had to enquire with someone else. I finally obtained the translation from Gulistan, after much winking and giggling. The fox, called penetrator of the vagina, clearly represents the penis; the second verse, though openly sexual in content, is somewhat enigmatic: it may be meant to tease men suggesting that they masturbate rather than copulating. But it was impossible to discuss the subject further with Gulistan. He only added that the girls sing that same song when in the morning they go to the forest where the shepherds are waiting for them.

Songs and dances continued on the roof of the temple until it was time for supper. It appeared to be a largely feminine celebration. The song leaders were all women and the few men present just joined occasionally in the choruses without taking any initiative.

In this day of preparations, some of the main themes of Chaumos are antici-pated. The boys gather brushwood near the *kot* to prepare the scene of the central

---

12 For a similar custom in pre-Islamic Waigal (Nuristan) see Klimburg 1999: 179.
13 Cf. Caillois [1939] 2001: 117; Sanga 1982: 5; Turner [1982] 1986: 83.

event of the festival, the race between runners of the two sections, and the women sing in the villages the song of the fox, which is sung only on the day of the race. The obscene and provoking song of the women has to do with the theme of fertility and human reproduction and is possibly aimed at stimulating male eroticism. With the morning excursion of the girls into the forest, the feminine sphere, exceptionally, expands beyond its borders: the male and the female pole live a moment of temporary integration in anticipation of the festival. But at the same time, the game accompanying the song represents the antagonism between genders and enacts female solidarity, as if it were intended to remind men that their power over women is not limitless. It has limits for what concerns the control of women's sexuality, a sphere in which Kalasha culture is at sharp variance with the Muslim world surrounding it (Maggi 2001). Another main theme of Chaumos is introduced in this day: that of renewal and regeneration, symbolized by the old baskets thrown in the fire.

Something to note is that in this first day of separation the two sections of the population remain neatly separated. The upstream one gathers in the temple of Biyou, while the downstream one, as we have seen, first in the temple of Aspar and then on the roof-tops of Guru.

Desh sucein and bhut ungush'ek – 14 December 2006

On 14 December the opening rite of Chaumos was held. It is called *desh suc'ein*, the purification of the country. It is a ritual carried out only by two elders and a couple of *'onjiSTa s'uda*, in which I did not participate. It was described to me as follows.

The group goes to a certain goat shed situated near Biyou, the uppermost village of the valley, in a place called *AU'e*, believed to be the scene of a famous mythical episode concerning the semi-divine ancestor of the Bangulè-dari clan,[14] the largest of the upper section. There the *'onjiSTa s'uda* burn juniper branches and sacrifice a lamb. The blood is gathered in a bowl that is carried up a mountain near Biyou where the rite of *suc* is held: a fire is lit with juniper branches and part of the blood of the lamb is thrown into it. The two elders then descend the valley separately accompanied by an *'onjiSTa s'uda*, each following one of the two banks of the river, so that the entire territory is covered. Taking a high path above the villages, they repeat the same *suc* rite for each settlement. Once they reach the last one at the extreme downstream end of Kalasha territory, they throw the skin

---

14 For a version of this myth see Hussam-ul-mulk 1974a: 82.

of the lamb they had brought with them into the river, and conclude their sacred duty by washing their arms.

With this ritual, the space of everyday life acquires an extraordinary quality in preparation for a form of communication that cannot take place just anywhere; it requires spaces that have previously been consecrated. The whole territory is consecrated with juniper smoke and with the blood of the lamb, which we may see as a scapegoat: its skin thrown in the torrent downstream from the Kalasha villages appears to symbolically take away all the ugly things of everyday life and the impurities accumulated in the course of the year. During the days of Chaumos, the *'onjiSTa* sphere expands beyond its borders of ordinary times, including not just the goat-sheds, but the villages as well; with the rite of *desh suc'ein*, the whole *desh*, that is the whole Kalasha country, is symbolically included in it. The environment will be included in the 'ritual text'[15] and must therefore be accurately prepared.

Every four years, my assistants continued, at the end of this day another ritual takes place, called *bhut ungush'ek* (exciting the *bhut* spirits). It is a nocturnal rite. A band of men runs through the villages after dark dancing the *bhut nat*, the dance of the spirits, which is danced backwards. They wreck havoc, for example by carrying away the ladders needed to go from one roof to the next, by taking the heavy wooden funnels for the grain out of the water mills, or by throwing rocks at the houses while the people remain locked inside. The *bhut* are believed to be spirits who live by the stream, near water-mills or springs, in the vicinities of the villages. In the extraordinary time of the feast, the ordinarily invisible presence of these low-valley spirits can manifest itself.

As *desh suc'ein* creates a sacred space, so does *bhut ungush'ek* install a sacred time, regulated by an order that is the opposite of that of ordinary life, as symbolized by the tricks they play and by their backwards dance. In this symbolic subversion we may see a representation of the Chaos/Cosmos dichotomy, typical of New Year celebrations;[16] Chaos seen as a return to the beginning, to the Unformed preceding creation, as a necessary point of departure for the regeneration of the world New Year rituals seek to accomplish.

Ruzhias – 15 December 2006

The day of *desh suc'ein*, is followed by that of *ruzh'ias*. The theme of purification is still in the foreground. In the morning the women sweep the houses and wash

---

15 For an analysis of ritual communication see Miceli 1989: 131–4.
16 Eliade [1949] 1968: 77–94; Cardini 1995: 21, 192; Buttitta, A. 1996: 268.

kitchen utensils. In the course of the day juniper branches are burnt for the *bhut* spirits. *ruzh'i* are evil female spirits that recall European witches, who on that day are believed to wander unleashed after dark. At the beginning of the 1980s Jean-Yves Loude and Viviane Lièvre recorded the following story from a man of Birir:

> The wife of Nadui was a witch. She had the habit of eating human beings.
> One day she wanted to devour her own husband. But Nadui was hiding on
> an oak tree and was observing the doings of his wife. The woman owed her
> powers to Warin. She implored him: 'Allow me to eat my husband!'. But
> Warin rejected her request: 'Nadui is a good man, he has always offered
> me nursing goats, no, I shall not hand him over to you!'. After these words
> the witch found herself catapulted at once in her house, lying on her bed.
> Nadui arrived and nailed her to the four legs of the bed, and the woman died.
> (Loude & Lièvre 1984: 323).[17]

The man related also that in the night of *ruzh'ias* his Panei-dari lineage offers a sacrifice on the terraced roof of the house of the descendants of Nadui as atonement for that crime, and he added that the people of Birir shoot in the air to chase away demons and witches. The same authors specify that this is also the day of the descent of the dead for whom offerings of bread are prepared in all the houses (Loude & Lièvre 1984: 323, 344).

My assistants, strangely, did not mention witches or the story of Nadui – traditions that seem to have a solid base in the name itself of the day (the day of the witches) – but they said that on that night two important sacrifices are celebrated: one of the two was indeed the one offered by the Panei-dari, one of the smaller lineages, considered to be autochthonous; the other one, they said, was the responsibility of the Razhuk-dari, another autochthonous lineage. The two sacrifices lift the prohibition on the consumption of the wine from the last grape harvest, which from then on can be drunk freely: wine and Chaumos are closely associated in the mind of the Birir people, and we shall see that elation from wine drinking is one of the main traits of the festival.

The Razhuk-dari seem to enjoy a special status among the lineages of Birir. According to tradition, we have seen, they descend from Gordimìu, the first Kalasha of Birir. Their houses differ from those of other lineages because they all have the prestigious *kumbAp'ur*, the elaborate lantern ceiling typical of temples.

---

17 An English translation of the work quoted here does exist, but is not at my disposal. This is therefore my own translation from the French original.

They are the custodians of the semi-god Grimùn, whose open-air mountain sanctuary is located near the settlement of Nozhbiu, where the most numerous branch of the lineage has its residence (Map IV). That night the Razhuk-dari were going to sacrifice a lamb specifically for Grimùn, in addition to a billy goat to celebrate the first wine of the year. The sacrifice of the goat was supposed to take place at the goat sheds by the *shin*, a cistern accurately lined with flat stones, dug in the floor of a small construction, where the must is poured and left to ferment. Since wine is *'onjiSTa*, all activities connected to wine making take place in the area of the goat sheds where, as we know, women are not admitted.[18]

Baras Khan proposed going to the Razhuk-dari goat shed, a forty minute walk downstream from Guru, to participate in the ritual to be officiated there. A few nights before, indeed, a young man of the Razhuk-dari lineage, after a number of glasses of wine, had warmly invited us to go. We reached Nozhbiu just before dark. The houses of the Razhuk-dari were grouped together one beside the other, in two lanes. We were received in the house of the patriarch, a man perhaps in his sixties, with two wives, ten sons and so many grandchildren he could not keep track of their number. They explained to me that they had recently built three new houses for the newly-formed families, which, however, were used only for sleeping: for meals they still gathered all together in the house we were in. Four houses made therefore one *kush'un*; with two more units of the same kind they formed a small hamlet of about twelve houses. We enquired about the rite, but we saw immediately that they were hesitant. The warm invitation of the tipsy young man had apparently been rash. His father, to all appearances, was not pleased by our visit. Finally the patriarch, forced in a corner, explained that the rite was a very *'onjiSTa* one, and that strangers could not be admitted. Baras Khan as well could not be admitted, because he belonged to a different lineage. That was the only time, in the whole cycle of winter feasts, when I was expressly denied participation in a ritual. To other semi-secret rites, considered to be particularly *'onjiSTa*, I simply never asked to assist.

The patriarch excused himself and the women begged me not to be offended. I replied that I fully understood their point of view, because I believed *dast'ur* had to be respected. It was decided that we could be allowed to go to the goat shed, once the rite was over, to participate in the sacrificial meal. A boy guided us along the icy little path leading to the goat shed. The space inside was full of men crouching

---

18 For descriptions of the wine-making procedures in Birir see Loude & Lièvre 1987, Fentz 2010: 403–10, and Klimburg 2014 who describes them in the context of a broader research devoted to viticulture in Kafiristan.

around the fire while in a corner the billy goat, that was hanging from the ceiling head down, was being skinned and cut to pieces. The same had already been done with the lamb, and a few small pieces of meat were cooking on the fire in a pan. The rite had been over for a while.

That same night, a short walk downstream from Nozhbiu, the inauguration feast (*hansar'ik*) was going to be held for the new house of *kaz'i* Saidan Shah, the father of my host in Guru. It was a ritual I had never participated in and that, therefore, I did not want to miss. But, feverish as I was from the day before, I had already made a huge effort to reach Nozhbiu in the cold of the night. Unwillingly I had to decline the invitation to go. The men in the goat shed, about twenty of them, were all planning to join the party. They were going to leave on the fire the big cauldron with the meat of the billy goat so that they would find it ready to eat upon their return. I heard, the next day, that the celebration had gone on until the morning. The house was packed with people, I was told, and they had been dancing and singing throughout the night.

Goshtsaraz – 16 December 2006

On the third day of the festival the divinity of Chaumos arrives in the valley. The day takes its name from the purification rite with juniper (*s'araz*) smoke that is held in the afternoon in all goat sheds (*goST*), with offerings of wine and *'onjiSTa* flour, obtained from grains brought to the mills by virgin boys. The rite is performed on the roofs of the goat-sheds, or at times inside, in front of the symbol of Surizan, the divinity protector of the herds. But the most spectacular event are the great torchlight evening processions that, from the various hamlets, flow to the three main temples of the valley, those of the villages of Guru, Aspar and Biyou.

In the morning, men and women, in the goat sheds and in the houses respectively, were busy preparing the filling to make *jA~'u* – thick bread cakes of wheat or maize flour filled with mashed walnuts – for the feast. The flour must be prepared in advance, because on the days of Chaumos it is not allowed to grind grain – the job that symbolizes ordinary everyday life, we may infer, must be suspended in the extraordinary time of the feast. At dusk I decided not to wait for the procession in Guru but to follow it from its departure, from the places, that is, where the torches were being made. So I went with Baras Khan to Grabanisar, one of the new hamlets around Guru, where his family lived. In the veranda of the house a young man was cutting long splinters of wood from the trunk of a pine tree with an adze. Inside the house other splinters were ready, lined up against a wall. It was a special type of torch (*Ca~J'a*) made only on this day. The long splinters are joined in a bundle tied up with a ring of intertwined willow catkins. The bundle must be made by as many elements as are the members of each *kush'un*, to symbolize the unity of the family and its full participation in the ritual event. The longest torch was as tall as a man. We continued to wait. From the darkness of the valley bottom came voices of young people shouting. Their cries, disorderly at first, faded away in the end with a crescendo of a long ohohohoh, voiced in unison. The young people were the *prabal'on g'Uak*, the Praba boys, a strictly male group composed of the novices themselves and of a band of adolescent boys, already initiated but still virgin (*'onjiiSTa s'uda*), who were going to spend the period of seclusion beginning the next day together.

On that day the *prabal'on g'Uak* were starting to emerge as an autonomous group and to become the protagonists of the feast. It was their task, Baras Khan explained, to signal the starting off of the processions, making the round of the villages. The torches were being lit as they arrived. Two processions were to converge on the *rikh'ini* of Guru: one formed by the people of the hamlets along the main Birir valley, and the other one by the inhabitants of the Grabet side valley (Map IV).

At a certain point, from the village of Grabanisar we saw a string of lights starting to move on the other side of the torrent. The first procession was already in motion. We saw groups of torches merging together and finally forming a single procession that suddenly started to run, swiftly crossing the bridge and climbing up Guru's small path, shouting insults at the people of the village. The second procession left shortly afterwards:

> We remain waiting until we see a fire being lit. We go down. There were some boys waiting with their torches around a small fire. There were some women as well. At a certain point we hear shouts far away in the dark and soon afterwards we are reached by a wave of lights held by men and women whistling, shouting, singing, at times even in unison. We join them. The procession was virtually running, led by Saidan Shah with his white beard, his chitrali *cug'a* [a long woollen embroidered overcoat] and a twig of juniper in his *kash'ong* [woollen cap], *gund'ik* [walking stick] in hand. There was a brief halt in a flat space just before the bridge, and there the volume of the singing was raised and several people, women and men, began to dance. And then everybody raced up the steep path leading to Guru, all the way up to the *rikh'ini* amid shouts, shrill whistles and gunshots. We manage to precede them with difficulty, because they are running fast, and we reach the temple

with the head of the procession. The drums are beating already. (*From my field journal – Guru. 16 December 2006*).

The shouts mostly appeared to be provocations or insults, addressed to the people of Guru and the surrounding villages. The following is the text I managed to record in the midst of the running stream of shouting torch bearers:

People of Guru, fuck you!
People of Guru fuck you!
Let's shout it out loud!
Fuck you!
People of Bashalitada, fuck you!
People from downstream, fuck you![19]

Strong words. Addressed in general to all the inhabitants of the surrounding villages and to the people of the other procession who were marching up the valley toward Guru and its temple, but at times they were directed even at specific people, particularly esteemed in the community. While I was observing from afar the third procession I had heard also the cry *lambard'ar zh'awi!*, seemingly a provocation addressed to old Sherbek (*lambard'ar* was his title), one of the most respected men of the valley who, in addition, at that time was laying sick in bed with an appendicitis. 'These are traditional cries' Baras Khan reassured me, when we were translating those lines. Young people, novices included, were mostly doing the shouting, but adult men would also intermittently join in.

With Goshtsaraz day, the peak of the pre-liminal stage of the celebration approaches. The purification rites of the first two days of the festival, which marked the separation from ordinary space and time, concerned the entire community. In this third day, instead, while rites for the entire community (offerings of juniper smoke at the goat sheds, the processions) continue, the initiates, we have seen, begin to emerge as a distinct autonomous group, which will take full form in the liminal stage with the physical isolation from the rest of the community: when they roam around the valley shouting, they are appropriating the territory; when

19 In the Kalasha original we have the verbal form *zh'awi*, which means to copulate, in the imperative, without any pronoun. But Taj Khan, a young Kalasha man studying in Greece, whom I consulted about this verse, replied that the exact meaning is that 'the act itself should be done by someone to the inhabitants of Guru' (email message 19 April 2016). The most correct interpretation would then be 'fuck you' rather than just 'fuck'.

they order the departure of the processions they play a leading role that youngsters ordinarily do not have; and when they insult adults and respected men they violate one of the basic rules of Kalasha society, that of treating elders with respect.

These are typical traits of initiation ceremonies and of New Year feasts. There is the trait of the liberty allowed to novices – or rather of the obligation imposed on the novices – to perform acts of aggression against the community, like insulting elders, that Van Gennep ([1909] 1981: 98) sees as a rite of separation, in which ordinary social ties are modified, and at times even severed. We can also see, in these ritual insults, the manifestation of one of the two poles of the 'increased solidarity/exacerbated antagonism' dichotomy that Lévi-Strauss ([1952] 1995: 67–8) indicates as a characteristic trait of the 'December feasts': young people join in an autonomous body and perform acts of violence against the community. The purpose of such ritual behaviour is to enact a subversion of the normal order preluding the sacred time of rebirth and regeneration (Rappaport 1999: 381 2), which founds – like in African rites of rebellion or in European Carnivals – a temporary 'world turned upside-down' in which the positions of status are inverted: in an essentially egalitarian community like that of Birir, the main hierarchical relation – apart from that between genders – is between youngsters and elders.

But at the same time the other pole of Lévi-Strauss's duality also appears. Though somewhat in the background, the theme of solidarity also emerges: the members of the lineages belonging to each temple celebrate the ties uniting them with the songs and dances of the night. The climax of the pre-liminal stage, and the imminent passage to the subsequent stage, is marked also by the element of fire, which appears in a moving form, as a procession of torches. Fire is, in fact, an essential element in every Kalasha rite, but here its form is grand: in place of the normal sacrificial flame, we have a true torrent of fire.

The use of fire in ceremonies connected to the solstices is a widespread ritual custom.[20] The flames of torches and bonfires mark a fracture in ordinary time. They are especially characteristic of New Year celebrations and are deemed to stimulate the fertility of nature and of human beings. In this general frame, their functions may be quite varied. In the processions of Goshtsaraz, fire plays an instrumental function because it lightens up the path, as well as, and especially, a function of expression because it is used to say something about the state of

---

20 In Europe from Ireland to Russia (e.g. Frazer [1922] 1987: 609–41; Van Gennep 1958: 3032–163, [1943] 1998: 841–84, [1949] 1999: 1439–580; Propp [1963] 1978: 49–50; Cardini 1995: 104, 118; Buttitta, I.E. 1999: 173, 213), as well as in India (e.g. Berreman 1963: 391–2) and America (e.g. Lanternari [1976] 1983a: 326–7).

things (Leach [1976] 1981: 23). It is a function of expression that is at once of communication and of goodwill because it signals the approaching of the central phase of the festival, and because fires lit in the wake of a solstice are aimed at helping the sun to resume its movement and at awakening the fertility of nature.[21]

When we arrived running at the *rikh'ini*, the drums were already beating. Under the porch covering the entrance to the temple, the women were welcoming the processions chanting *sh'ahi*, a slow and yearning hymn announcing the coming of Chaumos:

The glare of your many torches, shahiooo
A hecatomb of billy goats, shahiooo
Benedictions upon benedictions, shahiooo
The glare of your many torches
This is the sacred feast of Chaumos

The chant of the women was celebrating the coming of the central phase of the festival, hailing the processions, the animal sacrifices and the abundant benedictions. It was an exclusively female chorus. No male voice ever joined in. While the women out in the porch were chanting in the light of the pine torches still streaming up the hill, inside the temple the celebration had begun.

The great hall was full of people and filled with the fragrance of the cedar wood burning in a big fire. The temple has the structure of a house, but it is much larger. Like all Kalasha houses it is quadrangular in shape with four central pillars upholding the roof; only that the pillars are richly carved and the ceiling has an elaborate structure with intercrossing beams (*kumbAp'ur*).[22] The entrance door is carved as well and on its doorposts two wooden horse heads are fitted. Two fires were lighting the interior. The singing and dancing was already going on, and was going to continue for the whole night, until morning came.

Since this long night-dance is the chief attraction of Goshtsaraz, and given the importance of song and dance in Kalasha rituality it is worthwhile to pause briefly in our narration to analyze Kalasha verbal art.

---

21 See Buttitta, I.E. (1999: 202–3) for a typology of the functions of fire based on a study of the ritual use of fire in popular Catholicism in Sicily.

22 This is an element of Kalasha material culture possibly due to the influence of the great civilizations of the plains: the same pattern, but carved in sandstone, decorated the ceilings of the cells of the rock monasteries surrounding the Buddhas of Bamiyan. This type of roof is not peculiar to the Kalasha; it is found also in Chitral, in Nuristan and in the Hindu Kush generally (Illi 1991).

Kalasha song and dance

In the Birir Chaumos we must distinguish two broad categories of song/dance. One is formed by songs and chants directly connected to Chaumos, never sung on any other occasion, and the other by songs sung also at the other seasonal festivals (Joshi and Prun), and at social events like funerals or merit feasts. The former are songs of the women, stemming from the female world, to which men – apart from the case of *ajh'ona b'ayak* – usually only listen. The latter, in contrast, require the participation of both genders, but the initiative of the singing is prevailingly male. The chant *sh'ahi*, translated above, belongs clearly to the first group, while the songs and dances beginning in the temple on the evening of Goshtsaraz belong to the second one. Unlike the songs of the women, these songs are always accompanied by dancing and drumming. We shall see further on that in the other two Kalasha valleys, in contrast, these songs are forbidden during Chaumos; even the drums are banned altogether. Consequently, the Chaumos dances there take forms specifically related to the solstice festival. We shall come back later to the Chaumos songs. Let us consider now the typology of 'ordinary' songs and dances, those of all celebrations, which in the Birir Chaumos are inaugurated on the night of Goshtsaraz.

* * *

Kalasha singing and dancing is a complex social and linguistic event with a precise structure. In a corner of the temple – or of the dancing ground if the celebration is taking place outdoors – a predominantly male group of singers, formed mostly by mature and elderly men, stands in a circle (*magl'is*). At a certain distance, but always in sight of the singers, stand two drummers. One of the drums (*da~'u*) is large, cylindrical and is beaten with a curved stick; the other one, much smaller (*wa~c*), has the shape of an hourglass and is beaten with bare hands. The drummers are not specialized musicians; in the course of a celebration several men take turns at the drums. The dances take place in the space at the centre of the temple delimited by the pillars, or also beyond them when the hall is crowded. The whole event is directed by the circle of singers, because from their singing depends the rhythm of the drums and the type of dance.

There are only three types of song/dance: *ca~, d'ushak* and *drazha'ilak*. The first one, *ca~*, has the liveliest rhythm. The dancing prevails over the singing: the singers occasionally strike up a verse, but the beat of the drums overwhelms all voices. *ca~* can be a solo dance, with the dancer rotating with lifted arms: the women just make elegant movements with their hands, while men dance more vigorously, whistling shrilly with two fingers in their mouths and brandishing at times a ceremonial axe, a spear or a walking stick with the steps of a war dance. Otherwise, *ca~* can be danced in groups of three that rotate three times in each direction, and then dash forward moving counterclockwise in a circle. At times two trios face each other and charge head down, imitating a clash between male goats, and then lift their heads abruptly just before the clash, bursting in a loud, ritual laughter: *ah, ah, ah!* The trios may be composed of women only, or of men, or they may be mixed. With wine flowing, *ca~* may get out of hand, generating an overpowering Dionysian atmosphere. But when out-of-control dancers start bumping into the singers in the circle, an order is generally issued from the *magl'is* to the musicians, who switch to a slower rhythm. The lyrics of *ca~* are quite simple and composed only of a few verses. They are usually based on traditional formulae, freely adapted to the circumstances. In contrast to what is generally the case with the other two styles, they contain often explicit references to the celebration taking place. Here are the lyrics of one of the *ca~* I recorded in the night of 16 December 2006:

> *Oh ceremony of Chaumos, it is already two days since you descended among us*
> *My little girl shall be initiated*
> *It will be a party for the children of my village of Guru*
> *When the celebrations will be over I shall miss them*
> *The god is arriving; many he-goats will be sacrificed*
> *The god is arriving, the god has arrived; he announces the initiation of those*
>   *dear little girls*
> *The god is arriving, from the sacrificial fires the scent of juniper and of blood*
>   *will arise*
> *The god is arriving; the scent of juniper is spreading everywhere*
> *The god is coming, juniper smoke rises in clouds from the sacrificial fires*
>   *burning in the goat sheds.*

In fact, *ca~* is not really considered a song (*ghO~*) as much as a dance (*nat*). The singing is indeed reduced to a few verses that are not taken up and repeated by the crowd as we shall see is the rule both in *d'ushak* and *drazha'ilak*. The verses above were not sung by a single person, but were shouted in turn by the six singers – all men – who composed in that moment the circle, while everybody else was dancing wildly without paying them any attention. The text is largely composed of standard formulae. The first verse welcomes Chaumos, addressing it as if it were a person. The time reference is precise; it was indeed the third day of the festival. The other verses, like the chant of the women under the porch, recall the main ritual events of the celebration – the initiations of the girls and the many goat sacrifices for the initiations of the boys – and evoke the joyful atmosphere typical of those days.

From the point of view of the morphology of ritual, an important element is the smoke of the sacrificial fires, and especially the fragrance (*gand'uryak*) of juniper sprayed with the blood of the sacrificial victims – this also being found in the Zoroastrian (Parsi) cult of fire, as well as in the Homeric formula of the 'odorous altar', but not present, it seems, in the Vedic sacrifice (Heesterman 1993: 18–19). Concerning the contents, the most interesting point in the text is maybe the announcement of the arrival of a divine guest: *d'ewa 'ilo*, the god is coming – a god, however, who remains without a name. This is a central aspect of the ideology of Chaumos. Each of the three great cyclical festivals – it was once explained to me by Kaanok, a middle-aged man who often came to see me in the evenings for a chat   is characterized by a focal point, a central event: 'of Joshi' he said 'we say *zh'ew par'au*', the line (of goats) has left (for the summer pastures); 'of Prun *buD'alak g'Uaka ucund'iu*', the budalak boys, the fecundating shepherds, descend; 'of Chaumos' he explained 'we say instead *d'ewa 'ilo*', the god comes. The term itself used, as we shall see, to refer to the festival – *dewasamE~a* – implies this idea. I enquired about the meaning of this word with various people without obtaining a unanimous answer. According to Kaanok, *dewasamE~a* means 'the *dewal'ok*, the gods, descend on Earth'.[23] To this he added that, however, now they no longer descend because Kalasha land has become *r'ela*, impure. Formerly, when no one ate chickens or eggs, when Islam had not arrived and everything was very *'onjiSTa*, then the *dewal'ok* really descended and people could see them; today, he concluded, at most they observe us from a distance. His view recalls the general idea of the divine entering the human sphere in the sacred time of the New Year, when a cycle ends, a new one begins, and profane time is suspended. The words of Kaanok seem to echo the 'longing for a paradise lost' discussed by Mircea Eliade ([1949] 1968: 93, 120), the longing, that is, for a mythical golden age when the channels of communication between humans and gods were open. A golden age evoked also by Kalasha oral tradition as a mythical time when humans, animals and gods were living side by side and could communicate.[24] Kaanok, however, adds to it an historical

---

23 A possible etymology is *d'ewa* (dio) – *sam'E* < *samana*, 'meeting', 'reunion', i.e., the meeting with the god.

24 Snoy 1974: 84; 2008: 45; Lièvre & Loude 1990: 145–6.

connotation, by placing it before the arrival of Islam with its disruptive influence on the *'onjiSTa* sphere.

If *ca~* is considered a dance and not a song, *d'ushak* and *drazha'ilak* are, in contrast, true performances of verbal art. The beginning of a performance and its type is signalled to the hall by the tempo of the drums. In the case of *drazha'ilak* the drummers beat a slow and paced rhythm, while the dancers – mostly women – hold each other by the shoulders and hips and form a long line (*tren*) that moves slowly anticlockwise around the *magl'is*. In the case of *d'ushak*, the pattern of the dance remains virtually unchanged, but the tempo of the drums and the rhythm of the step are much faster than in *drazha'ilak*, while the lines of the dancers are much shorter; but in structure the two performances are exactly the same.

An event of *d'ushak* or *drazha'ilak* can be divided into two phases.[25] A singer, of his own initiative, or exhorted by the *magl'is*, starts a chant in a low voice, while the other members of the circle lend their ears, and the crowd literally piles up around them to listen and learn the lyrics. The chant is then repeated in a chorus by the *magl'is*. This binary sequence soloist/chorus is subsequently repeated twice more, but at the third repetition the solo singer adopts a different, simplified style, which makes the verses easier to understand, facilitating the choral singing of the chant. The singers in the *magl'is* are then gradually joined by the line, or lines, of dancers, so that the original song of the soloist finally becomes a collective chant resonating in the whole temple.

At this point the second phase begins. One of the members of the circle grasps a stick and, brandishing it in the air, voices a song of his own in the simplified style of the third repetition of the soloist. This will be a new composition that takes the form of a panegyric praising the composer of the original song, mainly by recalling the feats of his ancestors and meticulously listing their names: *nom nom'ek*, 'to name the name', is indeed the expression used to refer to this type of eulogy. A second choral repetition of the original song follows. The sequence could virtually be repeated indefinitely, because there is no limit to the number of panegyrics that could be composed, but generally the event is concluded after the third, or fourth, *nom nomek*. The complete performance may last more than one hour. The structure just described has been schematically summed up by Di Carlo (2007: 71) as follows:

---

25 For an analysis of Kalasha verbal art and a detailed description of *ca~*, *d'ushak* and *drazha'ilak* events during the Prun festival of 2006 see Di Carlo 2007: 65–76, 2010a, 2010b. For Kalasha verbal art see also Parkes 1996a.

1- solo singer intones a song (original or traditional) in ornamented style (style A);

2- *magl'is* repeats the song (specific choral style);

3- solo singer repeats the song in style A;

4- *magl'is* repeats the song (specific choral style);

5- solo singer repeats the text of the song in a less ornamented style (style B);

6- *magl'is* repeats the song (specific choral style);

7- one out of the *magl'is* components makes *n'oman nom'ek* (style B);

8- *magl'is* repeats the song (specific choral style).

At the second choral repetition of the *magl'is*, the chant starts spreading in the temple, taken up by the lines of dancers who, looking towards the central fire, revolve with a lateral step around the small circle of the singers.

From the formal point of view *drazha'ilak*, as well as the other two genres, is a performance strictly guided by *dast'ur*. The structure of the singing and the dancing follows traditional patterns, as well as the gestures of the singers and the listeners. As for the contents, in contrast, the lyrics of *drazha'ilak* and *d'ushak*, unlike those of *ca~* that are always traditional, may be traditional but also original new compositions, created expressly for a certain circumstance. The singers prepare themselves beforehand and for every festival new songs are created. The lyrics may refer to the festival being celebrated but they may concern also issues that have nothing to do with the celebration for which they were composed. The text presented below is an example of traditional composition. It is a song in *d'ushak* style followed by a *nom nom'ek*:

> *Oh celebration in every way I praise you*
> *For two days now you have been our guest in our village temple*
> *When we celebrate, the peak of Pachaemundik is clad in dense smoke*

Nom nomek

> *Oh offspring of Shurasì, look! This Chaumos celebration*
> *Oh offspring of Shurasì, look! Your ancestors came here from Majam*
> *Chaumos was not celebrated here then*
> *Your ancestor Sinwashal brought it here after crossing the Durik and*
>   *Sarawat passes*
> *Oh Kalasha king, look! This whole Kalasha country is under your control*
> *Oh descendant of Lataruk, the words of your tongue have told the truth*

Oh descendant of Lataruk, look! This is how you make beautiful this whole
*   Kalasha country*
Your celebration has taken place here in Guru, it did succeed
This is your celebration
Oh descendant of Lataruk, my son in law, look how safe this whole Kalasha
*   country is!*
In every way I praise you
With the full autumn moon
Down in Sandik Nisar you built a mansion where your bee-hive will thrive
Now the whole Kalasha country is gathered here, look! and everyone is
*   seeking you, oh descendant of Lataruk*
Now look, you are gathering together your noble stock
Oh descendant of Lataruk. oh brave man
Restored is this whole Kalasha country, here is your holy house
Oh descendant of Lataruk, what else can you say, let us make beautiful my
*   celebration.*
Oh brave man it has become solid here your holy house
This very feast you are making together with the descendants of Babura
You with the support of the descendants of Babura are awakening this whole
*   Kalasha country*
Oh descendant of Lataruk! If the lineage of Lataruk has given the biramor
*   feast, the lineage of Babura gives the precesh feast at the shrine of great*
*   Mahandeo*
The harmony between you made happy the gods who dwell on the crests
What other beautiful words can we pronounce? work well for the success of
*   this joyful feast, ololéee!*

                    (Recorded in Guru temple – night of 16 December 2006)

As can be seen from the text, the initial song is very simple and short while the panegyric that follows is long and fairly complex in its content. If this were a *drazha'ilak* instead of a *d'ushak*, the song of the first soloist would have been longer, but still much shorter than the panegyrics sung in response. The song was sung in the night of Goshtsaraz, in Guru village temple, by the *kaz'i* Saidan Shah, of the Lataruk-nawau, the father of my host Erfan. The panegyric following it was intoned by Goarnement,[26] of the Razhuk-nawau. After two days of

---

26 It is a name clearly inspired by the the English word 'government'. Similar names are quite common among the Kalasha. In Rumbur there is an Enginier Khan, a Komandér and a London

mere ritual activities, that was the first night dedicated to dancing and singing. Like the *ca~* analyzed above, this *d'ushak* also welcomes the festival as if it were a person. From the point of view of content, the only difference is the reference to Mount Pachaemundik, an imposing massif delimiting to the north the sacred valley of Jagar, with a verse evoking the image of a great cloud of smoke rising from the sacrificial fires of Chaumos, so great as to envelop the rocky crests of the mountain. The song, after the usual repetitions, was followed by two panegyrics.

The first one, reported above, recalls in the beginning the mythical ancestor Suwashai, forefather of the Shurasi-dari clan, to which the Lataruk-nawau belong. Quite appropriately, considering the occasion, Goarnement reminds me that the founding of Chaumos is attributed to Suwashai. He brought the festival with him – the lyrics say – from his previous homeland, Majam, beyond the present-day Afghan border, on the other side of the Durik and Sarawat passes. Majam, in fact, is only a summer pasture, just beyond the passes, but the name seems to be used to refer to the country beyond the mountains to the west, ancient Kafiristan, where until the end of last century, as we know, the majority of people were still polytheistic. According to the text, Chaumos would have, to some extent at least, an external origin.

We explained in the beginning that Kalasha culture was in the past an integral part of a much larger polytheistic world, which in the nineteenth century had its main centre of resistance in north-western Afghanistan, in present-day Nuristan. A winter solstice festival was also celebrated by the people of the neighbouring Bashgal valley,[27] in Nuristan, with whom the Kalasha have been in close contact for centuries. It does not seem very likely, however, that the whole complex of the Birir winter solstice festival was imported from outside. Certainly, at any rate, the text posits a privileged connection between Chaumos and the Lataruk-nawau, since they have the duty to announce the beginning of the festival. A similar privileged link also appears to be recognized, as we shall see, between the Aliksherdari lineage and the Prun festival. Though special relations do exist between cyclical festivals and specific lineages, it must be remarked, on the one hand, that such privileged positions are not concentrated in any one lineage; and on the other, that in the context of each feast, as is the case with Chaumos, the most significant ritual tasks are assigned to different lineages, to prevent any single group from enjoying a sort of monopoly on one or the other festival, not to mention the ritual system, in general. Such a monopoly that would bring with it so much prestige (Miceli

---

Bibì.

27 Robertson 1896: 583; Cacopardo A.M & R. Laila Schmidt 2006: 38–42.

1989: 135) as to favour the emergence of hierarchical relations – an outcome that Kalasha *dast'ur* seems constantly intent on avoiding.[28]

After praising Saidan Shah's ancestors, the singer goes on to celebrate the personal accomplishments of the elder. Especially the most recent one, the building of a new house in Sendik (and the connected feast, the *hansar'ik* mentioned earlier) where his 'beehive' – a metaphor for the home and the family – was growing in size and strength. He then concludes by praising the harmony between Lataruk-nawau and Babura-nawau – branches of the same macro-lineage of the Shurasi-dari – which pleased 'the gods who dwell on the crests', a reference to the location of their shrines, and which had allowed each of the two groups to give great merit feasts, like *biram'or* and *prec'esh*.

Particularly manifest in the panegyric is the function of language that Malinowski called 'pragmatic', that is, the use of words to highlight social ties, and to strengthen social relations. Reciprocal panegyrics renew the solidarity between lineages, which recognize themselves and each other as members of one and the same community. While in everyday life, in informal conversations, there is a tendency to exalt the feats of one's own lineage, in the extraordinary time of feasting only the feats of other lineages can be praised by a singer. Indeed, it must be stressed that panegyrics are exchanged solely between members of different lineages. Never is a praise-song addressed to a member of one's own descent group. A good singer must therefore know the genealogies and the oral traditions of other lineages, almost better than those of his own. In a *drazha'ilak* or a *d'ushak* there is therefore an exchange of collective memory and a fusion of identities.[29] On the other hand, the forefathers of the other lineages are also, due to the exogamic rule, the ancestors of the wives and the mothers of one's own lineage.

The words of the songs, therefore, are words pronounced to strengthen ties, not to describe events; therefore they amount to actions. In the terms of the philosophy

---

28 Scarduelli (2007: 22–3) observes that although in British social anthropology the tendency to consider ritual activities as a symbolic representation of social differences aimed at founding the legitimacy of hierarchical social relations has prevailed, Firth has also remarked that ritual may be aimed as well at attaining exactly the opposite objective, by distributing, for example, ceremonial activities between different groups to prevent an unequal distribution of prestige. This seems to be indeed the case of Birir.

29 Peter Parkes (1994) has argued that Kalasha singing is implicitly structured in its poetic, musical and choreographic expression, to manifest and progressively integrate the personal, the lineage and the collective identities of the valley communities.

of language of Austin and Searle, a panegyric would be an expressive illocution-ary act because the act of praising expresses feelings and attitudes.[30] But in our case the 'inner' state of a person is not relevant. Concerning the practice of eulogy in Hindu India, Appadurai has written that praise does not require any direct com-munication between the 'inner' states of the persons involved, but it has rather to do with the public negotiation of some gestures and some replies. It is only when the entire event has a positive outcome that a 'community of feeling' is created that requires the emotional involvement of the singer, of the praised, and of the audience that witnesses the eulogy (in Duranti [1997] 2000: 210). In our case the complete event is formed by the song of the first singer, by the chorus and by the dance that accompany it and by the panegyrics that follow. A positive outcome, something to note, cannot be taken for granted: in a *nom nom'ek* praise-song, negative evaluations of the singer and his lineage are at times hidden under the poetic formulae of the composition.[31]

But *d'ushak* and *drazha'ilak* are performative linguistic acts also in another sense. In the field of folk studies and of arts in general, the term 'performance' is usually given a quite different meaning than the one it is given in the theory of linguistic acts. Performance is seen as designating a sphere of action in which special attention is paid to the modalities of communication acts (Duranti [1997] 2000: 25). We are dealing here with what Jakobson has termed 'poetic function' of language (Foley 1997: 362–4). There is a high degree of formalization in the language of *d'ushak* and *drazha'ilak* and of the praise-songs they comprise. There is a true language of praise-songs with its formulae and its terminology. A lan-guage probably unchanged for a lengthy period of time, as indicated, on the other hand, by its archaic forms. The new residence of Saidan Shah is a fairy house (*bararih'an*), and his family is compared to a hard-working swarm of bees in its hive (*mac'erikmO*). The verses, also, have a very well-defined metric structure – a point, however, that remained outside our analysis.[32]

---

30 Duranti [1997] 2000: 201. A locutionary speech act is an utterance describing a situation ('it is raining'), an illocutionary act is a speech act with which an action is performed: in the case of a Kalasha praise-song that of strengthening social ties.

31 In one of the praise-songs recorded, for example, the eulogy turns at a certain point into a reproach for the high number of conversions that had taken place in the lineage of the initial singer.

32 Interestingly, Parkes remarks (1996a: 327–8) that there are hints that Kalasha metrical structure may go back to forms of early Indo-European metrical organization and expresses the wish to demonstrate,' though this is highly speculative', that 'Kalasha recitation may be related to some forms of Vedic meter like *anustubh* and *tristubh*'.

The singing also has its own body language. At the beginning of each verse the singer rests the lifted stick vertically on one of his shoulders and then raises it, pointing it now in the direction of the places mentioned in his song, and now in the direction of the person being praised, to finally move it back at the end of the verse. The other members of the *magl'is* plant their sticks firmly on the ground and rest on them their left hand and the elbow of their right arm, holding up their chin with their right hand, while lending their ears in a listening position. Occasionally, at the end of a verse, from the circle may raise cries of encouragement and approval: *S'abaS*, 'Bravo!' *she~h'e~*, 'So it is!'

This poetic function, however, important as it is, does not seem to have an influence on the pragmatic function. In other words, the positive outcome of the event, the actual strengthening of social ties, does not depend on the skill of the actor. Badly-executed songs normally produce the desired effect, while conflictual elements can very well emerge also in the replies to a formally perfect song. Yet, though not underscored by any specific form of approval, skill in the execution of a singing performance is a highly appreciated talent, a skill that does not have to do only with formal aspects, but also with the creative power expressed in the contents.

There is finally an experiential aspect to the Kalasha performances of song/dance that deserves to be highlighted. Roy Rappaport, in a comprehensive and ambitious treaty on ritual published posthumously in 1999, analyzed in depth this aspect of ritual. Referring to the 'communitas' of Victor Turner ([1969] 1990) – a condition of more than fraternal conviviality that would take form especially among novices in initiation rites – he suggests that 'as distinctions of mundane structure are reduced in the condition of society that prevails during rituals…so may the distinctions of discursive logic be overridden' (Rappaport 1999: 219). He remarks that states of trance and other altered states of consciousness are often a component of ritual participation, and he examines also neurophysiologycally its genesis (ibid.: 226–30). Rappaport's reflection focuses on the issue of the performative effectiveness of dancing and singing in unison, and on their ability to erase the borders between the individual and the environment surrounding him, especially in a ritual context. For him participation in rites encourages alterations of ordinary consciousness and can lead to states that, taking inspiration from Rudolf Otto, he calls 'numinous'. 'Communitas', he proposes, is also a state of mind, indeed typical of ritual. Therefore 'the state of communitas experienced in ritual is at once social and experiential.' (ibid.: 220).

Similar considerations had, in fact, been made also by Victor Turner in a later work – strangely not quoted by Rappaport – where he remarks that 'communitas' has to some extent the characteristics of a flux (Turner [1982] 1986: 109), a term he borrows from Csikszentmihalyi and MacAloon, for whom it denotes the holistic sensation generated by a state of total involvement in which the distinction between the subject and his environment becomes blurred. A sensation that extends to the natural environment and to other humans, generating in the subject the perception that all men, and even all things, form a unity (in ibid.: 105, 108–9). This experience, for Turner, has been transferred in post-industrial societies to leisure activities like art, sports or games, but in 'archaic', non-industrialized societies, the main cultural mechanisms producing the experience of a flux were provided by ritual (ibid.: 110).

Stanley Tambiah also reasons along the same lines; for him, as we saw in the introduction, ritual is a performative act also for the fact – in addition to the two senses mentioned above – of being characterized by a structure that aims, through stereotipity and redundancy, at producing an elevated and intensified feeling of communication, the aims of which have often been expressed as the shift to a supernormal, transcendental, 'altered' or 'numinous' state of consciousness, or as a euphoric communion between participants, or as a submitting to a collective performance. If this is actually so, he adds, anthropologists should investigate more in depth the interaction between the 'vertical' and the 'horizontal' dimensions of ritual to understand in which way means like singing, music and dancing are used to elevate communication (Tambiah [1985] 1995: 159).

If among the Kalasha the vertical dimension of ritual has yet to be investigated, the structural characteristics of the song/dance event indicate that the conditions exist in full for an 'intensified and elevated communication', or to achieve 'an altered state of consciousness' in which the borders between individual participants are blurred. The search for unison discussed by Rappaport is an important trait of Kalasha song – both in the *d'ushak* and the *drazha'ilak* style – since the structure of the event has exactly the purpose of allowing all participants to learn the verses intoned by the singer so that they can be sung in unison.[33] The *tren*, the human chain that rotates around the circle of the singers, proceeds laterally with waving movements as if it were a single being. In *ca~*, in contrast, where the singing is reduced to the minimum, the beating of the drums dominates the scene in an atmosphere of collective exaltation. Many, on the other hand, intentionally

---

33 Naturally, this does not always happen in practice. Di Carlo (2007: 68–9), analysing his recordings, found that in the choral singing the words of the original song were hardly intelligible because they were replaced by a generalized humming emitted by the many who had not understood them.

seek an altered state of consciousness through the consumption of wine. The atmosphere of a Kalasha dance, at its climax, has therefore definitely something Dionysian, connected to its communitarian character.

A little-known passage by Radcliff Brown on Andamanese dancing, quoted by Rappaport (1999: 221), aptly highlights the link between these two aspects:

> The Andaman dance, then, is a complete activity of the whole community in which every able-bodied adult takes part, and is also an activity to which, so far as the dancer himself is concerned, the whole personality is involved ...
> In the dance the individual submits to the action upon him of the community; he is constrained, by the immediate effect of rhythm, as well as by custom, to join in, and he is required to conform in his own actions and movements to the needs of the common activity. The surrender of the individual to this constraint or obligation is not felt as painful but on the contrary as highly pleasurable. As the dancer looses himself in the dance, as he becomes absorbed in the unified community, he reaches a state of elation in which he feels himself filled with an energy beyond his ordinary state ... at the same time, finding himself in complete and ecstatic harmony with all the fellow-members of his community ...

This was indeed the atmosphere that seemed to dominate in the temple when the whole crowd filling the hall was piling up, everyone leaning on each other's shoulders, around the *magl'is* to catch the words of the new song. The headdresses of the women, all covered in cowrie shells seemed to be forming the shell of a huge turtle that then dissolved into the wide circle of the *tren*, from which the lyrics of the song, finally acquired by all, were raised in powerful unison.

On the night of Goshtsaraz, 16 December 2006, the dances went on in the temple of Guru until three in the morning. Similar celebrations were being held at the same time in the temple of Aspar, as well as in the temple of Biyou for the upstream section.

Nongrat – 17 December 2006

The ritual events of this fourth day of Chaumos, in extreme synthesis, were a round of collection by the neophytes, sacrifices at the goat sheds, dances in the *rikh'ini* temple and finally a nocturnal rite preceded by a fast.

The name of this fourth day of Chaumos is rather enigmatic because it does not seem to have any explicit reference to the ritual activities carried out. The literal meaning of the name is 'the night of the *non~g*'. The *non~g* was described to me as a monstrous being that lives near springs. At times it is represented as one-eyed.[34] According to Morgenstierne (1951: 165, 1973a: 157) it is imagined as a dragon whose breath is the rainbow, and its name could be derived from Sanskrit *na:ga* (T-7039). Fussman (1977: 37) agrees with Morgenstierne on this point,[35] but believes it to be a genius of water and cold (ibid.: 36; cf. Jettmar 1986: 75). 'Naga' is a generic term, which in Indian mythology signifies the Serpent, or also serpent spirits connected to rain, venerated in shrines found throughout India.[36] It is a very ancient cult, extending beyond the borders of India all the way to China. Its origins are debated.[37] For Karmakar[38] it is an autochthonous cult that has undergone a process of Arianization begun with the introduction of the Rig-Vedic myth of the primordial Serpent Vrtra,[39] enemy of India and of the *d'eva*. *Vrtra* as well, in fact, like the *na:ga*, is connected to the water element: in the Vedic myth he confiscates the waters and keeps them imprisoned in the recesses of the mountains (Eliade [1949] 1968: 37).

In the context of a New Year festival like Chaumos, the temptation to see the *non~g* of the Nongrat as reminiscent of the primordial Serpent of the Rig Veda is strong. Vrtra represents Chaos (Stutley & Stutley [1977] 1980: 496). Following Eliade ([1949] 1968: 37) we could see in the *non~g* the symbol of the 'non-manifested formless' and in the Nongrat, the time of chaos before creation that precedes the rebirth and renewal of the following days. This is the beginning, indeed, of the central phase of the festival when, as we shall see, the victory of light over darkness and the beginning of a new cycle are celebrated. We would be faced, in that case, with a trace of the central myth of Indra, the main one in the Rig Veda. Something that would not come as a complete surprise, if we consider that for Buddruss (1974) there are traces of this great Vedic complex in a myth of

---

34 Hussam-ul-mulk 1974b: 101; Parkes 1986: 154; Trail & Cooper 1999: 221.

35 '…avec intrusion d'une nasale non étymologique, phènomène très frequent surtout lorsque la syllable précédente commence par *n*-…' (Ibib: 36–7).

36 See, as examples, Crooke 1894: 24, 262–3; Berreman 1972: 107; Schmidt Laila 2006; Nicoletti 2006: 105–69.

37 Sergent (1997: 387–9) believes that it is the fruit of East-Asian influences. For Fussman (1977: 38), in contrast it is based almost for certain on an Arian belief. The presence of these divinities in a notoriously 'archaic' Indo-European context, as that of the Hindu Kush, lends some support to his thesis.

38 In Stutley & Stutley [1977] 1980: 289–90.

39 Eliade [1975] 1979: 226; Stutley & Stutley [1977] 1980: 496–7.

the Kafirs of the Prasun valley, the religious centre of pre-Islamic Nuristan,[40] and that Lentz suggested that the Prasun myth may be connected to the winter solstice (in Buddruss 1974: 37). For Eliade the myth has a cosmogonic structure and he believes that in ancient times the fight between Indra and Vrtra was probably the mythico-ritual scenery of New Year festivals that guaranteed the regeneration of the world.[41] For Witzel (2004: 598), too, this is a very ancient theme, present already among the ancient Indo-Europeans but found also, in similar forms, in the great civilizations of Bactriana and Margiana, which were connected, as we have seen in Chapter 1, to the Mesopotamian ones. In his view, such parallelisms stem from even older, underlying, Euro-Asiatic paradigms found from Ireland to Japan, and even further.

What is certain is that in the structure of Chaumos the evocation of the primordial monster could not have a more appropriate position. However, if this is the theme hidden behind the name 'Nongrat', its memory today seems to be completely lost. No one mentioned it among my assistants and informants, nor did anyone posit a connection between the name of this day of Chaumos and the monster the Kalasha call *non~g*.

* * *

On the morning of Nongrat, animal sacrifices started in preparation for the initiation rites of the following day. For each initiate, three he-goats had to be sacrificed. An ox, which was supposed to compensate for the insufficient number of he-goats, had already been sacrificed in the morning by the Lataruk-nawau of Grabanisar. From the terraced roof of the goat shed where the rite had taken place, we could hear people shouting down by the stream. The *prabal'on g'Uak*, the Praba boys, were carrying out their collection. A group of virgin boys was formed for each of the three main temples, those of Guru, Aspar and Biyou. The group we could hear shouting was the one of the Guru temple. We were approaching the end of the pre-liminal stage. The initiates were being integrated in the group of the *'onjiSTa s'uda* of which they were going to become rightful members the following day. They were making the round of the homes – Baras Khan explained to me – to collect walnuts and grain[42] for the bread they needed during the days of

---

40 An important reference point for the Kalasha as well: see Parkes 1991.

41 Eliade [1975] 1979: 228–9; cf. Kuiper 1970: 99, 105–6, 111, 117, 123.

42 Only the *prabal'on g'Uak* are allowed to use the water mills during Chaumos. As we have seen, the everyday activity of grinding grain is forbidden during the festival.

their seclusion. We waited for them in Grabanisar. The shouts got louder until a band of boys appeared, the oldest ones in early adolescence. One of them, with a commanding tone and a stick in hand, started to make the round of the houses of the tiny settlement collecting grains and walnuts in a basket that was immediately emptied in a large sack. We followed them for a little while. Along the way they yelled: *r'ela moc zh'awi!* 'Impure people, fuck you!', an insult addressed to all adult men who, because of sexual relations with women, are no longer *'onjiSTa*; and they yelled also: *pishm'otray j'ita!* 'Hail homosexuality!'.

The hailing of homosexuality may be interpreted on the one hand as a way to reaffirm the separation from the world of the *r'ela* people based on the contaminating contact with the female sphere: it is not sex in itself, it would seem, that is the cause of impurity, but the contact with women. On the other hand, homosexuality may be seen also as an aspect of the liminal condition the neophytes are in, a transitional state in which the oppositions of ordinary life are suspended, the male and female poles are integrated and the initiates are represented as androgynes: they are, as reads the title of a famous essay by Victor Turner (1967: 93–111), 'betwixt and between', that is, neither this nor that, and yet both at the same time. Initiatory androgyny is a well-known phenomenon and homosexual practices are attested in the initiation rites of many speakers of Indo-European languages (Sergent 1996), and not only among them (e.g. Godelier [1982] 1986: 53–5). For Eliade ([1962] 1971: 102, 104–5) the idea is that of the non-differentiation and non-determination characterizing the Unformed; the still unformed individual would correspond to the Unformed that precedes creation. For Victor Turner, since the liminal period represents an interstructural stage in social dynamics and 'since sex distinctions are important components of structural status, in a structureless realm they do not apply' (Turner 1967: 98).

The collection round of the *prabal'on g'Uak* may also be seen as a rite of separation. Whoever, like the neophytes, is on the verge of undergoing a change in status must be separated, first of all, from his former status (Leach [1976] 1981: 106). The group of boys carrying out the collection was indeed already posing as a distinct and separate body, in preparation for the actual physical separation from the community due to take place the next day. The boy leading the group had an imperious attitude that was the exact opposite of the one normally expected from a Kalasha youth. The collection resembled an extortion, because the boys offered nothing in return – as is usually the case in singing collection rounds where gifts are given in exchange for well-wishing – but demanded grain and beans as if they were exercising a recognized right. As remarked by Van Gennep ([1909] 1981: 98), the neophytes are outsiders; society has no power over them and no defence against them. The arrogance and the insults of the *prabal'on g'Uak* are expressions of an inversion of status accepted because the boys are playing the role of messengers of a world that is 'other':[43] the boys of Birir are not ordinary kids; they are the boys of the god Praba, and as such they are envoys of the *'onjiSTa* sphere.

The boys reached Guru village in the early afternoon and deposited their sacks full of booty on the roof of a special house, which is *'onjiSTa* and therefore off-limits for women. The sacks contained the food for the days of their seclusion and had to be kept in a safe place, where it could not be reached by contaminating influences. Though they had not yet left the villages and the *r'ela* society, the *prabal'on g'Uak* were already moving like an extraneous body in search of *'onjiSTa* places that could give them refuge. The boys spent the afternoon playing on the terraced roof, and were still there in the evening when the dances began in the temple, just a few yards away. They told me they were going to stay there only a while longer and were ready to run away as soon as the women arrived for the evening dance. Pointing at a pile of juniper branches in a corner of the terraced roof, they added they were first going to purify the path with juniper smoke (*suc k'arik*) to cleanse it after the passage of the women, because they had to keep themselves *'onjiSTa*. Subsequently, they were going to take the grains collected in the morning to the mill, to make flour for the bread of the days of their seclusion. For the flour to be *'onjiSTa* they had to carry out with their own hands all the grinding operations (which are ordinarily a female task).

In the late afternoon the sacrifices began in the goat sheds of the families who had male initiates. I went to a goat shed of the Lataruk-nawau in Grabanisar, where there were three novices. That evening only three he-goats were going to be sacrificed – the rest, the next day. The rite took place on the terraced roof of the goat shed. A small fire had been lit; a *'onjiSTa s'uda* had washed his arms up to the elbows and was standing ready with a knife in hand. A man grabbed the first he-goat by the fleece on its back and all participants (maybe six or seven men) turned towards the ridge closing to the west the valley of Grabet, where the main shrine of the god Warin stands. The victim shook its back with a movement called in Kalashamon *biT'Oik*, which is deemed to be a proof of its assent to the sacrifice.[44] The man who was holding it still by the fleece uttered a brief prayer:

---

43 Cf. Caillois [1939] 2001: 122–4; Ginzburg [1984] 2008: 167; Buttitta I.E. 2006: 177.
44 For a similar custom among the ancient Greeks, see Detienne ([1977] 2007: 130).

Oh ingenious and valiant Warin; you valiant Warin of the rocky crests
We are celebrating the Chaumos festival
Accept this offer, oh ingenious and valiant Warin
Bring peace, oh valiant Warin
Give him [to the neophyte] *peace of mind and well being, much health and*
    many children
Give him your blessings, oh great and valiant Warin
You wise and valiant Warin, who are a friend of the holy Creator God

In the prayer Warin is addressed with the traditional epithets of 'ingenious' and 'valiant'. In the beginning he is also called 'Warin of the rocky crests' because his shrine is located on a high ridge. The god is asked in the first place to accept the offer, and then to grant health and many children to the neophyte. He is reminded, finally, that he is a friend of the Creator and, implicitly, that he can therefore intercede with him. This last point is in line with the modern interpretation of Kalasha religion which, as we have seen in Chapter 2 when discussing Kalasha polytheism, tends to represent the gods of the traditional pantheon more like angels or messengers of God than as fully-fledged divinities.

After the prayer, the first he-goat was forced to lie on the ground and two men held it still. When the *'onjiSTa s'uda* slit its throat all the participants made with their lips a sound like the one we make to call a cat. The blood gushed out and the boy caught it in his cupped palms and threw some of it on the fire and some on a bough of oak held up by a small pile of stones a couple of yards away on the roof. He then cut a tiny piece of the ear of the animal and threw it in the fire as well. At this point everybody started to watch the movements of the body of the victim to make sure it was dead. Only when the he-goat lay completely still did the boy sever its head to set it at the edge of the fire so that the blood would coagulate. The other two sacrifices followed immediately, with the initiates and their male kin always present. Counting adults and children, there were about a dozen people altogether. Once the rites were completed, the slaughtering of the animals began there and then on the roof of the goat shed. The liver and the entrails were going to be eaten that same evening, the meat the next day.

As is often the case in traditional societies, among the Kalasha domestic animals are only killed for ritual requirements. An animal is never slaughtered expressly to procure meat for ordinary meals. It is sacrificed only for cyclical, social or therapeutic rituals. We may see in Kalasha sacrifice the traits of a communion: between men, because the sacrifice and the communal meal have the effect of strengthening the ties within the social group; and between humans and the supernatural because the gods are believed to take part in the sacrificial meal. The blood of the victim is their share in the banquet.[45]

Ritual activities did not finish that day with the sacrifices at the goat sheds. In the homes, on the evening of Nongrat, the women wash all utensils, then set them aside and avoid touching them once they have been washed. In the temples, moreover, singing and dancing went on for the whole night. When I returned to Guru and climbed the slope to the temple at the top of the village, the large hall was filling up quickly. Lighting their way with pinewood torches, people were flocking in from the many hamlets downstream. The *magl'is*, the circle of the singers, was already in place, the drums were beating and the dancing had started. Like the preceding night, *ca~*, *d'ushak* and *drazha'ilak* followed one another until late in the night. Standing in the circle, I recorded for hours on end surrounded by a dense crowd.

The dancing finished with an endless *ajh'ona b'ayak*. The circle of the *magl'is* dissolved and two groups – a male and a female one – were formed that exchanged verses for over an hour and a half. Each group had a lead singer who improvised verses that the others repeated. The singing required also some poetic skill for the new verse had to rhyme with the one of the rival group. Many singers, especially among the men, had been drinking much wine and each of the two groups was determined not to leave the last word to its rival.

Similar celebrations, I was told, were taking place that same night in the other temples of the valley. In the long nocturnal dance the social ties between the members of the lineages belonging to each *rikh'ini* were being consolidated. In the Guru temple the three lineages of the village – Lataruk-nawau, Babura-nawau and Ghilasur-nawau – were gathered, plus the Changanchai-nawau who are not genealogically related but live in hamlets around Guru. While the dances went on in the temple, in the homes some rice was being cooked that was not to be touched until the early hours of the morning, at the end of the dancing. This time of fasting, called *idr'O~ai gren*, literally 'the knot of the bowels', marks the exceptional character of the time of the feast: the evening meal, which pertains to the ordinary, is skipped. The end of the fast is signalled by a rite – to which I did not participate – carried out individually on the roofs of the houses around 4 o' clock in the morning. The ritual is called *pact'i s'araz*, the rice *s'araz*, because on the sacrificial fire where juniper (*s'araz*) boughs are burning a small offer of rice is thrown together with some grapes and a few walnuts. Only after the rite is

---

45 For sacrifice as a communion and for the share of the gods see Grottanelli's comparative essay (Grottanelli 1999: 12, 49).

completed can the kitchen implements be handled again and the rice finally eaten. This nocturnal rite introduces one of the main themes of Chaumos, that of fertility. The grains of rice are seeds, which contain the energy of reproduction; for the Kalasha rice is an exceptional food, the food of the times of plenty. With this rite of good omen the community prepares for the holiest time of the year.

The Nongrat, the vigil of the great day, closes the first part of the festival, the pre-liminal one, characterized by rites of preparations, purification and separation. Once the pre-liminal stage is over, the festival enters its liminal stage, that of the seclusion, which lasts three days. Ritual activities took on at this point an extremely intense rhythm. The day following the Nongrat – called *ist'on~gas rat* – is the day of the initiations. This is the central, focalizing element (cf. Smith [1979] 1988: 131) of the whole solstice festival, around which all the other rituals are organized: rites of fertility and regeneration that are perfectly parallel to the initiation rites. The renewal of nature is assured together with the regeneration of the human society (cf. Caillois [1939] 2001: 110).

Istongas rat – 18 December 2006

On this and the following day, Chaumos reaches its climax. Ritual activities went on for thirty-six hours in a row, continuing virtually without interruption throughout the night. A last day of celebrations held entirely in daylight followed, at the end of which the neophytes came out of their seclusion and were reintegrated into the community.

Ritual activities start at dawn. At the first lights little girls go to deposit offerings for the deceased at the *kuraw'at dur*, a place in the vicinities of the villages described by Gulistan as 'a bit *'onjiSTa'*, because it is off-limits for women who have recently given birth and for the whole time they are nursing, and it is off-limits for their fathers as well. The rite is performed by prepubescent girls who, as we have seen, in the female world are the closest to the *'onjiSTa* sphere. The offers are miniature bread cakes (*kush'urik*) together with some walnut kernels and grapes. The fact that it is a duty assigned by *dast'ur* to girls, and not to boys, who would be more *'onjiSTa*, can be explained if we consider that the sphere of death belongs, like that of birth, to the *pr'agata* (or *r'ela* in the Birir language) pole, to which women also belong. It is significant, furthermore, that this simple rite is carried out in the day of the initiations, the nature of which implies a death and a new birth (Eliade [1949] 1968: 95).

The process of initiation is fairly complex and differs for the two genders. Before resuming our narration we shall give a brief outline of it. The male initiation has two stages. The ceremony of the first stage, held when a child is two or three, consists in dressing the boy in the *ceL'ik*, a woollen hand-woven dress, of the same type of the one worn by the women, but white in colour. Black and white were traditionally the colours of the clothes of women and men, respectively.[46] This first initiation ceremony marks for male children the beginning of the separation from the female world; a passage in which they are assisted by their maternal uncle (*m'oa*), the male representative of their maternal line, who is in charge of dressing him up. The maternal uncle receives in exchange the *push*, a gift of metal utensils, like tripods for the fire or kitchenware, the same type of goods, that is, as those given in payment for a bride price, the ones given to affines. Among the Kalasha, the maternal uncle is a protective and sympathetic figure contrasting with that of the father, who embodies absolute authority. At the time of the initiatic trial it is his duty to symbolically accompany the neophyte all the way to the threshold. In the evening, at the goat sheds, the child undergoes for the first time the *ist'on~gas* rite, a true blood baptism, as we shall see. The first stage ends a couple of months later when, for the Raistam (*ra'istam*) celebration, at the end of the winter ritual sequence, the child undergoes the same ritual for the second time. After having spent his early childhood in the orbit of his mother and the other women of the house, by dressing in the *ceL'ik*, the child starts to move closer to the male sphere. But as his dress indicates, he remains in an intermediate stage: he wears a dress of the colour worn by men, but of the form worn by women (a woollen gown with no trousers); the name itself of the garment, on the other hand, is a diminutive of that of the female dress (*c'ew*). The true entrance in the male world takes place five or six years later, when the boy will undergo the second stage of the initiation process, once again on the same day of Chaumos. Always with the assistance of the maternal uncle, the *ceL'ik* is then replaced by the *bhut*, a pair of white woollen trousers.[47] In the same day, as we shall see right away, the neophyte undergoes again the *ist'on~gas* rite, after which the period of seclusion begins. When he rejoins the community on the last day of Chaumos he is considered to all effects an adult male: he can no longer touch cups and plates used by women, he can go with the herds to the high pastures, and, as *'onjiSTa s'uda*, will now officiate in rites, including animal sacrifices.

---

46 It is no longer so because, while the women continue to wear the traditional Kalasha attire (though brown hand-woven wool has been largely replaced by black bazaar cotton) the men have, for decades now, adopted the Pakistani *shilw'ar kam'iz*, which can be of any colour.
47 Today boys, though they always dress in the *bhut* for the intiation ceremony, start wearing trousers, the Pakistani *shil'war*, from an early age because of school attendance.

Girls are initiated at the same time as their male counterparts. Assisted by their maternal uncle they dress for the first time in the *kup'as*, the female headgear (Photo 1). While at the goat sheds the *ist'on~gas* rites are being held for the boys, the girls undergo in the homes the parallel rite of *shish a'u*. Just like the boys who dressed the *ceL'ik*, they will undergo again the same ritual – in the same year – on the day of Raistam. *shish a'u* means 'head-shaped bread': for each initiate seven round bread loaves with little ears are prepared, which the girl, standing by the hearth, must hold between her two hands. The mother, or another woman in the family, holds some water in her cupped left hand and with her right hand lights a bough of oak (*bonj*) in the fire; she touches with it the water she is holding in her left hand, she passes it over the head of the girl and then behind her back, to finally throw it in the fire.[48] With this rite, the little girl exits the world of early childhood, when she was completely dependent on her mother, and starts moving autonomously in the female world gradually learning all related tasks. The female initiation ritual does not have a second stage.

The morphology of the initiation rites mirrors in its material traits the fundamental dichotomies of Kalasha worldview. For the girls, who will be entrusted with the care of the fields, the material object of the rite is bread; for the boys, who will be herders of goats, the material substance is the blood of the sacrificed he-goats. The male rite takes place in the *'onjiSTa* space of the goat sheds, while the female one takes place in the homes. We can discern here one of the senses in which, for Tambiah ([1985] 1995: 178), ritual may be seen as performative, i.e. its 'indicality', which means its forms refer to the social context, and can only be understood by taking into account that connection. The indical characteristics we just highlighted indeed confirm, and realize, the symmetrical relations between some of the fundamental polarities of the Kalasha symbolic system: *'onjiSTa/r'ela*, herding/agriculture, male/female.[49]

It must be noted, finally, that the 'social puberty' established with the rite, does not coincide among the Kalasha with physiological puberty. This should not surprise us: Van Gennep ([1909] 1981: 59) has already observed that physiological

---

48 Since I was following the male initiation rituals, I could not observe this rite. I did observe it, however, in 1973 during the Chaumos of Rumbur, where the *shish a'u* rite is held in the open (in a field) and is officiated by a male member of the family.

49 As Leach ([1976] 1981: 73) also remarked, 'the material topographical (human and natural) aspects of the space where ritual performances take place...form a series of indexes for metaphorical distinctions...' (my translation from the Italian edition) of the type, indeed, we indicated in our case.

and social puberty rarely coincide because they are substantially different things. But it is now time to see how the events of this holy day enfolded in the Chaumos of 2006.

* * *

In the morning I was woken up hastily by Erfan: the dressing of the initiates had already begun in their homes. I staggered to my feet with some effort because the dancing of the previous night had gone on, as mentioned, until the early hours of the morning. We ran up the steep village path to the house of Danok, whose son was undergoing the dressing-of-the-trousers (*bhut sambi'ek*) ceremony. The house was full of people. The guests were being served wine and walnut-stuffed bread (*jA~'u*). The boy had already been dressed in his ceremonial attire. He was wearing the *d'ashak bhut*, the traditional hand-woven white woollen trousers, with a fringed and embroidered upper part covering his chest like a pair of overalls, making a strange contrast with the manufactured wind-jacket[50] the boy had kept underneath. While the guests feasted on bread and wine, an elder seated on a low chair by the hearth was declaiming a panegyric in which a key role was attributed to an ancestor of the Lataruk-nawau, the child's lineage, in a famous episode of Chitral history. It was an *ishtik'ek*, a recited – not sung like the *nom-nomek* – eulogy typical of funerals and merit feasts.

When the panegyric ended, the people started swarming over the roofs. Down below, a small procession of women was crossing the bridge intoning the *sh'ahi* chant. They were the *jam'ili* of the Lataruk-nawau – the married women of the lineage who, being that marriage is virilocal, had left the home of their fathers for that of their husbands – who were temporarily rejoining their lineage of origin to participate in the celebration. Once they reached the village, they were given as a gift a cotton mantle (*sad'ar*) each. An incredibly polychromous crowd was now filling the terraced roofs of the village. It was a clear and extremely bright day. Over their usual clothes, many men and women were wearing robes of honour (*cap'an*)[51] decorated with arabesques in gold, red and other vivid colours shining in the morning sun. Several neophytes were wandering around in the crowd. They

---

50 Used clothes coming mostly from Europe are sold at low prices in all the bazaars of the Indian subcontinent.

51 These are industrially-produced robes, made of synthetic materials. In 2006 one of these robes could be bought in the Chitral bazar for 500 rupees, not a low price if we consider that Baras Khan's monthly salary as school teacher amounted to 2,500 rupies.

wore the upper part of their *d'ashak bhut* folded down with the fringes dangling at knee level. On their chests they wore sideways the *kamarb'and*, a strip of material decorated with cowrie shells, buttons and little bells, and, crossing it, the *shok'ekband*, decorated only with cowrie shells. For headgear they wore a sort of turban (*dap'ari*); their shins were wrapped in the *kutaw'ati*, woollen leggings worn by shepherds, especially in winter. Their attire was an exact reproduction of that of the *ganD'au*, the wooden effigies made for givers of merit feasts. They were wearing, in other words, full Kalasha ceremonial dress (Photo 4).

The atmosphere was joyful. The younger boys, the ones who were going through the first stage of the initiation, were not, however, wearing the *ceL'ik*, but were dressed in ordinary, though new, *shilw'ar kem'iz*. Apart from their new clothes, they stood out among their age mates only for the fact that their woollen chitrali cap (*kaS'ong*) was adorned with rupee bills (Photo 5). The hand-woven *ceL'ik*, still worn by many children in the 1970s, had apparently fallen into disuse.

At a certain point Saidan Shah appeared wearing an embroidered woollen Chitrali coat (*cug'a*), and began to summon the people to the temple. The chatting and laughing came abruptly to an end and the roofs soon stood empty. Gathered all together under the porch of the *rikh'ini*, the women intoned in unison the melody of the *sh'ahi* chant. The younger initiates – I counted two of them, a boy and a girl – were in their mothers' arms. The crowd was made mostly of women. The celebration seemed to be mainly female.

The notes of the *sh'ahi* chant at a certain point were transformed, without an interruption, like a sound wave changing form, into another chant celebrating the central event of the festival, the descent of a god and the initiation rituals just begun with the dressing-up of the initiates.

Bring peace, oh Bidrakalen, you descended [among us]
Blessings and blessings, oh Bidrakalen you descended
Fragrance of blood and of juniper [smoke], *oh Bidrakalen you descended*
The sacrifices of the initiations, oh Bidrakalen you descended
Bring peace, oh Bidrakalen you descended
Bring celebration, oh Bidrakalen you descended
A whole night on the White Trail, oh Bidrakalen you descended
A joyful celebration, oh Bidrakalen you descended
Your large sacred bread cakes, oh Bidrakalen you descended
The markhor hunt, oh Bidrakalen you descended
Your celebration, oh Bidrakalen you descended
Bring peace, oh Bidrakalen you descended

Your powerful whistle. oh Bidrakalen you descended
Your ox that ploughs, oh Bidrakalen you descended
Your tended lawn, oh Bidrakalen you descended
Your garden in bloom, oh Bidrakalen you descended

The women were wearing their most beautiful ornaments. The singing was slow and solemn. Only women were in the chorus. Like the *sh'ahi* hymn, this is a typical Chaumos chant, never sung on any other occasion. The lyrics of chants of this type, as already remarked, may be very ancient: always sung in a chorus they are known to everyone, and tend therefore to root themselves deeply in collective memory. The archaic character of the chant seems also to be indicated by the name of the divinity invoked. The name Bidrakalen does not occur in any other context. There are no shrines dedicated to a god with this name. The answer to my enquiries was that Bidrakalen is the god who descends to Earth for Chaumos. Etymologically the name may be traced back to Vrtra, the monster obstructing Creation killed by Indra in the central myth of the Rig Veda. Linguistically, a plausible hypothesis may be the following: *b'idra-kal- (k'aw/k'aluna = year, in the year)*, where the second element is a time reference and the third one a locative.[52] The semantic outcome would be 'in the time of Vrtra', that is, the times of the beginning. The name Bidrakalen would mean in this case something like 'the god of the times of the beginning'. Otherwise, possibly an even more fascinating hypothesis, the connection could be with Vrtraghan or Vrtrahan, 'killer of Vrtra', a name rooted for Witzel (2004: 599, 601) in Indo-Iranian times, which became in the Vedas an epithet of Indra.[53] A solution that would agree with various other ritual elements indicating that the god of Chaumos is indeed Indra, who in Vedic times was considered the founder of the New Year celebration (Dumézil 1929: 111, 122–5), and to whom was dedicated the Vedic winter solstice festival (*Indradhvaja*) (Witzel 2004: 593). Both hypotheses, at any rate, are quite coherent with the context: a reference to Vrtra in the day following the Nongrat, the night of the monstrous Serpent, when with the initiations a new beginning is going to be celebrated, could not be more appropriate. And just as appropriate would be the reference to the 'killer of Vrtra', to Indra; which would give support to Witzel's (2004: 614) idea that the pre-Islamic world of the Hindu Kush, apart from mirroring many aspects of the Vedic religion, takes us back even further, to the still undivided Indo-Iranian world.

---

52 I must thank Pierpaolo Di Carlo for this suggestion.
53 See also Sergent 1997: 193.

The chant recalls the various stages of the male initiation, naming the individual rites one by one. The first verses refer to the sacrifices and to the fragrance of the smoke of the sacrificial fires on which juniper is burnt and the blood of the sacrificial victims, the share of the gods, is poured. The Visitor god is invoked to bring peace and give his blessings. The verses that follow refer to the activities and to the trials of the initiates during the time of seclusion. The 'White Trail' of verse 7 is the impervious mountain path they have to follow on the night of their initiation (*ist'on~gas rat*) to reach Praba's shrine where they are to celebrate the holiest rite of Chaumos, a holocaust sacrifice in honour of the god. It is named the 'White Trail' because the *prabal'on g'Uak*, reach Praba's shrine at the first pale lights of the day.

As *r'ela moc*, an adult non-virgin man, I could not follow them on that trail. But some time after Chaumos I asked Gulistan to show it to me. Above Guru village the trail climbs steeply until it reaches a very high water channel, along which it continues, remaining therefore well above the goat sheds, in *'onjiSTa* space. Past the village of Gasguru a tract begins that in the past must have required some real climbing. At certain spots, Gulistan related, the boys held each other by the hand as if they were roped together. Presumably, the difficulties of the trail, the nocturnal rock climbing in the light of the torches, the confrontation with the mountain, in brief, were part of the initiatic trial. Today, a relatively comfortable, though still rugged, stone trail has been built.

The large consecrated bread cake of verse 9 is a specially-decorated bread cake the initiates take to the shrine of the god, a ritual element with a name – *indr h'arik*, 'to bring to Indra' – which is a quite explicit reference to the god Indra, to all appearances identified with Praba. As for the hunt of the markhor – the wild mountain goat of the Hindu Kush (*capris falconeri*) – of verse 10, it was explained to me that in the past these animals were hunted especially at the beginning of winter, just before Chaumos, because at the first snows they descend to lower altitudes becoming easier to hunt; their meat was then consumed during the festival. The whistle of verse 13 is the whistling of the shepherd who calls his goats, the same whistle dancers make in the tumultuous *ca* dance, a few rounds of which the initiates have to dance, as we shall see, under the eyes of the whole community. The last three verses remained without an explanation: in all likelihood the 'fox that ploughs' is a metaphor for the male sexual organ, while the 'tended lawn' and the 'garden in bloom' are allusions to the female one. Unsurprisingly, since fertility and reproduction are among the main themes of the festival, references to the sexual sphere, as we have already seen, are quite frequent in Chaumos.

Shortly afterwards, the initiates of the second stage arrived in a body. Like Danok's son, they had undergone the *bhut sambi'ek* ritual and were wearing the traditional white woollen trousers. I counted six of them. They were to dance inside the *rikh'ini*. They danced in the middle of the temple holding their sticks upright, while everybody crowded around them to get a close look at their *ca* dance (Photo 6). At the Chaumos of Rumbur in 1973 I had seen the neophytes holding their sticks between their legs in a manifestly phallic position while some adults were doing the same to encourage them. In 2006 I did not see in Birir a similarly explicit mimicry, but the upheld sticks were probably meant to express the same meaning concerning fecundity and reproduction. Once the dance of the neophytes was over, the habitual songs and dances began and went on for the whole morning. Danok sang the following *drazha'ilak*, of his own composition:

> *I shall now sing a verse, lend me you ears sun and moon of mine*
> *My companion descended the valley*
> *He went downstream to the city of Islamabad*
> *For three full years he battled in the courts of Swat and Peshawar*
> *The government had issued an ordinance; the seat of president was at stake*
> *His Kalasha name, Turap Khan, shun in the three Kalasha valleys*
> *He unified our community and then he went to Rumbur and Bumburet*
> *He reached the Sajigor shrine during a ceremony*
> *An assembly was held and all the elders of Rumbur promised to support him*
> *But when the day of the elections came old Katasing was left alone*
> *Ratmalai brought gold and silver to Rumbur, beloved valley*
> *Having shared it between them, rich became Munir and Saifullah*
> *The votes of the Kalasha were given away to the Chitralis, to Ayun and to*
> *   Awari*
> *Sorrow grabbed the souls of the people, here in my village of Guru*
> *What other beautiful words can I utter?*
> *Life goes on but disappointment remains.*

In contrast to the other text presented, this song makes no reference to Chaumos. As is quite clear from its content, it is not a traditional song. Danok composed it to lament the defeat of Erfan (Turap Khan is his official name), the Kalasha candidate in a recent local election, due, according to him, to the 'treason' of some influential elders of Rumbur who cast their votes for a Chitrali Kho candidate. The verses suggest – we do not know, of course, if with good reason – that their votes were bought. The way in which the song uses traditional poetic forms to express the point of view of the author on a contemporary political issue, shows to what extent this form of verbal art allows for individual creativity (cf. Parkes 1994: 175, 181–2). Moreover, Danok's lyrics indicate also that the Kalasha political arena is quite modern and not dominated by a traditional authority – which ritual singing and ritual in general, according to Bloch ([1974] 1989), would have the function of legitimizing – but is, in contrast, the scene of struggles between competing factions.[54] In the holiest day of the year, during one of the central ritual events of the festival, the ordinary, profane, world had made an incursion into the temple.

At the end of the morning the male part of the community headed towards the goat sheds. Baras Khan led me to a goat shed of the Changanchai-nawau where we found four initiates ready to undergo the *ist'on~gas* ritual. Three he-goats had been sacrificed the night before and three more were going to be sacrificed shortly. The four initiates wore the ceremonial attire described above, and had their heads shaved. With some curiosity I observed their sticks: one boy was holding an ordinary axe, another one the curved stick of an old umbrella, the third one a sort of ice-axe of local production, while the fourth one – I noted with surprise – held in his hand a car radio antenna, possibly from the 1970s. Carried by three men in large funnel-shaped baskets, the skinned carcasses of the he-goats sacrificed the previous night arrived; they were rapidly cut to pieces that were plunged to boil in a few big aluminium pots. After a long wait, the first sacrificial victim appeared. The rite was held in a roofless little chamber of the shed, because the beaten earth of the terraced roof – the most *'onjiSTu* place – had been turned into a muddy swamp by the melted snow. The animal gave its sign of approval by vigorously shaking its fleece and, after the ritual prayer (text below), was forced to the ground. While two men kept it still, a boy – who had washed his arms with snow because there was no water available in the vicinity – cut its throat, gathered in his cupped hand some blood and poured it on the sacrificial fire; he then gathered more blood in the same hand and poured it on a bough of oak (*JaC-shon~g* = bough of the *JaC* deity) which had been fixed on the wall. The neophyte was standing close; he bent until he almost touched the neck of the victim, from which a gush of blood spurted out onto his shaved head. The *ist'on~gas* rite was completed – a true blood baptism. The same rite was repeated for two more boys. The fourth one was only at the first stage of his initiation, the dressing of the *ceL'Ik*. He

---

54 In contrast, Parkes (1994: 182) believes that Kalasha songs and dances legitimize the traditional authority of influential elders, which gives partial support to Bloch's view. But he adds this 'is a specifically ceremonial ideology that appears to have little persuasive power outside of festival performance'.

was a toddler about two years old who remained in the arms of his father for the whole time; the man bent down and held the head of the child to the victim's neck until it was stained with some blood. All four initiates belonged to the Changan-chai lineage. The neophytes of each lineage undergo the ritual all together in the same goat shed, as if to highlight the unity of the descent group.

The slaughtering operations soon began. As usual, the liver and the entrails of the animals were going to be eaten on the spot, while the meat was for the evening feast. The neophytes were not going to eat with us. From that moment on they had to avoid physical contact with *r'ela* people, like us married adults, and could not therefore share our food. That night they were going to sleep all together in a goat-shed just above Guru village. For two days they were going to be confined in the area of the goat sheds, and they were going to follow the celebrations only from above, moving along the high path from goat shed to goat shed, never entering in contact with the women or with the *r'ela* world in general. They were to return to their homes only on the last day of Chaumos, the *dah'u tatt'u*.

These are two of the three prayers recited before the sacrifices:

Prayer n.1
Oh Allah, you are one, oh my Allah
for these sons of mine I carry out the duty I am assigned
give us welfare, keep misfortune away
you are one, oh Allah
nobody can do without you
Allah, you are one, bring peace to my family

Prayer n. 2
...give a long life and many sons, give health and welfare
if you accept the offers of humans, if you are the tutelary deity of the
    ist'on~gas rite
give a long life and many sons
give them also many sons and keep them in good health
so that their lives may be long, give them welfare

Let us consider the second prayer first. Unfortunately the initial invocation was missing in the recording, and it is not possible therefore to say to which divinity the prayer was addressed. The god invoked is defined as *baS zhu'aw*, 'eater of a part of the sacrificial offer'; in other words he is seen as a participant in the sacrificial banquet. It is an epithet designating the gods, the *dewal'ok* (T-6540) in general. They are seen, that is, as receivers of a part of the sacrificial victim, just like men, with whom they therefore share the sacrificial meal. The offering they receive creates a tie with human beings, who recall it at the moment of making their requests. 'If you accept the offers of humans' the prayer says, then 'give a long life and many sons'. This may seem to confirm the theory that in sacrifice the gods are debtors and men are creditors. A theory formulated by the French linguist Emile Benveniste on the basis of a semantic analysis of the Sanskrit term śraddhā, which is referred in the Rig Veda to those who make offerings to Indra and has the meaning of setting one's trust in a god, but with the assurance of a return (in the form of a guaranteed divine favour).[55] However, despite this important common trait, Kalasha sacrifice, it is hardly necessary to say, differs profoundly from the Vedic sacrifice, which was held for the sole benefit of the patron and could be celebrated only by a Brahmin. In particular, it was not a communal rite in which participants shared the sacrificial meal, but an individual rite (Malamoud 1976: 8) that depended on the munificence of the patron, and was officiated by Brahmins who were its (remunerated) celebrants and its guests; the meat of the sacrificial victims was not distributed to the community but only to the Brahmins.

If this prayer seems to be fully in line with Kalasha tradition, the first one may leave us perplexed for its repeated invocation of the name of Allah and for its insistence on his unicity – as if the person reciting it had the deliberate intention of radically denying the polytheistic character of Kalasha religion. We have already seen that a reinterpretation of Kalasha religion is now established that identifies the Creator God of tradition with the God of the Quran, and reduces the dewal'ok to mere messengers or intermediaries. Still, the text of the first prayer appears to go a step further: the God of the Quran is invoked directly, without intermediaries, insisting expressly on his unicity; the dewal'ok seem to have vanished altogether.

The third phase of the sacrifice was about to take place: after the consecration and the ritual killing of the he-goats, the distribution of their meat was to follow. If in the first two phases the act of communion had joined humans and gods, in this third phase the act of communion was going to concern the relations between men. That evening, according to what I was told, about twenty boys in the whole valley underwent the ist'on~gas ritual. About a dozen belonged to lineages affiliated to the rikh'ini of Guru, three to those of the Aspar temple, and four to lineages of the Biyou rikh'ini. Just over half were at the first step of the initiation process and were therefore (symbolically) wearing the ceL'ik; the rest were at the second step and were dressed in the bhut. More than thirty he-goats were sacrificed in

---

55 Grottanelli 1999: 19–20; see Benveniste [1969] 2001: 134; Campanile [1993] 1997: 26.

the goat sheds of Guru, six in those of Aspar, and fourteen in Biyou. The animals offered came from the herds of the parents of the initiates (but maternal uncles also contribute, as mentioned, a he-goat). Yet, since it is quite normal for the herd of a set of brothers to remain undivided even after the division of houses and fields, the sacrificial victims were in effect offered by an entire extended family. Some lineages, naturally, had more boys to be initiated than others, and they contributed therefore to a greater extent to the distribution. The Ghilasur-nawau had, for example, as many as seven initiates while the Lataruk-nawau had only three. But since the frequency of births is governed by chance, in the course of the years the amount of goods destined by each lineage to initiation banquets will presumably tend to level out. The quantitative data I collected indicate, further, that the number of animals offered tends to decrease with the increase of the number of initiates, often not reaching the amount of three per boy prescribed by *dast'ur*; while the opposite is the case when there are only few boys to be initiated. It is therefore an exchange of the type termed 'balanced reciprocity' by the US anthropologist Marshall Sahlins ([1972] 1980) in which, in the long run at least, each group receives in the end more or less as much as it has given. There is no redistribution of wealth therefore, but with the sharing of the food and wine the ties between lineages are strengthened and confirmed.[56]

A meal for the guests was prepared in each of the goat sheds where the sacrifices had been held. The whole male population of the Guru temple was going to visit them in turn. The itinerant banquet started at dusk in a hamlet near Guru, called Bashalitada. When we reached the spot, we found several dozen men crouching in the open in the December cold intent in eating *tas'ili* – thin unleavened wheat bread cooked on an iron plate[57] – which they dipped in the *ishp'on~ac*, a flour mush cooked in the broth of the meat, enriched with clarified butter (*prac'ona*). Chunks of meat and cups of wine were also being distributed. The meal was almost at its end. Soon everybody stood up and the group marched on to a goat

---

56 With a reference to Robertson Smith, Van Gennep ([1909] 1960: 28) writes: 'The rite of eating and drinking together…is clearly a rite of incorporation, of physical union, and has been called a sacrament of communion…Often the sharing of meals is reciprocal, and there is thus an exchange of food which constitutes the confirmation of a bond.' (*published English translation; from the internet*)

57 Flour is mixed with water to obtain a very liquid mush subsequently poured by hand in small portions on an iron plate (*'onza*) set over an open fire. Propp ([1963] 1978: 43), who describes this technique used in Russia to make a type of ceremonial bread (*bliny*), remarks that this is probably the most ancient method for cooking something made of flour.

shed in the side valley of Grabet Kui. With Baras Khan I followed the crowd. In the Grabet Kui goat shed, after some waiting, the same foods were distributed to the visitors, who this time gathered around a lively bonfire. There were guests coming also from the other two Kalasha valleys. Wine was generously served. Many men were tipsy and some were definitely drunk. The people of Birir have a very indulgent attitude towards drunkenness, especially during Chaumos. Everybody patiently puts up with obnoxious drunkards and everybody drinks, women and children included. In one of my visits to Sherbek, a most respected elder, I found his wife, a quite mature lady, literally rolling on the floor seized by a fit of laughter she could not control, and unable even to reach her bed; 'She drank too much and now her head is spinning.' was the general amused comment.

At the goat shed, in the course of the meal, Saidan Shah suddenly stood up and started declaiming at the top of his voice. It was a long recited panegyric (*ishtik'ak*), acclaimed at intervals by the crowd with shouts of *Sab'aS* (bravo!). The eulogy was addressed to the owners of the goat shed and to their lineage, the Changanchai-nawau; it praised the munificence, the prosperity and the wisdom of their ancestors. Here is a fragment of it:

...to him a son was born, Changanchai was born
and to him six sons were born, in a row
From them the Changanchai lineage descends
who settled in the Grabet valley
Oh your power!
Behold on one side the waving ears of your wheat bending [from the weight
    of the grain]
Behold on the other side the wave of the tangled horns of your goats!
In your Kundeavis pasture
crumble under their weight
your piles of cheese moulds
Honour to you, descendants of Changanchai!
The harmony with which you carry out your activities
is known to all the people of this country, and of the world at large...

Once the meal was finished, the group resumed its journey. Erfan was staggering under the effect of wine to the point that he had to be supported when the icy path got too steep, until he thought it wiser to halt in a nearby goat shed to try to recover. That night virtually the whole male population of the Guru temple made the full round of the goat sheds of the families of the initiates. At each stop a meal

was offered, at the end of which the leftovers – always abundant – were distributed for the visitors to take home. There were five stops. The meat and the bread
distributed were enough to satisfy the needs of an average family for several days.
For many nights, indeed in all the homes of Guru, the people ate *a'u pac'aLa*, a
much-coveted dish consisting of pieces of meat and shreds of bread boiled and
re-boiled in large aluminium pots. As for the neophytes, the *ist'ong~as* rite marked
the beginning of their period of seclusion. Immediately after undergoing the rite,
they all retired to a goat shed above Guru village, together with the other virgin
boys, the *prabal'on g'Uak*. For the following two days they were going to live in
an intermediate space, neither here nor there, in a condition, that is, of liminality, during which they had to officiate, and to enact, the most sacred ritual, the
Chaumos holocaust sacrifice at the shrine of the god Praba, the true climax of
their trial.

At the end of the itinerant banquet the people all flocked to the temples of the
main villages. It was 10.30 p.m. when I reached the temple of Guru. The drums
were beating. The hall was full of men and women of all ages, toddlers included.
No one was missing. The *gaderak'an*, the most influential elders, were all present.
From the *magl'is* circle they took turns in the lead of the songs and dances. The
ca~, the *d'ushak* and the *drazha'ilak* followed by the long praise-songs, were
alternated as usual.

Until this phase of the festival the communion through sacrifice had concerned
only the lineages belonging to the same temple. But that very night the whole
population of Guru was going to march in a procession, lit by the long pine torches
(*Ca~J'a*) made on the day of Goshtsaraz, to the temple of Aspar. Two larger social
units were thus going to be joined, the two macro-lineages of the Shurasì-dari,
the most numerous clan of Birir. The procession, Baras Khan informed me, was
going to depart from the temple of Guru in the depth of night, around 3 a.m. Songs
and dances went on in the *rikh'ini* more or less until that time. The ludic dimension was quite manifest, especially in the rounds of *ca~*, but since ceremonial
behaviours, as already mentioned, are dictated by tradition, the dancing was also
considered mandatory, as amusing and gratifying as it may have been. The physical exertion was taking its toll. Every so often someone was asking me (as one of
the few wearing a watch) what time it was. At a certain point a wave of excitement
ran through the crowd:

I step out of the temple and I see a group of women standing at the beginning
of the trail leading to Aspar, holding their torches ready to be lit. All of a
sudden, the procession departs. At the beginning we can see high up on the

mountain slope the torches of the *prabal'on g'Uak* that have left the Guru
goat shed and are heading to Aspar along the higher path. I find myself in
the midst of a grove of crackling torches that thins out along the narrow
path while the women intone the *sh'ahi* chant. I hold my tape recorder in
one hand and with the other one I try to take some photographs, not an easy
task. Shortly after the departure from Guru, in a spot where the trail crosses
a deep indent in the mountain, an enchanted scene opens before my eyes:
the whole slope facing me is on fire with the torches that tinge of red the
polychromous attire of the women holding them, who had made a halt to
light up the impervious crossing or maybe just to see who was following. I
am not fast enough to take a photograph. The spell lasts only a moment; the
women hurry forward. But other fabulous and surrealistic scenes – if perhaps
not as grand – suddenly take life along the path in the light of the torches.
(*From my field journal – Guru 18 December 2006*).

As the procession got closer to Aspar, the crowd erupted in the obscene cries
of *zh'awi*! already heard during the previous torchlight procession on the day
of Goshtsaraz. In the distance we could hear the drums beating. Shouting ritual
cries the long procession finally reached the Aspar *rikh'ini*, where the dancing
was already in full swing. At the centre of the temple a large fire was burning;
the great hall was suddenly lit up with innumerable torches. Several people, men
and women, started dancing torches in hand. The *magl'is* circle was already in
position. The lineages of the downstream half (*pr'enaw*), were now united in
the celebration; the people of the upstream half (*w'enau-moc*) that night were
gathered in the Biyou temple. The dances, however, did not last very long. After
roughly forty minutes, a group of women resolutely entered the temple, torches
in hand, pushed their way through the circle of the singers standing around the
fire, lit their torches in the flames and departed abruptly towards Guru. We hiked
back in the light of the torches along the muddy and icy path and reached the
village around 5 a.m.

When we reached the village the celebration was not yet over. A fire was
already lit on the terraced roof of the temple, and a circle of singing women had
formed around the fire. A girl in the centre was threatening with a (extinguished)
torch the women who were preventing her from beating another young girl who
was standing outside the circle and was shielded by them all. It was the game of
the angry husband threateningly pursuing his wife without ever managing to get
hold of her. I had already observed the game in the preparatory day of *achar'ik*
and *gandalik'an* which anticipates many themes of Chaumos. The obscene song

accompanying the game is presumably meant to stimulate the reproductive energy that produces fertility.

Right from the departure from the temple of Guru the women appeared to have taken the lead. In the nocturnal procession the women were the majority and were mostly carrying the torches and, as we have seen, it was a group of women who gave the signal for the return to Guru by lighting their torches in the fire burning in the Aspar temple. Now that we were back in Guru they were again dominating the scene, filling up the roof of the *rikh'ini* and singing the obscene song accompanying the game that jokingly represented the male/female contrast. The population of the valley seemed to be ideally divided in two parts. Together with the mainly female procession leaving from the temple, as we have seen, the male procession of the *prabal'on g'Uak* had left the Guru goat shed following a higher trail, in the *'onjiSTa* area of the oak forest. The community appeared to be moving in unison, with the initiates following their itinerary along the valley bottom. Even if only a few adults were reportedly accompanying the initiates and the other virgin boys, and the majority of men had remained therefore on the valley bottom with the women, it seemed that the division between the *prabal'on g'Uak* and the adults corresponded not only to that between *'onjiSTa* and *r'ela* but also to that between male and female. While the quintessential representatives of the male world, the virgin boys, were secluded in the area of the goat sheds, the women seemed to have taken possession of the villages that had become their undisputed realm (cf. Parkes 1994: 180). In the Rumbur/Bumburet Chaumos, as we shall see, such contraposition is made absolutely explicit by a rule obliging all men to sleep at the goat sheds during the most holy days of the festival.

Before dawn the *prabal'on g'Uak* would have reached Jagar ga (*jag'ar ga*), the sacred side valley where Praba's shrine is located. The group, according to what I was later told by one of its members, did not include only virgin boys – who were about fifteen, including ten neophytes – but also several adults, fathers and older brothers, who accompanied them. In the open-air enclosure of the Guru goat shed the boys had prepared the *'ushak kushur'eak* – thin moulds of bread made with *'onjiSTa* flour (*'ushak*) from the grain gathered in their rounds – which were to be consumed at Praba's shrine. The procession reached the shrine at 5 a.m. At the first light of dawn they sacrificed a kid they had taken with them and smeared the altar with its blood.

Since I could not participate in the sacrifice at Praba's altar I cannot say how it was carried out exactly. It is certainly the most *'onjiSTa* rite of the whole festival. The hour itself of its celebration, the brief moment between night and day, indicates that it is a secretive rite that must be kept hidden from any extraneous gaze.

I was told that the body of the sacrificed kid was burnt in the fire. The blood of the victim, to be smeared on the altar, was first mixed with water coming from a particular *'onjiS'la* spring, the one to which Gordimiu, the first Kalasha of Birir, had connected his tower-house, as we have seen, through an underground pipe made of markhor horns. The fact that the blood is smeared, rather than sprinkled, on the shrine, seems to indicate that the extent to which the sacrificial offer is attributed to the god – expressed through the contact of a part of the victim with the shrine (Hubert & Mauss [1899] 1909: 51) – is in this case total. If we consider that, in addition, the carcass of the victim was entirely burnt in the fire, it seems quite certain that the rite was a true holocaust sacrifice.[58]

Victor Turner observes that the neophytes are frequently 'brought into close connection with divine or with superhuman power, with what is, in fact, often regarded as the unbounded, the infinite, the limitless' (Turner 1967: 98). This may be explained by their 'unstructured' position, which, escaping all classifications, makes them appear in a certain sense as formless. In Birir this is materially the case, for the neophytes are initiated as executors of rites, and will therefore come in direct contact with the divine. The same applies, however, as we know, to all initiated males, who can officiate in rites as long as they remain virgin. It would seem that the condition of liminality is implicitly extended to the whole period of life when having been initiated, a boy is already a man but, not having had sexual relations with women, he is not quite a man yet. In Turner's words he is 'betwixt and between' or 'neither here nor there'.

Kot shatek – 19 December 2006

After a virtually sleepless night the village rose later than usual. The day of the true climax of Chaumos was about to begin: the whole (non-Muslim) population of Birir was for once going to be reunited in the open-air dancing ground (*gri*) right at the embouchure of the sacred valley of Jagar. While in the previous days

---

58 Kalasha sacrifice recalls the Jewish one in some of its forms (cf. Hubert & Mauss [1899] 1909: 52; Bell 1997: 112--13; Grottanelli 1999: 24), and for the fact that the share of the gods is the blood of the victim; it differs from the Greek one, in which the share of the gods were the bones and the fat. For Grottanelli (1999: 48–52), however, in both cases the same principle is at work, demanding that the most noble and vital part be offered to the god, for bones embody the quality of permanence as opposed to the ephemeral nature of the flesh. The Greek and the Jewish sacrifice ideologies also share the idea that the deity materially consumes the part it is offered (Hubert & Mauss [1899] 1909: 52–3), a notion, we have seen, well documented among the Kalasha.

the dances were held mostly at night in the closed spaces of the temples, now they were going to be held in the open, in broad daylight. The night had been the 'deep heart' of the festival. There had been a 'sacral pre-eminence of night over day'. Though such notions are not explicit among the Kalasha of today, the fact that darkness precedes light in the architecture of the festival may be seen as symbolically mirroring the precedence of primordial Chaos over Creation (cf. Cardini 1995: 90). Quite manifestly, at any rate, the rituals of the new day were to sanction the victory of light over darkness, represented in the race between runners of the two sections of the valley community. The reign of obscurity was over: the festival was going to reach its climax in full daylight.

There was great excitement and expectation for the beginning of the race. The *prabal'on g'Uak* of the two sections, in the morning, had piled up in the two *kot* the branches (*acar'ik*) collected during the preparation day before the beginning of Chaumos. Everything was ready for the celebration. No processions were scheduled. Everyone was going to reach the dancing ground in his/her own time.

I set off from Guru around midday. At the beginning of the path leading to the open-air dancing ground a small group of men were singing *ajh'ona b'ayak* led by Kaanok, a specialist in the genre. After a few joking verses the group moved on. A first stop was made near the *bash'ali* to address the women confined there, who responded in song. Then we proceeded slowly upstream. Almost at every house Kaanok would stop to apostrophize the owners with his improvised verses. Behind the doors of their houses, we would sometimes spot Muslim men or women, furtively peeping out. When we reached the hamlet of Bishala, where the valley bottom is rather level and open, a group of women came forward to exchange with us their verses, dancing and laughing. Men and women reciprocally accused each other of causing love pains:

Women:
If your sister[59] suffers, oh brother, then you will suffer as well
Oh my dear brother, little brother of my heart
Men:
Oh my dear sister, little sister of my heart
Your voice is sweet like the singing of the oriole, why do you make me suffer?
Women:
You become sad and to your little sister you do not give even a look

---

59 'Brother' and 'sister' are the ordinary terms of address used between men and women of the same generation.

Oh my little brother, little brother of my heart
Men:
I dispelled your sadness with the spell (of love) and now I am your prisoner
Oh my dear sister, little sister of my heart

...

It took us more than two hours to cover a distance that could be walked in half the time. As we approached the dancing ground the soothing and solemn chant of the women became louder and louder. When we at last reached Grom, we found the *gri* dancing ground crowded with people. The *gri* is spectacularly situated on the flat top of a protruding rocky ridge reaching out to the middle of the valley. A splendid view opens to the east with the imposing mountains and the tiny villages hanging on their lower slopes. Paradoxically, this most important ritual space is found at the edge of an entirely converted village – Grom – which is in all likelihood the earliest settlement of the valley. The Birir *gri*, I was told, in the past was not situated where it is now. It was located at the other end of Grom village, in a vast space close to the last houses, at the feet of the steep rocky spur (*koTT'on*) on top of which, according to tradition, Gordimìu had built his tower-house (*dup'uri koT*). On the flat top of the spur, still in recent times, *uph'or* was celebrated, the ritual dance of the victorious warrior upon his return from an incursion into enemy territory. There were seven stones, and the dancer had to jump from one to the other, firing his gun at each jump. Gulistan, who provided this brief description, recalled that his own uncle had performed the ritual.

In that space, probably the symbolic centre of the whole territory, in the shade of the spur of the apical ancestor, a mosque was built several decades ago, once the village was entirely converted. Gordimìu's rocky spur is now left in Muslim territory and converted Kalasha girls climb on its *'onjiSTa* top, formerly off-limits for women. When the old dancing ground was occupied by the mosque, a new one was created in its present site at the opposite end of the village, in a much smaller, though very spectacular, place.

The crowd filling the dancing ground was mainly female. The drums were not there, but I could hear them beating somewhere further up, I could not quite tell where. Someone summoned Kaanok, urging him to 'accomplish *dast'ur*'. I was slow in following him. When I finally climbed up the ladder leading to the place where the drums were beating, it was too late: I just managed to see the heads and the points of the sticks of the initiates who were dancing surrounded by a thick crowd. They had danced three rounds of *ca~* and this one was their last. We were gathered in a large level space in the area of the goat sheds, called *pasg'ut kh'aw*,

'Pasgut's threshing floor'. The neophytes had danced the *iCh'oa nat*, 'dance on the hind legs', which imitates the movements of a goat when it stands on its hind legs to graze on the leaves of the lower branches of a tree. My assistants later dictated to me the lyrics of the song accompanying the dance. They celebrated the participation in the feast of the mountain spirits and of a god:

> *I gaze at the mountains and I see the markhor grazing*
> *I turn my eyes towards Praba's valley and I see a line of young fairies*
> *The god arrives in the shade of that fecund valley*
> *The god is arriving, the lord of Pachaemundik* [the mountain closing Praba's
>   valley to the north-west]
> *I look at my shrine and I see it alight with a thousand torches.*

Ritual events took place in succession at a fast pace, almost without interruption. The rite that followed the dance of the neophytes was called *nog'or grik*, 'to capture the fortress'. It enacted the fundamental *'onjiSTa–r'ela* opposition. Two adult, and therefore *r'ela*, men had crossed the border marked by a small water channel dug sideways in the mountain above the goat sheds, invading the more *'onjiSta* territory where the boys were symbolically entrenched. The *prabal'on g'Uak*, as personifications of the *'onjiSTa* sphere, had the duty to defend it by repelling the invaders and restoring the separation between *'onjiSTa* and *r'ela*. The rite unfolded more like a game than a ceremony. The two trespassers were rudely pushed away and sent tumbling down the slope amid great laughter and shouting.[60] Immediately afterwards, the band of boys, who were joined by the two drummers with other adults, swarmed up the mountain in what seemed like a chase after some wild animal. The rite is called *Law'ak bih'ik,* 'the fox is scared'. At the end of their round, the boys, from afar, again attacked the *r'ela* people below shouting at them and trying to hit them with snowballs hurled from the slope, a further enactment of the fundamental opposition.

We have seen that in a song of the women the fox is called 'penetrator of vaginas'; it represents therefore the male sexual organ in the act of copulation. The rite of its chase by the virgin boys appears to enact the symbolic expulsion of what is considered the main source of contamination, to confirm the separation

---

60 Winter ritual games of the type of 'the assault on the fortress' are documented in various European contexts. See Propp [1963] 1978: 216–18; Van Gennep 1988: 3353; Toschi [1955] 1976: 156, 277; Burke [1978] 1980: 180.

between *'onjiSTa* and *r'ela*;[61] a repetition in different terms, it would seem, of the same theme already expressed in the *nog'or grik* rite.

The neophytes had initially joined the chase, but had subsequently gone on to the Praba dur, after executing another round of *ca~* on the mountain slope. They had to be inside the sacred enclosure when the runners arrived with the torches to light up the wood stacked up between the poles of the two *kot*. The race was about to begin.

We descend on the *gri* [from the goat shed area where the preceding rites were carried out]. In a moment the ritual race of the *kot shat'ek* will take place. Meanwhile the singing goes on. I would like to find a good spot along the itinerary of the runners, but who knows when the race will actually start. After a short while the women [and the few Muslims present] are sent away from the *gri*. They must not even gaze upon Jagar ga, which is partially visible from the dancing ground. I hurry in its direction. I see a young man running with a torch in his hand. I follow him, from afar I see him reaching the *kot* of the downstream half and setting it on fire. But the other *kot*, the one of Biyou village, has already been lit; the wood is already all burnt. Biyou has won; last year the *w'enau* (the upstream ones) also won. At this point a true fight erupts. A young man tries to attack another one. Three men hold him putting their arms around his shoulders and waist. Other men get involved, until the turmoil is generalized. 'They have been drinking' some people tell me. 'It happens every year', Erfan says, 'it is *dast'ur*'. Gulfurus as well confirmed to me today that it happens every year. I do not think they were all drunk, because among them was Mir Badca, who did not seem to be drunk at all and later sang for hours on the *gri* with his powerful voice. (*From my field journal – Guru 19 December 2006*).

The race had a bad end, everybody was saying; worse still, it practically had not taken place. The upstream people – the others contended – had set their *kot* on fire before it began. When I enquired about the issue in Biyou, the *kaz'i* Wali Khan said they had done it because otherwise they would not have had any chance of winning, for the downstream people are much more numerous and they would have tackled their runners to prevent them from reaching their *kot*. It is part of the competition, he added, to resort to any means to block the runners of the opposite

---

61 In European folklore, the fox is often considered a diabolical animal (Caro Baroja [1979] 1989: 349–51).

side. The victorious team receives a he-goat, or its equivalent in cash, from the villages it represents. At stake is the good fortune of the coming year (cf. Schomberg
1938: 193). Gulistan and Erfan explained to me that the teams did not have a fixed
number of runners. Whoever so wishes, can run. But the torches used in the race
must be *'onjiSTa Ca~J'a*. They are fabricated using only the root of the pine tree
(*kw'erik*), which is the most resinous part of the tree. They are *'onjiSTa* torches
because they remain in the *'onjiSTa* space of the goat sheds, without ever coming
in contact with the world of the villages below. The *prabal'on g'Uak* themselves,
take them to Pasgut's threshing ground, which is the centre of the ritual activities
of the day. Erfan showed me some of them, tucked in between the beams of the
roof of a nearby shed, while we were waiting for the beginning of the race. Each
runner had one. They were much smaller torches than the long *Ca~J'a* I had seen
in the processions; they could be easily held in one hand while running. I counted
three or four of them. Gulistan remembered that when he was a boy he saw as
many as twenty-five torches, only for the downstream half. That year there were
only six of them, he lamented. He had run the race three times, he said, and twice
he had been first.

It may seem surprising that the climax of a feast that seemed to celebrate the
unity of the community through rites aimed at reaffirming the ties between its two
sections, should consist in a competition regularly ending in a brawl. But, as some
scholars have remarked (Lanternari 1983b: 56; cf. Caillois [1939] 2001: 126),
in traditional contexts group cohesion is frequently reconfirmed and celebrated
through a dialectical process made of antagonisms, divisions and ritualized competitions. We have already seen how the processions heading to the Guru temple
on the first night of the festival, were accompanied by shouts and insults. Just as
shouts and insults were addressed to the people of Aspar when the people of the
Guru *rikh'ini* flocked to their temple in a torchlight procession in the night of the
initiations and all the lineages of the downstream half danced together for the first
time.

We are again faced, it seems, with the dual rhythm of increased solidarity/exac-
erbated antagonism, noted by Lévi-Strauss ([1952] 1995). Through a dramatic
representation of conflict, a superior unity is reaffirmed. In Eliade's perspective,[62]
the race and its outcome may be seen in the light of the Chaos/Cosmos dichotomy:
on the one side the competition that sparks the brawl and therefore represents
Chaos, and on the other the return to the Cosmos represented by the unity and
solidarity expressed by the communal dancing and the reciprocal panegyrics on

62 Eliade [1949] 1968: 78ff., 93, [1948] 1976: 324, [1975] 1979: 211.

the *gri*. At the core of the ritualistic symbolism there is, however, quite manifestly, the light/darkness dichotomy. The winner of the race, in the imminence
of the solstice (it was 19 December), lights the fire that symbolizes, and is meant
to favour, the return of the sun and the end of the darkest season. The race is a
representation of the victory of light over darkness. On one side we have therefore
obscurity, disorder, conflict and chaos; and on the other we have light, ordered
cosmos and solidarity.[63] Only through a return to the undifferentiated, can renewal
and regeneration be accomplished:[64] the Chaos represented in our case by the
brawl, generates vital energy.[65] Hence, the race has also the traits of a fertility rite
(cf. Frazer [1922] 1987: 316–17). Abundance of crops and of offspring is indeed
the reward of the victorious section.[66]

Around the fire where the *magl'is* had formed, *ca~*, *d'ushak* and *drazha'ilak*
alternated as usual. Though the soloists and the members of the *magl'is* are mostly
men, women can also play these roles. In the course of that day I repeatedly saw
women taking the lead as soloists. The members of the circle listened to them with
the same attention given to male singers, and they would reward in the same way
the singer with rupee bills. But around another bonfire only a few yards away a
group of women was singing songs of a different type. I stepped closer to listen to
their lyrics. Gulistan noticed my move and, skipping all formalities, ordered the
women to sing the traditional songs of Chaumos, so that I could record them. In
contrast to what was the case with all the other lyrics presented so far, those songs
were not sung spontaneously, even if, in all likelihood, a number of them at least,
would have been sung also without Gulistan's intervention.

They were typically feminine songs, with relatively brief lyrics composed of
only a few verses, which could, however, be repeated at will. We have already seen

---

63 For Witzel (2004: 585, 591, 593) the ritual clash between two opposed sections at the time of
the winter solstice is connected to the dichotomy Deva/Asura, which would reflect in his view a
more ancient dichotomy between two groups of divinities already present among the Proto-Indo-
Europeans, and even in a larger Eurasian context.

64 Eliade [1949] 1968: 117–18; Cardini 1995: 192; Buttitta A. 1996: 268, 276.

65 For Eliade ([1948] 1976: 214) ritual fights are meant to stimulate the reproductive forces of
nature, and they are rooted in the 'archaic concept' that competitions and brutal games increase
and nourish 'universal energy'.

66 For similar forms of antagonism/cooperation in European folklore see Toschi [1955] 1976:
438–42; Marinelli 1982; Sordi 1982: 28–30; Lanternari 1983b: 57–9; Gianotti & Quaccia 1986:
32–43; Van Gennep 1988: 3346–7; Giallombardo 1990: 13; Buttitta I.E. 2006: 192, 196. For the
frequent erupting of violence in Italian medieval feasts see Cardini 1995: 59; for a Tuscan example
Addobbati 2002: 64–7; in general Caillois [1939] 2001: 98.

that there is a category of songs quite different from *ca~*, *d'ushak* and *drazha'ilak*, that belongs specifically to the cultural world of women and is typical of Chaumos. In this category we may distinguish two genres: songs celebrating Chaumos, and obscene songs. I had already heard the main songs of the first type, Shahi and Bidrakalen, in the preceding days. What follows is another example of the kind, a chant celebrating specifically the ritual activities of the *prabal'on g'Uak*:

> *Your fox hunt, oh Praba boys*
> *Your bread and your apple-mush you must eat them while standing*
> *Your dance of the grazing goats, oh Praba boys*
> *Your bread and your apple-mush you must eat them while standing*
> *A full night on the white trail, oh Praba boys*
> *Your bread and your apple-mush you must eat them while standing*
> *Your thick bread cakes, oh Praba boys*
> *Your bread and your apple-mush you must eat them while standing*
> *A walnut kernel and an ear of corn (only), oh Praba boys*
> *You mash them and eat them.*

The chant is addressed to the *prabal'on g'Uak*. The refrain seems to refer to the hardships of their trial: the boys must eat standing up because – according to Gulistan's explanations – they are numerous and inside the goat shed there is not enough space to sit down.[67] The other verses celebrate the ritual activities of the initiates during the time of their separation from the community. The first one recalls the fox chase already discussed. The second one refers to the dance preceding the chase that imitates, as we have seen, the movement of the goats standing on their hind legs to graze on the lower leaves of the oak trees. There is also a reference to the 'White Trail' the boys have to follow on the night of their initiation, and to the large flat bread cake (*cAh'aka Dh'ou*), that we already mentioned when analysing the Bidrakalen chant, called *indr-h'arik,* 'to be taken to Indra'. The last verse refers again to the hardships of the trial by underlining the scarcity of the food at the disposal of the initiates.

The name of Indra appears also in another song I recorded that same night; a song I had already heard in 1973 at the Rumbur Chaumos:

---

67 In fact, both Gulistan and Erfan were uncertain about the meaning of the refrain. As an alternative Gulistan suggested it could perhaps refer to the meal at Praba's shrine where, because of the snow, it is not possible to sit down.

Photo 1
The female headgear (kup'as) worn by a little girl (Birir, 12.09.2006).

Photo 2
The shrine of the god Praba (Birir, 12.09.2006).

Photo 3
Guru village with my lodging on the bottom left corner (Birir, 01.16.2007).

Photo 4
Chaumos, an initiate in ceremonial dress (Birir, 12.18.2006).
© Martino Nicoletti 2007

Photo 4a
Chaumos, an initiate in ceremonial dress (Birir, 12.18.2006).

Photo 5
Chaumos, a child at the first stage of his initiation in his father's arms
(Birir, 12.18.2006).

Photo 6
Chaumos, dance of the initiates in the rikhini temple (Birir, 12.18.2006).

Photo 7
Lagaur celebration, the game of the wife threatened by her husband (Birir, 01.05.2007).

Photo 8
Lagaur celebration, the girls head to the temple to deck it with evergreen boughs
(Birir, 01.05.2007).

Photo 9

Animal masks appear for *Lawa'k bih'ik*, one of the last days of Chaumos
(Bumburet valley, Bruhn village, 22.12.2006)

Photo 10

Lawa'k bih'ik, one of the last days of Chaumos (Bumburet valley,
Bruhn village, 22.12.2006).

Photo 11
Kalasha girl (Birir, 12.18.2006). © Martino Nicoletti 2007

Pilimsho's mother in law, Pilimsho's mother in law went to Indra's fortress
You sacrificed a chicken and offered it to me
And what can I do with it?
Sacrifice an initiation ram and give it to me
When something comes to me, I give that to you.

The mention of Indra's fortress is seemingly a reference to the holy place where in the neighbouring Bumburet valley the central rite of Chaumos is celebrated on the night of the descent of the god, a holy place called, indeed, 'Indrunkot' (Jettmar 1975: 356).[68] The meaning of the remaining verses is quite clear. They express, in the simplest way, the principle of reciprocity formulated in the form of a joking reproach addressed to those who give the worst of what they have: among animals, chicken are for the Kalasha the true incarnation of the *r'ela* principle; their meat and their eggs are forbidden food.[69] The reproach is followed by the exhortation to give the best that can be given to a girl, which is the initiation ram, called 'ram of the braids', because when a girl first puts on the traditional headgear (*kup'as*), her hair is also plated for the first time in the five traditional braids. The song, with a very lively rhythm, finally ends with a warning reminding the direct connection between giving and receiving, because what we give is what we receive. A warning that recalls closely the Maori saying reported by Marcel Mauss at the end of his famous *Essai sur le don*, 'so much Maru gives, as much as Maru takes, and this is good, is good' (Mauss [1923–4] 1965: 277); as well as the less-famous Sardinian proverb 'piattu ki andata, piattu ki torrara', 'a plate that goes is a plate that comes back' (Buttitta I.E. 2006: 153). In the Rumbur Chaumos, in 1973, this song was accompanied by a dance in which the dancers, facing each other, mimed with their hands a flux going from one to the other and then coming back. The communion is here at the human level.[70]

The theme of reproductive power emerges instead in a series of other songs called *Lac ghO~* (shameful songs), of which I had recorded, until then, only one example, the song of the fox 'penetrator of vaginas'. They are called 'shameful songs' because of their crude lyrics that include terms never used in ordinary

---

68 It may be that this song was imported from Bumburet; a not-unlikely possibility, if we consider that inter-valley marriages are common.

69 A ban today not always respected, especially in the two northern valleys.

70 Victor Turner would probably see in the lyrics of this song the expression of the basic principle of his *communitas*, which condemns those who give in to the desire of keeping for themselves what should be shared for the good of all (Turner [1969] 1990: 104).

language; and especially not by women who normally have a very modest attitude towards everything concerning sexuality.[71] Here is the text of one of them:

> *The crow ran after the walnut*
> *He put it underground and it sprouted*
> *A penis grew to him*
> *Lever up and lever down*
> *With a dom[72] of your scrotum's hair, Salamdin will make his leggings.*

Walnuts are an immediate symbol of fertility and sexuality (Maggi 2001: 142). The crow burying a walnut, which subsequently sprouts, is a quite clear represen-tation of the process of generation and reproduction. The song alludes to sexual intercourse by giving a double meaning to the term designating the lever used to regulate the level of the grinding stone of the water mills, and it ends with a shameless reference to the pubic hair of the man the women want to make fun of, with which a certain Salamdin can make his *kuTaw'ati*, the goat-wool leggings used by shepherds in the mountains. The tune was lively and the singing was accompanied by rhythmical claps of hands.

A recurring theme of these songs are the relations between men and women, and especially the game of conquest and refusal, which is represented with recur-ring sexual allusions that provoke general fits of laughter. Another example of *Lac ghO~*:

> *Falling sideways between the ropes at the end of the bed,*
> *With his trousers thrown across his shoulders*
> *He said to the spirit of Sengil:[73] since she rejects me, you will have to act as*
>   *my sister-in-law*
> *(Watch out that) I'll set the hair of your scrotum on fire and I'll burn it all –*
>   *the mother-in-law said – and forget about this sister-in-law business!*
> *So he shaved, he trimmed his moustache, and went to look for a woman in*
>   *Rumbur and Bumburet.*

---

71 Maggi 2001; Wutt 1983: 133.

72 A measure for sheep and goat wool weighing about 1kg.

73 This is a verse that remained in part obscure. Baras Khan, who was assisting me in the translations, had never heard of the spirit of Sengil and could not figure out why it was mentioned, since the request that follows is clearly addressed to the mother-in-law.

The song makes fun of a man who tries to get his mother-in-law to have sex with him to make up for the refusal of her daughter. But since sexual intercourse between a woman and her son-in-law is considered a form of incest, the man suggests she plays the role of a sister-in-law, with whom sexual relations, though illicit, are permitted. The woman, at any rate, rejects him and pushes him away to the end of the bed where the ropes holding the bedding are distanced so much that the man falls in between them with one leg, and remains there half naked with his trousers across his shoulders. In addition the woman threatens to set his pubic hair on fire and makes it quite clear that there is no way he can get her to replace her daughter. Her threat is successful because the young man, after taking good care of his looks, goes in search of a woman in the other two valleys. The scene, we must keep in mind, is not as absurd as it may appear to a Western eye. Since traditionally the marriage of a Kalasha girl is arranged when she is little more than a child, a mother-in-law can easily be a young woman, possibly not much older than her son in law.

One last example of a shameful song:

Hiding behind a corner he throws walnut shells at me
But what do you want from me, old man with a shaking beard?!
You have your pipe and all the rest
They put tobacco into it
But your organ is coarse, they say
Leave women alone
Your shrivelled scrotum may fall to pieces.

We have here another ironic scene in which a woman makes fun of an older man who courts her in a childish way throwing walnut shells at her from behind a corner. The pipe and the tobacco are possibly sexual allusions. Sexual organs, at any rate, are explicitly named in the verses that follow, in which the woman urges the man to forget about women because his penis is coarse and his scrotum all shrivelled. As in the preceding song the woman rejects and ridicules the man. Both songs make fun of men's virility, giving full expression to the male/ female opposition. Once again antagonism is staged at the time of integration and unification.

The obscene character of these songs, manifested especially in their making explicit reference to male sexual organs, has, however, also another symbolic value. They are an expression of the orgiastic dimension of the festival, which had already made its appearance in the preparatory day of *acar'ik* and *ganDalik'an* and, in the form of the food orgy,[74] in the long itinerant banquet that followed the first sacrifices on the night of Nongrat. The magical value of obscene insults is well known. There is ample evidence, also, that orgiastic themes are typical of fertility rites in general and of New Year celebrations in particular, for the rites of men are meant to support and favour the work of nature.[75] The group of women recruited by Gulistan moved from one song to the other without interruption. One of them came close to me to tell me that they were singing all the Chaumos songs, really all of them, without leaving even one out. I could be assured.

But the most sacred moment of the celebration was approaching:

At a certain moment Gulistan calls me. He pushes me precipitously up the ladders leading to Pasgut threshing ground. An important ritual is about to begin. I am not too late, this time. But Saidan Shah signals a 'no', those words must not be recorded. About twenty men are gathered on the threshing ground. I turn around making a move to go away, but they conclude that I can stay, as long as I stand at a distance. I see in front of me a group of about a dozen men facing the Jagar valley, their shoulders turned towards me. I cannot see what they are doing. A man is holding a bough of a tree I do not recognize, called *zar'ori*. A fire is lit, or maybe someone is holding a pine torch. They murmur some words. A few other men are standing, like me, at a distance. Suddenly the rite is concluded and everybody leaves swiftly the *dram'i* [the terraced roof of the goat shed, used as threshing ground]. That is the holiest moment, someone tells me; the Muslims have been sent away from the dancing ground. (*From my field journal – 19 December 2006*)

Gulistan had come to fetch me accompanied by another man. Night had already fallen and they were both holding a torch. Nobody had mentioned this rite to me before. At my arrival on the roof of the goat shed a short discussion took place and I was asked to leave. I started down the ladder thinking my condition was not considered *'onjiSTa* enough, but I was called back and allowed to stay as long as I stood at a distance of about ten metres from where the ritual was held, on a nearby roof. I understood they were not objecting to my presence, but to my recording,

---

74 For comments on, and examples of, food orgies see Caillois [1939] 2001: 120; Lanternari [1976] 1983a: 510–11, 1981: 142; Giallombardo 1990.

75 Cf. e.g. Caillois [1939] 2001: 117; Eliade [1948] 1976: 373–5, 412, [1949] 1968: 44–5; Propp [1963] 1978: 209–11; Lanternari [1976] 1983a: 517–19; Buttitta A. 1996: 282; D'Agostino 2002: 175.

for they were going to recite the *ghaC*, the secret prayer, of Chaumos. Since I was standing at a distance from which I could not record the words of the rite, I felt free to leave my recorder on for the whole time to record the natural sounds of the event and my voice describing its unfolding. From the recording, other details emerged that, due to the overwhelming intensity of the events, had not found their way into my notebook.

The rite began between 7 and 7.30 p.m. and lasted less than half an hour. Among the performers of the ritual were some *gaderak'an*, including Saidan Shah who as a *kaz'i* led the ceremony, but there were also several boys, probably the *prabal'on g'Uak*. Some were holding torches. At a distance of three or four yards from the group, two elders were beating the drums to a very slow and regular rhythm. From the dancing ground, attenuated by the distance, flowed the melodious and solemn chant of the women intoning Bidrakalen, the chant announcing the descent of the Chaumos god. At the head of a small line of men looking towards Praba's holy valley, there was a man who was covering his head and face with a mantle. He was the custodian of the secret prayer and must have been therefore from the Aliksherdari lineage. The secret prayer – *ghaC* – he was about to utter, Gulistan later told me, was dedicated to Indr.

The officiating man, the one covering his face, held in his hands a bough of a plant I did not recognize, which surprisingly was not juniper, normally used in rituals. I learned it was called *zar'ori* and that it was a parasitic plant. It was a very *'onjiSTa* plant – explained to me Gulfurus, a young man standing by my side – that had been collected and brought over by the *prabal'on g'Uak*; it was going to be used, he added, also the following day for the final ritual of the festival. The next day I saw it in the light of day: a bough with little green leaves and small transparent whitish berries. It was mistletoe! Frazer's 'golden bough'. An augural plant, as is well known, also in Europe since remote times.[76] In the European continent great virtues were attributed to mistletoe, and especially those of ensuring fertility to fields, animals and human beings and of protecting them from all threats. In Birir I did not hear of any special property attributed to it. I was just told it was a parasitic plant that could only grow with the support of another tree. But can there be a better symbol of fertility and regeneration than an evergreen plant that gives its fruit, the little whitish berries, in the coldest and darkest period of the year, just when a new cycle is about to begin? As Propp ([1963] 1978: 43) remarks, berries are basically seeds covered with the pulp of the fruit and they express, therefore, the same reproductive symbolism.

---

76 Miles [1912] 1976: 273; Frazer [1922] 1987: 658–63; Van Gennep 1988: 3476–80, 3492; Cattabiani 1988: 78–9; Hutton 1996: 36–7.

While the rite was being carried out Gulfurus kept on repeating to me that what we were watching was very difficult and very *'onjiSTa* work (*krom*) and that *r'ela* people who eat chicken and eggs, as we were, had to stand at a distance. From where we were we could hardly hear the murmur of the prayer. Suddenly the rite was over and its end was marked by choral shouts of *zh'awi!*, an exclamation we already know; the reference to reproduction and fertility is quite manifest. We quickly left the roof of the goat shed and returned to the *gri*. In the meantime the dances had been resumed. Two fires were burning and around one of them the *magl'is* had again been formed:

> At a certain point a long line of dancers was formed, men and women, who, holding hands, started making volutes around the *magl'is* without locking it in a circle. The leader of the line was holding the mistletoe bough I had seen during the rite. Many men were wearing a little bough of mistletoe or of juniper in the fold of their woollen caps. The lines at one point appear to be two. They intersect, all movements become increasingly accelerated and chaotic; there is pushing and bumping in all directions. I climb for refuge on the rock closing the dancing ground towards the valley. The commotion increases until the man holding the *zar'ori* bough breaks into the circle of the *magl'is*, reaches the fire and starts stumping on it almost putting out. That is the signal: the great day when the whole community is gathered together on the *gri* is over. (*From my field journal – 19 December 2006*).

The chain dance is called *granz'uliak*.[77] The line, which at some point must have split in two, formed by men and women, made coiling spiral volutes. The dance was accompanied by a chant called *sharacat'aki*. It is the song of the arrival of the markhor (*sh'ara*). These are the lyrics I recorded:

> *Clear the way! The markhor is coming!*
> *The time has come of the markhor dance!*
> *The markhor is coming and will mix with us*
> *In the high pastures he arrives walking in the snow, my little markhor.*

For the Kalasha, the markhor are the goats of the *s'uci*, the mountain spirits, who are represented as a pastoral community in a mirror image of the human one. Among them, women take care of herding and their domestic animals are the wild animals

---

77 Cf. Trail & Cooper 1999: 111.

of men. A much-coveted prey, markhors cannot be killed by a hunter without their consent, which is granted only if a series of ritual prescriptions aimed at protecting the *'onjiSTa* sphere from contact with the *r'ela* one are respected. The markhor (*sh'ara h'ira*) is therefore the quintessential *'onjiSTa* animal, not only because it inhabits the *'onjiSTa* territory of the mountain peaks, but because it is directly connected to the spirits who are seen as the true personification of that sphere; it is therefore a living expression of the sacredness of wild nature. The descent of the markhor announced in the *sharacat'aki* song represents the irruption of the purity of the wilderness in the symbolic centre of the domestic domain of the villages, the dancing ground. The wild/domestic polarity is ritually integrated.

At the moment when the celebration reaches its climax, all the oppositions – human/divine, male/female, upstream section/downstream section, wild/domestic – are brought to unity. In the course of this long day the communion with the divine is first represented in the holocaust sacrifice at Praba's shrine, at the first lights of dawn; then the communion between men is enacted with the overcoming of the contraposition between the two sections; and finally the communion with wild nature is achieved with the symbolic descent of the markhor that mix with humans, as sung in one of the verses of the *sharacat'aki* song. Condensed in the rituals of a single day are expressed, it seems, the essential concerns at the heart of the festival.

For Izard and Smith ([1979] 1988: 14), these concerns animate all cultures, for all need to offer a view of the relations of man with nature and society, and, ultimately, of his individual destiny. We have witnessed, as the festival unrolled, a gradual descent of the *'onjiSTa* sphere into the *r'ela* one. A gradual penetration of the male principle into the female one, from which life springs. With the integration of all polarities, the beginning of the new cycle and the regeneration of all things living is celebrated. After the symbolic enactment of Chaos in the preceding days of the festival, from the backwards dance of the *bhut* to the brawl on the *gri* after the race, on this pivotal day, with the symbolic integration of all polarities, an ordered Cosmos is represented. In the sacred time of the feast, the *illo tempore* of the beginning is relived when Cosmos triumphed over Chaos, and life came into existence. Significantly the secret prayer is dedicated to Indr, the god who in the Vedic myth defeats the monster obstructing creation.

With the dance hailing the descent of the markhor, the day marking the climax of Chaumos is over. It seems significant that the final act should be entrusted to the bearer of the mistletoe bough who, by extinguishing the fire[78] burning on the *gri*,

---

78 The power to extinguish fire was among the virtues attributed to mistletoe in Europe (Frazer [1922] 1987: 659, 662).

signals the end of the old time in the very moment when, with the green leaves of the mistletoe, he announces the beginning of a new time. But the solstice festival was not over yet. The seclusion of the *prabal'on g'Uak* had still not come to its end and one last day of dancing and rituals still awaited us. The crowd dispersed. I walked back to Guru in the light of a couple of pine torches with Saidan Shah, Gulistan, Gulfurus and another young man who was so drunk that he could barely stand on his feet. The valley was covered in snow and we had to be very careful not to slip on the icy trail. At Erfan's house we again ate the *'onjiSTa* food distributed in the night of the sacrifices. The wheat bread handed out then had been broken into pieces and warmed up in a pot together with the meat to make *a'u pac'aLa*, the Chaumos delicacy. Since it was *'onjiSTa* food, women did not eat any of it.

That evening I had a chat with Saidan Shah, who had decided to stay the night at his son's house. He told me he spent several years in Karachi, where he was employed as a construction worker. In those times he used to spend six months there and six months in Birir. He had been also to Lahore, Multan, Islamabad, Rawalpindi and Murree, in other words all the big cities of Pakistan. With some surprise I found out thus that the old *kaz'i*, one of the most jealous custodians of tradition, knew the outside world maybe better than anyone else in the valley.

Aspar nat – 20 December 2006

The following day, the triumph of light having been celebrated, ritual activities took place again in full daylight. I started out for Aspar in the company of Baras Khan, who was reappearing after two days of absence due to the fact that his wife had delivered a child exactly at the climax of the festival, on *ist'ongas rat*, the night of the initiations. Everything had worked out fine and the new mother was now in the *bash'ali* with the baby, to whom, as is the custom, no name had yet been given. Indeed, names may not be given until after several months have passed, when the baby has already started to interact with the world around it. The woman was going to spend at least twenty days in the *bash'ali*, until she was 'clean' (*saph'a*) again. Some women, I was told, remain there even a month and a half.

We reached Aspar around midday. In the temple the dances were in full swing. Only the downstream half was participating, the upstream people that day were gathered in the Biyou *rikh'ini*. After the rites of integration of the preceding day, each group was separated again. The female songs typical of Chaumos were not heard that day; only the ordinary songs of all festivals – *ca~*, *d'ushak* and *drazha'ilak* – were sung. The dances continued in the early afternoon.

In the meantime the seclusion of the *prabal'on g'Uak* continued. They had spent the previous night in the goat sheds around Pasgut threshing-ground. In the morning they had descended the valley (always keeping to the *'onjiSTa* area above the irrigation canals) as far as Aspar, when the dancing was taking place in the temple. Along the way – I was later told by Shujauddin, a twelve-year-old boy who was part of the group – they had stopped in various goat sheds where they were welcomed with walnuts, dried mulberries, grapes, pears and wine. For the whole time of the dances they stayed in a goat shed above Aspar, and only in the evening they proceeded to Guru for the *zar'ori s'araz*, the final rite of Chaumos in which mistletoe boughs are burnt, celebrated in the same goat shed above Guru from where they had started out.

When, some time after Chaumos, I followed the 'white trail,' a detail emerged that had not been mentioned by Shujauddin. Exactly above Gasguru village, Gulistan showed me a rocky spur where the neophytes, on their way back to Guru, stage a torchlight dance to the beating of the drums – a dance of relief, it would seem, at the conclusion of their trial. It is a trial made of sleepless nights, of mountain climbing in the dark, and especially of ritual acts they have the responsibility of carrying out correctly. It is certainly not a trial of suffering, as those documented for initiations in other contexts, but still a trial for children aged about ten, as indicated by the lyrics of one of the songs sung by the women on the *gri* the preceding day:

> *You have been to the goat shed; you have been to the goat shed*
> *How is he feeling my baby boy?*
> *Is he feeling well or not, my baby boy?*
> *Maybe his legs are aching*
> *He has to wake up early in the morning.*

It is the song of a mother, worried for the hardships her son will have to face in the days of his seclusion: he will be uncomfortable, he will get cramps, he will have to leap to his feet. The woman is anxiously asking how her son is doing up there at the goat sheds. But on the day of the Aspar dances (Aspar *nat*) the trial is over: the neophytes will come out of seclusion to be reintegrated, with a new status, within the community.

The dances in the Aspar temple were supposed to last, Baras Khan told me, until the sun went down, which meant around 4 p.m. I walked back to Guru slightly earlier, in time to spot a line of little girls singing as they climbed up the steep path leading to the temple, each carrying a piece of wood. They had just made the round of the houses of the village collecting beans. I followed them to the *rikh'ini*. Under the wooden porch, between its carved columns, the beans were already cooking in two large cauldrons. The wood carried by the little girls was going to be used for the fire. Here below is the translation of the lyrics of their song.[79] It was the song of *dA'u tat'u*, the feast of beans, which concluded that day and was going to be one of the last ritual events of Chaumos.

> *Make beans and their seed abound*
> *Make the markhor multiply*
> *Make black-speckeled beans and their seed abound*
> *Make the markhor multiply*
> *Make the 'imo' beans and their seed abound*
> *Make the markhor multiply*
> *Make white lentils and their seed abound*
> *Make the markhor multiply*
> *Make goats and their seed abound*
> *Make the markhor multiply*
> *Make kids and their seed abound*
> *Make the markhor multiply*
> *Make cows and their seed abound*
> *Make the markhor multiply*
> *Make calves and their seed abound*
> *Make the markhor multiply*
> *Make female offspring abound*
> *Make the markhor multiply*
> *Make male offspring abound*
> *Make the markhor multiply*
> *Make virile energy abound*
> *Make the markhor multiply.*

This was the song sung during the collection of which I had observed only the last act. The little girls, I was told, had done the round of the houses in the afternoon, separately in each village.

No god is mentioned by name in the lyrics, but the fact that in all the verses the verbs are always declined in the second singular person of the imperative/

---

79 I could not record the song. These lyrics were dictated to me the following day by the wife of my host Erfan

exhortative indicates that the song must, at least implicitly, be addressed to some divinity. The most natural addressee of similar invocations would surely be Jeshtak, goddess of the family and of reproduction in general, who is indeed invoked with very similar lyrics in the *dA'u tat'u* rituals of Rumbur (Loude & Lièvre 1984: 302–10). Reproduction, and therefore fertility, is the manifest theme of the song. The last verse asks for abundance of male energy, without which there is no procreation, while the other verses pray for abundance of everything: fruits of the earth, offspring of humans and animals. The song asks in particular for abundance of all sorts of beans and lentils because, we may surmise, beans are the main everyday food in winter. Beans and lentils, however, are symbols of abundance, a symbolism that inspires also the custom, widespread in Europe,[80] of eating lentils – or, at any rate, cooked seeds – for New Year as a wish for abundance. Beans and lentils are seeds, and as such they contain life in potential. They preserve life and they have the potential for reproducing it; the circle seed-plant-seed bears witness to the eternity of life, and humans, by eating seeds, become part of this process (Propp [1963] 1978: 47).

The song, repeated at each halt by the girls, has a well-wishing function because abundance of all goods is invoked for the donors. It is significant, as well, that the prayer for plenty is sung by little girls who, among humans, are the most suitable to represent the idea of a budding seed. We may note, also, that the *dA'u tat'u* collecting ritual is morphologically quite different from the 'extortive' rounds of collection made by the *prabal'on g'Uak* in the afternoon of Nongrat. We have here, perhaps, a more common instance of a collecting ritual in which the gift is demanded in return for the well-wishing verses sung for each family.

While the legumes were cooking in the pots under the porch, little girls were playing inside the temple or dancing and singing in threes. There were also a few male children, but the atmosphere was decidedly feminine. Two adolescent girls were supervising the cooking of the beans.

A couple of hours earlier the *prabal'on g'Uak* had returned to the goat shed above Guru from which they had started out, where was held the closing rite of the festival, the *zar'ori s'araz:* boughs of mistletoe burned on the fire together with offerings of grapes and walnuts.

The *zar'ori s'araz* ritual is clearly a rite of integration, since it marks the end of the period of seclusion of the neophytes. In this last day the great rite of passage enters its final stage. The passage is completed. From the moment of their descent

---

80 Propp [1963] 1978: 46–8; Bakhtin [1965] 1984: 219; Cardini 1995: 191–2; Buttitta I.E. 2006: 96–102.

from the area of the goat sheds, the neophytes re-enter the community with the new status of young adults. But their return is not ceremonious. Divested of their ceremonial clothes, the boys, silently and swiftly, go to mix again with their peers. The reintegration of the neophytes in the community, and the return of the community to ordinary time, should not, however, be seen as a mere return to the condition of departure. A lasting quality has been acquired. The return may be seen – as Maurice Bloch suggests in his revisitation of Van Gennep's three stages – 'as a conquest of the here and now by the transcendental' (Bloch 1992: 5–6). In the case of Birir the initiates have become *'onjiSTa s'uda* and can, from then on, officiate in rites. In the same way the entire community returns to a renewed condition that differs essentially from that, worn out by the daily here and now, preceding the initial phase. The ritual reaffirmation of the *'onjiSTa* principle brings with it regeneration.

Once the neophytes had been reintegrated into the community, the scene of the village was at once totally occupied by the women. The few men present were all gathered in the only space to which the women had no access, the *'onjiSTa* roof of Sherbek's house.[81] Two groups of several scores of girls and women were formed, one headed by Erfan's wife on a higher roof-top, and one led by Gulistan's wife on a lower roof-top. In an atmosphere of great hilarity the two teams exchanged, maybe for over an hour, improvised verses. The women seemed to put all their energies in the singing. That was the last *ajh'ona b'ayak* of the season: with the end of Chaumos, the song was going to be forbidden until the following autumn.

That evening the space of the temple was left to the young; some boys started to show up while the beans continued to cook in the two cauldrons and groups of girls sang lively songs. From the voices of one of these groups I recorded the following song:

> *You want to buy me with an iron cauldron, oh Gakshingoyak*
> *But my daughter in marriage I shall give you not, oh Gakshingoyak*
> *You want to buy me with an iron tripod, oh Gakshingoyak*
> *But my daughter in marriage I shall give you not, oh Gakshingoyak*
> *You try to buy me with a few apricots, oh Gakshingoyak*
> *But my daughter in marriage I shall give you not, oh Gakshingoyak.*

The song clearly belongs to the world of women and it is a manifest expression of female solidarity. The issue is that of the choice of a husband. According to

---

81 The question of why this particular roof is *'onjiSTa* remained unanswered.

traditional Kalasha custom, a girl's wedding (Maggi 2001: 167–212) is organized by her father when she is still a child, in reply to proposals advanced by the family of her future husband. Kalasha girls often accuse their fathers of selling them off, when they do not like the choice he made for them; iron tripods for cooking, and iron cauldrons to make cheese are the objects that traditionally form the *mal*, the bride price. The lyrics of the song feature a mother who wants to protect her daughter. The name *gakshing'oyak* is probably a nickname with a pejorative connotation designating an unwanted suitor; its literal meaning is 'little cow horn', a clear phallic allusion. The woman addresses him saying that if he thinks he can convince her with his gifts – cauldrons, tripods, apricots – he is mistaken: she'll never give him her daughter in marriage. The song expresses therefore the plight of Kalasha girls who are often given in marriage to much older men who take them away at a very young age from their family and friends. Kalasha marriage, it is true, is a process rather than a single act, and a girl goes therefore back and forth from her father's to her husband's home for years, but this is not enough to soothe the pain of an imposed choice. However, Kalasha *dast'ur* offers a way out of situations of great unhappiness. Young women have a culturally-sanctioned way to break up an unwanted marriage decided by their father: a girl can elope in *aLaS'in~g* with the man she loves, if he is able to give to the abandoned husband twice the bride price he originally paid to her father. *aLaS'in~g* is the choice of the heart.[82] In the 1990s when Wynne Maggi conducted her research on the Kalasha female universe, two-thirds of the women of Rumbur had been 'given' in marriage by their fathers when they were still children, at an age between six and twelve, and 43 per cent of the women married in this way, had later eloped with a man of their choice (Maggi 2001: 177–8), though only in seven cases had this happened after the birth of a child (ibid.: 185). For Maggi, *aLaS'in~g* is the 'prototypical act' defining a woman's freedom which, in its turn, is in her view one of the main traits of Kalasha ethnicity (ibid.: 198). The possibility of *aLaS'in~g*, indeed, more than a mere vent-hole for otherwise unbearable situations, seems to be a true instrument of empowerment for Kalasha women. To the point that today – according to what I was told by various informants – family-organised weddings do not appear to be any longer the rule.

The female element appeared therefore to dominate the village in that last part of the last day of Chaumos. The girls were entrusted with the task of taking care of the cooking of the beans without adult supervision. The temple was in their hands and as the evening progressed, boys were flooding in for what appeared to

82 For an in-depth analysis of this institution see Parkes 1983, as well as Maggi 2001.

be a proper teenage party. There were no drums, but the party went on late into the night.

Dau pachein – 21 December 2006

The following day was not seen as being part of Chaumos, but ritual activities did not come to a standstill. 'Today they cook beans and that's it' (*mic dA'u pac'ein*), had been Gulfurus's reply to my enquiries about the happenings of the day. In the morning the beans, together with some maize, were still cooking in the two cauldrons under the columned porch of the temple, and the whole day was indeed dedicated to the cooking and to the distribution of the beans. Though the collection had been carried out in a group by the girls of each village, the goods gathered were not consumed collectively in the course of a common meal, but separately by each family in their home. In the ritual, the time of sharing was the time of the cooking, rather than that of the consumption, of the product of the collection. A time enjoyed by the youngsters, rather than the adults. Though the consumption is not collective, the founding structural element of the collection, the abundance of food (Giallombardo 1990: 29), remains quite visible. A somewhat miserable abundance, perhaps, if we compare it to what has been observed in other cultural contexts (Ib.), or to the abundance, reserved for men, that we have seen displayed on the night of the initiations, but still, a form of abundance is there. We can also discern the propitiatory value of the abundance of food, which carries meanings functionally connected to life and regeneration (ibid.: 30), just as is also quite evident the social function of the ritual which, through the series of exchanges it generates, contributes to the strengthening of social ties between the women of the village. Finally, by making the time of sharing coincide with the collecting rounds and with the cooking, rather than with the eating, the ritual allows for the young to be set apart from the adults in a way that could not have been possible if the moment of sharing were that of the common meal. As for the consumption of the legumes collected, though no explicit prohibition was mentioned, it was clearly reserved for the women, who were excluded, we must recall, from the meat distributions of the night of the initiations.

The idea that that was a day of plenty was perceived also outside the community. In the course of that morning three Muslim beggars appeared in Birir, with their sacks and walking sticks. They separately made the round of the houses of the village collecting grain and legumes. One after the other, they entered Erfan's house without asking permission; they took their seat around the fire and intoned a sing-song prayer that went on until they received something to put in their sack.

It was quite a surprise to see Muslim men begging from the Kalasha who, as we know, are generally looked down upon. The beggars, however, were Gujur, a population of transhumant herders originating from the plains of the Punjab who, in the hierarchy of ethnic groups in Chitral, hold possibly the lowest status.

Lévi-Strauss ([1952] 1995: 71–2) puts in relation the autumn/winter collecting rounds of European children with the cult of the dead typical of that time of the year:

> the unfolding of autumn, from its beginning until the solstice, which marks the release of light and life, is accompanied, hence, on the ritual plane by a dialectical movement with the following main phases: the return of the dead, their threatening and persecutory conduct, the determining of a *modus vivendi* with the living consisting in an exchange of services and gifts, and finally the triumph of life when, at Christmas, the dead loaded with gifts abandon the living to leave them in peace until the following autumn. (Lévi-Strauss [1952] 1995: 72)[83]

The connection between the cult of the dead and the time between Halloween and Christmas is stressed also by Davidson (1988: 114) with regard to the ancient Celtic and Germanic peoples. Eliade ([1948] 1976: 364) adds to it the element of fertility. According to A. Buttitta, the connection – highlighted by Lévi-Strauss – between the dead, the rounds of children, and fertility, can be explained by the analogy relating them both to the seeds: the dead because like seeds they are buried under the earth, and children because 'in the archaic world-view they represent for the continuity of society what seeds represent for the rebirth of vegetation' (A. Buttitta 1995: 22). 'The dead' he adds (ibid.: 24) 'are reborn through the children: hence to give children offerings is like giving them to the dead themselves'.[84] Lévi-Strauss observes that among the living not only the children, but anyone who is only partially incorporated in the group, like strangers or slaves, can be an appropriate incarnation of the dead because they 'participate in that otherness that is the distinctive sign of the supreme dualism, that between the dead and the living' (Lévi-Strauss [1952] 1995: 73).

In Birir the theme of the descent of the dead appears to be ritualized rather weakly, but still it is present: we have seen that on the evening of *ruzh'ias*, the second day of Chaumos, offerings of bread for the dead are placed on the shelf

---

83 As for all texts in French, German and Italian (see fn. 25, Ch. 1) the translation is my own.
84 See also Buttitta A. 1996: 245–55.

(*maD'ir*) running along the back wall of every house, and that on the day of the initiations little girls deposit offerings for them at the *kuraw'at dur*, the special place where they are honoured.[85] This connection between children and dead ancestors, at the end of Chaumos, is extended to foreign beggars. The collecting rounds of prepubescent girls on the last day of Chaumos are followed by the visits of foreign beggars the very next day. Like uninitiated children who are not yet full members of the community, foreign beggars too are marginal figures, and 'to give to the poor and to the children amounts to giving to the dead'.[86]

I did not record any reference to the dead in those last two days of the festival. But it is perhaps implicit that with the return to ordinary time, the ghosts of the dead, greeted at the beginning of the festival with the offerings of *ruzh'ias*, should at that point part, with their gifts, from the living, to 'leave them in peace until the following autumn'.

---

85 The theme is more effectively ritualized in Rumbur and Bumburet, where a whole day is dedicated to the ghosts of the dead who are the focus of a collective ceremony celebrated in addition to the individual offerings just recalled for Birir. For descriptions see especially Loude & Lièvre 1984: 234–40; but also Jettmar 1975: 382–3 Cacopardo A.S. 1985: 733–5; Snoy 2008: 48.
86 Buttitta I.E. 2006: 106; cf. Ginzburg [1984] 2008: 17.

5

The Narration: the Other Winter Feasts

Lagaur – 5–7 January 2007

Just after the solstice, a great snowstorm announced the final settling-in of the winter season. It snowed almost without pause for two days and two nights. It was a particularly cold winter. For Pakistan – I found out later – it was the coldest in eighty years. A sprinkling of snow even reached Lahore – something unheard of. Rabijan, Erfan's wife, one morning spoke very angrily against the elders and the *kaz'is* who, in her view, were not fulfilling their duties because they had not performed any rite to stop the blizzards.

In those days, by word of mouth, news arrived of further deaths. First, the death of a converted Kalasha woman was announced. She died in Chitral, while she was visiting one of her daughters. Rabijan erupted in exclamations and prayers, with her open palms behind her ears, a typically Muslim prayer gesture. The sad news of the death of a child followed. He had not even put on the *ceL'ik* yet, the first phase of the initiation, and he was going to be buried therefore without any ceremony. One or two days of intense visits to the parents, and nothing more. I went as well: a prostrated mother, a house full of people, food for the guests, only a few words. The wish they might conceive another baby soon seemed the only possible consolation. Nobody could explain what had been the cause of the child's death. When he began to feel ill he was taken to the Chitral Hospital. He was discharged after a few days but he died at home shortly afterwards.

On 29 December Lagaur, a festival closely following Chaumos, was announced. The announcement is made by the *kaz'is* – Baras Khan explained me – who give the news going from home to home. That night the rite of *ishper'i* was going to be held in all the houses, which consisted of a special meal with wheat bread (*gum tas'iLi*) and cheese (*caman'i*); the following evening the ritual food was going to be *an~guc'ui*, a dish made with beans dried in their peel and subsequently boiled, mashed and mixed with walnut kernels, also mashed and made into a paste (*jA~*). The next day in all homes miniature animal figurines were going to be made with bread dough (*sharabir'ayak*). In the evening the men were going to cook two large bread cakes to take to the goat sheds at first light. In the last hours of that night the women were going to gather in the village temple for a nocturnal prayer for fertility and plenty. For six more days, afterwards, the drums were going to beat for the children in a clearing at the top of the village.

In the afternoon of that same day, however, news arrived of another death. This time a non-converted Kalasha man had died. He was not old, but he had been ill for a while and the doctors of Chitral Hospital were not able to cure him. A fully-fledged Kalasha funeral was going to be organized, and the Momola (*m'omaLa*) and Rukmula (*rukm'uLa*) – the people of Bumburet and Rumbur – were going to be invited as well. Preparations had therefore to be made for four days of ceremonies – a sizeable effort for the lineage of the deceased as well as for the whole community after the intense celebrations of Chaumos, which had already been preceded, as will be remembered, by other funerals. The beginning of Lagaur, by necessity, had to be postponed a few days.

A Kalasha funeral is such a complex ritual and social event that I cannot attempt to relate it here; its description and analysis would take us too far away from the theme of this work.[1] It was an intense ceremony that ended on 2 January 2007 with the departure of the guests, after three days of uninterrupted celebrations. On the evening of 4 January we at last ate the *an~guc'ui*. The *ishper'i* ritual meal had been skipped because of the funeral, at least in Erfan's house. The next day was the first day of Lagaur.

Lagaur – day 1

In the morning children of all ages, boys and girls, were going out to 'call the crow'. A line of little girls, dressed in their best, all wearing the *kup'as* [the head-dress for festivities they normally do not wear], descended the village path of Guru singing the song of the crows. They headed downstream in the valley for a few hundred yards until they turned to their left hiking up the mountain slope to reach the *bonj* forest where they halted in the vicinity of a goat shed. Each girl carried a provision of walnuts, *s'icin* [*ziziphus jujube*, a

---

1 For a detailed narration, characterized by an intense emotional participation on the part of the author, of a Kalasha funeral see Cacopardo, A.M. 2009: 192–200. For other descriptions see Guillard 1974: 165–74; Jettmar 1975: 375–7; Loude & Lièvre 1984: 149–61; Graziosi 2007: 42–4.

rather dry berry] and grapes, as well as of *bats'a w'elik*, a mixture of walnut
kernels and dried grapes cooked in must. As soon as they reached their
destination, they immediately discarded their *kup'as* and rested them on the
trunks of some grape vines hanging from the surrounding trees. A symphony
of colours, that line of *kup'as* shining together in the morning sun. In a
rush the girls laid a *sad'ar* [a cotton mantel] on the ground and poured their
personal provisions of dried fruit into it. The boys went up the mountain slope
in search of boughs of *c'iin*, an evergreen bush that grows among the *bonj*. The
girls lit a small fire with some dry branches, and waited singing traditional
songs or running in circles singing the obscene song that accompanies the
game of the husband trying to beat his wife (Photo 7). After about an hour the
shouts of the boys could be heard as they returned with *c'iin* boughs, which
they gathered on the terraced roof of the goat shed a short distance up the
slope. Apart from two adolescent girls, the children were entirely on their
own. They accomplished playfully their ritual duties, without any guidance
from anyone. At a certain point, like a gush of wind, they rushed down to
where the girls were. The girls had opened their *sad'ar* and were distributing
the dried fruit they had collected. Nothing had been brought by the boys.
The male children then returned with their booty to the roof of the goat shed,
which seemed to have become their base, while the girls remained among the
bonj, just below the building. Another precipitous charge and the boys joined
the girls and they all started playing *nog'or grik* [to capture the fortress], one
of the ritual games of Chaumos. Two of them climbed on a tree and the rest
of the children had to try to pull them down; girls were actively participating,
fighting amongst themselves as well as with the boys. They were the children
of the families of the temple of Guru. At a certain point – 12.30 by my watch
the girls suddenly ran all together towards the goat shed and halted at its
entrance. The boys, from the roof, started throwing to them boughs of *c'iin*.
In the end every little girl had a bough in her hand. The girls then recovered
their *kup'as* and headed back upstream towards Guru (Photo 8). They entered
the village singing and they walked up to the *rik'ini*. They stuck their boughs
in the outside front wall of the temple, under the porch and then inside the
building, on the capitals of the columns and wherever they could reach. This
done, they swarmed through the tiny alleyways of the village and reached
their homes. (*From my field journal – 5 January 2007*)

While the ritual was unfolding before my eyes, what struck me the most was
the fact that the actors were all children: kids mostly not yet ten, who enacted

the ritual on their own as if it were a game, or rather, they carried it out while playing. After participating in Chaumos mostly as spectators, the children now had the opportunity to learn to celebrate the rites by direct experience, guided only by their more experienced peers. A practice of *peer education*, we might say, in line with the most modern pedagogic trends. This educational objective is to some extent a peculiarity of Lagaur as compared to Chaumos. A young woman confirmed that this was indeed an objective of Lagaur when she spontaneously explained to me that Lagaur is like a 'training' (she used the English term) for the children, because in this way they learn to play the drum. 'This is why we do it', she added, 'if they do not learn to play the drum, then they become Muslim. This is why we do Lagaur, to train them.'

Some rites of Lagaur are indeed a repetition of those of Chaumos in the form of a game for children: that morning the boys had played the ritual game of *nog'or grik*, the fight between the initiates and the impure adults that precedes the race, and the girls had played the game of the wife chased by her husband – two ritual games of Chaumos. But more than a miniature repetition of Chaumos, Lagaur is a continuation of it. It is the next ring in the sequence.

As for the final result of the children's ritual, the decking of the temple with boughs of *c'iin*, is interesting to note that the custom of decorating buildings with green boughs is quite characteristic of European December celebrations, from antiquity to the Middle Ages,[2] as a popular British Christmas carol also testifies. But in the Kalasha context we also have the exceptional event that the girls enter the *bonj* forest, thus penetrating the *'onjiSTa* zone of the goat sheds. The male/female opposition is weakened and almost dissolved in the person of the children, together with the polarity *'onjiSTa/r'ela* which, at their level, takes on more blurred traits. In the female world prepubescent girls are the closest to the *'onjiSTa* sphere, hence it is their privilege to be allowed, though only exceptionally, to have physical access to its spatial expression: the area of the *bonj* forest and of the goat sheds. The separation, on the one side, remains: the male children have their base in the goat shed, and the girls, though approaching it, do not enter. But at the same time it is overcome: boys and girls are involved together in the ritual task of decorating the temple. The girls bring the necessary food, while the boys provide the green *c'iin* boughs from the forest, their territory. Once the boughs are distributed, it is the task of the girls to fix them on the walls and the pillars of the

---

2 Lévi-Strauss [1952] 1995: 67; cf. Miles [1912] 1976: 272–6; Owen [1981] 1996: 48; Van Gennep 1988: 3492; Hutton 1996: 34–5. The custom is reported also for the Roman January Kalends by the fourth-century Greek sophist Libanius (in Miles [1912] 1976: 169).

temple, which is located among the houses of the village, a predominantly female space, opposed to the strictly male space of the forest and the goat sheds.

The joining of the masculine and the feminine worlds in the common ritual work is accompanied by chants invoking fertility. These are the lyrics of the song I recorded from the voices of the little girls as they were leaving Guru in the morning to 'call the crow':

From downstream he brings male energy
Come to call the crow
From downstream he brings sweet beans
Come to call the crow
From downstream he brings the seed of cowrie shells
Come to call the crow
From downstream he brings the seed of virile energy
Come to call the crow
From downstream he brings necklaces of ludum-pearls
Come to call the crow
From downstream he brings iron vessels with seven handles
Come to call the crow.

The chant refers to a mythical white crow, bringer of fertility and abundance. A crow – Baras Khan explained to me when we were transcribing the words – 'formerly men maybe saw it, but today it is no longer seen and is quite different from normal crows'. A version of the myth concerning him has been collected in Rumbur:

In former times, the Creator decided to divide good luck between all human beings, on equal terms. In the course of a single night he sent the spirits in his service everywhere in the world, to make sure that nobody had fallen asleep, like he had demanded. Everyone in fact was asleep, save for a Kalasha man intent in carving a small statue, a task that had kept him awake until dawn. The spirits reported to God that only a Kalasha man had not slept for the whole night. God decided then that every year he would send an envoy to collect the wishes of the Kalasha.

The following year, on the appointed night, the Kalasha had not gone to sleep, they waited. But nobody knew under which form the spirit was going to arrive. They expressed their wishes, which were granted, but they never discovered the identity of the envoy. (Loude & Lièvre 1984: 312).

We may wonder whether in this text the now-current monotheistic reinterpretation of Kalasha religion may have been grafted onto a polytheistic narrative context. We see, on the one hand, the divinity that bestows rewards and sanctions represented as the god of a monotheistic system, but on the other we note that the man who is granted the award, obtains the favour of this Creator God by staying awake to carve a small statue. What sort of statue? The text does not say. Could it be that he was carving the effigy of one of the *dewal'ok*,[3] who probably occupied, in a former version of the story, the place of the Creator? Surely the divinity mentioned in the myth could not have been *D'izila D'izaw*, the Creator god of Kalasha tradition who, as we have seen, is a *deus otiosus* who does not interfere in human affairs. Be this as it may, the story goes on to tell how only a long time afterwards, a man of Birir, after celebrating a series of rites that made him achieve an extremely *'onjiSTa* state, lay in wait on a high ridge on the night the envoy was expected and saw a white crow descending from the sky (ibid.).

In the Kalasha symbolic system the crow is, in fact, a bird of the *pr'agata* sphere, connected especially to the world of the dead (cf. Wutt 1983: 140–1) – an association already present in the Vedas, and still documented today in some areas of India and Nepal.[4] But here we find the crow converted into its opposite, which can only be a mythical white-feathered bird. If the black crow of ordinary times has nothing to give and only eats the leftovers of humans, the white crow of holy times, in contrast, brings all things in abundance. The white crow may be a solar symbol reasserting, once the solstice is over, the triumph of light over darkness.[5] We may be dealing with a representation of Indra. Virile energy (*moch kwat*), i.e. power of generation – the main trait of Indra in the Rig Veda[6] – is what the song is asking first of all from the white crow. Or it may be, also, that we are dealing instead with an Iranian element, because in Iranian contexts the crow was seen as the bringer of the seed of spring and as symbol of the good news of the arrival of holy *nawruz*, the Iranian New Year celebration.[7] Certainly the ritual invocation pertains to the female world, because, apart from the power of generation, it asks

---

3 For a discussion of anthropomorphic representations of divinities among the Kalasha see Cacopardo A.S. 2006.

4 De Gubernatis 1872: 253; Witzel 2004: 609. The crow as an envoy of the world of the dead appears also in Italian folklore (Di Nola 1993: 30).

5 The white crow as a solar symbol appears in Greek mythology, as well as in some Estonians oral traditions (De Gubernatis 1872: 255–7).

6 Stutley & Stutley [1977] 1980: 170

7 Karamsahyef 1997: 290 in Cristoforetti 2002: 234.

for items that all belong to the world of women: the cowrie shells used to decorate the headdresses of Kalasha women, the precious necklaces called *L'uDrum
gaD'uLai* worn by women for celebrations, or the iron vessels to make cheese
(*cid'in*) that are one of the main articles traditionally included in bride prices.

* * *

In the afternoon, Erfan's wife started making *sharabir'ayak*, bread-dough figurines representing sheep, cows, goats or markhor (*sh'arab'ira*).[8] The animals
represented are the ones, wild or domestic, that the community wishes to see
proliferate. The little menagerie taking shape on the shelf (*mad'ir*) running along
the back wall of the house, did not include, for example, bears, wolves or snow-
leopards. Rabijan moulded the dough with her hands and once the desired shape
was obtained she lay the dough figurine to cook on the iron plate of the stove.
The neighbour from the house below – a woman from Rumbur – hurried up with
her baby boys, and the two women continued the job together while their children followed their every move with great trepidation. As she was working, our
neighbour explained to me that if you do not make *sharabir'ayak*, you will fall ill
and everything will go wrong; but if you make them you are quite safe. I made a
round of the houses of the village and everywhere I found women busy making
bread figurines. But for the children the most desired moment was probably the
evening, when it would be the turn of the men, who were going to make bigger
figurines stuffed with walnut kernels.

Late in the afternoon I went to Gulistan's house and found him busy moulding
an imposing markhor with two long horns held up by small sticks. The figurines
made during the day were lined up on the shelf, but the one he was making was
going to be kept in a special place, away from the other ones, on a specific beam,
called *sat'ar*. It was the chief, the leader of the herd who – it is believed – at night
leads the animals to the distant Sarawak pasture, way up the valley, past the Durik
pass, in the Nuristani valley of Bashgal. A few days later, as an answer to my
questions about the rite, Kaanok told me the story of a man from Biyou, called
Pachà, who had not made the *sharabir'ayak*. On his *mad'ir* there were only a few
figurines his sons had received from their relatives. That night Pachà dreamed that
the *s'uci* spirits were rejecting the animals of his sons, judged to be faulty, while
they were taking to the Sarawak pasture all the other ones. As soon as he woke
up in the morning he immediately made a large quantity of *sharabir'ayak*. He had

---

8 For dough figurines among the Kalasha see Siiger, Castenfeldt & Fentz 1991.

not carried out his ritual duties and the gifts of his relatives could not compensate for his fault.

The smaller figurines, the ones made by the women, with no filling, remain on the *mad'ir* shelf for three days and are finally given to the goats. The ones made by the men, filled with walnut mush, are left on the shelf until the last day of the festival. Apart from the chief, who remains in his place until the following Lagaur, the rest of them are given to the children. On the last day of Lagaur, while the girls waited eating their *sharabir'ayak* in the clearing at the top of the village, where for six days the drums had been beating for the children, the boys take their dough animals to the top of the ridge overhanging Guru in a place called *La~STaT'alaka*, 'level plateau', accompanied by the drummers. To reach it – I went to inspect it a few days later with Baras Khan – they go up a goat path that, in some places, requires almost some real climbing on the edge of a dangerous ravine, but for the Kalasha such a climb is indeed no more than child's play. Once they have reached the plateau, the boys play for a while, imitating the game of the chasing of the fox (*Lawakbih'ik*), one of the various ritual games played, as we have seen, on the main day of Chaumos; finally, they break the dough figurines into pieces, eat some of them, and give the rest to the crows.

In pre-Islamic times the custom of making dough animal figures for winter rituals must have been widespread in Peristan and possibly further to the east, for it is documented in New Year celebrations of Lamaist Ladakh (Dollfus 1987: 69–70). The *sharabir'ayak* also curiously recall the *kozuli*, dough figurines collectively called 'little goats' but representing, in fact, various domestic animals, that were made in Russia for Christmas, and were in the end fed to the beasts. For Propp ([1963] 1978: 66–7) the rite is clearly a 'magical procedure' to favour the reproduction of the animals, independently of the final destination of the bread figurines.[9] That, for the Kalasha, the figurines are also made to ensure the fertility of the animals, seems quite certain, not only for the morphology of the ritual but also for its structural position at the end of a day begun with the invocations of fertility made by the little girls. Also, if it is significant that it is a female task to make the figurines to be given to the goats to favour their reproduction, it is true that among the Kalasha the final destination of the figurines is also of secondary

---

9 There is some other sparse European evidence of the custom of making animal figurines at Christmas time. For example, sweets in animal form are a Christmas tradition in Scandinavia (Motz 1984: 160) and Frazer ([1922] 1987: 461–2) mentions a Swedish and Danish custom 'to bake a loaf in the form of a boar-pig' at Yule. Owen ([1981] 1996: 49), believes that it is possible that the pagan Anglo-Saxons 'baked birds, boars or horses in honour of their gods'.

importance: as Pachà's story tells us, what matters is that you make them; otherwise, as our neighbour had explained to me, you fall ill and everything goes wrong.

That evening I moved on from Gulistan's house to the home of Tarok, another member of the Lataruk-nawau lineage, where the *goSTj'uzhi* were being made. These were two thick, flat bread cakes, about two palms in diameter, to be taken to the goat sheds at dawn the following morning. It was necessary for them to be made by men for they had to be *'onjiSTa* bread. As if to justify the prohibition Gulistan, who had followed me, explained that women were not able to make them because, due their size, they were difficult to cook. When the first flat cake was finally deposited on the stove, a little girl pressed some small circles into it with the shell of an oak acorn. No other object could be used for those decorations; Erfan (who had joined us as well) explained that since they were to be *'onjiSTa* bread cakes, to be brought to the goat sheds, they had to be protected from contact with objects belonging to the sphere of the village, the home and the women. It was probably also quite significant that the decorating had to be done by a pre-pubescent girl. Gulistan pointed out two groups of little circles on the surface of the flat cake that were meant to represent the kids and the lambs. The decoration evidently represented a goat shed, where the little ones are kept separate from their mothers, so that the shepherds may have enough milk to make cheese. In the morning, at the first lights of dawn, one of Tarok's brothers was going to take the two flat cakes to the goat shed hosting their goats, to offer them to the *walm'uc*, their family members who were there to take care of them. Earlier still, in the dark of night, the women were going to gather in the *rikh'ini* for the true invocation to the White Crow. Gulistan took the responsibility of waking everybody up. I asked him to wake me up as well.

Lagaur – day 2 and 3

Last night I went to sleep with the fear of not being awoken, and at 4 I am already awake. After an hour or so, I hear the stout voice of Rabijan's mother, and shortly afterwards Gulistan comes to wake me up wrapped up in his goat fleece coat. I jump to my feet and follow him up the muddy path to the *rikh'ini*. The sky is absolutely cloudless and the moon shines on the roofs of the houses and on the fields white with snow. In the temple I find a dozen women and girls singing in a circle around a small fire. Gulistan brings some wood. Their singing is solemn and imploring. They make room for me around the fire and I squat with my recorder in my hands. The chant continues for a half-hour at least ... *(From my field journal – 6 January 2007)*.

It was a rite conducted at the village level. The women in the temple were all from Guru. The chant was very similar to the one sung by the little girls the previous morning when they were going to collect the boughs to decorate the temple. But the intonation was completely different. The girls had sung the same lyrics joyfully, as in a game. Now the women were singing them in a sorrowful, imploring tone. A soloist began a verse and the other women took it up in a chorus. Danok later explained to me that it was not a song (*ghO~*), but a prayer (*suw'al*). What I had heard from the girls the day before, those were songs, he specified, but what I had heard in the temple, that was a prayer, to express the wishes to be fulfilled. Only one woman per *kush'un* – the family group that shares the same fire – had gone to the temple and each brought the wishes of all her family. Anything may be asked for, Danok's mother added, good health, peace, prosperity.

This is the translation of the words I recorded that night:

Make us prolific with numerous offspring, come oh crow!
Show us joy upon joy, come oh crow!
Give us well-being, come oh crow!
Bring sacrifices of he-goats, come oh crow!
Make the population of our village numerous, come oh crow!
Bring iron tripods, come oh crow!
Give me virile energy, come oh crow!
My brother's daughter cannot walk, come oh crow!
Keep sorrow away from us, come oh crow!
Bring us good health, come oh crow!
Pray Allah for us, come oh crow!
From downstream bring the seed of barley, come oh crow!
Make us numerous, come oh crow!
Keep all anxiety away from us, come oh crow!
Give us a long life, come oh crow!
May our children be good, come oh crow!
To this brother of ours give soon a male child, come oh crow!
Fulfil the wishes of the soul, come oh crow!

Though many verses were identical to those of the morning song of the girls, the structure of this chanted prayer is rather different. The girls were inviting the crow to join them, and were listing all the things he would have brought, while the nocturnal prayer was addressed to him directly. As the text shows, the women prayed for happiness, well-being, good health and a long life; they asked to be freed from sorrow and anxiety; and especially they demanded fertility and reproduction. But the prayer also contains two specific requests: one was pronounced by a woman for the healing of her niece who was not able to walk; and the other one was advanced on my own behalf, so that I could soon become a father (a wish that indeed was fulfilled). The White Crow is seen as a messenger, as an intermediary between humans and the supreme God, called with the Muslim name Allah; the identification of the ancient Creator God Dizala Dizaw with the God of Islam, as we know well, is by now an established fact. The prayer finally ends with a verse asking the crow to fulfil all the wishes of the soul. We may discern here a theme typical of winter feasts: the arrival from another world of a beneficial being that fulfils all desires. It was the morning of 6 January.

While the prayer was still going on in the temple, I went outside and took a short stroll on the roof just below. The moon was lighting up the snow-clad valley. It was 5.30 in the morning. From afar I heard the voice of the *muezzin* calling from the mosque for the early morning prayer. From the temple behind me came the chant of the women praying. Certainly a non-Muslim chant, but for them it was addressed to the same God. When I walked back to the temple the prayer was finished and the hall was resonating with the notes of a completely different, very lively, song that sounded like children's music:

Crow, crow, come little crow
For you they prepare excrement
For me they prepare curd.

It was the song that concluded the ritual. A song calling the crows – the black ones, of flesh and bones, this time – with affectionately ironic tones, mockingly recalling that they eat excrement.

Every woman had a *kh'Ui* [a small aluminium vessel a woman always keeps in the fold of her dress] in front of her filled with walnuts; in one of them there was also a little bun in the shape of a crescent. They give a couple of walnuts to me as well. At a certain point they interrupt the lively and playful singing that had followed the prayer, and they walk out of the *rikh'ini* each with a burning peace of wood from the fire. Under the porch they empty their cups of the walnuts, which they had cracked in the meanwhile, calling the

crows with a sound of their tongue, 'ts, ts, ts'. After that, we all went home.
(*From my field journal – 6 January 2007*)

The ritual ended rather abruptly. From the balcony of the porch of the temple, I
threw down the slope the walnuts I was given, like all the women were doing, and
I strained to see if any crows were appearing, but the valley was still plunged in
darkness. Shortly afterwards, I knew, a man from each house was going to take
to the goat sheds the two large cakes made the previous evening. Danok invited
me to go with him to a goat shed in Grabet Kui, about a half hour away. We were
joined by his son, the boy who had just been initiated during Chaumos.

The *'onjiSTa* bread cakes for the goat sheds were made in all houses, Danok's
mother assured me, and are sent to the shepherds together with two *sharabir'ayak*,
markhor-shaped bread figurines. In the goat sheds, where they usually make their
own bread, men were receiving that day bread produced in the heart of the female
world – the home – and on the surface of that product of the labour of the fields
was represented a herd, the fruit of the work of the shepherds. Opposed poles were
being integrated. The two bread figurines were sent to favour the reproduction of
the animals.

On the way my eyes are filled with tears because of the cold, but inside the
goat shed a fire is lit. There are two men and many children. The goat shed
belongs to the Changanchai-nawau. We hand over the two large *jA~'u* and
we take a seat. Shortly afterwards the two flat cakes are cut with a knife and
the pieces are offered to everybody present on a *saw'ew* [tray made of willow
boughs] along with a metal beaker full of wine. The bread is not well baked
but is good anyhow and the wine suites it perfectly. The children also drink
wine, Danok tells me. 'It is good for them,' he adds, 'but it happens that they
occasionally get tipsy.' Danok drinks three or four large beakers in a row and
he starts singing. He sings a song called *khondameshal'ak*. He sings it well
with the children joining him in a chorus. (*From my field journal – 6 January
2007*)

A Kalasha goat shed is a stone building with only a single floor; on the terraced
roof there is a little wooden shelter used for stocking hay or other animal fodder.
The building is entered through a small courtyard delimited by a low wall and partially covered by a roof, where the goats can stay in the open. The interior consists
of a single space, a corner of which, delimited by some large beams set on the
ground, is reserved for men; the rest is for the goats, apart from a raised platform

(*kaTTh'ar*) made of wooden boards that serves as a bed for the shepherds. At the centre of the small square space off-limits for the animals, a couple of men and a bunch of children were sitting around a lively fire. After the meal, without any solicitation on my part, Danok started singing. This is the translation of the lyrics I recorded:

> The hornless ram wanders on the high mountain lawns
> The hornless ram hits you with his horn, the hornless ram
> The hornless ram runs inebriated
> The hornless ram hits you with his horn, the hornless ram
> The hornless ram in crazy search of a female
> The hornless ram hits you with his horn, the hornless ram
> The hornless ram wanders all the way to Surawak, the hornless ram
> The hornless ram hits you with his horn, the hornless ram
> The hornless ram wanders among peaks and crests
> The hornless ram hits you with his horn, the hornless ram
> The hornless ram mixes with the fairies, the hornless ram
> The hornless ram hits you with his horn, the hornless ram
> The hornless ram leads the pure herd
> The hornless ram hits you with his horn, the hornless ram
> The hornless ram grazes on mountain grass, the hornless ram
> The hornless ram hits you with his horn, the hornless ram
> The hornless ram dances in the snow, the hornless ram
> The hornless ram hits you with his horn, the hornless ram
> The hornless ram eats insects, the hornless ram
> The hornless ram hits you with his horn, the hornless ram
> The hornless ram grazes on the low branches of juniper trees, the hornless ram
> The hornless ram hits you with his horn, the hornless ram.

The chant was not new to me though I had not heard it yet in Birir. I had heard it in 1973 at the Rumbur Chaumos during the night at the climax of the festival, and I had been struck by its solemnity. Danok sang it to a much less solemn tune, but the chant was no doubt the same one. Though not solicited, it did not seem to be in its regular ritual context. It could be that it was a loan from the Chaumos of the northern valleys. The apparent contradiction of the verse of the refrain – the hornless ram hits you with his horn – was solved when we got to the translation and it was explained to me that the horn is a metaphorical horn, representing the male sexual organ.

A *meshal'ak* is a ram between a year and a year and half, which is often still hornless. The chant thus evokes the image of a young ram searching madly for a female, wandering inebriated (*naksh'a ti*) among the peaks, mixing with the mountain spirits (*s'uci*), dancing on the snow, grazing on mountain grass, ready to hit anyone with his penis. An image of virile energy, it would seem, seen as emanating from the *'onjiSTa* sphere. If we recall that in a verse of a Vedic hymn Indra is represented as a famous ram (De Gubernatis 1872: 403), we may conclude that the hornless ram that fecundates with his metaphoric horn is possibly none other than Indra himself.[10] Inebriated by the wine, Danok told us that our hosts, the Changanchai-nawau, had a special relationship with Warin. It was one of their ancestors, Matuzal, who 'brought' the god to Birir from Suwir, a former Kalasha settlement in the main valley, when the people there converted to Islam. Warin was the first among the *dewal'ok*, he asserted, to 'arrive' in the valley; the rest of them had been 'brought' afterwards. And he told also about the terrible punishment the god had delivered to Matuzal because he had not complied with his order to make sure no one would see him when in the evening he came riding his horse to drink a glass of wine with him. His son had sensed there was something special taking place, and one night he caught a glimpse of the god from a hiding place he was spying from. Warin knew immediately and caused Matuzal, once he was drunk, to kill his only son by throwing him in the fire. He had no other male offspring. All the Changanchai-nawau descend from a brother of Matuzal. This myth probably fuels the atmosphere of 'holy terror' that hovers, as mentioned, around Warin's shrine.

We walked back to Guru late in the morning. In the afternoon, in a clearing near the top of the village, Tarok and another young man were beating the drums for a large band of children, including even toddlers. For six days the drums were going to be beaten for the children to teach them, as I was told, the *dast'ur*. In the final day the boys were going to stage an imitation of the torch race to Praba's altar (*koT Sat'ek*). After the race, they were going to take the *sharabir'ayak* to La~sht at'aLaka, the little plateau at the top of the ridge overhanging Guru, and that ritual would have marked the end of Lagaur. I went to Chitral, at this point, for a couple of days, and when I came back Lagaur was over. The period of six days for the dances of the children had been reduced to three, probably because of the delay in the beginning of the celebration. The ritual activities of this last part of

---

10 An hypothesis that would be confirmed by the structural position of the chant in the Rumbur Chaumos: it is chanted on the night of the departure of Balima-In, the visiting god of Chaumos who, as we have seen, is none other than Indra.

the festival seemed to especially concern the boys. But soon another celebration was approaching, specifically dedicated to the learning of female ritual activities, the Jhanì (*jhan'i*).

Jhanì – 23–25 January 2007

If the time of the beginning of Chaumos was determined through the observation of the sun, for the feasts that followed it the reference point was provided instead by the moon. The Jhanì was supposed to begin between the fifth and the seventh day of the January new moon. It was still therefore about a couple of weeks away – fifteen days during which I hoped ritual activities would pause so that I could arrange and record correctly the data I had gathered thus far. But those days did not pass idly. Once Lagaur was over the *ghul* season began.

This is a traditional game played on snow that could be the ancestor of hockey or golf. The participants form two teams each to attain its goal with its ball. The players head in the same direction and there are therefore both two goals and two balls. I asked what the prize was, hoping – for a personal ideological preference – that related by Robertson (1896: 586) for Bashgal, according to which in a competition it is the winner who must offer a banquet to the loser. But I was disappointed. It was the duty of the losing team to sacrifice a he-goat or an ox, and its members were to act as hosts arranging the banquet and serving the winners.

The first game was played in the side valley of Grabet. The itinerary, divided in eight stations, started from the mouth of the little valley, and followed it upstream along the snow-covered fields. At each station stood a man – or several men – from each team who, as soon as the ball reached him, had to hurl it with his stick to his team-mate at the next station. The players had handmade bats (*paC'ew*) of oak (*bonj*) or willow (*b'eu*) wood, with a round hollow space in the hitting edge, used to set the ball (*prinz*) – which the players must not touch with their hands – on the spot (a small mount of snow) from which it is hurled to the next station with a powerful blow of the bat. The ball was wooden as well, a bit smaller than a tennis ball, and had a rather irregular surface, due to its being handmade. The players were the team of the Guru *rikh'ini* against the team of the Aspar temple. In this case as well, as in *kot Sat'ek*, the number of the players was not fixed. In any moment, anyone could join in the game. Baras Khan, who came with me, when we reached the first station grabbed a bat and gave a couple of blows. The action in the game was rather slow because the ball, due to the length of the itinerary, once sent to the next station, took quite a while to come back. The players, in the meantime, had time for a chat, but always with an eye on the game, because when the ball arrived – a moment of frenzy with much shouting and laughing – it had to be immediately spotted in the snow, lifted using the hollow space of the bat and set on a mount of snow to be hit with all possible strength before the player of the opposing team. Spectators like myself had obviously to be careful not to find themselves in the way of the small wooden bullet; in Rumbur there was a young man who had lost an eye playing *ghal*. The team that reaches its goal first gets one point. With 12 points the game is won. *ghal* is quite a long game: it is played for three days in a row and each game takes up a whole day. That day the winner was the Aspar team, but Guru had won on the previous day and subsequently also won the game on the third day. The season was just at its beginning. The main challenge was in preparation. It was played the following week on the fields at the centre of the main Birir valley with great participation of both the young and the old.

A similar game was apparently played in Nuristan in pre-Islamic times (Robertson 1896: 401; cf. Court 1840: 94), and, until very recent times, in Chitral as well, especially by children and young boys. Since in Chitral and Gilgit the game of polo, called *ghal* as well in Khowar, has also ancient roots (Parkes 1996b), one may wonder whether the traditional Chitrali polo could be an equestrian version of the Kalasha game. However, the Kalasha *ghal* seems similar, rather, to a variety of games with wooden bats and balls, non-equestrian, widely spread in Europe, from which are probably derived both golf and hockey. Sergent (2005: 279), noting that games of this sort are attested in the European continent from Ireland to Greece, concludes that they must be derived from an inherited model, at least 'européen ancien', that is with ancient European roots. On the basis of the Kalasha *ghal*, and especially of the existence of a similar sport among the Nuristani, we may imagine an even more remote origin of the game, possibly dating back to the undivided Indo-European world. But, of course, games with bats and balls are attested in other contexts as well. Be that as it may, in 2007 Birir was probably the last Hindu Kush valley where this ancient game was still practised; in Bumburet and Rumbur *ghal* had been replaced by cricket, a legacy of colonialism that has become today the national sport of Pakistan.

Although general attention, of males especially, was now concentrated on the games of *ghal*, and even though those were not festive days, ritual activities did not halt completely. The young lady from Rumbur living in the house below ours told me that a woman had made a divination, using a bracelet, for her baby son who had not been well for some days. The response was that a certain *bhut* who lives by the mill, for a reason I could not ascertain, was offended and had caused the sickness of the child. Years before, I had observed a couple of times the male version of this divinatory rite. The diviner, sitting on a stool, holding with his fingers the string of a little bow made there and then, had given his response watching the oscillations of his divinatory tool. In the female rite, a bracelet – it must be an old one, made of iron, the woman specified – replaces the bow and the response is deduced from its oscillations. A few days later I related to Rabijan the story of the offended *bhut*, to try to understand what could have been the cause of the wrath of the spirit. Erfan's wife exchanged a knowing look with her mother, sitting opposite, which I interpreted as an ironic comment of the type: 'Just look what sort of bullshit they give him.' For a moment, I expected a modernist denial of the whole story, until Rabijan resolutely turned back to me to explain instead that the spirit was not a *bhut* but a *non~g* that lives by the spring, adding with a tone of reproach, and derision, that it is the Rukmula, the people of Rumbur like our neighbour, who mix things up, because they cannot tell a *bhut* from a *non~g*. I could not ascertain the cause of the spirit's anger, nor could I find out what was the atonement suggested by the woman diviner.

In addition to occasional individual rites such as this one, other communal ritual activities were in preparation, independently of any feast. After Lagaur, the *wel'atay khoda'i* or *d'eshay khoda'i* had to be held, a ceremony consisting of four sacrifices dedicated to the gods of the valley: Praba, Warin, Mahandeo and Grimun. The name of the ritual means 'sacrifice for the whole population (*wel'at*) of the valley' or 'for the whole country (*d'esh*)', that is for the well-being of the entire community, as Kaanok explained to me, adding 'not for the animals, only for the human beings'. The four sacrifices were going to be celebrated in four different places. The he-goats were supposed to be offered by the people of the village closer to the spot where the sacrifice was to be carried out.

On the morning of 18 January we woke up in an intense blizzard. Early in the morning Saidan Shah appeared, followed by two venerable old men holding their walking sticks. They were the three *kaz'is* of the Guru temple. They sat around the stove. They were heading to the Jagar goat shed for the sacrifice dedicated to Praba. The rite was not going to be held at the shrine of the god, Saidan Shah explained to me, because, for *dast'ur*, the only sacrifice that can be done there is the one celebrated for Chaumos. The three elders drank a cup of tea (*c'ay*) and walked out under the dense snowflakes. They reappeared only in the evening, and empty-handed. They had not found anyone, they explained, who was ready to offer the animal to be sacrificed. But the following day, Saidan Shah added, the rite was going to be celebrated at all costs, because if no one else would volunteer, the he-goat was going to be offered by one of them. While the banquet at the end of the *ghal* tournament was considered a certainty, it was apparently not as certain that the animals could be found for the sacrifices in favour of the whole community. But sooner or later the he-goats were going to be produced. The *wel'atay khoda'i*, Kaanok assured me, is celebrated every year.

Meanwhile I was trying to find out when Jhanì was going to start. Nobody, however, could tell me with any precision. The *kaz'is* were going to announce it having observed the course of the moon. Between the fifth and the seventh day of the January moon, Gulistan told me. It so happened that the first day of Jhanì fell exactly on the day on which I had arranged to go on the 'White Trail' of the *prabal'on g'Uak* with Gulistan. As we were leaving, we just managed to catch a glimpse of a group of little girls setting out for their round of gifts. About ten of them gathered around the little fountain just below my lodging; they intoned the song of Jhanì and then started down the path singing:

Get up and braid your hair, mummy's little girl
In the day of Jhanì there are tigers and fierce beasts.

The first verse is the affectionate invitation of a mother who urges her daughter to get up and get ready for the feast. The second one, in contrast, is rather enigmatic. It announces the arrival of tigers and other beasts of prey on the day of Jhanì. None of my assistants offered any explanation of this verse. We have seen that the chants of Chaumos, especially those of the women, may be very ancient because, for being sung mostly in a chorus, their lyrics are known to all. With just about no room for individual innovation, such texts may very well be transmitted virtually unchanged down many generations. It is quite possible, therefore, that words are transmitted of which the meaning is lost and the ritual context forgotten. This is not the case for the majority of the chants of Chaumos, but it may very well be for this verse of the Jhanì song.

We may detect in the lyrics of this ritual song of the girls, an echo of the array of beasts of the *gody* – the New Year feasts of the Slavic world – of the Christmas folklore of the Celtic-Germanic world, and of many other places: animal masks that in a vast Euro-Asiatic area appear in the course of the famous twelve days (or at times removed to the first two weeks of January) when the new year sets in.[11] For Dumézil (1929: 36–50) they are representations of spirits who are at once genii of time, for their connection to the time of the changing of the year, genii of

---

11 Dumézil 1929: 12–13; Motz 1984: 159–60; Ginzburg [1989] 2008: 161–77; Buttitta, I.E. 2006: 110–16; Kezich 2015: 96–130.

nature because they represent the guardian spirits of the resources of the natural environment, and genii of the world of the dead, because they appear in the time when the spirits of the dead are believed to descend among the living. Carlo Ginzburg, a renowned Italian historian, highlights especially this last aspect of them, specifying that they are 'mediators with the world of beyond' (Ginzburg [1989] 2008: 167) and recalling 'the almost universal association of masks with spirits of the dead' (ibid.: 249).

Animal masks do not appear today in the Birir winter festival, but they are not completely absent from the Kalasha Chaumos: as we shall see, they appear, though in a rather marginal position, in the Chaumos of Bumburet (Wutt 1983: 120, 137; Snoy 2008: 63). The Jhani song may therefore preserve the memory of a lost rite: it would not be surprising to find out that in past times the children made their round in animal disguise, or were accompanied by adults wearing animal masks. Such an association between children and animal masks on New Year's Day is documented in an immense area stretching from France to East Asia (Ginzburg [1989] 2008. 165). For Ginzburg, children's rounds and animal masks are just different ways of relating to the dead in the crucial time of the changing of the year, because the begging children, like the masks, are to be seen as portraying the cohorts of the dead (ibid.: 163), an identification we have already considered.

As genii of time and mediators with the World Beyond, the fierce animals of the song could be seen as spirits representing the dangerous forces of primeval Chaos, which breaks out in the moment when the old world is dissolved and the new Cosmos is not yet formed. Perhaps what is expressed here is the terrifying aspect of the sacred. What, at any rate, seems quite certain is the connection, here too (cf. Dumézil 1929: 40), of this virtual animal procession to the time of the changing of the year. For the Kalasha, the New Year – though Chaumos has all the traits of a New Year celebration – at the time of Jhani has not come yet. But its arrival is imminent. It will be celebrated with the *sal gher'ek* (turning of the year) ceremony only a few days later.

In their round the little girls were going to collect flour and red beans. In the evening Kaanok told me that they first descended the valley and then walked back upstream stopping at every hamlet. The round was therefore conducted at the level of the whole downstream half of the valley, and not separately at the village level, like the one of the last day of Chaumos.

When I returned from my tour of the White Trail, I headed directly to the *rikh'ini* temple with Gulistan. It was already well after dark:

The scene was similar to that of *dA'u tat'u*. Under the porch, a group of girls was sitting around two cauldrons where the beans were cooking with their casks. Inside the temple children playing. Another ceremony with children as protagonists expected to carry out almost on their own the *dast'ur*. Only two or three girls in their teens. At a certain point the girls gather around two boys who sing Chitrali songs, crouching on the floor. I listen for a little while until Gulistan steps in ordering the girls to sing the Jhanì songs. The two boys disappear, the girls form a group and a session at Gulistan orders – for my benefit – begins. I record for a bit. Their singing is dragged out. Gulistan and Jamil, who had showed up in the mean time, scold them repeatedly, urging them to give vent to their voices and to carry out the *dast'ur* correctly. I ask them to set them free and after a little while the two men finally let them go. (*From my field journal – 23 January 2007*).

Inside the temple there were mainly girls of all ages, while the boys stayed mostly under the porch. Gulistan had not demanded from the girls any specific song; he had just urged them to sing the songs of Jhanì. His attitude was imperious as that of a teacher with a class of somewhat recalcitrant pupils. The girls, in fact, did try to obey, only they did not seem to know for sure which ones were the songs of Jhanì. They sang various songs I had heard on the day of the race; but they sang also two songs that are surely Jhanì songs. One of them was the same one we just discussed, while the other one was a song I had heard some time before when I had once asked a little girl to give me an example of a Jhanì song:

> *Brother is gone to shoot with his gun*
> *Brother has wiped out Kamdesh*
> *Brother has gone to dance at Joshi*
> *Brother has left for the mountains with the herds.*

The text is incomplete because it was not possible to transcribe all the verses of the recording: a couple were incomprehensible. The song celebrates the feats of men, who go about armed with their guns, destroy their enemies, and dance at festivals. In a moment we shall compare it to another song of Jhanì about the life of women.

The following morning was still dedicated to the cooking of the beans, which were mashed and mixed with mashed walnut kernels. With the flour collected in their round, I was told, the girls, taking their mothers' places, had made bread for all the families. In the evening each home received a portion of beans and bread, presumably in proportion to the number of females in each household; like the food of *dA'u tat'u*, this dish too appeared to be reserved to women. The next morning the ritual of the purification of the dolls was going to take place. Men gave no importance to the ritual. For them it was women's business. The rite was held in various houses, where the girls gathered in groups of three or four.

> They had brought their dolls. They were made of a wooden skeleton in the shape of a cross with arms that could be moved by pulling a string from below. This skeleton is covered with a dress and around the neck of the dolls there were necklaces of tiny red beads; one of them was wearing an exact miniature of the Kalasha women's costume, another one had completely different attire. The little girls were laughing and chatting and helping to turn around the flat bread cakes cooking on the stove. One of them, maybe seven or eight years old, turned to me and said: 'Brother [you see?] We are women, we go fetch water, and we make bread...' (*From my field journal – 24 January 2007*).

The dolls are called *kumbA'uchak*. Their wooden structure, as shown by the description, is very simple, but the clothing probably required quite a bit of work on the part of the mothers. I expected to witness a miniature female rite of purification, with a burning bough of juniper circled around the head of the dolls. But I saw nothing of the sort. The mother handed the bread cakes to the three girls, two each, and that was the end of that. The girls grabbed the bread and immediately ran away with the dolls.

For the men, we have seen, the Jhani was an event of no significance, but for the girls those three days were quite intense: the round of the houses, the nocturnal cooking at the temple, the preparation and the distribution to all households of the food, and finally the making of the bread for the purification of the dolls. The most obvious function of Jhani seems to be pedagogical. The girls take up responsibility for another person, fictitious as it is, for whom they bake bread and, supposedly, carry out the rite. Not only must they make the round of the villages to collect flour and beans, but they must also make bread for their families, the main female task, and fetch water, as one of the little girls had explained to me. Even if it is not included in the formal rites of initiation, Jhani has an initiatic character, because it is aimed at introducing the girls to their future duties as women. But the purification of the dolls is also a game, a game that includes a present, the doll, for the girls – perhaps another trait characterizing Jhani as a New Year celebration.[12]

---

12 In Europe the custom of gifts for children at New Year has ancient roots. Already at the end of

In this case the gifts do not confirm generic social ties, but rather the ties on which the fundamental social unit, the family, is based (cf. Van Gennep 1988: 3495). In particular, the purification of the dolls is a rite reserved to prepubescent girls, who are just beginning to look at their future life as women. A sad glimpse of a woman's life is given by the lyrics of a song later dictated to me by Kaanok, who said it was an ancient song the girls had forgotten:

> *You make for me a doll but I will show you a treasure*
> *Either you will give me to a Pashtun and I shall cook salted vegetables*
> *Or you will give me to a Kom and I shall eat bread and rennet cheese*
> *You give me away in exchange for dark iron, my dear father*
> *My heart is frozen with sorrow.*

The words of the song are those of a girl telling her father that he makes a doll for her, but she will give him much more than that, a true treasure. Probably the reference is to the fact that a daughter is like a treasure because, when she is married, her father receives a bride price. Juxtaposed with the preceding song telling about the feats of the men who kill enemies and earn glory, this song appears to express the grudge of the women for their destiny of subordination. You will give me to a Pashtun or a Kom, the song says, and I shall have to eat their food. You give me away in exchange for iron, it adds, referring to the iron items that, as we have seen, are traditionally the main items in a bride price. The song ends with the powerful image of the girl's heart frozen with sadness.

These lyrics also, therefore, express the drama Kalasha girls used to live until very recently – and possibly to some extent even today – when their fathers assigned them at a very young age to a man of their choice, forcing them to leave their native village or even their native valley, if not, as feared in the song, the very world of the Kalasha, in the case of them being given to a foreigner.[13]

---

the third century CE it was condemned by the Church as a pagan practice (Ginzburg [1984] 2008: 162; Barthélemy in Van Gennep 1988: 3493). See also Lévi-Strauss [1952] 1995: 67, and Miles [1912] 1976: 170, who quotes the text of a sixth-century Latin sermon, where such gifts are condemned as 'diabolical', as well as ibid.: 276–9 for a brief overview of present-giving in European folkore.

13 The fact that the possibility is contemplated of a marriage with members of other communities now Islamic, could be seen as proof of the ancient character of the song, because such marriages would conceivably have been possible only before these communities were converted, but if the Kom were still unconverted only a century and half ago, the Islamization of the Pashtun is surely much older. We must also accept the idea that Kalasha fathers occasionally gave their daughters in marriage to Muslim men, even if this entailed their conversion.

Jhani seems thus to be the feast of the little girls about to grow up, to become women. It is a celebration heralding a change in status, and therefore quite coherently included in the festive sequence of the beginning of the year.

Salgherek and Benjistem – 31 January / 1 February 2007

The winter sequence was not yet concluded. The *b'asun don* (spring bullock) sacrifice still had to be celebrated on the day of *salgher'ek*, the turn (*gher'ek*) of the year (*sal*). On the morrow, the New Year was going to be welcomed in all the goat sheds with the rite of *benjisht'em*.

A beginning of the year in February should not surprise. As Dumézil (1929: 6–10) observes, the winter season, with the pause (in temperate climates) in agricultural chores, though typically a time of very intense social activity, does not provide the temporal points of reference, for rites and feasts, offered by the other seasons. Lacking direct connections with productive activities, ritual events, comparatively observed, show 'uncertainty of date' and tend to fluctuate depending also on historical circumstances. Yet, in the Indo-European world, the French scholar observes, the dates of New Year's Day remain included between the two thresholds of winter, i.e. between December and March.[14]

However, if there is nothing exceptional in a New Year falling in February, what may appear puzzling is the non-coincidence of the beginning of the year with the solstice, when the event is celebrated with a festival as grand as Chaumos. As mentioned, *salgher'ek* falls instead in the lunar month that comes *after* the one of the solstice, at the full moon. The logic behind this circumstance may be that the end of a cycle, celebrated with Chaumos, must be kept distinct from the beginning of a new one, celebrated with the *b'asun don* sacrifice. Beginning and end, though indissolubly connected, is not the same thing. Between the two is therefore inserted 'a marginal period' (Van Gennep [1909] 1981: 157), 'a crepuscular phase'.[15]

For the name of its main rite – *b'asun don*, 'springtime bullock' – and for its position at the end of the coldest period, *salgher'ek* seems to have the traits of a springtime rather than a wintertime New Year celebration, though it is celebrated

---

14 Cf. Propp [1936] 1978: 44–5; Van Gennep 1988: 3471–2.

15 There is an analogy here with what Cardini (1995: 191) highlights for the religious folk festivals of Italy, from the Epiphany to the two following feasts of Saint Anthony the Abbot (17 January) and Candlemas (2 February), a sequence with a temporal rhythm quite close to that of the winter sequence of the Kalasha of Birir (see Appendix).

still in winter (on 31 January in 2007). This was the prevalent trend in the Iranian world,[16] the influence of which seems to be indicated by the name itself of the celebration: if *gher'ek* is a Kalasha word, *sal* is the Persian term for 'year', which is not normally used by the Kalasha in everyday speech. Possible Iranian influences, however, should not be seen as stemming from the official Iranian New Year (*No-ruz, Norouz, Nawroz*), celebrated already by the Achaemenians (Eliade [1975] 1979: 346–8) and later becoming a national holiday under the Arsacids (248 BCE – 224 CE), which is celebrated at the Vernal Equinox, i.e. on 21 March, and which was formerly a ritual of royalty (Gnoli 1980: 196–7, 217) that has little to do with the Kalasha world. We should rather think of the celebration called *sada* (or *sadeh*), held in many places on the 10th of the month of Bahman, which corresponds to 31 January and coincides therefore exactly with the date of *salgher'ek*. The Iranian *sada* is an ancient pastoral festival (Cristoforetti 2003), including themes possibly even of pre-Zoroastrian origin. Though not considered as such, it has the traits of a New Year ritual complex, in which bonfires are lit and the end of the coldest time of the year is celebrated. We have here a further lexical correspondence: in Iran *sada* marks the end of *čilla-yi buzurg*, great *čilla*, and the beginning of *čilla-yi kūčak*, little *čilla* (ibid.: 75). In the same way the Birir celebration takes place at the end of the period called *gh'ona cil'a*. The first word is the Kalasha term for 'big', 'great', while the second one – which was interpreted by informants as meaning 'cold' – is quite manifestly the Persian *čilla*, meaning 'the forty days', which was used to subdivide the Iranian sequence of winter pastoral feasts (ibid.). In this light, it seems quite significant that between the end of Chaumos and *salgher'ek* there is an interval of just about forty days.

Such a surprising correspondence may be taken as an indication of further parallels between the winter feasts of the Kalasha and the ancient Iranian pastoral winter cycle. In no other instance, however, do we find mention among the Kalasha of the term *cil'a*, nor have I heard any reference to subdivisions of time in periods of forty days in winter or, for that matter, in the rest of the year. The Kalasha traditional calendar is a lunar-solar system in which the year is divided into twelve months – for which the same term as 'moon' (*mastr'uk*) is used – with names mostly coinciding with those of the main seasonal festivals. According to

---

16 Dumézil (1929: 9) remarks that in the Indo-European universe there has been, in historical times, a century-long conflict about the beginning of the year between the Roman and the Iranian worlds, the former in favour of a wintertime date and the latter of a springtime one. In Rome as well however, until 153 BCE the first day of the year was 1 March. For the beginning of the year in Europe see Cardini 1995: 85–6, for Russia in particular see Propp [1963] 1978: 44.

Peter Parkes (1983: 183), who conducted a year-long systematic investigation of Kalasha time-reckoning in 1975–7,[17] the count of the days starts with the new moon, which is said to remain 'hidden' for a period varying from one to three days, with the result that the number of days in all months may vary from twenty-eight to thirty-one.[18] While the progression of the year is generally followed by the people by keeping track of the moon cycles, the exact timing of religious celebrations, as we have seen for Chaumos, is determined by observing the place where the sun sets along the crests of the mountains closing the valleys to the west. The elders, after comparing their observations, reach an agreement on the date for the beginning of the festival, which is then officially announced.[19]

In 2007, immediately after Jhanì the great cold seemed to suddenly retreat. On 26 January the air changed. It was certainly not warm, but the freezing cold that had settled in since Chaumos appeared to relent. The terraced roofs of Guru village were suddenly filled up with women and children playing in the sun. The *gh'ona cil'a*, the great cold, everybody was saying, was over, and for that year it was not going to return. The ice-cold heart of winter had passed. The warm season was still far away, but a first signal of its approach had arrived. It is not by chance, perhaps, that the rite marking the 'turn' of the year is called spring sacrifice (*b'asun don*, 'spring bullock').

It seemed therefore that there was still a week to go before *salgher'ek*, and I was again looking at the pause in ritual activities as a precious moment to fully record and reorganize the data I had collected. But if ritual activities did actually halt for a few days, social activities were resumed with great intensity, taking advantage of the pause.

I had gone with Baras Khan to a distant goat shed to interview an elderly man, when a child messenger hastily dispatched on our tracks brought us the news that

17 More generic data collected by us through informants in 1973 coincides pretty much with his.
18 He adds that 'there seems to be a hiatus in reckoning days after the end of the Chaomos festival at the midwinter solstice; and there is some suggestion that an intercalary month is (or was) inserted every seven years at the Dewaka rite in January' (ibid.); Dewaka is the name of a sacrifice celebrated in the Rumbur valley at the end of January, like the Salgherek of Birir.
19 Parkes (ibid.) relates that the observation is conducted by specifically appointed elders (*suri-jagaw'au*) with the aid of 'sun pillars' (*s'uri thū*) erected in a few goat sheds in each valley. He notes that the system is fairly accurate because the climax of Chaumos always coincides with the solstice and the dates of the other main seasonal festivals have only varied in a range of three or four days in the forty years preceding his observations. In 2006–7, however, fixed dates had been introduced in Bumburet and Rumbur, but not in Birir, where the traditional system was still in use.

a group of guests had arrived at Baras Khan's house. We concluded our interview and descended rapidly to Grabanisar, where we found the new arrivals, about fifteen people in all from Bumburet valley, where Baras Khan's wife was born. They were his *kaltab'ar*, his affines, who had come to wish his new-born baby well. They were going to spend the night in his house to leave the next morning. That evening a grand party was held in Grabanisar, and adults and children flocked in from all the surrounding villages.

In the Kalasha valleys people dedicate a good part of their time to the strengthening of social ties. Visits are exchanged for births, initiations, marriages, and especially for funerals. As the group of Momola guests arrived in Birir for Baras Khan's baby, a large group of Birila, as the people of Birir are called, had just left for Bumburet to attend a funeral. And there is no discrimination between converted and non-converted relatives: the deceased in this case was a Muslim.

The end of my stay was by now approaching. Only two weeks remained before my departure for Italy. I had to bid farewell to my friends in Rumbur. I joined therefore the stream of people in movement. I left early the next day, shortly before the guests, so that I could be back in time for the *salgher'ek* rite. I returned indeed just in time. The very morning after my return, three or four *kaz'i* elders headed upstream announcing that they were going to the *d'ewa dur* to celebrate the rite of *b'asun don*. I followed in their tracks with a younger 'colleague' of theirs.

The ritual was going to be held at the shrine of Mahandeo, located near the village of Gasguru in the shade of some great plane trees. The shrine of the god is of the conventional type: a small construction of rough stones, with an overhanging plank with two roughly-hewn horse heads. Mahandeo, as we have seen, is the only divinity worshipped in all three valleys. According to tradition, we said, he taught to the Kalasha many of their techniques including the one, of fundamental importance, for making cheese. At his shrine various rites are celebrated in Birir in the course of the year and especially those of the end of summer pastoral festival – the Uchaw – in which the male community shares the first cheese brought down from the mountain pastures and offers it to the god. The holy place is approached with no fear and the rituals are celebrated in an atmosphere of relaxed familiarity, quite different from the 'holy terror' inspired by the shrines of Warin and Praba.

Together with the nocturnal one at Praba's shrine, to which I could not participate, that was the only sacrifice of the whole winter sequence celebrated at the shrine of a divinity; the other ones were all held at the goat sheds. It is a quite complex ritual and one of the most important of the whole year cycle. It is worthwhile therefore reproducing here in full the description of it recorded in my field journal:

There were maybe ten of us altogether, or a few more. Preparations are made
for the sacrifice. The *'onjiSTa s'uda* goes to wash his arms up to the elbow
in the water of the spring just beside the altar. The kid is forced to lie down
and, while a man holds it still, the *'onjiSTa s'uda* slits its throat. He throws
some of the blood on the juniper fire burning in front of him, and some of it
on the shrine, while the rest of the men pray. He then cuts the tip of an ear of
the victim; he dips it in the blood gushing out of the throat and throws it in
the fire. Finally he severs the head and he lays it for a few moments on the
edge of the fire so that the blood will coagulate. The boy then starts kneading
flour and water to make *tas'iLi* wheat bread. It will be *'onjiSTa* bread.
Meanwhile, the kid is skinned and cut to pieces which are put in a large pot.
It was a beautiful day and those who were not involved in any operation were
lying on the lawn by the shrine warming up in the sun. The big plane tree
shading the altar, dominated the scene. Once the bread was ready a second
rite (*baz'aek s'uraz*) began. after setting some boughs of juniper on the fire
the *'onjiS'Ta s'uda*, with all the men standing behind him in a semicircle, he
threw a piece of *tas'iLi* in it, and another piece towards the shrine; the same
he did with a few pieces of cooked meat, and with some 'wine' obtained by
squeezing a few bunches of grapes inside a beaker and mixing it with some
water. Adinà was leading the prayer:

> *Mahandeo the wise, give well-being to the community,*
> *Give wealth of offspring to the community*
> *Give harmony to the community*

First the entrails of the kid were cooked. Meanwhile two men started
to crack walnuts to make *jA~* [paste of mashed kernels of walnuts] on a
large flat stone slab, located at the foot of the shrine, that had been carefully
washed by Adinà. On that slab – installed by Murat Bek, a famous shaman
of the past – the food for the sacrifice is deposited. To mash the kernels
Adinà (who is not a *kaz'i*) had brought a special polished stone brought by
a Lataruk-nawau ancestor from Maskor, a place in the main valley between
Nisar and Ayun. It is called *istil'ak*. It is in the custody of Adinà. It is used
to make *jA~*. Meanwhile the meat was being boiled in the pot. When the
jA~ and the bread were ready, they were mixed with the meat in the same
vessel used to mix flour and water to make bread, obtaining a mixture called
tsipan'a, which we ate there and then. Quite tasty, though the meat was tough
as usual or maybe a little less than usual because the kid was only one year

old. The left-over bones had to be burnt in the fire, and not thrown on the ground around the shrine. *ishpon~ak* [flour cooked in the broth of the meat] was also made, but we did not eat it on the spot. It was brought to the goat-shed, I was told, for sure the one of Adinà, who had offered the kid. Once we finished up the meat, when the sun had already set behind the mountains to the west, and the air was getting colder, we got ready for the final rite. For the last prayer, juniper was first set on the fire, and then the *onjiSTa s'uda* poured some grape juice on the flames and on the shrine. Adinà held in his open palms a large wheat *tas'iLi* on which were set the heart (*h'Iia*), the spleen (*pr'EA*), the kidneys (*bruk*) of the kid, spiked in a ring made of vine shoots, which was afterwards hung on the shrine and left there. Again the *'onjiSTa s'uda* squeezed some grapes in the beaker and mixed the juice with some water taken from the spring nearby the shrine.

Altogether, therefore, three rites and three prayers: (a) *marikw'eo*, (b) *baz'aeks'araz*, (c) *prec'esh*.

(From my field journal – 31 January 2007).

In the presence of a dozen men, in the shade of the plane tree facing the shrine of the god, three distinct rites had been celebrated. The atmosphere was far from ceremonious, however.

The first rite was the animal sacrifice. The kid is offered in turn by all the goat-sheds. The donor, as we have seen, takes back to his goat shed the *ishp'on~ak* and the meat not consumed on the spot. The offering of the tip of an ear of the victim dipped in blood, could mean that the entire animal, and not only the blood is offered to the god. In this sense, must probably also be interpreted the command of burning the left-over bones in the fire – an obligation not in force for the sacrifices held at the goat sheds – something reminiscent of a holocaust.

The second rite is called *baz'aek s'araz* or *zh'An~gu s'araz*, because the pieces of meat thrown in the fire and on the shrine are pieces of the liver (*zh'An~gu*) and a piece of the front leg (*baz'aek*) of the victim. The flour used to make the bread must be *'onjiSTa* flour, obtained from grain brought to the mill not by a woman – as is normally the case, because it is a female task to take grain to the mill – but by the same *'onjiSTa s'uda* who is due to officiate in the ritual. While with the first rite the sacrificial victim was symbolically offered to the god, with the second one the deity was given its share of the food we were about to consume. The prayer was recited in the name of the whole community, for good health, harmony, and many children. The food for the meal that followed was prepared according to very precise rules. The use of tools belonging to ancestors indicates the repetitive character of the ritual: a ritual act does not imitate that of the ancestors, it repeats it. It takes place, that is, in a time 'other' than that of profane duration.

The third ritual was the material offering to the god of the most vital organs of the victim – the heart, the spleen, and the kidneys – strung on a couple of vine shoots bent to form a ring. Holding with his hands, as if it were a tray, the big flat bread-cake on which the offerings were laid, Adinà recited another prayer:

Oh Allah Creator
Bring peace and good health to the community,
Make sure that everything goes well
Give us your blessings, heesh!
Oh Allah, holy Creator
You, Mahandeo the clever, pray God on our behalf
Once the summit is reached, from the peak you must descend heesh!

While the first prayer was addressed to Mahandeo, this one was addressed to Allah; the Kalasha god is only mentioned as an intermediary who is asked to intercede with the Creator – something consistent with the now prevailing reinterpretation in monotheistic terms of the Kalasha religion. The requests are the usual ones, but what makes this prayer special is the cry 'heesh!' concluding the invocations, which I had never heard in other sacrifices. The last verse is also rather peculiar , and no explanation was available for it. In all likelihood it is a traditional formula that may be interpreted as a reference to the ending of the old cycle and the beginning of the new one. As a formulation, that is, of the idea of cyclical time: once the end – or maybe the climax – has been reached, you can only go back, and hence begin again. The 'rotation' of the year had been celebrated.

That night a final rite was held in the homes in honour of the goddess Jeshtak, guardian of the house and the family. I followed the ritual at Gulistan's house. A mixture of mashed walnuts and cheese was prepared with wheat bread. The ritual food (*ishper'i*) was gathered in a wickerwork basket and set on the wooden shelf along the back wall of the house, while Gulistan addressed a prayer to Jeshtak:

We have done this b'asun don *ritual to ask for peace and a numerous*
    offspring
Now we consume this ritual meal
You, Jeshtak, goddess of the home, who shares with us our food
Give us peace
Keep troubles and sorrow away from us.

The goddess is called 'goddess of the home' because her symbol is found, as we know, in all homes, as well as 'eater of a share' (*baS zhu'aw*), like all gods we have seen are defined. The requests again are the usual ones: peace and well-being, protection against trouble and sorrow. The rite has, however, something unique about it, because that very night the prohibition is lifted of consuming food from the new crops. The meal offered to the goddess was, materially, the first meal of the new year. The ritual food on which Jeshtak's blessings were invoked consisted of bread made with maize from the last season, and the walnuts were those gathered the previous autumn. From then on, all the products from the cycle just ended, could be consumed. The lifting of that prohibition on New Year's Day – a custom documented in a great variety of cultural contexts – confirms that the beginning of the year is seen as a true beginning of life.[20]

However, the real New Year's Day was going to be celebrated the following day; the day just passed had started out still in the old cycle, and only in the evening, with the lifting of the prohibition on the fruits of the new crops, had the new cycle been entered. In other words, it was New Year's Eve. The next morning the rite of *benjist'em* was going to be celebrated in all the goat-sheds. I had arranged to follow it at Baras Khan's goat shed, just above the village of Grabanisar. In all homes, that morning, boiled pumpkin was the ritual food. At Baras Khan's place, the family was sharing a large orange pumpkin:

Around 11 o'clock we go up to the goat shed, just along the slope above the house. Baras starts mixing flour and water to make bread. A half hour later we climb on the *dram'i* [roof] of the goat shed where two brief rites take place. The first one is celebrated at the feet of a great oak tree above the shed up which a vine was creeping. A ring made of braided vine shoots is hung on a walnut bough stuck in a crack of the trunk of the great tree. A small fire is lit. A child puts a bough of juniper on it. On a small flat stone a little heap of wheat is ready. Sharakat, an uncle of Baras Khan, passes it to the child. While Sherakat recites hastily a prayer, the child pours on the fire some of the grains and throw the rest of it towards the ring of vine shoots: he then squeezes some grapes on the fire and throws them in the flames, and he does the same in the direction of the ring, besides which he lays the grapes after squeezing them. He repeats the same gestures with some walnuts, throwing some in the fire and some towards the ring. The same rite is repeated immediately afterwards under the *daran'O~*, the shelter [for hay and other

---

20 Eliade [1949] 1968: 73, 98.

fodder] found on the roofs of all Kalasha goat sheds. Meanwhile Baras had stopped making bread and his brother was mixing mashed walnut kernels and cheese to make *sambar'i*, a very tasty sort of mush which we ate together with the bread made by Baras accompanied by abundant wine. (*From my field journal – 1 February 2007*).

On the meaning of pumpkin as New Year's ritual food we can make some speculations. Apart from possible symbolic values of the fruit itself – as expression of abundance, for example – what seems essential is that it is non-ordinary food, not normally eaten in the morning meal and has therefore the function, as is generally the case with the food of feast days, of signalling the 'otherness' of this special day.

The ritual celebrated at the goat sheds is, in some of its aspects, quite peculiar. The supernatural recipient of the offerings, rather than by a bough of juniper or oak, is represented by a vine shoot bent and braided to form a ring as big as a hand, hung on a short stick of walnut stuck in a crack of the bark of a tree or of a wall. The offerings are of three types: wheat, grapes and walnuts. The objective of the rite, Erfan explained to me, is the increase of fruit crops.

The rite seems to have a magical component. A cascade of fruits is poured on a ritual object representing the two plants of grapes and walnuts, as if to stimulate their fertility. Not only are the materials meaningful, however. We must consider also the morphology of the cult object, of which, maybe not surprisingly, no explanation was offered to me. The ring should probably be seen not as hanging on the walnut stick but as being penetrated by it, with a quite explicit symbology: the upright stick and the ring may very well represent the male and female sexual organs, and the ritual object appears to be, in all likelihood, a representation, of the simplest kind, of the sexual act.

The symbol would certainly fit the occasion: on the first day of the year, to celebrate rebirth and regeneration, it would be quite appropriate to invoke the power of generation itself, as source of energy and life. At the time when nature is about to start waking up, humans try to stimulate it and to support it in its wakening.

Raistam

Shortly after the day of Benjishtem I had to leave Birir. But the winter sequence was not over yet. About two weeks later, just before the new moon following New Year's Day, the feast of Raistam (*ra'istam*) was going to be celebrated. The fulcrum of this last ritual event – as described to me by old Sherbek – is a repetition of the initiation rite of the girls and of the younger boys, those who had put on the *ceL'ik* for Chaumos, that is, at the first stage of the process. The children, boys and girls, are washed and then dressed again in their ceremonial attires. In the homes of the children, meanwhile, walnut-filled bread cakes are made, to be offered to the people of the village; two for each household. The girls then undergo again the *shish a'u* ritual, and the boys the *isht'on~gas* at the goat sheds, where a he-goat is sacrificed for each initiate. The boys will spend the night at the goat sheds, in the isolation of a brief liminal stage. The next day a group of *'onjiSTa s'uda* – that is, fully-initiated boys – goes to the holy place called *ra'istam pr'aba*, which is located on a spur at the mouth of the Jagar valley where the main Praba shrine is located. A lamb is sacrificed there and the blood, mixed with flour, is smeared on a stone deemed to be the 'sign' (*nish'an*) of the divinity. The meat of the sacrificial victim is eaten in part, and the rest, bones included, is burnt in the fire: another instance of a holocaust sacrifice.

The *'onjiSTa s'uda* then join the adults who have gathered in the meantime at the Mahandeo shrine. A kid is sacrificed there by one of them; some of its blood is sprinkled on a leaf of the sacred plane tree overhanging the shrine on which are laid some grains of millet, held in his hand by another initiated virgin boy. The rite of *zh'an~gu s'araz* (with which the liver of the victim is offered to the god), already held for *salger'ek*, is then repeated, and finally all the participants move to a nearby field where the boy scatters the blood-stained seeds on the snow with a rite that, lifting the prohibition, inaugurates the season of sowing. The ritual then ends with a meal at the shrine of the god shared by all the participants.

Raistam, the last act of the winter sequence, announces the spring sequence with this final ritual. Once again we see the cycle of human life joined to that of the seasons, and the course of individual existence to the course of collective life. As the children, having completed the first stage of their initiation, will continue to grow, so it is wished will grow the crops from the imminent spring sowings.

After Raistam, which marks the end of the long winter sequence, periodical rites halt for a pause that is maybe the longest in the ritual calendar. At least two months will go by before the beginning of the spring sequence focussed on Joshi, the great spring festival announcing the departure of the herds for the mountain pastures and the summer dispersion of the community to exploit in full the resources offered by the environment.

6

The Deep Meaning of the Kalasha Chaumos

The Chaumos of Birir and Bumburet/Rumbur: structures in comparison

To fully understand the complex nature of the great winter solstice festival and to do justice to the richness of the Kalasha symbolic system, we must now compare the Chaumos of Birir with the Chaumos of the two northern valleys. Since quite detailed accounts exist of the Chaumos of Rumbur as well as of that of Bumburet,[1] we shall only focus here on the traits differentiating them from that of Birir. We shall carry out our comparison at the structural level, considering the details of the single elements only when necessary: we shall do that, therefore, just for the central rite of the festival, for the focal event around which the whole structure is organized.

A comparison between the two complexes shows noteworthy differences not only in some elements, but in the structure of the ritual event itself. In fact, there are differences also between the festivals of Bumburet and Rumbur, but within an essentially homogeneous pattern, while the Birir Chaumos differs from those of the other two valleys especially in structure. Naturally, we must keep in mind that the differences between Birir and Bumburet/Rumbur concern not only the winter solstice festival but the whole yearly ritual cycle. In the perspective of this work, we must focus, however, just on Chaumos.

The structure of the festival is different in the first place because the Bumburet/Rumbur Chaumos includes some rites celebrated in Birir for Lagaur which, as we

---

1 For Rumbur see Cacopardo A.S. 1974, 1985; Loude & Lièvre 1984; Cacopardo & Cacopardo 1989; for Bumburet see Jettmar 1975: 379–87; Wutt 1983; Snoy 2008.

have seen, is considered a separate feast. The solstice festival of the two northern valleys is therefore longer. It lasts twelve days interrupted here and there by some 'empty days' (*mic 'adua*) used for preparations, for a total of over two weeks. The whole structure of the winter sequence thus appears different. One of the most macroscopic differences is that in Bumburet and Rumbur the drums are forbidden for the whole duration of the festival, which means that *ca~*, *d'ushak* and *drazha'ilak*, the usual songs and dances of festive occurrences which, as we have seen, characterize not only the other two sequences of cyclical festivals – the spring one and the end of summer one – but also social celebrations like funerals (*cik*), feasts for the delivery of the dowry (*sari'ek*), and the feasts connected to the system of rank, are banned. It is a prohibition that gives Chaumos a character of absolute uniqueness that transcends the intrinsic exceptionality of all festive events, setting it neatly apart from all other celebrations. For Chaumos, the Kalasha of Rumbur and Bumburet sing and dance without the aid of any musical instruments, just to the simple rhythm of the singing and clapping of hands. The chants are all traditional Chaumos songs never sung at any other event. Many are contrast songs for which small groups of men and women engage each other in a duel of improvised verses with very explicit sexual references. Other ones are choral chants to be sung in unison. Some of these chants are the same in the three valleys.[2]

Another major structural difference concerns the seclusion of the liminal phase. While in Birir only the novices and the other *prabal'on g'Uak*, with the few adults accompanying them, are secluded in the goat sheds, in Bumburet and Rumbur the whole male community sleeps in the stables for the central days of the festival,[3] where men make their own bread, baking it on stone slabs to avoid using any implement that has been in contact with women. Sexual relations are forbidden and men must even avoid sitting on a bed when they go down to the villages during the day for the celebrations. The *'onjiSTa* and the *pr'agata* must be kept separate. These however, as mentioned above, are relative concepts: though Kalasha women are *pr'agata* in relation to Kalasha men, the whole Kalasha people are *'onjiSTa* in relation to the Muslims. Hence in Bumburet and Rumbur the whole community isolates itself from the external world through a series of additional prohibitions which remain in force throughout the holiest days of the festival: Kalasha converts must leave the villages, tea and cigarettes are banned,

---

2 The French translations of some of these texts from Rumbur are published in Loude & Lièvre 1984; some texts of the Bumburet Chaumos are published in the original Kalasha language with a German translation in Wutt 1983, and only in English in Snoy 2008.

3 Already in 1973 this requirement was not strictly adhered to in Rumbur.

as well as soap, radios and any other item coming from outside; recently, I was told, a prohibition on speaking Khowar has been added. The community enters into a sort of 'valley cloistering'[4] aimed at avoiding all contact with the external world and with the Muslims, seen as a source of contamination. The *'onjiSTa* sphere extends its reach to include the villages, from which *pr'agata* influences must be kept away.

If in Birir the community identifies only symbolically with the novices and the other *prabal'on g'Uak* in their seclusion, in Bumburet and Rumbur the identification is ritually enacted. Not only the novices, but all males undergo the purification ritual of *ist'on~gas* in the goat sheds, and all women are purified with the *sh'ish au* ritual.

This period of separation of the sexes and isolation from the external world – called *diC* – covers the whole liminal phase of the festival in Bumburet and Rumbur.[5] The community as a body undergoes, as it were, the initiatic ordeal marking the passage from one stage to the next. In other words, the crucial moment in the individual life of the novices is made explicitly to coincide with the crucial moment in the life of the community represented by the end of the yearly cycle. It is particularly interesting, in this regard, to note that the term *diC* is connected to the Sanskrit word *diksha*, which designated the elaborate preparations for the great Vedic sacrifice of soma (Dumont & Pollock 1959: 16). The word *diksha* means 'initiation', 'consecration', 'dedication'. It is associated with the idea of rebirth; the rebirth that takes place through the sacrifice.[6] Different as the context may be, the Kalasha term appears to cover the same semantic field: a period of preparation in the wake of a ritual event consisting in a rebirth – of the novices who are reborn with their initiation, and of the community as a body which celebrates its rebirth with the rituals of the New Year.

At the apex of this liminal period we have the main structural difference between the Chaumos of Birir and that of the two northern valleys. In the time

---

4 Such ritual isolation, termed 'village cloistering' by Macdonald (in Nicoletti 2006: 137), is quite a common practice in the Himalayas.

5 Until very recently the period of seclusion lasted seven days in Rumbur, but only three in Bumburet (Loude & Lièvre 1984: 256; cf. Wutt 1983: 144). In 2006, I heard that since many infringements of the rules had taken place in Rumbur, *kaz'i* Koshnawaz (one of the leading ritual elders of that valley), following instructions received in a dream, ordered a number of atoning goat-sacrifices and declared the period of seclusion should be reduced to three days the following year, but the proscriptions were to be respected in full.

6 Kuiper 1970: 117; Stutley & Stutley [1977] 1980: 114–15.

when the community is all projected towards the *'onjiSTa* sphere, the human and
the divine plane are joined: a god called Balimain (*balima'in*) descends into the
Bumburet valley. To this focalizing event are due all the other structural differences: the drums must stay silent because this is the command of the Visitor god
who has expressed his will through a shaman (*deh'ar*), and the period of 'valley
cloistering' and of separation between the genders is conceived in preparation of
his arrival. We have seen that in Birir as well the descent of the god is announced
in the chants, but there are no sacralizing prohibitions and the ritualization of his
arrival is reduced – if it is at all present – to the night sacrifice at Praba's shrine
(in which, as will be remembered, I could not participate).

Balimain, the Visitor god of Bumburet and Rumbur, arrives on a winged horse
with hooves of burning embers[7] in the most sacred days of the festival, during the
period of separation. From his name the figure of Indra emerges, because *bal'ima*
is an epithet borrowed from Kati, the geographically closest Nuristani language,
meaning 'most-powerful' and used in hymns as an attribute of divinities,[8] while *in*
stands for Indr.[9] Just as Indra is depicted as the founder of the New Year festival
in Indian epic literature (Dumézil 1929: 111, 122–4), so is Balimain considered
the refounder of Chaumos in this version of Kalasha mythology.[10] It is believed
he established the prohibitions mentioned above and instructed the Kalasha in
the rituals to be performed for his arrival. In fact, the identification of Balimain
with Indra, if we consider the festival as a whole, appears to be quite explicit: he
is called often In or Indr in songs and prayers;[11] the holy place dedicated to him,
in Bumburet, is called *indr'eyn*; the place where the sacred fire is lit for the ritual
performed to receive him is called *'indras kot* (cf. Jettmar 1975: 356), the fortress
of Indra; and the name of his horse, we were told, is *'indras*, which is a genitive.
We have already seen, on the other hand, that also in Birir Indra emerges, though
not as explicitly, as the god of Chaumos.

---

7 He was so described to us in 1973 by our main informant Shahjuwan.

8 Morgenstierne 1951: 180, 184; cf. Jettmar 1975: 358. In Rumbur we have another instance of the
use of this adjective for a deity: *bal'ima JaC*.

9 In my view this is the most likely etymology. My assistants offered no suggestions. Morgenstierne
(1973: 154) hypothetically suggests a derivation from **Bala-mahendra*, which, Di Carlo remarks
(personal communication) would anyhow lead to Indra, because *bala-mahendra >bala-maha-indra*;
for *bal'a*, 'huge', in Kalasha, see T-9161 *b'ala*, 'power', 'strength' (Trail & Cooper 1999: 26). A
very different etymology is proposed by Loude & Lièvre (1984: 262). For a still different proposal
formulated in the past by the present author see Cacopardo A.S. 1985: 740–1.

10 Jettmar 1975: 354–5; Snoy 2008: 50–64.

11 Jettmar 1975: 384; Wutt 1983: 123, 132; Loude, Lièvre 1984: 261.

Though Indra is a complex deity, to whom many activities are attributed by the texts, some of his main traits can be discerned in Balimain. In a hymn of the Rig Veda (VIII, 3, 6) Indra sets the sun alight, in the Satapatha Brahmana (VI.i.i, 2) he is described as 'the one who inflames', and the original meaning of his name is possibly, as we have seen, the one stated in the Rig Veda where generative power and vigour are indicated as his main characteristics.[12] Balimain is explicitly connected to fire, as shown by the burning embers of his steed and the bonfires and torchlight processions that welcome him, while his connection to the power of generation is stated clearly in the prayers addressed to him: '*gum bi zhe putr bi de*', 'give us seed of wheat and seed of children'. If we further consider that the reproductive power of Indra is identified with the energy of the stallion and is associated with his bay horses (Stutley & Stutley 1980: 170), we find in Balimain's representation as a rider – or at times as a god appearing in the form of a horse, or in mixed human and equine form, almost a centaur[13] – another strong indication of the basic identity of the two figures.

Most interestingly, another Vedic divinity is associated with Balimain. The attendant of the god, we were told in Rumbur, is called Pushaw (*p'ushaw*), a name leading quite directly to Pushan (*p'ushan*) 'a divinity whose name derives from the root *puS*, to nourish, with reference to his role of divine dispenser of fertility' (Stutley & Stutley [1977] 1980: 350). Pushan is a deity associated with the sun and the partition of the solar year, and he is the guide of wayfarers (Ib; cf. Sergent 1997: 318–19). The etymology of his name is connected to the term *puSya*, which in the Rig Veda indicates vigor (T-8306) as well as the month of December–January (T-8307). There could have been no more appropriate companion for a god like Balimain who brings reproductive energy and arrives for the winter solstice; further, it is interesting to note that the two deities are found associated in a Vedic hymn (RV, VII. 35, 1) where Indra and Pushan are reunited in a dual divine being, called Indra-Pushan (Stutley & Stutley [1977]1980: 174).

Though the Balimain complex is present both in the Bumburet and in the Rumbur Chaumos, the real centre of the cult is in Bumburet, because it is in a precise place in that valley that the god is believed to descend to Earth, while in Rumbur the Visitor deity does not have its own shrine and is welcomed at the altar of the god Sajigor, of whom he is said to be a guest.

The place of the god's descent in the Bumburet valley is called, as we have

---

12 Eliade [1975] 1979: 228; Stutley & Stutley 1980: 170.
13 Wutt 1983: 132; Snoy 2008: 57. On the importance of the horse in the New Year festivals of the Indo-European world see Dumézil 1929: 34–6.

just seen, *indr'ein*. By expressed will of Balimain, oral traditions state, no altar
was to be built there, for the god wished his worship to be different from that
offered to the other divinities (Jettmar 1975: 355, 362). The holy place is only
a stony clearing surrounded by a thicket of evergreen oak trees, at the foot of a
steep rocky cliff. On the west side of it, by a holy oak tree, a level grassy space
has been created through some terracing where the god's 'nest' – a small structure
of willow reeds[14] – is prepared, while on the east side a stone set upright marks
the place where a lamb is sacrificed on the night of his arrival. The holy place
is located in the side valley of Batrik, which parallels the sacred Jagar valley of
Birir, and is considered the main ceremonial area of Bumburet. We may further
recall that on Praba's altar as well is found an upright oblong stone. Like *indr'eyn*
in Bumburet, in Birir Praba's shrine is the altar of Chaumos.

The descent of Balimain into the Bumburet valley

The rites performed at *indr'eyn* on the Nangairo night, the night of Balimain's
visit, are complex. Only a very brief synthesis of them is possible here. As far as
we know, we have only two eyewitness accounts of the events of that night, by
Peter Snoy and Karl Wutt, who participated in the Bumburet Chaumos in 1955
and 1973 respectively.[15] We shall follow here the earlier one, that of Peter Snoy
(2008),[16] who was, with Adolf Friedrich in 1955, the first ethnographer to participate in a Kalasha Chaumos.

In the evening, torchlight processions of people coming from the whole valley
proceeded to Batrik. While the women stayed behind at the village, the men went
on to the holy place where, after a rite with offerings of bread and wine, seven
pure boys – the *inw'aw g'Uak* (In's boys) who correspond to the *prabal'on g'Uak*
of Birir – brought some consecrated wheat grains (*h'ushak*) which were sprinkled
with the blood of a lamb sacrificed for the purpose. The bloodstained grain was
to be used for the rite inaugurating the sowing season, as we have seen is done

---

14 For Propp ([1963] 1978: 112–14), ritual use of the willow is due to the fact that its reeds are the
first signs of spring.

15 Wutt 1983: 135–6; Snoy 2008: 58–62. However, neither Wutt nor Snoy were allowed to spend
the night at *indr'eyn*, just like we have seen I was not allowed to witness the nocturnal sacrifice at
Praba's shrine.

16 The essay quoted here is the English version of a German manuscript written by Snoy back
in 1960 (personal communication by Snoy to the author), which is the source of the account of
Chaumos given by Jettmar (1975: 384–6).

in Birir – but with millet instead of wheat[17] – for Raistam, the last of the winter feasts.

At this point, the *deh'ar*, the shaman, fell into a trance: he revealed the wishes of Balimain and made divinations for the coming year. Contextually a functionary was nominated (*r'oy*) who is charged with a number of ritual duties for the year to come. All men then withdrew to the village where obscene songs and dances were staged, while the seven pure boys, chaperoned by some adult guardians, stayed at the holy place where, having lit seven fires representing the seven gods of the valley gathering there to greet Balimain, they remained in vigil to welcome the god. The climax of the event was reached in the early hours of the morning. The impure adults (*m'Aka moc*) left the dancing ground of Batrik village and headed back to *indr'eyn* as a menacing throng, bragging of having raped the women (in spite of the prohibition forbidding sexual relations), and launched an assault on the virgin boys, threatening to rape them as well: a ritual enacting on a grander scale the same theme of the pure/impure contrast played out in Birir's *nog'or grik*. The *inw'aw g'Uak* then struck up the Nangairo song welcoming the return of Balimain, while their guardians defended them with sticks and stones. At this very moment Balimain discharges his blessings on the boys and leaves the valley. The resistance of the guardians then relented, and the *m'Aka moc* finally succeeded in symbolically touching the boys, thus participating in the benediction – a conclusion that seems to differ from that of the Birir rite where the impure adults were repelled. The merging of the two basic opposites – *'onjiSTa* and *pr'agata* – had now taken place and a long line was formed by the men, each holding from the back the hips of the person in front. With a wordless chant the long line slowly proceeded with explicit copulating movements down to the village where the women were waiting, singing with a clear sexual allusion, the chant of the horn-less ram (*konDameSal'ak*)[18] 'who will pierce you with his horn' (Jettmar 1975: 384–6), the same chant intoned by Danok at the goat shed on the last day of Lagaur.

The theme of fecundity and reproduction is quite obviously in the foreground here. In one of his main aspects Balimain is no doubt a god of fertility. His cult is

---

17 A significant difference, because in the myth wheat was brought to Bumburet by Balimain (cf. Jettmar 1975: 354).

18 According to information collected by Wutt (1983: 135–6), who, like Snoy, could not witness this part of the rite, ritual events were somewhat different in 1981: instead of the menacing throng of *m'Aka moc* the assault on the pure boys was enacted by two shepherds, notoriously uninterested in women, who had blackened their faces and were wearing goat horns on their heads.

connected specifically to the cultivation of wheat, as shown by the rite just briefly described and by the circumstance that, in the myth, he presents the first Kalasha who welcomes him with two ears of wheat.[19] This trait of Balimain is confirmed by the obscene songs typical of Chaumos and of his cult in particular (Loude & Lièvre 1984: 272, 282–5); according to the myth, the god himself taught them to humans.[20] The songs are accompanied by dances with explicit sexual allusions:[21] in 1973, in Rumbur, we observed a dance in which the women twisted a strip of their ample robe in the form of a male organ and, laughing loudly, advanced towards the men, who, seeing them approaching, joined in their turn their thumbs and their indexes to represent a vulva and danced laughing in their direction.

But the most intriguing aspect of Balimain is that he is represented as a hermaphrodite deity, (Snoy 2008: 51) appearing as male when turning to the right and female when turning to the left (Jettmar 1975: 354, 412), probably meaning that his right side is male and his left side is female; a representation which may have something to do with the association (made in ancient India) of the pupil of the right eye with Indra, and of the left eye with his wife Indrani (Stutley & Stutley 1980: 174). In the account of one of our informants his female part was played by his horse, which was described as woman-faced.

The male-female contraposition is portrayed as relative in the mythical symbol; this fundamental polarity has been termed by Sherry Ortner – a pioneer in gender studies – 'a root metaphor'[22] because, for being inscribed in the very bodies of the human beings who classify, it is the most obvious conceptual tool to indicate opposed classes. In the divine representation this 'mother of all distinctions' is dissolved, revealing itself as ephemeral, tied to the world of forms. It is the supreme unification: the *'onjiSTa* principle manifests itself and it includes its opposite. We have here a symbolic representation of the mystic notion of '*coincidentia oppositorum*'.

The principle is again expressed, after the god has left, in the day called *Lawakbih'ik*, the same name given in Birir, as we have seen, to the rite of the

---

19 Jettmar 1975: 354; Snoy 2008: 52, 54.
20 Jettmar 1975: 357; Loude & Lièvre 1984: 199; Snoy 2008: 41.
21 Wutt 1983: 133; Loude & Lièvre 1984: 197–8, 272, 282–5,; Cacopardo A.S. 1985: 743; Snoy 2008: 43–4.
22 In Rappaport 1999: 247–8; cf. Bell 1997: 101. It may possibly be also the most archaic of all metaphors of distinction, if it is true that it can be traced back to the Paleolithic (Eliade 1979: 32–3).

chase of the fox. A similar rite is celebrated also in Bumburet for *Lawakbih'ik*,[23] but the central event of the day is a cross-dressing dance. In Bumburet the whole population of the valley gathers in a large level space just below Bruhn village for a great collective dance – in which animal masks also appear – focused around the exhibition of a few couples where the man is dressed as a woman and the woman as a man.[24] Cross-dressing, a widespread custom in the agrarian feasts of Asia and Europe[25] has been seen as a symbolic representation of primordial androgyny (Ivanov 1984: 16). For Eliade ([1948] 1976: 440) this ritual represents '... the condition of perfect humanity, where the two genders coexisted, as they coexist, together with all other qualities and all other attributes, in the divinity ... The man dressed as a woman ... attained for a moment the unity of genders'. Once the hermaphrodite divinity has departed, the community replicates in this manner his/her androgyny. The beginning of the New Year coincides with the beginning of the world: the rite reflects the deepest level of the sacred, beyond all dualities, to attain a total regeneration.

Structure and History in the Kalasha Chaumos

We can now wrap up our synthetic comparison of the two versions of the Kalasha Chaumos. As suggested by Lévi Strauss ([1992] 1995: 69), it is important to distinguish here between the historical and the structural point of view. We shall now take up the latter, leaving the former aside for the moment, keeping in mind that to highlight a structural transformation does not amount to a statement about its historicity.

Available data seem to suggest that we should see in the Bumburet Chaumos a structural transformation of the Birir feast, because in Birir, we have seen, a Visitor god is hailed, but his arrival, strangely, is not the focal ritual event of the festival, which is rather the celebration of the initiations. A logical development of the implications of such a system would be the full ritualization of the coming of the god. This is exactly what we have in Bumburet. Resorting to a parallelism that fits only partially – because the god also arrives in Birir – we may say that the relation between the two versions of the Kalasha Chaumos reminds us of that between

---

23 Wutt 1983: 137; Snoy 2008: 63.
24 In 2006 I had the opportunity to participate in this event.
25 Cf. Miles [1912] 1976: 169, 170; Dumézil 1929: 27; Caillois [1939] 2001: 119–20; Van Gennep [1943] 1998: 789–90; Eliade [1948] 1976: 440; Propp [1963] 1978: 204–5; Leach 1971: 135–6; Caro Baroja [1979] 1989: 88–9; Hutton 1996: 96.

the Old and the New Testament: in the former we have the mere announcement of the coming of the divine, in the latter its actual arrival.

To understand the relationship between the two systems we must probe here into the deepest level of meanings in the Kalasha system, the one most removed from the conscious appreciation of the actors. The fear that the world may not re-emerge from the depths of darkness and coldness in which it is plunged at the heart of winter has been highlighted as characteristic of archaic thought.[26] A true regeneration can only be ensured by a renovated contact with the source of life, which lies in the supernatural. For the Kalasha this means an immersion into the *'onjiSTa* sphere, where gods and pure spirits dwell.

In Birir the task of re-establishing contact with the source of life is entrusted to the children, the novices, and the other *'onjiSTa* boys, the *prabal'on g'Uak*. The society, as we noted, identifies symbolically with its children. The novices face the trial that will give them a new individual status, just as they perform a ritual duty for the whole community. Their rebirth coincides with the regeneration of the society. In Bumburet the virgin boys – though not the initiates themselves – play a similar focal role. Like the *prabal'on g'Uak* in Birir, the *inw'aw g'Uak* bear the responsibility of performing the most sacred rituals on behalf of the community in the course of the Nangairo night, when they are confined in the holy place dedicated to Balimain. In Bumburet too the virgin boys are mediators between the world of humans and the world beyond. But there the success of their task is more fully ensured by the descent of the god in the very place of their confinement.

In both cases the virgin boys have to go through a symbolic ordeal when they are attacked by the *pr'agata* (or *r'ela* in the language of Birir) forces: an attack enacted in Birir in the ritual games of the storming of the castle (*nog'or grik*) and of the fox chase (*law'ak bih'ik*), and in Bumburet especially with the assault on the pure boys by the *m'Aka* men, who try to get hold of the *inw'aw g'Uak* and symbolically rape them. The outcome, however, does not seem, as mentioned, to be quite the same. In Birir the *r'ela* forces, impersonated by the attackers, are repulsed, while in Bumburet the assailants eventually manage, once Balimain has showered his blessings over the boys, to catch hold of them. In one case, it would seem, the *'onjiSTa* principle simply overcomes the *r'ela*, while in the other there is a final merging of the two, which is further symbolized by the line of men, including the boys, heading with copulating movements towards the village where the women are waiting, and by the obscene singing that follows once the village is reached.

The idea of the integration of the opposites, we have seen, is present in Birir

---

26 Eliade [1948] 1976: 359–60; Buttitta A. 1996: 280; Brelich 2007: 57.

as well. There too the festival is pervaded by the theme of unification through the integration of all polarities. But the system appears to lack the idea of their essential coincidence in the divinity, which in the festival of the northern valleys is expressed by the bisexuality of Balimain. Could the full assertion of the *coincidentia oppositorum* be the focus of Balimain's cosmologic message?

It may be. But let us see now if this structurally conceivable transformation, can in any way be traced at the historical level. In other words, is it possible that the Bumburet/Rumbur Chaumos is a historical development of the Birir morphology? Given the lack of any documentation, we can unfortunately only venture in the hazy realm of conjecture.

Karl Jettmar, apparently somewhat startled by the presence in the Kalasha system of such a deep insight – the *coincidentia oppositorum* – in which even he saw a reflection of a system of thought reminiscent of the Greek philosophy of the late classical period, ventured to explain it by suggesting possible external influences of distant Greek/Dionysian and Iranian/Zurvanist origin, possibly transmitted through contacts with the Ismaili Muslims, who have long been present in north Chitral (Jettmar 1975: 357–8).

Though we cannot, of course, rule out some external influence, it does not seem necessary, however, to resort to what appear rather far-fetched speculations to explain the presence in the Kalasha religion of such a profound vision. As noted by several anthropologists,[27] and as Jettmar (1975: 473) himself remarks in the conclusions to his work, religious thought is not the monopoly of literate civilizations. Divine androgyny is a well known notion in the history of religions. For Eliade ([1948] 1976: 434) it articulates in biological terms the coincidence of opposites, and is 'one of the most archaic ways in which the paradox of divinity was expressed'.

In this light we must equally reject Jettmar's further suggestion – formulated in quite contradictory terms – that the Balimain complex may be a very recent development – a suggestion based on the circumstance that at the time of Friedrich's and Snoy's first visit in 1955–6 the cult of the Visitor god appeared to be shrouded in secrecy and limited to a section only of the Kalasha population, while, at the time of Snoy's second visit in 1970, it turned out to be widely acknowledged (Jettmar 1975: 358–9). Such a difference can, in fact, be easily explained with an understandable wish of the people not to disclose to those early Western visitors the details of a cult they were probably used to keeping to themselves for the fact that it was in sharp contrast with Islamic tenets (cf. Snoy 2008: 50, 62). As Jettmar

---

27 For example, Douglas [1966] 1975a: 25; Griaule [1966] 1972: 10.

himself (1975: 396) in the end recognizes, the Kalasha of Bumburet/Rumbur must have known Balimain for a long time.

More cautiously, Snoy suggests that the cult of the Visitor god may indeed pertain to a second phase in the development of the festival, but not such a recent one: for him it could belong to a layer of Kalasha culture associated with the cultivation of wheat, as opposed to an older layer, represented by the other rites of the Chaumos festival, associated instead with the cultivation of millet and beans.[28] The idea that millet preceded wheat in the agricultural world of the Kalasha seems correct. According to our most knowledgeable informant in Rumbur in 1973, millet was the main cereal crop of the Kalasha until less than a century ago; and the fact that the sowing ceremony of Birir is done, as we have seen, with millet instead of wheat would seem to confirm this point.[29] Snoy's hypothesis, in brief, appears to give some historical quality to our structural analysis: the Chaumos of Birir (which Snoy did not know) could be seen as belonging to a more archaic cultural layer reflected in its morphology, which remained unchanged even after the diffusion of wheat, while the morphology of the Chaumos of Bumburet and Rumbur was transformed by the introduction of the cult of Balimain.

The data from Birir seem to indicate, however, that this was not due to outside influences, but rather to the development of an element already present in a latent form in the system: for the descent of a divinity is an example of what has been termed 'the cultic complex of the visitor', which for Eliade ([1949] 1968: 96) is rooted in prehistory. It is quite possible, therefore, that the introduction of the Balimain cult in the Chaumos complex, was a development internal to the Kalasha world, the seeds of which were contained in the older model, still in function in the Birir festival.

If we do not need to resort to influences from literate civilizations to explain the presence of this complex among the Kalasha, we cannot, however, rule out the possibility of influences from the other polytheistic religions of the Hindu Kush, before they were submerged by Islam. In pre-Islamic times the cult of a Visitor god descending once a year, existed in other parts of Peristan, namely in Gilgit[30] and in southern Nuristan. An influence on the Kalasha is more likely from the latter area, where a similar complex existed in Wama (Klimburg 1999: 146,

---

28 In Jettmar 1975: 394; Snoy 2008: 52, 64.

29 Interestingly, there are indications that millet was for a long time, and until the dawning of historical times, the main grain cultivated by the speakers of Indo-European languages (Sergent 2005: 187).

30 Biddulph 1880: 107; Müller-Stellrecht 1973.

177) and in Kattar (Masson 1842, 1: 234), both located in the basin of the Pech River, today in Afghan Nuristan. If the name given in Kattar to the divine visitor is not mentioned in our source, we know that in Wama he was Indra himself who, just like Balimain, was expected to return on horseback every year (Klimburg 1999: 147). Like Balimain, who according to the myth was barred from settling in Bumburet after losing a competition with another god (Mahandeo), Indra competes with Gish, the war god, for his position in Wama (ibid.: 146). In pre-Islamic Nuristan, Wama was the recognized centre of the cult of Indra, for it was the seat of the famous Indrakun vineyard garden, in the midst of which the *indr-ta~* was located, an open-air shrine comprising a large effigy of the god next to a sacred juniper tree,[31] the morphology of which the Bumburet *indr'eyn* appears to replicate, though in very simplified terms. Wama, however, is far south of Bumburet and the closest neighbours of the Kalasha, the Kati of the adjoining Bashgal valley, did not have – as far as we know – a Visitor god (cf. Cacopardo & Schmidt 2006: 38–42) and only knew Inthr (Indra) as a minor deity and not quite as one of their own (Palwal 1969: 66). Kati oral tradition relates, however, that Inthr originally dwelt in the upper Bashgal valley, from where he was expelled by Imra, the supreme god of the Kafir pantheon (Robertson 1898: 388). The myth therefore seems to convey the memory of a time when the cult of Indra was practised in that area. This could refer to the times preceding the arrival of the Kati from western Nuristan, a migration related by Kati oral traditions which should not have taken place much earlier than the middle of the second millennium CE. If it is actually the case that the cult of Indra was formerly practised in upper Bashgal – and the place name Indr-Zyul (Jettmar 1986: 64) lends some support to the myth – where accessible passes lead to both Bumburet and Rumbur, we can surmise that from there it may have spread to the two northern Kalasha valleys. Indeed in some accounts Balimain is said to come every year from Bashgal,[32] while the Kati origin of his attribute *bal'ima* would be a further indication in this direction. The circumstance that the myth explicitly refers to upper Bashgal and

---

31 Klimburg 1999: 147–8, 2014: 57–60. Four enormous vats, dug in four gigantic boulders, were another characteristic of this very special shrine, which must have been dedicated to the cult of wine. Interestingly, similar vats were also found in the upper reaches of two side valleys of the Swat River (Olivieri 2011: 136–7, 147, 149).

32 But in other accounts he is said to come from Waigal (see Loude & Lièvre 1984: 264, 268), i.e. from south Nuristan; or from Tsiam (Jettmar 1975: 386; Loude & Lièvre 1984: 286), the mysterious original homeland of the Kalasha. Tsiam, it is worth noting, is the place name mentioned in the account of our earliest source on Chaumos (Friedrich and Snoy, in Jettmar 1975).

not to the lower part of the valley, which adjoins the southern Kalasha area, could mean that his cult was not prominent there; the absence of the Balimain complex in Birir would thus be explained.

A third possibility is that the Bumburet/Rumbur model of Chaumos is simply the form typical of the northern variety of Kalasha culture, which in pre-Islamic times was centred around the present-day town of Chitral, as opposed to that of the southern area, centred instead around Drosh, represented by the Chaumos of Birir.

From the historical point of view we are therefore confined, as noted earlier, to the realm of conjecture. Some conclusions can, however, be drawn from our comparison of the two varieties of the Kalasha Chaumos. In the first place it is quite certain that Balima-In (or Indr) is to be identified with Indra.[33] Indr is without any doubt the god of Chaumos, both in the Bumburet/Rumbur and in the Birir versions of the festival, and he is conceived as a Visitor god of fertility.[34] Secondly, though it is confirmed that the Balima-In complex does not exist in Birir, we may say that the cultual complex of the Visitor god is latent in the Chaumos of that valley, because there are several references to Indr in the course of the festival and his descent is clearly announced, if apparently not fully ritualized. Yet the focalizing element of the two versions is different: in Birir the celebration is focused on the initiation rituals, while in Bumburet and Rumbur the focus is on the descent of the Visitor god.

Apart from the Balima-In complex, with the structural differences it implies, we find in the winter sequence of Birir just about all the elements of the winter solstice festival of the two northern valleys, though differently arranged. The emphasis on demonic forces, the dangerous forces of Chaos – the *bhut* spirits, the witches, the serpent-monster, which loom over the first pre-liminal phase of the festival – seem, however, to be a peculiarity of Birir. The descent of the dead, a typical trait of the New Year feasts of agrarian societies,[35] is, in contrast, much more

---

33 The close connection between the figures of Balimain and Indra has been highlighted already by Loude & Lièvre (1984: 261, 326). Their suggestions fall just short of an outright identification of the two figures, probably due to the doubtful etymology they propose for the name 'Balumain'.
34 As remarked by Fussman (1977: 32) with regard to the pre-Islamic pantheon of the Nuristani, the identity of origin of Indr and Indra is also assured by the presence in the Kalasha language of terms like *idr'O~*, 'rainbow' (T-1577), and *ind'ocik*, 'lightning' (T-1576) (cf. Trail & Cooper 1999: 127, 128).
35 See Dumézil 1929: 44–5; Eliade [1948] 1976: 363–8; Lanternari [1976] 1983a: 489; Buttitta A. 1996: 286–7.

simply ritualized in Birir, where only some offerings are prepared for the ancestors on the day of *ruzh'ias* and on the day of *isto'n~gas*. In Bumburet and Rumbur, instead, on a specific day dedicated to the return of the deceased, a complex rite is staged in which men, women and children gather in the temples and stay silent, holding a pine torch, while the dead descend to consume the offerings of dried fruit left outside the building. Also, a symbolic representation of the troop of the dead living the valley may perhaps be seen in the procession of *Law'ak bih'ik* in Bumburet, guided by the cross-dressed couples – which symbolize a non-human state – and the animal masks, of which we have already discussed the connection with the world of the dead. We could hypothesize that the symbology of death and rebirth of the initiatic complex at the centre of the Birir Chaumos, obscures the collective return of the dead, which belongs to the same semantic field.[36] As for the semantics determined by this differential structural morphology, it seems that the Balima-In complex brings with it a deeper appreciation of the quintessential identity of opposites, expressed by their coexistence in the representation of the divinity. In other words, it appears that the deep insight of the *coincidentia oppositorum*, remains somewhat implicit in the Birir Chaumos, while in the Bumburet/ Rumbur model it reaches full expression and articulation.

We have here a fundamental theme that may be seen as a further link with the religious world of India. Though the idea of the coincidence of opposites is widely spread in world religions, its role in Indian thought is particularly prominent.[37] Eliade (1971: 84–5) highlights indeed 'a mighty effort of the Hindu spirit to reach a single principle of explanation of the world, and from a spiritual perspective in which contraries may be united and oppositions cancelled' (ibid.: 84), an effort already present in the Vedas with the idea of the consanguinity of Devas and Asuras, and later developed in the classical metaphysics of Hindu philosophy. Could the androgyny of Balima-In be an early seed of that profound reflection? A comparison between the concept expressed by the Kalasha ritual system and the notions developed in Indian philosophy may perhaps suggest an answer to this question.

---

36 It is in similar terms that Lanternari ([1976] 1983a: 490–1) explains the absence of this theme in the New Year celebrations of nomadic herders and hunter/gatherers – a further indication of the possible greater ancientness of the Birir Chaumos.
37 Eliade 1979: 224; cf. Dumont & Pollock 1959: 34.

The coincidence of opposites in Indian philosophy and in the Kalasha system

Let us consider the semantic nucleus of the symbol, keeping in mind we are now moving on a plane definitely removed from the daily awareness of the Kalasha of today.

Corrado Pensa (1974),[38] an Italian scholar of Indian philosophies, attempts to go beyond Eliade's reflection on this issue. He remarks that we find in Eliade's work two differing ideas of the *coincidentia oppositorum*. One represents a well-known aspect of his thought conspicuously present in our analysis of Chaumos: the aspiration towards the integration of opposites expressed in the symbolic restoration of Chaos, representing the Formlessness that preceded Creation, i.e. the pre-cosmogonic One. The other aims instead at transcending the plane of opposites, as it happens for example in Tantric Yoga (Eliade [1962] 1971: 105–6). Pensa remarks that in the first case we are dealing with a *coincidentia* of a 'regressive' character, and in the second one with a *coincidentia* of a 'progressive' character, but that the outcome does not seem to be any different because in both cases, once the *coincidentia* is accomplished, the polarities dissolve either in the 'indistinct primordial chaos' or in a 'motionless luminosity'. And therefore their union does not lead to procreation but to annihilation.

Pensa subsequently shows how a third, fecund, form of *coincidentia oppositorum* may be conceived. It is a 'bipolar dynamism' that, though a minority trend, is firmly rooted in classical Hindu thought, especially in Samkhya Yoga, as well as in certain forms of Buddhism. Its basic idea is that the two opposites do not annihilate each other, but coexist in a *coniunctio* pervaded by a drive for generation, and which is thus always becoming: '… a *coincidentia* that constantly reproposes itself, at different levels' (Pensa 1974: 21). In Pensa's view we should make a distinction '*between co-presence of the opposites and inter-fecundation of the opposites* (i.e. true *coniunctio oppositorum*, in my view)' (ibid.: 28). The Italian scholar detects this notion already in the Vedic pantheon, in a certain representation of the god Agni as androgynous, and in the myth of the fight between Indra and Vrtra, whose death 'is also and especially a fecundation'.

The *coincidentia oppositorum* represented in Balima-In's hierophany appears to be of this third kind. The image of the god as a rider, male on the right side and female on the left side of his body, is a perfect representation of the *coniunctio*. As

---

38 Corrado Pensa was professor of Philosophies of India at Rome University and is now senior teacher in the Insight Meditation Center of Barre, Mass. USA, and since 1987 leading teacher of A.ME.CO. (Associazione per la meditazione di consapevolezza).

remarked by Alan Watts – a well-known British/American specialist in Oriental philosophies – in a work on the myths of polarity (Watts [1963] 1978), opposites do not meet as strangers, because there is between them something that unites them, like the two sides of a coin. In the same way, Balimain appears sometimes as male and other times as female, depending on the side of his body a spectator is looking at. The two poles are not strangers to each other; in the person of the god they coexist and they generate. Androgynous god of fertility, Balimain impersonates creativity at its highest degree. We know, on the other hand, that he is none other than Indra who, in the Rig Veda, performs the primordial act of creation by killing Vrtra. Pensa also remarks that 'the stage, quintessentially creative, of the *coniunctio* must be preceded by a *separation*', because there cannot be creation without two separate and distinct elements. Thus, in the Rig Veda, Indra separates the sky from the Earth, so that they may create. In the Bumburet Chaumos, the separation is ritually enacted by the community itself by separating men from women during the most sacred time of the year. Furthemorer, we have seen that the term *diC*, designating the time of separation, is connected to Sanskrit *diksha* which designates the preparations for the Vedic sacrifice of soma and means 'initiation' and 'rebirth'. In both cases, we have seen, we are dealing with the preparatory stage of a great ritual event.

The integration of opposites as symbolically enacted in the rites of the Birir Chaumos seems, in contrast, to be of a different kind. We have seen that in the game of the storming of the castle (*nog'or grik*), the impure adults are pushed out of the *'onjiSTa* area, while in Bumburet they manage in the end to break into it and to seize the *inw'aw g'Uak*. In Birir is represented the supremacy of one of the two poles, which annihilates its opposite, while in Bumburet we have the revelation of their junction in a superior unity. The *coniunctio* represented in the rituals of the Birir Chaumos belongs apparently to the 'regressive' type, in which the aspiration to reach the integration of the opposites is expressed through the symbolic representation of the primordial chaos preceding creation. In Bumburet, in addition to this 'regressive' notion of duality, we can seemingly detect also the third type of coincidence of opposites, the true *coniunctio* in Pensa's view. In this light, the difference between the two winter solstice festivals appears to be due to a true process of development – rather than divergence – with the Birir variety representing a logically earlier stage. As in the Christian vision of the relations between the Old and the New Testament, the structural transformation represented by Balimain would have brought to their full flowering ideas already present in the Birir Chaumos, enriching them with a deep new meaning.

Mircea Eliade ([1962] 1971: 84–5), it seems, was not mistaken when he wrote

that late Indian metaphysics did not do much more than re-elaborate and systema-
tize themes already expressed in a mythical-symbolical form in the pre-systematic
phase of Indian thought. Just like Mary Douglas was quite right when she wrote
half a century ago that 'The more we know about primitive religions the more
clearly it appears that in their symbolic structures there is scope for meditation
on the great mysteries of religion and philosophy' (Douglas 1966: 5).[39] Let us
consider then the overall meaning of the symbolic system ritually expressed in
Chaumos, to detect the perceptions that underlie it and the cultural ideals that
inspire it.

Kalasha cosmology

We have now reached the crucial point: the deep meaning of Chaumos. A lot, in
fact, has been anticipated because in the course of our narration we discussed the
meanings of the single ritual events we called 'ritemes', by analogy with morphemes. Although semantically autonomous, as bearers, like morphemes, of the
smaller unit of meaning, these ritemes are combined in Chaumos so as to generate
new meanings that transcend them, just like morphemes generate new meanings
when they combine to form words. On these relational meanings we shall now
focus our attention.

Due to the conservative power of ritual, the Kalasha Chaumos is in all likelihood
a ritual complex of great antiquity. We have seen that the name itself of the festival
derives from the four-monthly celebrations of Vedic times (*cāturmasyā*), and that
the Visitor god invoked in the most sacred days of the feast is none other than Indra,
the ancient tutelary deity of the Vedic Indo-Aryans, marginalized in later Hinduism. What transformations the festival may have undergone in the course of the
centuries we have no way of knowing. Certainly some rites may have been obliterated – as possibly indicated by the song of Jhani maybe referring to animal masks,
or by the name Nongrat perhaps containing a reference to the primordial serpent-
monster of which there is, however, no trace in the rituals – and others may have
been modified. Yet, it seems quite certain that what is documented in this work is
a constellation of ritual events celebrated in roughly the same form for many generations. Echoes of remote times undoubtedly resonate in the Kalasha Chaumos.
Yet, we are not dealing with a fossil, but with something very much alive where,
together with the voice of the ancestors, we can hear the voice of the Kalasha of
today, as shown by Danok's song about Erfan's defeat at the latest elections.

---

39 On this point see also Victor Turner [1969] 1990: 12.

For the Kalasha, Chaumos is one of the three great traditions (*tre gh'ona dast'ur*), together with *aLaS'in~g*, the love marriage by elopement, and *biram'or*, the main distributive feast. Since these two, however, both concern the social sphere, Chaumos alone occupies the central position in the religious sphere. As fulcrum of the ritual system, the winter solstice festival is the event that expresses in the most complete way the cultural ideals of the society, i.e. the vision of the world inscribed in the Kalasha symbolic system. It will certainly be clear by now, that we are dealing with an organic complex endowed with a unitary nexus expressing coherent values, which correspond to mental attitudes and behavioural models that give their imprint to Kalasha culture as a whole. We are talking, of course, about cultural ideals, independently of their actual implementation. As warned, we are investigating the plane of ideology, not the plane of practice.

Three great themes are intertwined in the rites of Chaumos and of the winter ritual sequence as a whole: regeneration, fertility, and unification or communion.

Regeneration is achieved through the rites of purification, but especially through the great collective rite of passage that relives the beginning of the world, and marks for the initiates the start of a new phase of individual life and for the community the beginning of a new annual cycle. It is a theme that runs through the entire sequence, from the burning of old baskets in the preparatory day of Chaumos (*acar'ik – ganDalik'an*) to the second phase of the initiation rites celebrated two months later for *ra'istam*, which concludes the winter feasts and inaugurates the season of sowing.

Fertility accompanies regeneration as its natural consequence. Rebirth brings with it the energy of procreation. Fecundity of humans, animals and fields is invoked especially in the second part of the Birir Chaumos as well as in the continuation of the sequence, until the descent of the mythical White Crow, bringer of abundance and until the rite of *benjist'em* on the first day of the New Year, in which offerings are made to a cult object possibly representing the sexual act.

Unification, forged in the clash between opposed groups, concerns first the minimal segments, the lineages, which gather in their temples, then larger units like the macro-lineages and, finally, the two sections – upstream and downstream – that challenge each other in the running race in Praba's valley. With the early morning sacrifice at the shrine of the god the unification with the divine is celebrated while, with the arrival of the markhor that symbolically mix with humans in the last dance of the central day of Chaumos, human society is joined to the *'onjiSTa* world of the mountain wilderness. At the climax of the festival, we have seen, unification, or better communion, with the divine, with nature, and between men is celebrated in a single day.

In Rumbur and Bumburet we have the descent of the deceased – commemorated in Birir only with some offerings – who are reunited with their descendants,
even if only for the brief time of a meal. Finally the god of life descends in the
valleys in the most sacred night of the year and the world of humans is united to
the world of the gods, as in the mythical golden age the event evokes. In the shamanic performance, like the one we witnessed in Rumbur in 1973, the channel of
direct communication is ritually opened, and in the trance of the dance the bodily
experience of that unity becomes accessible to everyone. In the Chaumos of the
two northern valleys a new symbol appears: the androgynous Visitor god that
represents the quintessential unity of all polarities. In Birir the notion of a Visitor
god is present, but is rather veiled and remains without a ritual expression, while
the idea of the coincidence of opposites, we have just seen, is apparently more
rudimentary than in Bumburet/Rumbur. On the whole, however, the two variants
of the Kalasha symbolic complex are based on a common pattern: we shall now
try to analyze it to bring to light the complete system of its implicit and explicit
meanings and their relations. The system appears to stem from a deep cosmogonic
level from which it expands to the most explicit and concrete levels of ecological,
social, and economic relations.[40]

At the deepest level – discernible in the system but far removed from the perception of the Kalasha of today – seems to emerge the opposition between the
world of forms and the Unformed preceding creation. An Unformed that has the
trait of ambiguity, because it can take up the antithetic qualities of Chaos or of the
Golden Age (Caillois [1939] 2001: 105): we have seen it with the disorderly traits
of Chaos in the backward dance of the spirits who wreak havoc in the rite of *bhut
ungush'ek*, held in Birir every three years, as well as in the insults addressed to the
elders, and with the harmonious traits of the Golden Age when humans, animals
and gods lived together, evoked by the descent of the god. If Chaos is ambiguous,
so too is its opposite, the Cosmos. If on the one hand it represents the reign of
peace and order, on the other it is also the reign of ruin and decay. Hence it needs
to be periodically re-fecundated by its opposite, because it is from the absence of
order of the Unformed that the vital force derives its energy.

The opposition between the Unformed, bringer of life, and the world of forms
subject to decay, mirrors the opposition between immortal life and mortal life that

---

40 The discussion that follows elaborates on an analysis of the Kalasha symbolic system
first outlined by Alberto M. Cacopardo in an article in Italian (Cacopardo A.M. 1985) and
subsequently synthesized by him in a joint article in English with the present author (Cacopardo &
Cacopardo 1989).

is at the origin of the universal experience of the transiency of human life. The passage suffered from the former to the latter dimension, which takes place with birth, is accomplished through the female function of generation. The male/female polarity occupies therefore the subsequent level. The identification of the female gender with the *pr'agata* (or *r'ela* in the language of Birir) sphere is based on the idea of her impurity. The impurity of women, especially in connection with the menstrual cycle and childbearing, is a notion widely spread in the Euro-Asiatic continent, as well as elsewhere,[41] and is present also in Judaism (Levitic 12, 2–4) and in Christianity. As it concerns the Kalasha, Peter Parkes proposes a sociological explanation of it. In his view the definition itself of a strictly masculine and pastoral sphere of the sacred would derive from the constant threat (in the male perspective) brought to the stability of marriages by the institution of *aLaS'in~g*, which allows a married woman to elope with a man of her choice (Parkes 1987: 652–3). Thence the idea of danger, expressed by the notion of the impurity of women, and the consequential definition of an anti-pastoral feminine sphere of the impure, to be kept strictly separate from its opposite.

Although the belief that women are dangerous at the time of menstruation may certainly be used, as remarked by Mary Douglas (1957b: 61–3), in interpersonal conflicts and in general 'for manipulating a social situation', the notion of female impurity among the Kalasha cannot be reduced to an ideological device aimed at justifying a hierarchical social relation between the sexes, as shown by the fact that virgin boys who, like all the young in general, have a low social status, are at the top of the hierarchy of purity among humans.[42]

We have seen that two places are absolutely *pr'agata*, the cemetery and the *bash'ali*. While the impurity of the former can be easily explained because it is the seat of death, it is not as easy to explain the impurity of the *bash'ali*, the house for giving birth, which would seem to represent its exact opposite. But the opposition here, rather than between birth and death, is between birth-and-death, the emblem of human transiency, and life-without-beginning-or-end. Hence the house where birth takes place is *pr'agata* like the place where death has its abode: Dizalik, Friedrich was told, is the goddess of death, as well as the goddess of birth (Jettmar 1975: 350). For their function in generation, women are therefore

---

41 For example,Van Gennep [1909] 1981: 39, 40, 43, 48; Harper 1964: 158–61, 167–9; Gluckman 1965: 248–50; Dumont [1966] 1979: 70–1; Owen [1981] 1996: 136; Chandra 1992: 258; Bell 1997: 96–7, 119; Nicoletti 2006: 99–100.

42 Cacopardo A.M. in Cacopardo & Cacopardo 1989: 327.

symbolically connected to the sphere of birth and death,[43] while men are symbolically associated with the opposed sphere of beginning-less and endless life. This is
the polarity expressed in Greek by the terms *bíos* and *zoé*. Karl Kerényi analyzed
its semantics: the former designates 'characterized life', the latter 'life without
any further characterization and without limits'; *bios* is not opposed to death to
the point of excluding it, while *zoé* is, because it rejects it: 'what clearly resonates
in *zoé* is "non-death"' (Kerényi [1976] 1993: 19). In other words we have on one
side mortal life that characterizes the human condition, and on the other immortal
life, of which the gods are a reflection. The impurity of the woman in the Kalasha
system appears therefore to stem from a profound 'cosmogonic view that ascribes
her the role of generating the world of mortal forms', of characterized life, indissolubly connected to death, 'by harnessing the immortal vital energy carried by
the male'.[44] This 'mother of all distinctions', the male/female polarity, in the case
of the Kalasha is reflected on the whole territory and takes on a concretely ecological aspect in the opposition between the higher and wilder realm of goat-herding,
and the lower and domestic reign of fields and villages.

   One of the fundamental axioms of the Kalasha symbolic system is an explicit
connection between the wild and the sacred: the quintessential *'onjiSTa* space is
that of the summer pastures and of the peaks of the mountains inhabited by the
s'uci spirits, and the shrines of the gods, as we have seen, are always located
outside the space of fields and villages, above them on the slopes of the mountains, or upstream from them in hidden thickets or other isolated places. It is a
connection that may have deep roots in the cultural history of humanity. Its most
archaic manifestations are probably to be found in the worldview that the late
Basilov (1999: 39) – a Russian scholar of Shamanism – has depicted as typical of
shamanic ideology,[45] the origins of which possibly hark back to the Palaeolithic
world of hunting and gathering. In that vision man '… is not a king of nature.
He is just one of the links in a chain of various forms of life' (ibid.: 26). In other
words, the relationship between humanity and the natural environment is seen in
terms opposed to those outlined at the beginning of Genesis (i, 26) where humans
are given 'dominion over the fish of the sea, and over the fowl of the air, and over

---

43 The 'perception of a contiguity between who generates life and the formless world of the dead
and the non-born' has been referred to also by Ginzburg ([1989] 2008: 282), who remarks that
the Celtic goddess Epona, like other related figures of folklore, is at once protector of delivering
women and emissary of the world of the dead (ibid.: 83).
44 Cacopardo A.M. in Cacopardo & Cacopardo 1989: 327.
45 See Descola 2005: 42–4 for a critique of the idea of shamanism as an 'archaic religion'.

the cattle, and over all the earth and over every creeping thing that creepeth upon the earth.' In contrast with this anthropocentric model,[46] the cosmological axiom we are considering implies that humans are beings among many, and that the resources of nature do not belong to them but to the spirits who are their guardians. In the space of the wild, men are guests, not masters.[47] The opposition that seems to emerge is that between the wild and the domestic.

The French anthropologist Philippe Descola (2005: 58–90) has harshly criticized this distinction, which he sees as an aspect of that between nature and culture.[48] He argues that it stems from a particular historical experience, that it is the creation of Western thought, and that many cultures simply do not conceive of it. While this can no doubt be said of the nature and culture opposition, we are not so sure that it is true for that between the wild and domestic. The meanings of the two antinomies do not necessarily coincide. In the Kalasha system the classical contrast between nature and culture cannot be discerned, while a distinction between the wild and the domestic is quite apparent. Linguistically it is expressed by the couple *pariL'oy/machiLoy*, respectively the wild world of the fairies and the world of the fields. The meanings associated with the two poles may be somewhat implicit, but they are certainly not those of the nature/culture opposition of Western discourse. The mountain wilderness is not seen as 'a residual sector, useless to men, or destined to fall in time under his domination' (Descola 2005: 84), or as a refuge for threatening enemies, nor is the domestic realm considered the reign of order and civilized behaviour. In contrast, positive values and qualities are attached to the wild rather than to the domestic. Untamed nature is the abode of the mountain spirits, an ideal world of harmony that humans strive to imitate, while the domestic world of the village is strewn with conflict and corruption. Certainly the opposition does not imply a partition between 'an anthropised homeland and an environment perpetuating itself outside human reach' (Descola 2005: 64). Humans inhabit both worlds but in different ways.

In fact, the meaning of the wild/domestic opposition in the Kalasha symbolic

---

46 Lanternari 2003: 53. See Descola 2005: 102–5 for a discussion of the role played by Christianity in the definition of the concept of the superiority of humans over nature, seen as a realm separate from that of humanity.

47 See Hultkranz (1961) for guardian spirits of nature, and Descola (2005: 37–50) for a characterization of this attitude on the basis of a vast array of ethnographic examples from a great variety of geographic contexts.

48 An opposition already much criticized: an 'artificial creation of culture' for A. Buttitta (1996: 34). See also Geertz [1973] 1987: 73–97; Ingold 2001: 77, 112–39.

system can only be fully understood if we relate it to that between animal husbandry and agriculture. Only the former, we know, is *'onjiSTa*. Though the wild, uncontrolled, space of animal husbandry is quite distinct from the controlled domestic space of fields and villages, animal husbandry is also a way of inhabiting a territory.

Husbandry belongs to the *'onjiSTa* sphere of the wild first of all because it depends from it materially, since it is in the wilderness of forests and pastures that the resources to nourish the herds are found. But at a deeper level, implicit in the system, husbandry belongs to the *'onjiSTa* sphere because it is based on a relationship with the natural environment very different from that implied by agriculture. Cultivation requires a profound manipulation of the land on the part of humans, who make fields by shaping the terrain according to their needs and by eliminating the plants they consider useless to make room for those necessary for their existence. With agriculture, humans become lords of nature and dispose of other species at their leisure, as envisaged by the anthropocentric model of Genesis. Animal husbandry does not require, in contrast, any manipulation of the land on the part of men, nor does it require the elimination of all plants useless for humans. The opposition, in fact, is not between a non-human and a human world – supposedly nature and culture – but between two different ways of 'inhabiting' (Ingold [1995] 2001: 113) the natural environment. In this optics we do not find among the Kalasha the opposition between herding and hunting that, for Descola (2005: 85), has nourished in the Mediterranean world the antinomy between wild and domestic. On the contrary, in the Kalasha symbolic system, not only hunting and herding both belong in the *'onjiSTa* sphere, but hunting in the 'graded' *'onjiSTa* category occupies a higher place, as the prototypical *'onjiSTa* activity. Hunting is practised in the mountain wilderness and requires the favour of the mountain spirits, who must be won over with the appropriate rituals. The hunter only appropriates from the natural environment what his guardian spirits allow him to take. As the least environment-affecting activity, hunting could be placed at one end of an ideal continuum that would have urbanization at its opposite end.[49]

The cosmological axiom that connects the two polarities – wild/domestic and animal husbandry/agriculture – includes an implicit ethical stance concerning the appropriate relation between humanity and the natural environment. An ethical stance that appears to be connected to what Lanternari (2003: 55–75) has defined as an 'ideology of sacrilege', an attitude widely documented in traditional

---

49 Cacopardo A.M. 1985: 722

societies, among hunter/gatherers as well as among stockbreeders and cultivators.[50] In societies of this type, the killing of an animal or in general the acquisition
of any type of natural resource is perceived as an unwarranted appropriation, or it
can even be experienced as 'sacrilege', a violation for which ritual amends must
be made. Among the Kalasha, rituals are prescribed before starting for the hunt
and only with a ritual, we have seen, can a domestic animal be killed.

We may see a reflection of the dialectics animating the Kalasha system in
the Biblical myth in which Yahweh accepts with favour the pastoral products
offered by the shepherd Abel while looks with disdain on the agricultural products
offered by Cain, tiller of the land. If the passage of Genesis quoted above presents
an anthropocentric model of the relationship between humans and nature, in the
episode of Cain and Abel may be reflected the opposed model, which condemns
the 'grand partage', to use Descola's (2005) expression, i.e. the 'great separation'
between humans and all other living beings that allows the subversion of the
natural environment inevitably implied by agriculture.

But we are not dealing here with a discourse concerning only the relations
between humans and nature. The message of the myth concerns also the plane
of relations between men: Cain, the tiller of the land, the first murderer in the
history of humanity, finally becomes the founder of the first city mentioned in the
Bible (Genesis 3, 17). A connection appears to emerge between the subversion
of the monistic perspective – which sees humans as part of one living whole and
not as dominators over a separate world – made possible by agriculture, and the
subsequent course of history that led, in some crucial parts of the world at least,
to the establishment of urban-centred civilizations with their emphasis on social
stratification and separation from nature (Cacopardo A.M. 1985: 722–3).

For the Kalasha, as we have seen (Chapter 2), agriculture is the sphere of
separation and appropriation, where private property is the rule, while husbandry
is the sphere of sharing. The opposition of animal husbandry/agriculture is therefore symmetrical to the one between sharing and keeping. If the first of these
two polarities is absolutely explicit, we may think that the second one should be
seen, rather, as only implicit in the logic of the system. This, however, is not the
case. We are dealing here with a fundamental cultural ideal of which the Kalasha

---

50 See Frazer [1922] 1987: 466–7; Evans-Pritchard 1956: 265–6; Di Nola 1974: 236–8; Lanternari
[1976] 1983a: 429–42, 2003: 62–3; Grottanelli 1999: 30; Descola 2005: 35–6; Buttitta I.E.
2006: 151–2; Nicoletti 2006: 215–16. It is an attitude, however, found also in some great literate
civilizations (see Hubert & Mauss [1899] 1909: 46; Heesterman 1993: 34; Grottanelli 1999: 11,
30–3, 41–2).

of today are totally aware. The words that follow have been recorded in 2006 by the Danish researcher and filmmaker Birgitte Glavind Sperber (Glavind Sperber & Yasir Kalash 2007) from the lips of one of the most authoritative elders of Rumbur, kazì Palleawan:

> Our lineages always help each other. We give to each other. Always, when there is a celebration someone gives *prach'ona* [clarified butter] and cheese. We Kalasha like goats very much. In our Kalasha tradition sharing is very important. We give to each other. Often we help each other for free, without any money. I help him, he helps me and him as well.

Palleawan obviously voices an ideal not always mirrored in the practice of social life – an ideal that lives especially in the ceremonial sphere of social rituals and celebrations, while is not infrequently set aside in the sphere of ordinary life, where conflictuality is certainly not unknown (Parkes 1983: Chapter 7). Nevertheless, there could not be a clearer and simpler formulation of the principle of sharing within the group and of its connection to the pastoral sphere. It is the same principle we found sharply expressed in a verse of a Chaumos song that celebrates reciprocity – ' when I receive then I give to you' – which reminded us of the famous sentence quoted by Mauss in his *Essay sur le don*: 'So much Maru gives, as much as Maru takes. And this is good, is good'. As remarked by Alberto M. Cacopardo (1985: 723) 'there is here a connection between the communion of humans with nature and the communion beween humans that is perhaps the most important contribution the analysis of the symbolic world of the Kalasha can offer to cultural-historical reflection'. The subjugation of nature by man is put in relation to the subjugation of man by man, because they both derive from an act of appropriation. Just as the appropriation of natural resources is perceived as a violation, so is perceived the appropriation – or the accumulation, if we want – of goods that should rather be distributed, which causes discord and conflict, and generates domination. It is not, however, a universalistic ethos open to all human beings. As is usually the case in traditional societies, we are dealing with an ethics limited to the members of the group, which even with allies exhibits different connotations. Beyond those limits, there is the enemy, who remains outside the horizon of ethics, against whom any act of violence is admitted and even exalted (Cacopardo A.M. 2011), as shown by the traditional system of rank that conferred the title of *sh'ora moc* for the killing of an enemy. But within the group, sharing and solidarity are the rule.

The most fundamental application of the principle of sharing, the one that perhaps comes before all others, we find it in the marriage system. We have seen that among the Kalasha whoever violates the exogamic rule becomes totally and irredeemably *pr'agata* and is expelled from society. Just as it is a violation the appropriation of natural resources and of goods that should be distributed, so is an even worse violation the appropriation of the women of one's own line of descent.

Therefore, *'onjiSTa* represents the cultural ideals on which Kalasha society is based: the idea that humans are not the masters of nature, that material goods can only be accumulated to be shared, and that the women of one's own group must not be appropriated. The deep philosophical foundation of this ethics of sharing can be found in the principle expressed in Balimain's theophany: the *coniunctio oppositorum*. As in Tim Ingold's mycological model,[51] what appears on the surface to be separate, like the individual mushrooms, is in fact connected underneath by a hidden network of which the individual organisms are an emergence: the other is not separate from the self, this is the deep meaning of the *coniunctio* (cf. Watts [1963] 1978: 68).[52] The monistic character of Kalasha cosmology is expressed in the ritual symbol. Sharing then logically follows and the harmony among men 'pleases the gods of the mountain crests', as the lyrics say of one of the songs of Chaumos. This is the vision at the core of the Kalasha symbolic system, ritually enacted in the great winter solstice festival.

We have here a true cosmology, in the sense of Tambiah ([1985] 1995: 132), that is, a coherent system that puts in relation 'man with man, man with nature and the animals, and man with gods and demons and other non-human entities', or, in the words of Izard and Smith ([1985] 1995: 132), a system aimed 'at accounting for the relationship of man with nature, with society, and in the last instance with his own individual destiny'. It is a cosmology, however, that is never fully applied in everyday life and that ritual periodically reaffirms. It is indeed the aim of ritual to reintegrate the condition of purity continually eroded by the reality of the human condition. In the winter solstice festival, more than in any other feast of the calendar, this reaffirmation takes place through the concrete, corporeal, experience of that unity, in the sharing of food, in praying the gods, and in the exaltation of the songs and dances that brings with it the experience of limitless life that only

---

51 Ingold 2004: 302–6; see also 2001: 79. Ingold is a British anthropologist with interests including human/animal relations and ecological approaches in anthropology.

52 A concept present in Hinduism (Watts [1963] 1978: 76), as well as in the Buddhist notion of *anatman*, non-self. In this perspective separation and hence contraposition of interests are the fruit of the limited perception typical of the human condition (Ib: XV).

in the sacred time of the feast can be fully lived.[53] The ideal is not only reaffirmed, but is enacted.[54] Such is indeed the power of ritual.

---

53 Cf. Kerenyi [1976] 1993: 21.
54 Cf. Geertz [1973] 1987: 168.

PART III

Intercultural Connections

Introduction

After this laborious analysis of the Kalasha ritual system, the urge comes quite spontaneously to seek broader horizons and to ask how this archaic complex – the expression, we must keep in mind, of a much wider culture area – might fit within the context of the Indian world and of the Indo-European universe in general. Although not only the Kalasha, but Nuristan and eastern Peristan as well, have been studied by anthropologists, linguists, historians and geographers for many decades, only a few steps[1] have in fact been made in the direction of a comparative approach aimed at exploring the broader cultural horizons to which Peristan must be in some way connected, either for distant common origins or, despite its historical condition of isolation, for subsequent contacts. We shall therefore dedicate the third part of this work to a search for intercultural connections that will concern the Indian world, archaic Europe and the Proto-Indo-Europeans. What we offer is, however, only an initial survey with no other aim than to suggest some possible lines of investigation for future research. We shall therefore only propose some possible parallels, without drawing any proper conclusions, limiting our analysis to the indication of some hypothesis that in our view deserve consideration.

What we propose are three possible directions that comparative research could follow. The first one is that of the comparison with the Indian world which, though already followed, and with some important results, would need to be extended, we suggest, beyond the Vedic world, to Brahmanism and popular Hinduism. The

---

1 For what concerns the Kalasha, see Parkes (1987), who proposes a comparison between agro-pastoral mountain cultures from the Hindu Kush to the Pyrenees

second one concerns pre-Christian Europe and its reflections on European folk-lore – an almost unexplored line of research on which we even attempt some provisional conclusions. The third one is that of comparison with the Proto-Indo-European world, as reconstructed by linguists and archaeologists. This direction has also remained quite untrodden. After a solitary article by the British social anthropologist Nick Allen (1991) who tried to apply Dumézil's trifunctional model to the Bashgali pantheon, only rather recently the Harvard Indologist Michael Witzel has taken into consideration the pre-Islamic world of the Hindu Kush in an essay dedicated to the roots of the Rig Vedic religious system (Witzel 2004). A fourth direction of research, which we consider here only fleetingly for lack of data, deserves, however, to be investigated at length, that of the relations of our area with the Iranian world. For Fussman (1977: 25) Iranic influences had only minor weight, but Jettmar (1974; 1986: 135–7), as well as other scholars,[2] did not hold the same view. In Birir, readers will recall, we did find some scant trace of possible Iranian influences, especially in the festive nucleus of *salgher'ek* and perhaps in the derivation – if correct – of the name *bidrakal'en* from *vrtragahn*, killer of Vrtra, a name possibly rooted in Indo-Iranian times.[3]

The interest of such research would no doubt be great. They are, of course, complex investigations requiring specific competences, but they can be an important line of development of the work conducted so far.

---

2 See Tucci 1963: 158, and Gnoli 1980: 70–4.
3 For a more in depth analysis of these elements see Cacopardo A.S. 2016.

7

Peristan and the Indian World

The pre-Islamic cultures of Nuristan and the Indian world

From the linguistic point of view, as we have said, Peristan belongs to the Indian world. Dardic languages are wholly Indo-Aryan languages that only a few features keep distinct from the languages of the plains, and even the Nuristani languages, in spite of their peculiarities, are on the whole closer to the Indo-Aryan than to the Iranic branch of the eastern Indo-European languages (Buddruss 1973, pp. 38–9). For Fussman (1977: 24–5), we have seen, the connection was not only linguistic, but cultural as well: in his view, even Nuristan, the westernmost inaccessible corner of our area, was once, culturally, a part of the Indian world, though only a very remote and marginal one.[1] This connection was seemingly perceived, at least to some extent, by the population: some of the earliest sources[2] relate that Hindu merchants were normally admitted, and hospitably welcomed, even in the fastness of ancient Kafiristan, where no Muslim could set foot. The traditional hairstyle of men who shaved their head letting only a short pigtail grow on the nape, also showed Indian affinities.

The attention of scholars who first embarked on the path of comparison focussed therefore on the Indian rather than the Iranian world. The efforts of these early researchers concentrated initially on the pre-Islamic cultures of Kafiristan (present-day Nuristan), as the last polytheistic stronghold of the Hindu Kush on which, in addition to the eyewitness account left by the British Colonel George Scott Robertson (1896), other important data could be collected through

---

1 A view also shared by Morgenstierne (1947: 240).
2 Mohan Lal 1846: 342; Gardner [1869] 1977: 50; Goes in Wessels [1924] 1997: 15.

interviews with elderly people who still had memory of the pre-Islamic world in which they were raised.[3]

The first steps were made in the field of historical linguistics. Georg Morgenstierne, who did pioneering work in the Hindu Kush beginning in 1924, investigated in many works[4] the etymologies of terms that could shed light on the cultural and historical background of the speakers of Nuristani and Dardic languages. His linguistic materials were used by Ralph L. Turner for his monumental work *A Comparative Dictionary of Indo-Aryan Languages* (Turner 1966).[5]

Morgenstierne's work was continued by the German linguist and Indologist Georg Buddruss who extended his research to the field of mythology, attempting this type of comparison for the first time. He (Buddruss 1960, 2002) highlighted significant correspondences between Vedic cosmology and the cosmology expressed in the mythology of the Kafirs of the Prasun valley, held to be the religious centre of Kafiristan. He saw a correspondence between the celestial sea of the Vedic Cosmos called *rtasya sadana* (the Abode of Truth) and the sacred *Sujum* lake of the people of Prasun, which in their symbolic system represents the Beyond and in its very name recalls the concept of fair law, justice, which in the Vedic system is a concept very close to Truth (Buddruss 2002: 131). He found also that one of their main myths showed the imprint of the Vedic theme of the fight between Indra and the primordial monster symbolizing Chaos (Buddruss 1974). In this connection, an important finding made by Buddruss in the field of etymology is that the Prasun word *bem* could be 'the only survival known so far, in a modern language, of the Rig Vedic meaning of Sanskrit *brahman-*' (Buddruss 1973: 42), which did not mean 'the absolute' as in later philosophical speculation, but belonged semantically to the sphere of 'religious hymn, poem, prayer' (ibid.: 41). Recently, Buddruss has made an invaluable contribution to Hindu Kush studies with the publication of his complete collection of Prasun texts (Buddruss, Degener 2015).

After him, the greatest effort was made by Gérard Fussman.[6] Through an

---

3 A written document containing such memories is the autobiography of Shaikh Muhammad Abdullah Khan Azar (Cacopardo Alberto M. & Ruth L. Schmidt eds. 2006).

4 Especially in Morgenstierne 1949, 1951 and 1973 (Fussman 1977: 27 fn.17). For a complete bibliography of his works from 1903 to 1972 compiled at the Indo-Iranian Institute of Oslo University by Knut Kristiansen and Inge Ross see Morgenstierne 1973.

5 See Chapter 2 ft. 13.

6 The topic of relations with the Indian world had also attracted the attention of Max Klimburg who, in an attempt to interpret the meaning of some wooden images of intertwined couples found

etymological analysis of the names of gods and spirits he concluded that the most ancient stratum of the Kafir pantheon is Indian (Fussman 1977: 33–4) and therefore comparable to the Vedic pantheon with which, on the basis of linguistic arguments, he highlighted several parallels. Yet, in his view, the roots of the cultures of Kafiristan are pre-Vedic, though post-Iranian: i.e. they date back to a time when the Iranian world had already begun to take form but the spiritual world of the Vedas was still not consolidated. In the centuries that followed, he believes, they developed in isolation without any contact with the Indian world, except through the Dardic domain which, in contrast, is wholly Indo-Aryan, both linguistically and culturally (ibid.: 35). In a later work Fussman (1983: 204) nuanced his position, recognizing that relations between Kafiristan and India had possibly been more complex than he had formerly thought, but he remained convinced that the proposals he had made in his 1977 article were still valid. Fussman, in that same article (ibid.: 61–5), extended his comparison beyond the pantheon, to the social structure, and he argued that pre-Islamic Nuristani societies were divided in social groups strongly reminiscent of the four original Indian castes: the *varna*. But data subsequently acquired showed that ancient Kafiristan was not a caste society and that the only true distinction was of that between a majority of free men and a small minority of slave-artisans – a division, as we have seen, found throughout Peristan.[7]

The Kalasha religious system and the Vedic religion

Due to the fascination exerted by the larger and richer cultural context of Kafiristan, only limited attention was at first given to the Kalasha by comparative research, though their culture was the only one still observable of the many that once composed the complex constellation of Peristan. In fact, if in the field of mythology the Kalasha compare quite poorly with the pre-Islamic cultures of the speakers of Nuristani languages, the contribution their culture can give from the point of view of ritual has been unjustly overlooked. Only more recently has Kalasha material been taken into proper consideration by Michael Witzel (2004) in the study mentioned above on the roots of the Rig-Vedic system.

---

in south Nuristan, advanced the hypothesis of a connection between Kafir concepts and Tantric beliefs (Klimburg 1976; 1999: 138, 313), a proposal already fleetingly aired by Edelberg (1960: 282).

7 For the complete argument against Fussman's proposal see Cacopardo & Cacopardo 2001: 43–4. On this point see also Klimburg (1999: 62, 346–8) who comes to the same conclusions.

Witzel refers in his comparison both to the pre-Islamic Nuristani and Kalasha religions, always specifying the position of each. Also, he analyzes the pre-Islamic religion(s) of the Hindu Kush as a system, considering not only the mythology, but also rituals and festivals. His conclusion is that 'In sum, the Hindu Kush area shares many of the traits of Indo-Iranian myths, ritual, society, and echoes many aspects of Rgvedic, but hardly of post-Rgvedic religion' (Witzel 2004: 614). His endeavour ventures far back into the Indo-Iranian world – and beyond that, into the Proto-Indo-European and even Eurasian universes – but the scope of his research brings him to investigate more in depth the Indian than the Iranian side. The traits he enucleates as Rig-Vedic antecedents include the existence of a creator god like Imra whose name is connected – as Fussman (1977: 30), and Morgenstierne before him (1951: 163), had already pointed out – to Sanskrit Yama Raja; the preponderance in myth and ritual of the typically South-Asian number 7 in contrast to the northern Eurasian 9; and, more importantly, the presence of an 'Indra-like figure' appearing in various forms and under various names (Witzel 2004: 606–7). Apart from the field of mythology, his contribution is particularly significant with regard to ritual and festivals; in his view, ritual in Hindu Kush religion is still of the Indo-Iranian type but South-Asian and Vedic influences can be detected. Among other features, he notes the exogamic rule mirroring the Vedic one, the importance of the concept of purity, as in India, which affects the status of women and prompts the exclusion from ritual of a group of artisan/serfs who form a caste of untouchables, like the Vedic Sudras; and he draws an interesting parallel between the role of virgin boys as semi-priests – they are the ones who should physically perform rites – and that of the Brahmacharins of the Atharva Veda.

Indeed, if we look at the Indian universe, the most manifest connections in the Kalasha system are with the Vedic world. We have highlighted many of these connections in the course of our narration (Part II), but it may be useful to briefly list them again here:

(a) The names of several divinities are etymologically connected to those of the Vedic pantheon, and especially to Indra. This is the case of the two main gods of the Birir valley, Warin and Praba, whose names can be derived respectively from *aparendra (unrivalled Indra) (T-444), and prabavhra, one of the names of Indra (T-8782). The very name Indra has also been preserved in that of the god Balimain (bal'ima-In, most powerful Indra) – the Visitor god of Bunburet/Rumbur – who is often invoked in ritual as Indr and presents many traits of the Vedic Indra. The name of Balimain's servant, Pushaw (p'ushaw), is connected to the Vedic Pushan, a pastoral

divinity connected to the winter months. Other Vedic connections concern
the goddess Jeshtak, whose name may be derived from that of the Rig
Vedic goddess *dēSTrī* (T-6556) or, possibly from *jyeSTha*, the first, the
eldcr (T-5286); the *JaC* spirit(s) connected to agriculture whose name is
etymologically related to the Sanskrit *yaksha* (T-10395), spirits venerated
since pre-Vedic times, possibly vegetation deities; the name of the *s'uci*
mountain spirits derivable from *sucikā*, one of the Apsaras (T-12510) or
from **suvatsika*, a goddess (T-13514), as well as, last but not least, the
two terms designating the gods: *d'ewa*, manifestly connected to Sanskrit
deva- (T-6523), and *dewal'ok* derived from *devaloka*, the abode of the gods
(T-6539).

(b) Equally important connections can be found in the field of ritual. As we
have seen, the name of the main event of the whole Kalasha ritual cycle,
the Chaumos (*caum'os*) winter solstice festival, is derived from Sanskrit.
The connection is with the *cāturmāsya* (T-4742) festivals which, in Vedic
times, were celebrated every four months in spring, in summer during the
rainy season, and in autumn; in fact, the Kalasha ritual cycle itself appears
to correspond quite closely to the Vedic one because it is subdivided into
three great ritual sequences, though their position in the ritual cycle, due
to climatic differences, obviously does not coincide with the Vedic one. A
further interesting correspondence in the field of ritual, is that of the term
diC designating the holiest period of the winter solstice festival when, to
restore a state of purity, the separation of genders is enforced: the men retire
to the goat sheds, and all outsiders are expelled from the villages. *diC* is
related to the Sanskrit term *diksha*, designating the elaborate preparations of
the great soma sacrifice.

(c) At the social level, an important trait connecting not only the Kalasha,
but the whole of Peristan, to the Indian world is the exogamic rule – already
present in the Veda (Witzel 2004: 615) – forbidding marriage between
two people who had a common ancestor in the male line up to the seventh
ascending generation, which governs the formation and the evolution of the
patrilineal lineages. Lineage exogamy is indeed widespread in India, and it is
codified in the *sapinda* system, which is based essentially on the same rule.[8]

As can be seen, parallels and correspondences also abound in the Kalasha case.
From what has been remarked so far it appears that the Indian traits in Kalasha

8 Karve 1953 in Berreman 1972: 158; Nicholas 1981: 371, 377; Goody 1990: 157.

culture are mostly due to common origins rather than to subsequent historical contacts. Nevertheless, we do find some stray traits indicating more recent Hindu influences. Of these the most prominent is the name of the god Mahandeo, that was a honorary title first of Vishnu and then of Shiva,[9] a divinity whose connection to our area, according to Tucci (1963:160), is quite certain.

Traces of more recent Hindu influences have been found also among neighbours of the Kalasha (Cacopardo & Cacopardo 2001: 160) and even in Kafiristan/ Nuristan where we have the seven Paneu brothers (Jettmar 1986: 75–6) that for Morgenstierne (1951: 165, 174–5) are etymologically connected to the Pandava brothers of the *Mahabharata*,[10] or the Kamdesh god Arom who's name, according to Strand (2001: 220 fn. 390), is probably derived from Rama. Quite predictably, more Hindu influences are found in eastern Peristan among the Shina speakers,[11] the alimentary prohibition of beef being the most conspicuous example.[12] In spite of geographical isolation, some contacts with the Hindu world must indeed have occurred before Peristan became encircled by Islam, and even after that. Ruins of a temple of the Hindu Shahi period, from the eighth or ninth century CE, were found as far west as the Kunar valley immediately to the south of Chitral (Lohuizen-de Leeuw 1959), and we know that still in the nineteenth century a sacred spring in Bajaur, just south of our area, formed a pond that once a year attracted many Hindus from the surrounding areas for a ritual bath (Raverty [1880] 1976: 183).[13]

---

9 Stutley [1977] 1988: 249; Gonda in Jettmar 1986: 60.

10 Some doubts are, however, expressed by Fussman (1977: 34) from the semantic point of view, though he recognizes that phonetically the etymology is perfectly viable.

11 Here, in Gilgit, Major John Biddulph was stationed as British Political Agent who, in an influential work, argued in favour of strong Indian influences on the region before the advent of Islam: he believed that Buddhism had been the religion of the area before it was superseded by forms of Hinduism brought by the Shina, whom he saw as immigrants from the south (Biddulph 1880: 109–15). Subsequently, Jettmar came, however, to the conclusion that the pre-Islamic religion of the Shina was 'very distant from the essential beliefs of Hinduism' (Jettmar 1975: 291), and it is quite clear now that, though Hindu influences were more evident among them, the Shina-speakers had a pre-Islamic culture of the Peristani type: see Jettmar 1975: 215–20, and Cacopardo & Cacopardo 2001: 27–8.

12 Cf. Göhlen 1997: 165; Cacopardo & Cacopardo 2001: 137.

13 Morgenstierne (1944: VII) even thought the pre-Islamic religion of the Pashai of the lower Kunar basin in Afghanistan, speakers of a Dardic language, might have been a form of Hindu-Buddhism, but his idea has been proved to be unfounded (see Cacopardo & Cacopardo 2001: 37–8).

However, such traits are few. It seems quite clear that the affinities and connections linking the Kalasha and Peristan to the Indian world point much more to the old Indic world than to Brahminical India. Accordingly, Buddruss, Fussman and Witzel have centered their comparative efforts on the Vedic world. Yet, it may still be interesting to adopt a broader perspective on the Indian world. Taking as a point of reference Kalasha culture, rather than the lesser-known Nuristani cultures, we could extend our gaze to post-Vedic Brahminical India, and therefore to Hinduism. A central role, in such a comparison, can be played by the polarity pure/impure.

The fundamental opposition in the Kalasha symbolic system and in Hinduism

If, finally, we consider the Indian system as a whole, the most significant affinity with the pre-Islamic cultures of the Hindu Kush is maybe the central role played at the symbolic level by the pure/impure polarity. The opposition has been developed in Hinduism in a very complex system obviously very different from the Kalasha and the Peristani ones in general: a system reflecting a highly stratified society that knew writing, the state, and money, and had a class of priests and sacred texts. But an analysis of the articulation of the polarity in the two systems indicates that those very different developments are the fruit of opposed applications of one and the same principle. A comparison between the Indian caste system and the Kalasha system has been recently carried out by Alberto M. Cacopardo (2009: 163–9)[14] on the basis of the famous work by the French anthropologist and Indologist Louis Dumont, *Homo hierarchicus* ([1966] 1979). The central thesis of Dumont's book is that the pure/impure dichotomy encloses the hierarchical principle which, with those of separation and interdependence it subsumes, represents the fundamental principle of Hindu society:

> Cette opposition sous-tend la hierarchie, qui est superiorité du pur sur
> l'impur, elle sous-tend la separation parce qu'il faut tenir séparé le pur de
> l'impur, elle sous-tend la division du travail parce que les occupations pures
> et impures doivent de même être tenues séparées (Dumont [1966] 1979: 65).[15]

---

14 Alberto M. Cacopardo is brother of the author and was director of the various research projects the two researchers conducted in Chitral under the aegis of the *Istituto Italiano per l'Africa e l'Oriente* (IsIAO, ex-IsMEO).

15 'This opposition underlies hierarchy, which means superiority of the pure over the impure,

Alberto M. Cacopardo argues that the same conceptual tools have been used, in the two cases, for radically diverging ends, because in India they generated the highly-stratified caste system, while among the Kalasha they were put at the foundation of an essentially egalitarian system. The principles of hierarchy, separation and division of labour in the case of the Kalasha – he observes – have been used to found the distinction between genders, instead of that between castes.[16] The opposition 'onjiSTa/pr'agata (pure/impure): a) puts the male gender in a condition of ritual superiority; b) founds the separation between genders by denying access to the goat sheds to women and by segregating them in the bash'ali house during menstruation and parturition; c) establishes the division of labour between genders on the basis of the relative purity of their respective occupations. The result is the exact opposite of what happened in India because, by confining the pure/impure distinction solely to the field of gender relations, the effects of the hierarchical principle are limited to that sphere and the principle of equality is conversely, and consequently, affirmed within the genders. Even in the disparity between men and women, the hierarchical principle is therefore rejected as a principle of social organization. The fact is that, in spite of this fundamental difference, the two systems are based on a common core of symbols which is indicated, Alberto Cacopardo also observes, by the circumstance that, in both of them, the prescriptions concerning purity have to do with the organic aspects of human life, which for Dumont ([1966] 1979: 70) are the immediate source of the notion of impurity. Indeed among the Kalasha, as is the case in India,[17] impurity is connected to menstruation and childbirth, as well as to death: women are segregated in the focal moments of their reproductive activity, and, as in India (Dumont [1966] 1979: 74), the relatives of the deceased are temporarily impure and they do not shave for the whole period of mourning. Further, Alberto Cacopardo notes, just as commensality is forbidden between untouchables and the 'twice-born', so are Kalasha women forbidden to eat from the same plate as men and they do not touch the drinking vessels used by males with their lips. The opposed application of the pure/impure polarity made by Brahmanic India has evidently much to do with power, because the ritual hierarchy replicates in the symbolic sphere

---

underlies separation because the pure and impure are to be kept separate, and underlies the division of labour because pure and impure occupations in the same way must be kept separate.' (the translation, as stated in the beginning for all textual quotations, is my own).

16 A similar remark was made also by Jettmar in his main work on the religions of the Hindu Kush (1975, p. 464)

17 Harper 1964: 158–69; Dumont [1966] 1979: 72–3; Nicholas 1981; Levy 1990: 388, 455.

the hierarchy established at the economic and political levels, founding the alliance and the complicity between kings and priests on which is based, as Dumont argues, the whole history of India (Cacopardo Alberto M. 2009: 165–6).

If Kalasha society and the known Peristani systems in general[18] tend to reject hierarchy as the founding principle of social organization, they do not totally expel it from their horizon – we may add – because the pure/impure dichotomy, apart from founding the ritual subordination of women, founds also a division known throughout Peristan between free men and artisan-serfs. If among the Kalasha these were serfs, among the speakers of Nuristani languages, in pre-Islamic times, the members of this group were mostly true artisans (*bar'i*)[19] specializing, as mentioned earlier, in advanced techniques that included wood-carving, metallurgy and ceramics. This subordinate minority was undoubtedly a caste: they formed an endogamous group, deemed inferior, connected to specific occupations; physical contact with its members could contaminate free men, and commensality with them was therefore forbidden; finally, it was an unchangeable status acquired by birth.[20] Furthermore, at variance with what is usually the case in class societies, where the groups of higher status are also the less numerous, here we have a vast majority of free men and only a small minority of serfs,[21] an inversion that, according to Leach ([1960] 1969: 4), is typical of caste societies. The pure/impure polarity did therefore lead in Peristan as well to the emergence of the notion of caste but, nevertheless – Alberto Cacopardo again argues – the principle of hierarchy was not developed in the mountains in the same direction as in the plains; in spite of the presence of this caste of untouchables, Kalasha society and the other known pre-Islamic societies of Peristan in general,[22] remain fundamentally egalitarian because the principle of hierarchy – outside the sphere of gender relations – had only a very limited application. We are certainly not dealing with caste systems. The presence of a small caste of untouchables is not enough to qualify them as such; as observed by Dumont, a society may be so qualified only if in its whole it is divided in a series of castes, which is definitely not the case for the Kalasha and for the other societies of Peristan (Cacopardo Alberto M. 2009: 169).

---

18 An exception is reportedly (comment by Max Klimburg) represented by the pre-Islamic society of the Prasun valley, in Nuristan.

19 A lower class of serfs, called *shūwala* also existed (see e.g. Klimburg 1999: 69–70).

20 We are referring here to the definition of caste given by Hutton (in Leach [1960] 1969: 2–3).

21 Robertson 1896: 102; Duprée 1971: 8; Jones 1974: 95; Klimburg 1999: 62.

22 An exception is reportedly (comment by Max Klimburg) represented by the pre-Islamic society of the Prasun valley, in Nuristan.

Chaumos and Indian religious festivals

Since we have seen that Peristan is close to the Indian world and that, in spite
of their radically different historical development, there is a common symbolic
nucleus at the core of the Indian and the Peristani systems alike, we might wonder
if there could be some affinities also in the cycle of yearly festivals, and, in particular, if there is in India anything resembling Chaumos. To deal with the enormous
complexity of India we must recall here the distinction made, among others, by
Srinivas between Sanskritic and non-Sanskritic Hinduism. By the former Srinivas
means Hinduism based on classical religious texts, usually called post-Vedic or
Brahminical and identified with the 'great tradition'; while by the latter, identified
with the 'lesser tradition', he refers to local or regional customs and beliefs, at
times even pan-Indian, not mentioned in the written religious tradition.[23]

Let us consider first Sanskritic Hinduism. Louis Dumont remarks that what he
calls Hinduism in its most restricted form – which seemingly approaches Srinivas' notion of Sanskritic Hinduism – lacks a characteristic trait of the so-called
'primitive' religions, that is, the subversion of the normal order. It lacks, in other
words, the subversion typical of festive periods – conspicuously present, we have
seen, in Chaumos – in which the sacred makes a temporary irruption in human
societies, overturning ordinary rules of behaviour and replacing prohibition with
licence, separation with union. For him, that subversion is represented in India by
the ascetic with his negation of all that is worldly; it is in the ascetic, rather than
in the feast, that Brahminical order has found its security valve (Dumont [1966]
1979: 342). In fact, a festival does exist in India that has as a central theme the
overturning of ordinary rules; it is the spring celebration called Holi. Dumont, of
course, does not ignore it but he remarks that it is not celebrated throughout the
south of the subcontinent, where the cycle of village life is devoid of all excess.

In the rites of the Holi festival, which takes place at the spring equinox, a
general overturning of social roles is staged, accompanied by abundant aspersions
of water and red powder on the members of the higher castes by the Shudras,
the group occupying the lowest position in the Hindu caste system. Holi is considered to be their festival, and in a sense all those who participate in it become
Shudras because in the days of the celebration everybody is brought to the same
social level. The rituals of Holi upturn the fundamental principle of hierarchy
and erase all differentials of status. The inversion takes place in an atmosphere
of licentiousness and promiscuity, fuelled by an orgiastic rituality expressed with
obscene songs and insults. The phallic theme plays a central role; there are ritual

---

23 Berreman 1972: 82; Das [1977] 1990: 109–10; Chandra 1992: 211–12, 241.

clashes between men and women and cross-dressing, and when the full moon rises huge bonfires are lit around which young men and women dance unrestrained.[24] That the Holi festival is celebrated mainly in northern India could be taken as an indication of a possible connection with the Indo-European world, though not necessarily with Peristan in particular; however, we are faced here with traits that, while conspicuously present in Chaumos, are quite typical of New Year festivals of agrarian societies in general.

Apart from the theme of subversion, the Holi celebration, in fact, differs markedly in its morphology from the Kalasha winter solstice festival. The whole ritual cycle of Sanskritic Hinduism, on the other hand, has little in common with the Kalasha one; this is certainly not surprising if we consider that the system of cyclical feasts is closely connected to productive activities and to the broader socio-historical context. In the Indian climate, with its three seasons regulated by the monsoons, where the sphere of production has completely different characteristics, and in a society with a radically different social structure, it was quite unlikely that, despite the existence of a common symbolic nucleus (the pure/impure polarity), affinities in this sphere would emerge. Still, the existence of such a common nucleus confirms the proximity of Peristan to the Indian world, indicated by linguistic data.

The Hindus of the Himalayas

If the affinities of the Peristani complex with Sanskritic Hinduism are limited to the fundamental symbolic nucleus, the parallels with non-Sanskritic Hinduism should be more numerous, especially with that of the peoples geographically closer to Peristan. From the cultural point of view, the pre-Islamic world of the Hindu Kush seems to have, in fact, many traits in common with that of the Indian people of the western Himalayas: the Pahari of Himachal Pradesh (Chandra 1992), Uttarakhand (Bhatt, Wessler & Zoller 2015) and Uttar Pradesh (Berreman 1972), the three Indian states closer to the border of Kashmir. Pahari, meaning simply 'mountain-folk' (from *pah'ar*, meaning 'mountain' both in Urdu and Hindi), is the name used throughout northern India to refer to the peoples settled on the slopes of the Himalayas, and is the term used also by linguists to refer to the Indo-Aryan languages spoken in this western corner of India,[25] which should be seen therefore as the natural continuation of the Indo-Aryan linguistic continuum past the

---

24 Crooke 1894: 387–93; Marriott [1966] 1968; Babb 1975: 168–75; Bell 1997: 127–8.
25 Berreman 1972: 21–3; Masica 1991: 10–13.

borders of the Dardic languages, which include Kashmiri as well.We should not be surprised, therefore, to find parallelisms and socio-cultural affinities between geographically contiguous and linguistically connected groups,[26] similarly settled in mountain environments.

The Pahari – according to the US anthropologist Gerald Berreman who conducted research in an Indian village of Uttar Pradesh in the 1950s – were rather unorthodox Hindus. Like the peoples of the Hindu Kush, they sacrificed animals, ate meat, drank alcohol, and had shamans and diviners (Berreman 1972: XXXIX, 87–90). Gender relations as well, appear to connect the Pahari to the pre-Islamic cultures of Peristan. Women moved freely in the villages, spoke to everybody but strangers and also enjoyed, to some extent, sexual freedom (ibid.: 167). Divorces were not rare, and were equally due to male or female initiative (ibid.: 161). If a conflict arose between husband and wife, it was quite easy for the woman to take refuge at her father's house or even to elope with another man (ibid.: 168, cf. 130, 154, 161) – the latter custom closely recalling the Kalasha institution of *aLaS'in~g*. At variance with the case in the plains and among the higher castes, the Pahari followed the practice of bridewealth (ibid.: 128) rather than dowry, as in Peristan. They had rules of lineage exogamy that produced a segmentary system closely resembling the Kalasha one, with maximal and minimal lineages. As among the Kalasha, lineages emerge as corporate groups in social and ritual contexts and they tend to be territorially concentrated (ibid.: 177–9) in settlements in which the basic unit is the patrilocal extended family composed of all those who share food from the same fire (ibid.: 144). Animal sacrifices (Chandra 1992: 237, 249), shamans (ibid.: 235, 245), use of alcoholic beverages (ibid.: 218, 247, 249), bridewealth (ibid.: 267), relative freedom of women (ibid.: 117, 211), and exogamous lineages, are traits attested also among the Kinner of Kinnaur, another Pahari population. Among the Kinner, moreover, a form of wedding (*haari*) is reported, almost identical to the Kalasha *aLaS'in~g*, which included the payment of the double of the bridewealth originally paid, to the abandoned husband (ibid.: 267).

Another important trait linking these Hindu mountain populations to the pre-Islamic societies of Peristan is the form of social stratification which, like in the Hindu Kush, has a dual structure with a vast majority of free men, owners of fields and animals, and a small minority of artisans, considered inferior (Berreman

---

26 The continuum, however, is interrupted because Pahari languages have affinities with the languages of Rajasthan, due to a long-lasting historical connection to that region (Grierson 1916: 13 in Berreman 1972: 17), but there are indications that in the past the ancestors of the Pahari spoke a different language connected to the Dardic ones.

1972: 14–21). In the village studied by Berreman, 90 per cent of the population belonged to the higher class – Rajput in majority with a small percentage
of Brahmins – and the rest was composed of tailors, basket-makers, smiths and
barbers. Although the Rajputs had a ritual status inferior to that of the Brahmins,
the difference between the two castes had little practical relevance: social relations
were intense and they appeared to the inferior castes as a single dominant group
(ibid.: 206–8). In the same way, Kinner society is divided in two main groups,
one of them numerically and economically dominant, the other one basically in
its service (Chandra 1992: 96).

   If we move from the socio-cultural sphere to the specifically ritual one, parallels
with the Kalasha and Peristan appear to be much weaker. The ritual cycle described
by Berreman is composed of twelve events, nine of which are local variants of
widespread Hindu celebrations, while the remaining three are local feasts (Berreman 1963: 388–94). The two most important festivals, Taulu and Diwali, take
place in May–June and November–December, at the end of the two yearly harvests
quite normal in the area. Though the second one, which is celebrated throughout
India, has absorbed elements of the 'great tradition', for Berreman (1972: 125–6)
they both probably derive from ancient non-Brahminical harvest festivals. Their
respective positions in the annual cycle – taking into account the different climatic
conditions that shape the productive cycle seem to correspond to that of the spring
and winter sequences among the Kalasha. The Pahari Diwali, especially, celebrated
a month later than in the plains and with quite different modalities, has some traits
of a New Year festival, even if Berreman does not define it as such. The element of
fire plays a major role in it and a rite is held in honour of Nag Raja, the serpent-god
that may echo the memory of the primordial snake; men and women dance and sing
and there is a general slackening of inhibitions. A transgressive nature, it is reported,
also characterizes the hill Diwali of the western Hymalayan village of Mausar in
Bangan.[27] The pan-Indian Diwali as well, on the other hand, though not considered
a New Year feast, has traits recalling the theme of the end and the beginning. With
the lighting of little flames in all houses, is celebrated the return of the sun hidden
by the evil spirit of the waters during the rainy season (Stutley & Stutley [1977]
1980: 115) and the return of the god Rama to Ayodhia after his triumph over the
demon-god Ravan – the victory of light over darkness is connected to the theme
of the duel with the primordial monster. A very apt shell, therefore, for a concealed
ancient New Year feast (rather than a harvest feast as Berreman suggests), that may
have had something in common with the Kalasha Chaumos.

---

27 Bhatt, Wessler & Zoller 2015: 103.

As for spiritual beings, if we compare those venerated in the Hindu Kush/Kara-korum in pre-Islamic times with those of the Central and Western Himalayas the differences are many, which is not surprising if we recall that Peristan is also inter-nally quite multifarious in this respect. The sole exception is represented by the god Mahasu identified with Mahadev or Shiva (Berreman 1972: 102) who seems to correspond to the Kalasha god Mahandeo. Yet there is a class of supernatural beings with remarkable similarities and several common traits in the two areas. These are the mountain spirits, the fairies of the mountains, the *peri*. A compara-tive study conducted by the German linguist and Indologist Claus Peter Zoller has highlighted many parallels, from the supposed physical appearance of the fairies, described as blond female beings with blue eyes and often with feet turned back-wards, to their being herders of the wild caprids of the mountains, to their golden or silver abodes on the peaks of the highest mountains, to their simultaneously attractive and irascible character, to their closeness to herders and hunters, to their belonging to the sphere of the 'pure' (Bhatt, Wessler & Zoller 2015: 83–5). Zoller, significantly, notes that though fairies are worshipped in other parts of South Asia, 'the features characterizing the fairies between Central Himalayas, Nuristan and Dardistan are limited to these highlands' (ibid.: 82). Indeed Zoller is himself of the opinion that the Central and Western Himalayas once belonged culturally with the Hindu Kush/Karakorum (ibid.: 115–21) to the point that he considers a form of 'non-brahmanic Hinduism' (ibid.: 127) the 'pastoral ideology' forming the common core of the Peristani symbolic systems, which is attested also in Bangan, in the Western Himalayas (ibid.: 115–16).

This hypothesis – of a former Greater Peristan reaching to the Himalayas – may not seem so unlikely if we consider that the upper stratum of the Pahari popula-tion is composed of Khasa or Khasiya people, deemed to be the descendants of a group of Indo-Aryan speakers superimposed on an older local population, from which the subordinate caste of the Dom is possibly descended (Berreman 1972: 14–15). The Khasia are often mentioned in Sanskrit literature. The texts locate them in Plinius' Indian Caucasus, i.e. in the Hindu Kush (cf. Tucci 1977: 82), and they described them as an Aryan population, composed of decayed Kshatrya who spoke a language close to Sanskrit, but had forsaken their Aryan identity because of their customs disrespectful of Hindu rules, especially in the alimentary sphere. According to George A. Grierson, director of the Linguistic Survey of India,[28] the sources concerning them locate them further west the more ancient they are

---

28 A project of the Government of India conducted between 1894 and 1928, consisting of a comprehensive survey of the languages and dialects of British India.

(Grierson 1916: 15, in Berreman 1972: 15). We may wonder if there could not be a connection between the ethnonym Khasa and the name Kasuo (*k(h)asu'o*) that, as we have seen, was the name the Kati of Bashgal gave to the people of Bumburet and Rumbur, or the name Kasi by which the Kalasha were referred to by the Dameli, a neighbouring population of southern Chitral;[29] also in view of the fact that certain wooden ancestors' effigies discovered by Tucci in Nepal in areas populated by Khasa people seem to suggest past contacts with the pre-Islamic world of the Hindu Kush (Tucci 1977: 82). Not enough, of course, to prove a direct connection between the Khasa and the Kalasha, but there are maybe sufficient elements to hypothesize that at least a component of the Pahari population may once have been part of the culture area of Peristan.

However, contaminations by Sanskritic and non-Sanskritic Hinduism are so numerous that the Pahari religious system appears to be markedly different from the Kalasha one. Although the Pahari are almost not considered true Hindus by the high castes of the plains, they have obviously long been exposed to strong Brahminical influences, totally unknown in Peristan. The Pahari have priests and temples, and the caste system, though regularly infringed, is certainly not unknown. Even if their practices are at variance with the tenets of the classical Brahmanism of the plains, the Pahari systems appear as forms of Hinduism, containing, however, elements of pre-existing religions seemingly akin to those of the pre-Islamic world of the Hindu Kush.

Summing up, the affinities we highlighted suggest the Peristani cultural complex extended in former times well beyond the Hindu Kush. We may think of a vast culture area of the mountains that could possibly have once embraced a large tract of the great Asian chain from its western reaches in the Hindu Kush to the Central Himalayas. Further research in this direction may yield interesting fruits both from the anthropological and the historical point of view. We could have the surprise of discovering that what is now an almost extinct model, peripheral for centuries, has been in the past a non-secondary component of the Asian cultural world.

---

29 For Damel see Cacopardo & Cacopardo 1995 and, especially, 2001: 145–71, which completely supersedes a contribution on the Dameli presented by the present author at the 3rd Hindu Kush Cultural Conference held in Chitral in 1995, and published in the proceedings of that conference thirteen years later (Israr-ud-din 2008) without contacting again the author.

8

Peristan and Archaic Europe

Affinities

Though Kalasha culture is part of the ancient Indian world or, more generally, of the Indo-Iranian universe, it also presents some affinities with the ancient European world. On a purely impressionistic plane, the atmosphere of the Kalasha valleys has for a European visitor something impalpably familiar that the Italian writer Fosco Maraini – author of a vivid account of a visit to Bumburet – has maybe described better than anyone else when he wrote:

> … all of the species of plants repeated to us the word 'home': the light was the same, as well as the colours, the scents of the resins of the trees and of the stepped-over grass, of the dead leaves and of the earth we picked up with our hands. Only the echo of a flute, resonating almost continuously far or near, instilled in the soul a vague fairy-tale suspicion. But whatever appeared as strange in the people, or their ways, was not so much exotic as ancient (Maraini 1997: 142).[1]

A sensation probably similar to the one experienced – according to Arrian's account – by Alexander's soldiers when they reached the Hindu Kush, where they believed they had found Nysa, the mythical town founded by the Greek god Dionysus.

But, apart from these impressionistic elements, it is possible to see some affinities with the pagan world that, to some extent, live on in European folklore and

---

[1] A similar remark, though in less poetic (and sympathetic) terms, was also made by C.G. Bruce, an English traveller of the nineteenth century: 'The Kafir is an unreclaimed savage and will always remain so … In his savagery one cannot compare him to the savage tribes on the eastern frontier of India … The Kafir is intensely ancient' (in Jones 1966: 103).

popular religion. In the course of our narrative we have highlighted some parallels between various elements of Chaumos and some customs widespread in
European folklore. It may be of some significance that many of these concern
Russian folklore, because according to Propp ([1963] 1978: 177) Russian material
is exceptionally ancient and '... gives us the image of agrarian religion in its most
ancient, original forms' – an idea shared also by Dumézil (1929: 10).

Here is a brief synthesis of the correspondences we mentioned: the ritual
game of the storming of the castle, like *nog'or grik*, of which there are parallel
examples in various European countries from Russia to Italy; the custom, again
Russian, of moulding bread figurines similar to the *sharabir'ayak*, to favour the
fertility of animals; the ritual use, once more in Russia, of willow catkins as
the first visible signs of spring, which appear in the central rite of the Bumburet Chaumos, the connection between the quests of the children, the deceased,
fertility and New Year, particularly explicit in Rumbur and well documented in
Europe; the custom, rooted in all the European continent, of decking buildings
with green boughs for the December feasts, just as we have seen it is done by
the children in Birir for Lagaur; the custom of eating lentils on New Year's Day,
which has its parallel in Birir in the feast of beans (*dA~'u tat'u*) and in the rites
of Lagaur; furthermore, the rituals of cross-dressing and the use of mistletoe in
well-wishing have also been found in Europe. We can add that the use of juniper
for New Year and other festivities, with the function of purification and atonement, is also documented in the European continent.[2] Furthermore, as highlighted
by Snoy (2008: 43), it may be significant that the tone system of Kalasha music
is similar to that of European music, because it lacks the numerous intermediate
tones typical of Indian music.

These are certainly sparse features, but since they are not typical of the New
Year complex in general (apart from cross-dressing), they could be seen – though
this is certainly speculative – as indications of a specifically Indo-European morphology of the 'Great Feast'.

If, as we have seen, the Kalasha pantheon is certainly almost wholly Indo-
Aryan, the ritual cycle shows more parallels with European ones than with the
festive cycles of Brahmanical India. Since, as we said, cyclical festivals are
closely connected to productive activities, this is surely due, to some extent at
least, to the environment. The climate of the Kalasha valleys, with its well-defined
four seasons, is indeed much more similar to that of European mountain areas – as
the vegetation also attests – than to the climate of the Indian subcontinent. Yet, it is

2 See Morelli 1982: 51; Van Gennep 1988: 3516–17; Cattabiani 1988: 76–77; Hutton 1996: 42, 45.

fascinating to consider the possibility (and there is no reason to rule it out before-hand) that the affinities may be due to a common heritage. That traces of such a remote past should be more visible in Europe than in India may not be so surpris-ing if we recall that the Christianization of the European continent is undoubtedly a later historical process than the synthesis between the Vedic system and the pre-Aryan religious forms, that in the Indian subcontinent gave rise to Hinduism (cf. Sergent 1997: 239–49). But let us now examine the morphology of the European festive cycles, to see to which extent it corresponds to that of the Kalasha cycle.

According to several scholars,[3] it is possible to detect in European folklore, in spite of the great diversity of its manifestations, a basic homogeneity of the festive cycles connected to the seasons. In France, Van Gennep distinguished six cycles according to a pattern that can be roughly applied, it seems, at least to the whole of Western Europe: Carnival-Lent, Easter, May, Saint John, summer-autumn, Twelve Days. The diverse historical conditions and the mixture of Christian and pre-Christian festivities have apparently produced in Europe a multiplication and fragmentation of the festive nuclei.

Among the Kalasha we identified only three sequences (or cycles in Van Gen-nep's terminology).[4] The winter one, the subject of this study, covers the span of time corresponding to the Christmas cycle of the Twelve Days plus the Carni-val-Lent one; the spring sequence of Joshi corresponds to the May cycle, in the obvious absence of Easter; the summer-autumn one of Uchaw-Prun takes place at a time when in the European rural world a series of rituals were held for the crops which, in France at least, formed a complex with a structure apparently more flex-ible than that of the other cycles.

As is to be expected, the match is not entirely exact. Not only for the smaller number of festive nuclei, but also because the Kalasha completely ignore the summer solstice, which in Europe is widely celebrated in the cycle of Saint John with rites focussed on the element of fire.[5] But it is interesting to note here that the main festive sequences were actually three in number in a vast section of pre-Christian north-western Europe, with a distribution in the yearly ritual cycle not

---

3 For example, Propp [1963] 1978: 167–8; Wittgenstein [1967] 1975: 39; Caro Baroja [1979] 1989: 280; Poppi 2006: 10–13; Kezich 2015: 15–16.

4 Unlike Van Gennep, we reserved the term 'cycle' for the whole complex of yearly festivities and call the festive nuclei he calls 'cycles', 'sequences'. In this chapter we use Van Gennep's terminology when referring to his work.

5 Van Gennep [1949] 1999: 1427–1737; Propp [1963] 1978: 155–60; Hutton 1996: 312, 321; Buttitta I.E. 1999: 84–98.

too different from the Kalasha one: October-November, December, April-May;[6] just as they were three, we have seen, in the Vedic year. A comparison between complete yearly cycles, however, is not possible on the sole basis of the materials presented in this work. We shall restrict therefore our analysis to the winter sequence which has been the object of our field research among the Kalasha.

Winter feasts in European folklore

Although the ritual cycles of pre-Christian Europe have been remoulded, fragmented and absorbed into the Christian calendar, the Kalasha winter sequence is based on a pattern that seems approximately discernible in the European sequence that goes from All Saints' to Carnival.

Van Gennep, at the folkloric level, distinguished in it two cycles: the one of the Twelve Days – from Christmas to the Epiphany – and the one of Carnival-Lent. These in fact are two cycles that can easily be reduced to a single one.[7] Van Gennep (1988: 3609) himself remarks that there are events of the Twelve Days cycle that are connected to the Carnival-Lent one. Indeed if the two cycles are perfectly distinguishable liturgically, they are not so easily distinguishable from the folkloric point of view. It is well documented that the dates for the beginning of Carnival are quite varied in Europe, and that in many cases they even coincide with Christmas, if not with Saint Martin's Day (11 November);[8] just as it is quite recognized that the morphology of Carnival is typical of New Year feasts.[9] Furthermore, between Christmas and New Year, in medieval times, the feasts 'of the Innocents' and of 'Madmen' were celebrated, which were true carnival manifestations of a 'world turned upside-down' right in the middle of the cycle of the Twelve Days. At the folkloric level, therefore, it is clear that 'the period of Carnival, in its broader sense' goes from November to February.[10] Equally

---

6 Davidson 1988: 38–9; Hutton 1996: 7.

7 Giovanni Kezich, author of a recent comprehensive study on European Carnivals, appears to be of the same mind, since he sees the imprint of a 'single ceremonial complex' behind the great variety of European winter feasts, which originally had to do, he observes, with the celebration of the New Year (Kezich 2015: 17).

8 Miles [1912] 1976. 349, Van Gennep [1943] 1998: 741; 1988: 3609; Toschi [1955] 1976: 114, 122; Burke [1978] 1980: 178, 187, 188; Caro Baroja [1979] 1989: 31–4; Barozzi 1982: 67–8, 69; Bausinger 1982: 88; Marinelli 1982: 112; Morelli 1982: 48; Brugnoli 1984: 49; Cattabiani 1988: 148; Cappelletto 1995: 97; Cardini 1995: 191; Kezich 2015: 21.

9 Toschi [1955] 1976: 122, 618; Sanga 1982: 7; Kezich 2015: 17

10 Burke [1978] 1980: 187; Cardini 1995: 191.

varied is the duration of the cycle of the Twelve Days; with initial dates ranging from 25 November (Saint Catherine's Day) to Christmas Day, and ending dates falling between 1 January and Candlemas (2 February).[11] We have therefore two cycles – or sequences, in our terminology – that clearly overlap. Seen as one, they cover exactly the same period of time as the winter sequence of Birir. It is likely that, in pre-Christian times, they formed one great festive cycle, probably centred on the winter solstice.[12] The present-day separation of the two cycles is due in all likelihood to the deeply-felt need of the Catholic Church to eliminate from the Christmas period the rituals that appeared to be more in contrast with the Christian spirit of the festivity.[13] A variety of ritual behaviours, condemned by the Church as pagan remnants, were thus channelled into the Carnival: a process that, according to the great Spanish scholar Caro Baroja ([1979] 1989: 280) seems to have taken place between the third and seventh century CE, and that brought about a complete restructuring of the festivities of the whole of Christianity (cf. Cardini 1995: 194). Similar considerations are made also by Bakhtin ([1965] 1984: 218) when he observes that Carnival celebrations have become like a deposit where obsolete genres are stored, and that in Carnival have merged a variety of local feasts of different origin, and formerly celebrated at different dates, which shared, however, the character of jolliness and popular merrymaking.

Carnival and Christmas

The basic trait of the Carnival cycle is undoubtedly its licentious character. It is a time of freedom and licentiousness when a suspension of the rules of ordinary life allows the emergence of the erotic and explicitly sexual dimension in acts and symbols, of the practice of insulting individuals or groups, of the public reporting of scandalous and secret deeds, of the hiding of objects to subvert the normal order and, especially, of the inversion of established hierarchies.[14]

A general model of the main traits, of the 'ritemes' we may say, that still today characterize Carnival celebrations has been proposed by the Italian anthropologist

---

11 Miles [1912] 1976: 350. In spite of his notorious reticence with regard to the remnants of the cults of classical civilizations in folkloric phenomena, Van Gennep (1988: 2868) recognizes a pre-Christian imprint in the structure of the cycle, agreeing in this with the majority of authors.

12 See Miles [1912] 1976: 174; Cattabiani 1988: 133; Hutton 1996: 8; d'Apremont 2005: 46–7.

13 Cf. Cattabiani 1988: 119–20, 142; Kezich 2015: 16–17.

14 Van Gennep [1943] 1998: 749; Caro Baroja [1979] 1989: 8.

Tullio Seppilli.[15] These are: (a) rounds for gathering donations; (b) parades of the various sectors of society; (c) the use of masks that may represent symbolic entities, such as King Carnival, or that are just worn to adopt a personality different from the ordinary one to better enact transgressive behaviours; (d) competitions of various types, which he sees as remnants of ancient and complex initiation rituals; (e) contrasts between opposed groups, possibly ritualizations of symbolic oppositions, as that between Spring and Winter, in many instances represented as a contrast between Carnival and Lent, or clashes between opposed groups generally characterized as 'good' and 'bad'; (f) numerous dramatic representations of the killing of a scapegoat charged with negative connotations that may extend over a very broad semantic field ranging from the ugly season finally departing, to the bad deeds done within the community; and (g) the subversion of the rules typical of the established social order, through sexual licentiousness, food orgy, inversion of hierarchies. For Seppilli as well it is in this last trait that the deep meaning of Carnival lies.

The majority of these traits were formerly also structural elements of the cycle of the Twelve Days: the licentious feasts of December presented exactly these same traits, which are notoriously typical of New Year celebrations (Eliade [1949] 1968), as Carnival is in its roots. These are in fact the same 'ritemes' we found in Chaumos. We found the rounds for donations, repeated several times, in different forms, in the course of the festival. We found also the race, connected, as Seppilli had correctly supposed, to initiation ceremonies, as well as the clashes between opposed groups in the game of the storming of the castle, in the fox chase, and in the general contrast between the pure, the *prabal'on gU'ak*, and the impure, all married adults. With the insults addressed to the elders and the obscene songs, we found the theme of the subversion of ordinary rules and hierarchies in Chaumos. The food orgy is present as well in the meat banquets following the sacrifices and in the unrestrained consumption of wine. In contrast, sexual licentiousness has only a symbolic expression, because in Rumbur and Bumburet, where the obscene is in the forefront, sexual intercourse is forbidden for the whole of the sacred period. There are no masks in Birir, but masks do appear in the Chaumos of the other two valleys, even if in a somewhat marginal position, at the end of the festival, with cross-dressing and animal masks. The use of masks certainly does not have the objective of hiding one's identity to favour transgression, because transgressive behaviours are performed by everybody openly in the dances accompanying the obscene songs.

---

15 Seppilli 1984: 16–20. But see also Sanga 1982: 5, who provides a similar picture.

On the other hand, a theme the Kalasha feast surely lacks is that of the scape-goat. The wrongdoings committed within the community are exposed in the salacious lyrics of the songs, but there is no scapegoat representing the accumulated negativity to be eliminated (apart, maybe, from the lamb sacrificed in Birir on the very first day of Chaumos). There is nothing like the Carnival dummies symbolically killed, or the kings of the feast symbolically dethroned. Negativity, which in the Kalasha view is identified with the contamination deriving from everyday life in which *'onjiSTa* and *pr'agata* are necessarily in contact, is everybody's responsibility and it does not have a symbolic concentration or personification. Everyone actively cooperates in eliminating it through the ritual purifications of the festival. The personification of Chaumos is different from that of Carnival and is closer to that of the cycle of the Twelve Days. In the European winter sequence we have, in fact, two distinct personifications, which correspond to the two cycles identified by Van Gennep in what, as we have seen, was presumably one single festive period.

The personifications of Christmas and Carnival

The personifications of the cycle of the Twelve Days have the traits of the 'visitor': they arrive in the heart of the most sacred period, they dispense their gifts and then they leave. A beneficial trait prevails in them, though they also have a darker side, because they can dispense punishments as well as prizes. European folklore displays a variety of these supernatural figures: from the French Père Chalande and Père Janvier, to the Germanic Frau Perchta and Frau Holda, to the Italian Befana and the Sicilian Vecchia di Natali, in addition to their Christianized versions like Saint Martin, Santa Claus and Saint Nicholas,[16] the most likely ancestor of Father Christmas who, with his present traits, is essentially a modern creation.[17] The personifications of Carnival, in contrast, are figures represented by dummies that are symbolically killed in a tragic-comic street act, and their remains scattered in the surrounding environment.[18] Other figures have been assimilated into the ephemeral Carnival-King,[19] figures of flesh and blood this time, like the Abbé de

---

16 Pitrè [1870–1913] 1978: 413; Miles [1912] 1976: 202–8, 218–11, 241–4; Motz 1984; Van Gennep 1988: 2981–3032.

17 Lévi-Strauss [1952] 1995: 57; Perrot [2000] 2001: 31–52.

18 Frazer [1922] 1987: 301–6; Toschi [1955] 1976: 228–9; Propp [1963] 1978: 138–141; Burke [1978] 1980: 181; Cappelletto 1995: 159.

19 Frazer [1922] 1987: 586; Cardini 1995: 195.

Liesse, the Abbas Stultorum or the Lord of Misrule, the Archbishop or Pope of the Feast of Fools who, in Medieval times, were chosen (especially in France, but also in Germany, England and Bohemia) as Christmas kings for the times of the December feasts – in the cycle of the Twelve Days therefore – during which they enacted, and legitimized, all sorts of behaviors that completely subverted normal order, like playing dice on the church altars or using them as dining tables for cakes and sausages, among obscene songs and lascivious behaviours, to be in the end dethroned.[20] These figures played the role of mediators between the reversed normal order and the realm of chaos inaugurated by the feast, in which they paradoxically represented the regulating authority.

In the Kalasha Chaumos we have only one of these types of personification that, in our view, are to be kept distinct. We find the beneficial visitor, but not the ephemeral king who is in the end eliminated. This figure is not present, neither in the form of the dismembered dummy, or in that of the dethroned mock king.

Lévi-Strauss, analysing the figure of Father Christmas in a brilliant essay written in reaction to a paradoxical and highly significant episode that had attracted the attention of the press, concludes that the beneficent old man is the relatively recent heir of figures like the Christmas kings of the December feasts, which he sees as 'the heirs of the *Saturnalia* of Roman times' (Lévi-Strauss [1952] 1995: 65), when a mock king was elected who used to be sacrificed, at the end of his brief reign, on the altar of the god Saturn, whom he impersonated (Frazer [1922] 1987: 584–5). For Lévi-Strauss, through a structural transformation, a flesh-and-blood figure, like the young Bishop of Fools, became a mythical figure, Father Christmas; the apostle of bad behaviour was put in charge of ratifying good behaviour and the imaginary mediator replaced the real mediator, changing its nature and acting in reversed fashion: 'the adolescents openly aggressive towards their parents are replaced by the parents masked with a fake beard to please the children' (ibid.: 69–70).

In our view, the great French scholar, as clever and fascinating as his interpretation may be, this time misses the point. The ephemeral Christmas kings of our Middle Ages, like the mock king of the *Saturnalia*, should be connected, rather than to the personifications of the cycle of the Twelve Days – the beneficent visitors represented today by Father Christmas – to the ones of Carnival: for their comical traits, for their being the lords of a reversed world, for the fleeting character of their reign; and, especially, for the fact that their dethronement amounts to a symbolic killing. Lévi-Strauss, it seems, mixes two types of personifications that, in our view, should instead be kept distinct.

---

20 Miles [1912] 1976: 298, 302–8; Van Gennep 1988: 3433–70; d'Apremont 2005: 42–4.

But if the figure of the Christmas visitor is not to be connected to the Christmas kings or the bishops of Fools of medieval times, and therefore neither to the king of the *Saturnalia* from which they are supposedly derived, to which other figures may it be related? If Lévi-Strauss, in our view, missed the point when he saw in Father Christmas àn antithetic heir of the medieval Christmas kings, he is quite right, we believe, when he remarks that his figure 'belongs to the family of divinities'.[21] He belongs to that family because he is neither a mythical being nor the character of a legend: there are no myths or legends about him. But Father Christmas is the object of a cult – the characterizing trait of a divinity – that should be seen as such to all effects, even if it is only practised by children. 'He is the divinity of a single age-set of our society', Lévi-Strauss observes, and as such 'he is the expression of a differential code that distinguished children from adults' (ibid.: 59), a circumstance that in his view reveals a connection with the contexts of initiation rites: the discovery, or the revelation, of Father Christmas' secret, i.e. that under the fake beard of the visitor from the unknown there is, in fact, a flesh-and-blood person, a well-known relative, would be, in this perspective, the event marking the end of childhood.

The arrival of supernatural visitors and the celebration of initiations are indeed deemed to be typical traits of New Year feasts (Eliade [1949] 1968: 92–3). In Bumburet the initiatic trial itself is centred, we have seen, on the ritual welcoming of the divinity descending in the valley, but instead of the revelation of the non-existence of the divine benefactor, as is the case with Father Christmas, we have here the opposed revelation of its epiphany.

If the benevolent visitor and dispenser of gifts who appears in the nights of the winter solstice belongs, as Lévi-Strauss believed, to the category of divinities, his roots rather than in the king of the *Saturnalia* and his medieval derivations, should be sought, it seems, in another direction. Saint Nicholas, Santa Claus, Saint Martin, Frau Perchta, Frau Holda, the Père Chalande, the Vecchia di Natali and their modern avatar, Father Christmas, could very well be the heirs of divinities of reproduction and regeneration like Balimain.[22] Such divinities, we have seen, in the Indian world generally lead back to Indra, the god that refounds the year, who frees the world from the monster of Chaos preventing its birth, and installs the Cosmos.

---

21 Van Gennep (1987: 3002) was not of this opinion.

22 Miles ([1912] 1976: 241) advances this hypothesis specifically for the Teutonic Frau who appears under various names – Holda and Perchta among them – during the Twelve Nights. One of her names is Frick, which in his view is probably a derivation from the name of the Germanic goddess Frigg to whom we owe the name of Friday.

The structural transformations that may have led from ancient Visitor deities to the Christmas Visitors of folklore can perhaps be seen as a process – in which ecclesiastical authorities surely took an active part – that has relegated true pre-Christian divinities, remoulding them, to the fable world of children. The gifts of vital energy dispensed by a Visitor god like Indr for the benefit of the community at large, become gifts for children. The god of reproduction, the personification of sexual energy, becomes the benevolent grandfather or grandmother, figures more appropriate to the world of infancy. It is, in fact, a well-known process of transformation: the unreal world of the fables becomes the final refuge of beliefs expelled from the social imagery.[23]

At least one of the European figures just mentioned, maybe the most pagan of all – Frau Perchta, nocturnal divinity of the December feasts, bringer of prosperity and ruler of the dead, whose cult is repeatedly condemned in medieval ecclesiastical documents[24] – has some additional traits, apart from that of being a divine visitor of the winter solstice, that recall Balimain. In particular, its figure appears to represent the *coincidentia oppositorum*, because she is in some cases described as young and beautiful on one side and old and ugly on the other (Motz 1984: 153, 156), half-fairy and half-witch. Like Balimain, furthermore, she is reputed to be a 'kidnapper of children'.[25] The god of Chaumos, indeed, according to the myth, at his first appearance took away with him the young novices who awaited him at the sanctuary of *indr'eyn*, and this is reportedly why today only older boys are sent there for the rites of the holy night of *Nangairo* (Snoy 2008: 55). This double, ambiguous, character of the visitor, seems to be expressed also in the figure of the bogeyman – Hans Träpp in Alsacia, Knecht Rupert in Germany and Piet the Black in Holland – who in some parts of Europe accompanies the benevolent Saint Nicholas, even merging with him in some instances.[26] In the case of Balimain this threatening aspect has rather faded in the cult, but is quite present in the myth: before kidnapping the initiates, the sons of those who worshipped him, he had destroyed with his whip a village where the people had unleashed, by mistake, their dogs on him.[27] The whip, by the way, is another trait he shares with several of the European Christmas visitors (Miles [1912] 1976: 207, 219, 242). The dual

---

23 Frazer [1922] 1987: 342, 701; Branston [1955] 1991: 9; Parkes 1991: 91.
24 Ginzburg [1989] 2008: 67, 79, 173; cf. Dumézil 1929: 45.
25 Perrot [2000] 2001: 37; cf. Miles [1912] 1976: 242; Motz 1984: 152, 155.
26 Miles [1912] 1976: 230–2; Perrot [2000] 2001: 36.
27 Schomberg 1938: 184; Shah 1974: 78; Loude & Lièvre 1984: 192, 1990: 182–4; Snoy 2008: 52–3.

character – benevolent and dangerous – of figures like Perchta and Holda, and their connection with children, has led to a hypothesis that envisages a tie with initiatic themes, which always include a trial to be faced. A certain isomorphism seems to emerge between these figures and that of Balimain. But what may be, we must now ask, the relation between the Christmas Visitor and the ephemeral Carnival King? Why did we insist on a distinction that apparently is not generally acknowledged?

The Visitor god and the Dying god

The slaughtered king, as is well known, is the central theme of the great fresco of Sir James Frazer's *The Golden Bough*. For the British scholar – whom Lévi-Strauss seems to follow on this point – the Carnival dummies, like the ephemeral kings of medieval December feasts, are heirs of the mock king of the Roman *Saturnalia*, whose rule, as we have seen, lasted only for the length of the festival.[28] In his view, in the most archaic period of Roman history, the king of the *Saturnalia*, at the end of the festive period, was dethroned and immolated as representative of a god of vegetation (maybe Saturn himself) who had to die to ensure the rebirth of nature.[29] A rite of magic based on the analogy with the rhythm of vegetation that every year dies and is reborn.

Caro Baroja remarks, however, that in the texts of the times of the Roman Republic no mention is made of the custom of electing a king, and that only after the establishment of the empire does a similar character appear, who is chosen by a group of young men by drawing lots in the course of a mock ceremony. In his view we are not dealing therefore with a custom belonging to archaic Rome, but rather with a tradition 'of non-classical derivation', fruit of the pronounced syncretism of the times of the empire, and hence in all likelihood of external origin: an analogous custom was followed, for example in the Babylonian feasts called *Sacaea*, where among the prisoners a king was chosen, who exercised full power for five days, at the end of which he was lashed and hanged.[30]

---

28 A theory still credited by some scholars (cf. Caillois [1939] 2001: 123; Cardini 1995: 194–5), but not by all: for A. Buttitta (1995: 22), for example, the supposed derivation of Carnival from the *Saturnalia* is unfounded, because the two festivals in his view are more likely to be derived from a common model, while for Kezich (2015: 397) at least two other major Roman feasts – the *Lupercalia* and the *Ambarvalia* – have contributed to the morphology of Carnival. See also Brugnoli 1984.

29 Frazer [1922] 1987: 585–7; cf. 315–16, 319.

30 Caro Baroja [1979] 1989: 292–3; cf. Brugnoli 1980: 52.

If we set aside this figure of apparent 'non-classical derivation', at the heart of the *Saturnalia* only Saturn is left, a divinity that presents indeed the traits of the Visitor. Macrobius, a fifth-century pagan Roman philosopher, author of an important work on the *Saturnalia*, relates that the statue of the god, that remained tied in his temple with a woollen band for the whole year, was liberated for the festival to symbolize the annual return of the god who revived, though just for a few days, the mythical golden age when all men lived in harmony and peace (in Cattabiani 1993: 62). That the Romans knew the figure of the Visitor is confirmed, at any rate, by the fact that 'in pre-Christian Rome *adventus* signified the arrival, once a year, of the deity in its temple' (ibid.: 49) for the length of the festival, which, according to some authors, in ancient times lasted seven days (ibid.: 339).

The Christmas Visitor and the Carnival King in fact appear to be personifications originating from two different worlds that in Europe had merged. Behind the Carnival dummies and the mock kings of the Middle Ages the profile seems to emerge of a markedly agricultural and socially stratified society. The triumph and the death of Carnival parallel the destiny of the seed that must die to generate new life, and reflect therefore the annual cycle of the crops, while the nature of the inversion that accompanies his reign, like the equally ephemeral one of the fake medieval kings, clearly mirrors a markedly stratified social structure. Therefore the hypothesis, covertly suggested by Caro Baroja, that we are dealing with a complex in some way connected to the great farming civilizations seems plausible.

Various authors,[31] on the other hand, highlight the connections of these ephemeral kings to the agricultural world and see in them the personification of the fate of the seed who must dissolve to produce new life. Vladimir Propp, for example, closely following Frazer, considers the corresponding characters of Russian folklore as 'incomplete divinities', which would represent a stage of the process that in the great Middle-Eastern civilizations has generated the figure of the god that is killed and resurrects.[32] A. Buttitta, in a similar perspective, explicitly connects the Dying god to a 'more complex type of organization, such as the State' (Buttitta A. 1995: 34–5). In his view the Dying god is related to the Mother-Goddess who 'through the death and resurrection of a creature she herself generated, regenerates animal and plant life' (Buttitta A. 1989: 106); he emphasizes that it is not by chance that these figures are found in the Mesopotamian basin, where agriculture

---

31 For example Frazer [1922] 1987: 325, 337; Propp [1963] 1978: 180; cf. Frankfort 1992: 7.
32 Propp [1963] 1978: 177; cf. Frazer [1922] 1987: 315–16, 319.

first became a pivotal economic resource,[33] and from where the complex would have spread to a vast area including southern Europe, the Middle East and northern Africa (Buttitta A. 1989a: 106–8). Indeed in the Kalasha system, where there is no place for a god who is killed and resurrected, we have not found a Mother-Goddess either. Similarly, a figure of this type has little space in the Vedic and Avestic myths (Witzel 2004: 601), just as there was probably no Mother-Goddess among the Proto-Indo-Europeans.[34]

If the personification of Carnival may perhaps be related – as a transformation of that of the Dying god – to the context of the great agricultural civilizations, it is possible, conversely, that the figure of the Supernatural Visitor was originated in societies in which animal husbandry prevailed over agriculture; as a travelling god he seems to have little to do with the vicissitudes of the seed and he appears, rather, to better reflect the cycle of summer transhumance.

Venturing a step beyond Buttitta's suggestion, we may hypothesize that as the Dying god seems to be connected to stratified societies organized in the form of the state, so may the Visitor of the winter solstice be connected to tendentially egalitarian and stateless societies; agro-pastoral societies in which agriculture has a subordinate role do not generally know the state as a form of political organization and are characterized by a low degree of social stratification.

The fact would thus be explained that in the Kalasha system like in the other Peristani cultures, characterized by a 'pastoral ideology' we find the Visitor of the winter solstice but not the Dying god, while in European folklore we have, as we have seen, both figures. In Europe, as mentioned above, the two complexes appear to have merged. A pastoral component of Asian origin is, on the other hand, deemed to be an integral part of the religious structure of the civilizations of Eurasia, as indicated by the historical course of the Greek religion, which was the fruit of the merging of an Indo-European pastoral component with an agrarian and urban Mediterranean one.[35] The Latin peasant-shepherds of archaic Rome, we have just suggested, probably knew the Visitor god, but not the Dying god.

Now that we have highlighted the differences between the two divine figures, we can move on to examine their similarities.

---

33 See Frankfort (1992: 8–9) on this point.
34 Devoto 1962: 220; Campanile [1993] 1997: 27.
35 Eliade [1951] 1974: 405; Lanternari [1976] 1983a: 530–1.

The deep meaning of the two figures

The themes at the basis of the two figures, in spite of their differences, appear, in fact, to belong to the same family. They both have to do with the regeneration of nature and society. Both are an integral part of the New Year complex.

For Eliade ([1949] 1968: 95) 'the mythical-ritual scenarios of the New Year ... were undoubtedly organized in their main traits since the times of the Indo-European community'. These main traits he lists as follows:

> (1) the twelve intermediate days prefigure the twelve months of the year (see also the rites mentioned above); (2) during the twelve corresponding nights, the dead come in procession to visit their families (apparition of the horse, pre-eminently the funeral animal, on the last night of the year; presence of the chthonic-funerary divinities ... during these twelve nights) ... (3) it is at this period that fires are extinguished and rekindled; and finally (4) this is the moment of initiations ... In this same myhico-ritual complex of the end of the past year and the beginning of the New Year, we must also include the following facts: (5) ritual combats between two opposing groups; and (6) presence of the erotic element (pursuit of girls, 'Gandharvic' marriages, orgies).[36]

Obviously, not all these traits are always present at once, and the relative weight of each varies in different contexts. Many of these traits are found in the Kalasha Chaumos. We have the descent of the dead and the presence of chthonic entities like witches as well as a trace – in the name of one of the days of the Birir Chaumos – of the primordial monster-serpent, the quintessentially chthonic divinity. The horse appears as the steed of the Visitor god, at least in the Bumburet/Rumbur version, in which the erotic element is also particularly evident. Chaumos is also the time of initiations and, also, features ritual combats between two opposing groups. The almost complete array of these traits is equally found in the European winter sequence that includes the cycle of the Twelve Days and the Carnival cycle in its broadest sense.

However, Eliade ([1949] 1968: 95) also adds that the New Year complex is more ancient than the Proto-Indo-Europeans and cannot be considered their exclusive creation, because the mythico-ritual scenario of the New Year was known to the Sumero-Akkadians and, in part at least, to the Hebrews and the Egyptians. In

---

36 From the 1959 English reprint (Harper & Brothers, New York) – entitled *Cosmos and History. The Myth of the Eternal Return* (available online) – of the 1954 English translation (Pantheon Books) entitled *The Myth of the Eternal Return*.

his view, the roots of the complex hark back to prehistoric times. The amazing similarities attested in the rituals of the New Year in the Middle East, among Indo-European peoples, and even in Japan, would thus be explained.[37] The profound and constant motif of the complex, as we have repeatedly seen in the course of this work, for Eliade, is the regeneration of life, which is achieved with a symbolic return to the Chaos of the beginning, to the *illo tempore* when the world came into existence. A theme elaborated in innumerable ways, but that for him always emerges, almost approaching the status of a cultural universal. But if we focus our attention on the symbolism of the two figures – the Visitor god and of the Dying god – other meanings may emerge.

Both divinities are not permanently installed. They come, they stay for some time, and then they leave. Both deities symbolize separation: the visitor departs and the god dies. It is the reality of death. Impermanence seems to be their first message. But death as well is not permanent, because life returns. In the symbolism of the Dying god, death even generates life. The Dying god is resurrected and the Visitor god returns. Life and death are a flux, they are not separate. The cycle's becoming always repeats itself. In this sense impermanence is eternal. Becoming is one with Being. This seems to be their second message. It is not by chance that, as we have seen, the Visitor has the trait of androgyny that symbolizes the *coincidentia oppositorum*. What is manifested here is the essence of the human condition, its transience and frailty, which is at the same time overcome. We are close to the interpretation given by Henri Frankfort, author of a specific study on the subject, who concludes that the Dying god does not only express 'the relation of man with the passing of the seasons', as scholars generally agree, but it has an 'intellectual content', a 'subjective aspect' connected to the fact that 'anywhere the withering of plants is seen as an image of human transiency. Consequentially, the myth of the Dying god mirrors the attitudes of men towards death and nourishes their hopes' (Frankfort 1992: 7–8).

If, following A. Buttitta (1989), we apply to cultural analysis the conceptual tools developed by Hjelmslev (1971: 81) for linguistic analysis, we would be here at the level of the schema, 'which, since it consists of logic procedures common to all men, leads to analogous outcomes in all cultures, given the same situations' (Buttitta A. 1989: 106). In other words, we are dealing with the symbolic expression of something universal. As Ginzburg ([1989] 2008: 224) remarks 'the universal element is not given by the concreteness of the symbol, but by the

---

37 For a discussion of the prehistoric substratum – Eurasian and Laurasian (Eurasia + the Americas) – of the Vedic religion, see Witzel 2004.

categorizing activity that elaborates in symbolic form the concrete (corporeal) experiences'. Indeed, what can be more universal than the experience of the transiency of life? No human being can escape from it. This, it would seem, is the universal meaning of the New Year ritual complex.

The marked analogies of its manifestations can be explained by its great archaism which has possibly kept it close to that *statu nascenti* in which the level of the schema can be more easily perceived. At the level, however, of the norm (always in Hjelmslev's terms), where cultural diversity arises, the schema is articulated in different forms. To this level seemingly belong the forms outlined by Lanternari ([1976] 1983a: 523–7) who distinguishes between New Year festivals corresponding to different 'cultural levels', that he defines on the basis of the 'economic regimes' characterizing them: those of hunter/gatherers, of fishermen, of nomadic herders and of agricultural societies, grouped in three sub-levels.

In the context of agricultural societies – in an area including perhaps a large part of Europe, Western Asia and North Africa – at the level of the norm, the schema represented by the idea of human transiency seems to have been expressed by the figure of a god who appears in the coldest and darkest time of the year, when plant life withers, to disappear again afterwards. In Hjemslev's model, after the plane of the schema and that of the norm, there is the plane of the use. It is here that 'the normative structures' of a certain symbolic universe 'are articulated … more neatly in relation to the different economic and social situations and to the different cultural traditions of the single territories' (Buttitta A. 1989: 107). To this plane seems to belong the distinction between the Visitor god and the Dying god, the former possibly emanating from agro-pastoral societies with agriculture in a subordinate position, the latter from the great agricultural civilizations. Both figures, furthermore, may assume, in their turn, peculiar forms depending on the contexts to which they may belong; a point that Frankfort (1992) most aptly illustrates for the Dying god.

Balimain and Dionysus

Among the gods of the Greek pantheon Dionysus is undoubtedly the closest to Balimain. Although, as we have seen, the god of Chaumos is to be identified with the Vedic Indra, several of his traits closely recall those of the Greek god.[38]

---

38 The German anthropologist Adolf Friedrich – who, as the reader will remember, was with Peter Snoy one of the very first ethnographers of the Kalasha – had already been struck by some similarities between the two divinities (Buddruss & Snoy 2008: 11).

Balimain's personality is obviously much fuzzier than Dionysus': there are only a couple of myths about him, in comparison to the very rich mythology developed around the god of wine. But even from this mythological poverty, thanks to the knowledge we have of his cult, various traits emerge that link him to Dionysus.

In the first place, both Balimain and Dionysus are Visitor gods. Balimain's yearly visit is brief because he leaves the Kalasha valleys before the end of Chaumos, while the Greek god remained among men for the whole winter, to finally leave in the spring (Eliade [1975] 1979: 390), but in both cases we have a god who arrives in the darkest time of the year and then leaves.

In the second place Balimain is a hermaphrodite divinity, just like Dionysus. In the representation of his person as half male and half female we have seen the expression of the principle of the coincidence of opposites, the *coincidentia oppositorum*. Dionysus too has a male and a female form (Daniélou [1979] 1980: 59); his spirit 'joins the two poles' (Otto [1933] 2006: 148, 129), and his nature 'expresses the paradoxical unity of life and death' (Eliade [1975] 1979: 402).

In the third place, both divinities are gods of fertility. To Balimain, as we have seen, the Kalasha pray for 'seeds of children and seeds of wheat'. Dionysus, in his turn, was seen as the god of trees (Jeanmaire [1951] 1972: 10–15, 18), and especially of fruit trees. He was the god of life that incessantly regenerates itself.[39] Both deities, further, descend among humans at the time when the wine vats are opened and consumption of the new wine begins. Among the Kalasha this is done for the winter solstice, while in ancient Greece the time was February–March, for the feast of the *Anthesterie*, which, like Chaumos, is a New Year celebration.[40] The fact that Balimain's arrival coincides with the opening of the wine vats seems to be a sufficiently clear indication of his connection to grapes and wine. However, he is connected more explicitly to wheat because he is believed to have brought its seed to the Kalasha. In the figure of Dionysus this relation is weaker, but a connection to the sowing of grains seems to exist in his case as well, because it was believed that he had taught men to yoke bullocks to the plough, rather than pulling it by hand.[41]

Furthermore, the myth narrating the first descent of the god, in both cases tells of an initial rejection on the part of some men, which were subsequently harshly punished. Balimain, we have seen, was ill-treated by the people of a village who,

---

39 Otto [1993] 2006: 165; Eliade [1975] 1979: 393; Merkelbach [1988] 1991: 18.
40 Jeanmaire [1951] 1972: 46–54; Kerényi [1976] 1993: 279–89; Spineto 2005.
41 Frazer [1922] 1987: 387–8; cf. Jesi 1972: 491.

mistaking him for a robber, unleashed their dogs on him and were incinerated by a lightning flash of his whip. The corresponding myths concerning Dionysus are so well known that we do not need to list them here. We shall just recall the horrible death of King Penteus, who was torn to pieces by the Maenads because he had forbidden the cult of the god.[42]

In the personality of Balimain there is a dark side corresponding to the terrific aspect of the cult of Dionysus, represented by the Maenads who in their fury devoured animals and humans, and especially children, ripping them from their mothers' arms; we have seen that, according to the myth, in his first visit Balimain not only burned to ashes the village that rejected him, but also carried off the children gathered for their initiation in his holy place, and never brought them back.

We find also in the celebrations in honour of Dionysus, like in Chaumos, macroscopic examples of subversion of the normal order: the partition of society into two groups corresponding to the two genders in the *Agionia* feasts; the treating of slaves as equals in the *Anthesterie* and the central role of the phallus in the Dionysian feasts.[43] The ecstatic-orgiastic element is present in these festivals just like in Chaumos.

Finally, an idea of Eliade's[44] is interesting for our comparison: at the root of the myth of the passion and resurrection of the boy Dionysus-Zagreus there is an archaic, forgotten, rite of initiation. In the scene of the Titans who, wearing masks of white chalk, kill, cut to pieces, cook and devour the body of the divine child, he sees an initiatic scene. In the death and resurrection of the god he sees a symbolic representation of the death and rebirth of the initiate in the Dionysian Mysteries (Eliade [1975] 1979: 400–2). In the case of the Kalasha festival, since the initiation ceremonies are one of its main focuses, the initiatic scenery is absolutely explicit. Balimain, however, does not die: the novices are there to face the initiatic trial. He is a Visitor god and not, like Dionysus, a Dying god as well.

Although the fading myth of Balimain can in no way be compared to the rich mythology surrounding the figure of Dionysus, the two deities seem to have several traits in common. How may these similarities be explained?

---

42 Otto [1933] 2006: 82; cf. Jeanmaire [1951] 1972: 64–5; Eliade [1975] 1979: 388–9.

43 Eliade [1975] 1979: 395–6; Bremmer 1994: 19; Graf 1995: 482.

44 An idea already proposed by Jeanmaire ([1951] 1972: 386–8).

The Silk Route and the Wine Route

A connection to India is one of the many peculiarities that set Dionysus apart from the other gods of Olympus (cf. Eliade [1975] 1979: 402). His 'conquest' of India and his triumphant return are well-known themes. There is, however, a previous journey of Dionysus through Asia that is not always mentioned. According to the various – and not always consistent – traditions, Dionysus was, in fact, born in India and travelled to Greece after a childhood spent at Nysa or on Mount Meros. Euripides is the first author to mention this journey (Grossato 2008: 278). The Italian Indologist and historian of religions Alessandro Grossato (ibid.: 280–1) suggests that the myth of the Indian origins of Dionysus may very reasonably be explained if we consider that the itinerary followed by the god seems to coincide roughly, on the basis of the available archaeological and ethno-botanical data, with the route along which the cultivation of the vine spread west from Central Asia. At the present state of research it appears that the cultivation of the vine was initially developed to the south of the Caucasus, where to this day prospers the wild sub-species *vitis vinifera Linnei*, which is the origin of 99 per cent of the wine produced today. This species of vine, however, is spread also further to the east, as far as present-day Tajikistan, immediately to the north, that is, of the Hindu Kush. The itinerary that was later to become the Silk Route, Grossato (Ib.) proposes, may formerly have been the Wine Route.[45]

If we consider that an autochthonous species of vine – the *vitis nuristanica Vassilez* – grows in Nuristan,[46] and that the southern flanks of the Hindu Kush would have been even more suitable for the production of grapes than the northern ones (cf. Olmo 2000), it follows that Peristan may very well have been, if not the very first, at least one of the first areas where wine was produced in the whole of Eurasia. That Nysa was located in Paropamisus, i.e. the Hindu Kush, is, on the other hand, part of the myth. Furthermore, Giuseppe Tucci, the great Italian Tibet-ologist and expert of Asian civilizations to whom we owe fundamental discoveries in the Swat valley, was sure of the existence of a historical Nysa that, in his view, should have been located exactly in the areas inhabited by Nuristani and Dardic-speaking peoples (Tucci 1977: 40). The fact that the goat is one of the animals

---

45 This hypothesis was first proposed by the present author at the International Conference on Language and Tradition held in Thessaloniki on 7–9 November 2008 (Cacopardo A.S. 2011). On this point and, more in general, on viticulture and wine in Kafiristan see also Klimburg (2014).
46 Neubauer 1974; Edelberg & Jones 1979: 35. For Olmo (2000: 36) the wild grapevine of Nuristan requires further studies, because the dioecy (allocation in separate individuals of masculine and feminine sexual organs) usually found in wild species, has still to be verified.

more frequently associated with Dionysus, could be seen as an additional element
pointing in this direction, because there are indications that the Hindu Kush is
the homeland of the species of wild goat considered to be the ancestor of all the
domestic species (Snoy 1959: 528).

To sum up, it appears that the similarities between Balimain and Dionysus are
probably to be explained by their connection with wine. Rather than of a Greek
influence on the Hindu Kush, we should maybe think of exactly the opposite, i.e.
of an Asian influence on Greek culture. The route followed by Dionysus in his
journey west would represent, in this case, the itinerary of the expansion of grape
cultivation from Asia to Europe.

But Dionysus, we know, is not only a Visitor god like Balimain, he is also
a Dying god, or, better, a god who is killed and resurrects. Possibly originated
among the shepherds and grapevine cultivators of Transcaucasia, the figure of
Dionysus may have absorbed the themes of death and rebirth typical of the great
civilizations of the Middle East, with which Greece was in contact.[47] The impression arises that in Dionysus are merged the two divine figures reflected in the
personifications of the Christmas and Carnival celebrations of European folklore.
This does not mean, of course, that we should think of the figure of Dionysus
– since it perhaps took shape in a cultural context that included our area – as a
direct development of that of Balimain or of other similar deities of Peristan. This
cannot be excluded, but it may be, on the other hand, that the two divinities were
both originated in an ancient religious *humus* common to Greece and the Indian
world, which could possibly be also at the roots of Shivaism. Like Balimain,
Shiva as well is at times represented as half male and half female.[48] The similarities between Shiva and Dionysus have been studied by some scholars,[49] but the
issue, as Sergent (1997: 321–2) remarks, needs further investigation; in his view,
at any rate, Shiva is a close equivalent of Dionysus, to the point that he sees the
profile of an ancient Indo-European divinity behind the two gods, a subverter
of the normal order (ibid.: 324), as is indeed Balimain for some aspects of his
cult. We have already suggested that it is a hypothesis worth considering that the
figure of the Visitor god may have taken shape in agro-pastoral societies and that

---

47 This is the opinion of Jeanmaire ([1951] 1972: 383), who highlights the differences between
the myth of Osiris and that of Dionysus, and suggests that the similarities in some versions may be
due, to some extent, to the contacts established from a certain time onwards between the priests of
Delphus and the Greek-Egyptian cults.

48 Watts [1963] 1978: 100; Daniélou [1979] 1980: 60.

49 For example, Kirfel 1953; Daniélou [1979] 1980.

these may have been the ones where Proto-Indo-European was spoken.[50] Such a divinity could be seen, in this case, as a characterizing trait of the Indo-European model of the New Year celebration. Although, as Eliade remarks, the structure of the New Year complex surely has roots that go beyond the Indo-European world, it is not unreasonable to ask whether in that context – at the level, that is, of the *use* – it could have developed a somewhat characteristic form. This is, of course, nothing more than a mere hypothesis. To test it, we would need an in-depth comparative study of European pre-Christian religions, which is made difficult by the poverty of sources on their ritual systems. Ronald Hutton, one of the main authorities on Northern European paganisms, only with difficulty managed to conclude that there are solid arguments in favour of the existence of an important pre-Christian New Year festival among the Anglo-Saxons, the Vikings and the Welsh, and he observes that data are scarce even for Ancient Rome, which is the best-documented case. If the mere existence of a pre-Christian New Year festival could only be ascertained with difficulty, we can imagine how little we are able to know of its morphology, which was certainly not uniform throughout Europe, or even just Northern Europe (cf. Hutton 1996: 1–8, 362).

As for the people who spoke Proto-Indo-European, we know, of course, even less. The only name we know of a cyclical feast – SEMEN – could, however, be connected to the Irish feast called *Samain* (Devoto 1962: 298), which took place in November (Hutton 1996: 360), and though it may not have marked the beginning of the year, it seems to have some traits of a New Year feast, or it must have opened, at any rate, the winter period. We know too little of course to say that SEMEN was the New Year festival of the Proto-Indo-Europeans – and anyway we know nothing of the morphology of that celebration.[51] Sergent (2005: 389–90) has made a tentative attempt at reconstructing the basic traits of a hypothetical Proto-Indo-European New Year celebration through a comparison between parallel feasts of various peoples speaking Indo-European languages; but due to the poverty of data, his efforts do not appear convincing. He himself remarks, on the other hand, that while Indo-European theology and mythology are, in his view, by

---

50 In this connection there is an interesting idea proposed by Gramkrelidze and Ivanov – who anticipate the beginnings of Indo-European migrations to a time around 5000 BCE – that the speakers of Proto-Indo-European already knew of wine (in McGovern [2003] 2004: 46) and may therefore have been among the first people to produce it.

51 It surely marked, however, a time considered to be particularly numinous because gods and fairies came close to human beings. It coincided with the time when the herds were brought back to their winter quarters and it marked the beginning of the winter sacrifices.

now largely reconstructed, the same does not at all apply to ritual (ibid.). Yet, if it does not seem possible, given the present state of research, to compare rituals, it may be interesting in this perspective to compare the Peristani complex with the cultural pattern of the ancient Indo-Europeans, as it has been reconstructed in Indo-European studies.

9

Peristan and the Proto-Indo-Europeans

The reconstruction of Proto-Indo-European culture

It is certainly surprising that Peristan, as the ultimate refuge of the last Indo-Aryan polytheisms which had escaped the deadly embrace of the great world religions, has not sparked the interest it deserves in the field of Indo-European studies; only the Indologist Michael Witzel, as mentioned, in an essay devoted to the investigation of the deep meaning of the Rig-Vedic system and to its antecedents (Witzel 2004), has taken into consideration the pre-Islamic cultures of the Hindu Kush. For Indo-European studies, the people of Peristan could indeed play a role at least as important as that played, for Dumézil ([1965] 1996), by the Ossetes of the Caucasus. As is the case with the Ossetes (Charachidzè 1987: 28) – the last descendants of the Scythian branch of the Indo-Iranians, i.e. of the Scythians and Sarmatians of Herodotus – Peristan offers a rare instance of a world virtually never reached by the influence of the great cultures of India and Persia. But, while in the Caucasus the Ossetes represent an Indo-European linguistic island in the midst of peoples of different origins, we have in Peristan, as we have seen, a whole constellation of speakers of a variety of Indo-European languages, who, in pre-Islamic times, had all been left, more or less to the same extent, outside the Indian and Iranian cultural spheres. In a similar context, the influence of non-Aryan cultural elements must presumably have been much weaker than in the Caucasus, and the Indo-European element should therefore emerge with greater clarity.

As remarked at the beginning, we have here a coincidence between linguistic and cultural data that deserves attention. The data available on the pre-Islamic cultures of the area appear indeed to agree with those of historical linguistics that, as seen, classifies Dardic and Nuristani languages as very early branches of proto-Indo-Aryan or, in the case of the latter, possibly even of the still-undivided

Indo-Iranian tongue.[1] As already stressed, we cannot obviously see the pre-Islamic cultures of the Hindu Kush as relics discarded by the stream of history, nor can we imagined them completely isolated from the world surrounding them; yet much seems to indicate that their roots hark back to the dawn of Indo-European expansion into the Asiatic continent, and that, in their isolation, they followed an autonomous cultural and historical development. For Witzel (2004: 614), we recall, the pre-Islamic world of the Hindu Kush shows in myth, in ritual and in the social dimension many traits of the Indo-Iranian universe. Mallory (1989: 47–8) even indicates, though with some caution, possible archaeological support for this hypothesis: in his view the 'Gandhara Grave culture' of the Swat valley (cf. Olivieri 2009: 36) – located as we know just to the south of Chitral – is one of the archaeological cultures that can more reasonably be attributed to the earliest Indo-Aryan speaking migrants into the Indian subcontinent, or to that even earlier wave of still Indo-Iranian speakers from which the speakers of Nuristani languages possibly descend.[2]

Since this ancient Indo-Aryan, or Indo-Iranian, world must have been in turn fairly close to the Proto-Indo-European one, it seems interesting to investigate whether, and to which extent, the pre-Islamic cultures of Peristan approach the cultural model of that world, as it has been hypothetically reconstructed by scholars. Certainly a comparison between worlds separated in time by more than five millennia may appear impracticable; the course of history cannot be ignored. Yet, history itself shows that there are social structures and symbolic systems capable of reproducing themselves, though not exempt from transformations, for centuries and centuries. Given the manifest archaic roots of the pre-Islamic cultures of the Hindu Kush, and given the fact that reconstructions of the ancient Indo-European world – hypothetical as they may be – do exist, it seems that the comparison is self-imposed.

All reconstructions have, of course, found their critics, but on some points there appears to be general agreement. The basic idea from which all works of reconstruction have started out is that, though the concept of Indo-European is

---

1 For Fussman (1977: 26), as we have seen, the common origins of the pre-Islamic religions of Nuristan and of the ancient Indo-Aryan religions emerge from irrefutable indications. See also Buddruss (2002: 120–1).

2 For the role of archaeology in Indo-European studies see Renfrew 1987: 20–41, Mallory 1989: 164–221, as well as Campanile 1990: 32–6, who, while recognizing the importance of the relations between ideology and economy, criticizes the tendency to connect, in an overly simplistic way, the concept of Indo-European with a specific archaeological culture.

merely linguistic, if we believe there was a former proto-language from which all Indo-European languages derive – a largely shared conviction – it follows that we should assume the existence of a community of speakers, bearers of a culture which must, to some extent, have been mirrored in that language (Campanile [1993] 1997: 19).[3]

This – obviously very reasonable – idea has induced many scholars since the middle of the 1800s, to attempt a reconstruction of that ancient culture through the means of linguistics. Thanks to the tools offered by linguistic palaeontology it has been possible to define a veritable 'compact vocabulary': the vocabulary of an hypothetical common Proto-Indo-European language – supposedly spoken before the migrations started towards Europe and India – reconstructed through the analysis of the connected forms appearing in the various Indo-European languages. The next step was to try to sketch a general picture of that *ur-kultur* on the basis of the reconstructed vocabulary and to attempt also to determine its geographical cradle.[4]

The main criticism of this 'lexicalistic' method is that linguistic reconstruction can only lead to a word, but not to its meaning, to the concept it transmitted: the fact that we can reconstruct the Indo-European lexeme for king and that we can therefore ascertain the existence of such a word in Proto-Indo-European, tells us nothing, for example, about the functions and the powers attached to that title, which are indispensable elements for an understanding of the true cultural meaning of the term.[5] This is, of course, a very serious objection, but in our view it does not totally invalidate the method, for the relation between meaning and its conveyer is not always as complex as in the classical example reported above.

There is, at any rate, an alternative to the lexicalist method. The Italian linguist Enrico Campanile (1990: 15, 19–32) proposes a method he calls 'textual', because the elements on which the reconstruction is based are derived from written texts of antiquity; the comparison therefore is not between lexemes but between full

---

3 According to Mallory (1989: 127) the earliest cultural horizon that can be assigned to this proto-culture, falls around the middle of the fifth millennium BCE. In the innovative hypothesis formulated by Colin Renfrew (1987: 205–10), it could be traced, instead, as far back as the seventh millennium BCE.

4 This has been a controversial issue. At present, according to Asko Parpola, the most widely-accepted thesis, both by linguists and archaelogists, is that it was 'in the Pontic-Caspian steppes in southern Ukraine and southern Russia' (Parpola 2015: 35). The main contrary thesis has been formulated by Renfrew (1987) who places it in eastern and central Anatolia; Merrit Ruhlen ([1994] 2001: 235–6) is among its supporters.

5 Renfrew 1987: 260; Mallory 1989: 112; Campanile 1990: 12, 43–8, [1993] 1997: 22.

texts. In other words, he proposes focusing attention on the contents and not only on the words used to convey them; if, in the absence of manifest proofs of borrowings or of parallel creations, corresponding contents are found in texts belonging to a plurality of Indo-European cultures, it will be quite legitimate to conclude that they are due to a common heritage. Such a method does not exclude the lexicalistic one, but it proposes a new version of it, which does allow lexical comparisons, but only between linguistic elements that present the same contents independently of the linguistic form in which they are expressed. In textual comparison, therefore, 'I dati addotti in comparazione non sono elementi linguistici di singole lingue, ma elementi culturali di singole culture' (ibid.: 19); the elements compared, that is, are not linguistic elements of single languages, but cultural elements of single cultures.

We shall refer here to cultural reconstructions based on both methods.[6] Though the textual method is certainly more refined and therefore heuristically more effective, it seems that also the traditional method based on linguistic palaeontology – as admitted even by the British archaeologist and paleolinguist Colin Renfrew (1987: 261–2), who has harshly criticized some of its reconstructions – has achieved some results.

Peristan and the Proto-Indo-Europeans

Before proceeding with our comparison, we must recognize that many of the traits defined on the basis of the compact vocabulary can, of course, be found also among other groups, and should not therefore be considered specifically Indo-European (Renfrew 1987: 8). It does not seem, however, that this should invalidate the cultural reconstructions on which our comparison is based. As remarked by Campanile (1990: 11), for the researcher who pursues the sole objective of reconstructing a culture, the question whether some traits are found, or not, among other non-Indo-European populations has no relevance. Traits shared with other groups, indeed, can very well combine to form at least the skeleton of a common cultural pattern, which is the very objective of the work of reconstruction (Campanile [1993] 1997: 25). But let us consider now the picture that emerges from the work of specialized scholars.

From the point of view of subsistence, the broad picture emerging from the compact vocabulary (Mallory 1989: 117–22) seems to correspond quite closely

---

6 Mainly to the works of Mallory (1989), Sergent (2005) and Parpola (2015), in addition to the classical studies of Devoto (1962) and Benveniste ([1969] 2001) for the lexicalist method, and to Campanile (1990, [1993] 1997) for the textual one.

to the traditional Peristani system. The speakers of Proto-Indo-European had a mixed agro-pastoral economy with herding prevailing over agriculture (Devoto 1962: 257, 261, 262); wealth was calculated in terms of livestock, and there are indications that herding was a male task while agriculture was the responsibility of women (Sergent 2005: 186–7). They produced butter and probably cheese (Mallory 1989: 117), and they possibly already practised transhumance (Sergent 2005: 182). They used a plough drawn by animals and they harvested with sickles. Millet, until recently the staple crop both in Nuristan (Robertson 1896: 546) and among the Kalasha, was probably their main cultivation (Sergent ibid.: 187). They produced pottery and they wove with a vertical loom (ibid.: 190).[7] They had smiths who worked bronze, if not yet iron, and carpenters who had developed woodcarving techniques that were probably quite refined (ibid.: 194). According to Sherrat the Proto-Indo-Europeans were a people who had gone through what he calls the 'Secondary Products Revolution', that is 'the second Neolithic revolution', which is marked by the emergence of secondary products of herding and farming, such as dairy products, wool and cloth, yokes and ploughs (in Mallory 1989: 126; Sergent 2005: 181). Their weapons, like those of Peristan, were the bow and the dagger. There are also indications that they played a form of hockey (Sergent 2005: 181), i.e. a ball game played with bats that recalls the Kalasha *ghal*. They had wheeled vehicles, of which, in contrast, there are no traces in Peristan. The horse had probably a more relevant role among them than it had in the Hindu Kush, but for them as well it was a precious animal, used only on special social occasions or in raids.

Several correspondences can also be found from the point of view of social organization (cf. Mallory 1989: 122–6). According to the reconstructions made by linguists, the speakers of Proto-Indo-European were divided in patrilineal descent groups and marriage was in all likelihood virilocal.[8] Settlements were a territorial reflection of the kinship system, for they were formed by clusters of houses hosting a group of lineage members, who also had a common burial place (Sergent 2005: 202). The maternal uncle was an affectionate and understanding counsellor for his nephews.

An important difference would have been found in the sphere of political organization if it had been confirmed that the speakers of Proto-Indo-European had kings, as is seemingly indicated by the well-known connection between Latin

---

7 The vertical loom was found throughout the Indian subcontinent and was used in Nuristan at the time of Robertson's visit (Robertson 1896: 543–4). It is still in use among the Kalasha.
8 But see the contrary opinion of Jack Goody (in Renfrew 1987: 258).

rex, Gallic *-rix* and Vedic *raj-*. The difference would have been quite significant because we would have been dealing with two completely different systems: one that knew the concept of the state and one that did not. Scholars, however, seem to agree that the political organization of the Proto-Indo-Europeans was of a 'tribal' and not of a state-like kind; for Renfrew it is possible that the 'common source word in Proto-Indo-European meant "leader", or "prominent man", without in any way implying the institution of kingship or even chieftainship of a formal hereditary kind.' (Renfrew 1989: 259); similarly for Scharfe (in Mallory 1989: 125) – who even argues that the word *raj* in the earliest Vedic texts was a feminine term indicating 'strength, power', and not the masculine noun meaning 'king' – the highest political role among the Proto-Indo-Europeans was of lineage leader. Even when scholars accept the idea kings did exist in the undivided Indo-European world, they remark they must have been religious more than political figures, akin to priests rather than rulers, that probably allowed space for elementary forms of democracy like assemblies of elders.[9]

Peristan and the tripartite ideology of George Dumézil

In this regard, it is interesting, and almost mandatory, to test the extent to which Peristani context can fit the famous theory of George Dumézil. The great French scholar had, in fact, planned to visit the Hindu Kush (apparently in the company of Morgenstierne), but unfortunately that trip never took place (Allen 1991: 146) – it would have been truly interesting to see in which ways and to what extent, his theory would have been influenced by the knowledge of our area.

Dumézil's work also aims at reconstructing the ancient Indo-European culture, but the French scholar moves on a plane very different from the one familiar to linguists and prehistorians. As is well known, following a huge work of comparison between the most ancient traditions from the different cultural contexts where Indo-European languages are spoken, Dumézil (1958: 5) thought he had detected a large reservoir of common elements organized in complex structures of which no equivalent was known among the other populations of the ancient world. Of these, the main one is a tripartite structure articulating the three fundamental functions of sovereignty/sacredness, strength/war and prosperity/productivity. Initially he saw this ideology in social terms, which prompted him to search for a corresponding tripartition in the social structure of the various Indo-European peoples; a tripartition of which the Hindu system of the three *Varna/Brahmans*

---

9 Benveniste ([1969] 2001: 295–6; cf Devoto 1962: 318; Campanile [1993] 1997: 34.

(priests), *Kshatrya* (warriors) and *Vaishya* (producers) – represents perhaps the best example.

The data from Peristan offer no support to such a view. No trace of the tripartite ideology has been detected at the level of the social structures. As previously mentioned, an attempt by Gérard Fussman (1977) to distinguish groups similar to the Indian *Varna* in the Nuristani pre-Islamic system, which could therefore be related to the three functions, yielded no results. The social division typical of the area, as we have seen, was that between a large majority of free men, owners of fields and herds, and a small minority of artisan/serfs, deemed impure, forming to all effects a caste of untouchables with whom commensality was forbidden. A type of social division that, according to Campanile (1990: 41–2), was also characteristic of the Proto-Indo-European society.

In this regard the critique of Dumézil's theory made by Renfrew (1987: 41–2) seems quite reasonable: he observes that the Proto-Indo-Europeans, for their chronological position – which cannot be set later than 2000 BCE and, according to his own theory, should be set much earlier – simply could not have yet known the type of social stratification implied by the tripartite ideology. Social stratification is one of the main elements of state-like organizations, and on the basis of available data it is inconceivable, Renfrew argues, that the Proto-Indo-Europeans could have had states and kings at that time. Certainly, the state as a form of political organization was quite familiar to the Romans, the Greeks and the Indians in the times to which Dumézil's studies refer, as well as to the Celts, at least starting from the first century CE, but for Renfrew institutions as complex as the state (1987: 253–4) cannot hark back to the times of the undivided Indo-European community which, in his view, could not have known the distinction between priests, warriors and producers, but must rather have been an egalitarian community of farmers. The similarities and parallelisms highlighted by Dumézil, in other words, in Renfrew's view are not the outcome of a common origin but, rather, the result of parallel evolution (ibid.: 8, 251). A response to such criticisms has come from Bernard Sergent (2005: 363–4), a French researcher in the Dumézilian tradition, who argues that, in his maturity, Dumézil had gone beyond the social approach to the three functions, typical of his early works, and had come to consider them as a way of thinking reality, as a system of classification[10] which, as such, would not be in any way beyond the speculative possibilities of a Neolithic population.[11]

---

10 Cf. Dumézil 1958: 18–19, [1968] 1982: XVII–XVIII.

11 But even this mature formulation of Dumézil's thought is criticized by Mallory (1989: 12) who argues that this civilization 'of the spirit', that may not necessarily have been reflected in the

For our purposes, at any rate, the most important point is that this more sophisticated version of the tripartite ideology, whether or not we deem it grounded or useful, is not in contrast with the idea – largely shared as we have just seen – that the Indo-European society must have been an undifferentiated, essentially egalitarian society, something that, on the other hand, Dumézil himself did not exclude (Dumézil 1958: 17–18).

If the early formulation of Dumézil's theory finds no support among the Kalasha – and, we may say, in Peristan in general – because there is no trace in the structure of their society of the functional tripartition, some support, though uncertain and rather elusive, may possibly be found for the later formulation of his theory. Allen (1991) sees a trace of it in the pantheon of the Kati of Bashgal (Nuristan), where in his view three of the main divinities – Mon, Gish and Bagisht – may be associated with the three functions. Allen's model manages to explain the data because he is convinced that the Indo-European Ideology included also a fourth function, that of otherness, which provides a structural position for yet another deity, Imrà, who is the chief god of the pantheon and would otherwise have been left, so to speak, 'unemployed'.

In the case of the Kalasha, as we said, it is not possible to detect a divine triad corresponding to the model of the tripartite theology in their pantheon. As we have seen in Chapter 2, Kalasha gods lack indeed a clear functional specialization. The function that can more readily be detected is maybe the second one, represented by Warin and Praba, especially for the etymology of their names which, as we know, leads in both cases to Indra, the warrior god *par excellence*; their connection to the function of strength/war is also indicated by the 'holy terror' inspired by their shrines, in comparison to the other altars. The third function could perhaps be represented by Jach, a deity invoked for the abundance of crops, who has, however, a very elusive personality. To the same function of prosperity/productivity seems to be connected also, on the other hand, to the god Mahandeo, addressed with the epithet *k'ushala,* 'ingenious', or 'crafty', because he is supposed to have taught humans how to make cheese and produce honey; the relaxed attitude with which his shrines are approached, appears to evoke the sphere of

---

actual world of the people that spoke Proto-Indo-European, is an untestable hypothesis that may have some explanatory function in the field of comparative mythology, but is quite useless for prehistorians. Such a criticism brings Mallory close to Renfrew (1987: 261), who of course did not ignore the changes in Dumézil's view, but believed that by setting aside the question of the historical reality of his model he had gone beyond the limits of scientific caution in his attempt to explain similarities always through the idea of a common origin.

the tranquil joys of peace, which for Dumézil (1958: 19) is a typical trait of the third function. On the other hand, the fact that Mahandeo is the only god who has altars in all three Kalasha valleys could suggest that he may be connected to the first function of sovereignty; however, nothing indicates that he is seen as standing above the other gods. The only paramount deity, certainly standing above the others, is Dizala Dizaw, the Creator god, but for his character of *deus otiosus*, aloof from the world of men, he cannot be seen as a personification of the first function. Indeed, the function of soveregnity/sacredness does not seem to have any representation in the Kalasha pantheon. If the tripartite ideology has ever been the classificatory principle of the deities composing it – which is far from certain – today we may discern only a few, faded traces of it.

Apart from these possible traces, there are, however, a couple of other indications which could appear more significant. A rather faded trace of the tripartite ideology seems to emerge in a theme recurring in various versions of the foundation myths of the three Kalasha communities: a legendary ancestor receives from the gods Praba or Warin in person, according to two versions from Birir, or from a famous shaman in the case of Rumbur, three arrows, marked in succession with a white, a red, and a black thread, to be shot from the passes closing the valley to the west. The black arrow would have marked the place where the *bash'ali* should have been erected; the red one the site where Warin's or Praba's shrine in Birir, or Sajigor's in Rumbur, was to be built; the white one would have marked the holy place of the Jach divinity in Rumbur and the site of the first village in Birir.[12] We find here exactly the three colours that are believed to already represent the three functions in the Indo-Iranian world, with a symbology that Dumézil has detected also among the Celts and the Romans: white is the colour of sovereignty/sacredness, red of strength/war, and black of prosperity/productivity (cf. Mallory & Adams 1997: 131). Among the Kalasha the symbology appears to be faded and the colours correspond only in part to the three functions; the connection of the third function with the *bash'ali* seems understandable because the house of birth is a place that represents women who are producers *par excellence*, both for their role in agriculture and for their function in generation; the red colour as well, in the Birir versions, appears to be correctly associated with gods like Warin or Praba, who are *avatars* of Indra. What seems to be missing is again the first function. The symbolic reference of the white-threaded arrow appears to be rather uncertain: in Birir it is the first settlement, which has little to do with sovereignty, and in Rumbur the holy place of Jach, a divinity connected to the sphere

---

12 Hussam-ul-mulk 1974: 82–3; Cacopardo A.S. 1974: 52; Parkes 1975: 12; Loude 1980: 54.

of production rather than to that of sovereignty. The tripartite ideology, maybe present in the myth, is not lineally reflected in the social reality. It is perhaps not by chance that in some versions the arrows are reduced to two:[13] The function of sovereignty/sacredness among the Kalasha does not emerge, even as a mere category of conceptualization of reality.

There is also another myth in which may be seen some trace of the tripartite ideology, though in an even more hypothetical way. According to a story related to us in 1973,[14] inside the stone building of the shrine of the god Sajigor, in Rumbur, are hidden three cult objects in which we may see a symbolic expression of the tripartite model. These 'symbolic talismans' – to use Dumézil's (1958: 25) terminology – are a hammer, a knife and a *nir'an*, a sort of short scimitar. The function of sacredness could be represented here by the knife as the tool of sacrifice, while the *nir'an* could symbolize the function of strength/war since it once belonged to a defeated enemy, and the hammer may be the third function because according to the myth it had been used by a divine being to chisel on a slab of stone the image of a large cheese, which can still be seen in the enclosure of a goat shed not far from the holy place.

Hence, in the Kalasha system we may tentatively discern only some faint trace of the tripartite ideology at the mythological level. Uncertain traces of course, but even if they were real it would not mean that the Kalasha have known, in their history, social stratification or the state, but only that they possibly did not ignore the tripartite ideology as a model for the classification of reality, in line with the more mature formulation of Dumézil's theory. However, even if in Kalasha mythology – especially in the myth of the three arrows – we may detect a faint echo of a time when the tripartite model *may* have been operational, today this is certainly no longer the case.

In the Kalasha symbolic system, in fact, is much more manifest and operational the bipolar ideology expressed, as we have seen, in a series of symmetric binary oppositions all stemming from the basic pure/impure polarity. It is a very different model, no doubt, but one that apparently has, in its turn, deep roots in the Indo-European world. Mallory (1989: 140–1) remarks indeed that Dumézil himself proposes a dualistic model intersecting the tripartite structure of Indo-European ideology. The doubling up of the first function attributed to coupled divinities as Mithras-Varuna or Odin-Tyr, and the divine twins of the third function (Dumézil [1977] 1985) would be examples of it. For Mallory the Indo-European ideology

---

13 Shah 1974: 77–8, Loude 1980: 61–2.
14 Cacopardo A.S. 1974: 53–4.

is not based on just one model: binary oppositions are part of its basic structure just as the tri-functionality. He considers fundamental the coupling of binary oppositions right/left and good omen/bad omen, which involves also the sphere of gender, associating the feminine gender with the left and therefore with bad omen, and the masculine one with the right and good omen (Mallory & Adams 1997: 130–1). If this is so, it seems that also at the level of the symbolic system the Kalasha model agrees to a good extent with that of the reconstructed ancient Indo-European culture. But let us see now what contribution may come to the knowledge of Proto-Indo-European religiosity from the textual method.

The religion of the Proto-Indo-Europeans

The religious ideology of the Proto-Indo-Europeans, as reconstructed by Campanile (1990), recalls the Kalasha one in some of its main features. In the first place because, in contrast to the religions based on the idea of a Saviour, it is not much concerned with representations of the World Beyond. It aims, rather, at regulating relations between humans and gods in reference to precise material objectives that have to do with life on Earth (ibid.: 93). For Campanile, representations of the Afterlife with roots in ancient Indo-European culture, are the idea of the Elysian Fields of the Greeks and that of the Land of the Living of the Irish. These are images of a place not open to everybody, nor necessarily to the most deserving, but to those who are led there by the free, and maybe impenetrable, will of the gods. The largest part of humanity is destined, in fact, to live in a sombre world of debasement where the body survives, enduring the horrors of old age and death (ibid.: 95–7).

Correspondingly, if we discard in the Kalasha system the traits clearly due to the influence of Islam, like the story of Adam and Eve and the notions of Paradise and Hell, the only traditional representations of the World Beyond are given by images like the shining Golden Houses of Palar, where the chosen ones dwell in bliss in the company of the *s'uci* spirits: a joyous place beyond the World of Time where all needs are satisfied, that recalls, indeed, the Elysian Fields and the Land of the Living. In contrast, we find no trace among the Kalasha of the sombre Afterlife awaiting common mortals. On the whole, their traditional notion of the Afterlife seems similar to that reconstructed by Campanile for the ancient Indo-Europeans, also for the role played in Kalasha culture by the 'path of glory', which appears to echo the 'heroic ideal' of the ancient Indo-European world that does not only refer to braveness in war, but also to the ability to solve disputes and to the generosity displayed in distributing goods to the people (Campanile 1990:

112). As the reader will recall, retribution for human deeds, in Kalasha traditional view, is not projected in a distant Afterlife, but takes the form of prestige and glory obtained in the course of one's life. Immortality has therefore nothing to do with the survival of an entity like the Christian-Islamic soul, but with the memory of a person's name, which will be perpetuated after his death by the generations to come in songs, chants and panegyrics. The only way to overcome death is therefore to accomplish feats that will make one's name immortal by engraving it in the memory of future generations. Hence the importance of genealogical memory and of the verbal art that transmits it, in the construction of Kalasha identity.[15] The *drazha'ilak* and *d'ushak* chants we analyzed in Part II, are genuine examples of a genre – genealogical poetry – that according to Campanile (ibid.: 107) is rooted in Indo-European times, and should therefore be ranked with the better known ones of religious and heroic poetry.

In addition to this notion of human destiny after death, Kalasha religion displays also another important similarity with the ideology of the speakers of ancient Indo-European, as reconstructed by Campanile. The Italian scholar (ibid.: 93–4) has indeed highlighted a contraposition between the mortal life of men and the immortal life of the gods, that is, in our own terms, between birth-and-death and life-without-beginning-or-end, and in Kerenyi's terms, between 'characterized' and 'non-characterized' life, *bios* and *zoè*; an opposition that in our view is at the core of the ritual complex of Chaumos and of the entire traditional symbolic system of the Kalasha. What appears to be absent, among the ancient Indo-Europeans as well as among the Kalasha, is the idea of an immortal soul. Some parallels seem to be emerging here at the deepest cosmological level, the one concerning the destiny of humans (cf. Izard & Smith [1979] 1988: 14).

Further correspondences appear to emerge if we consider the general picture of the religious sphere in the Indo-European world, as outlined by Mircea Eliade. The reconstruction of the great Romanian scholar seems indeed to be applicable in full to the Kalasha:

The Indo-Europeans had developed a specific mythology and a specific theology. They celebrated sacrifices and they knew the magical value of words and chants. Their religious ideas and their rituals enabled them to consecrate space and to 'cosmicize' the territories where they settled (this mythic-ritual scenery is attested in ancient India, in Rome and among the Celts), and they enabled them as well to periodically renovate the world

---

15 Parkes 1996a; Di Carlo 2010a.

(through the ritual clash between two groups of performers, a rite of which traces are attested in India and in Iran). The gods were believed to be present at the celebrations, together with humans, and the offerings reserved to them were burnt. The Indo-Europeans did not have sanctuaries: in all likelihood their cults were celebrated in a sacred enclosure, in the open air. Another characteristic trait was the oral transmission of tradition … (Eliade [1975] 1979: 211).

If mythology and theology, as we have seen, appear faded among the Kalasha, we know they were more developed in pre-Islamic Nuristan, and that they were therefore certainly present in Peristan. We have seen how central is the role of sacrifice in the rituals we described and what great value is given to spoken words and chants, even though we might not call it magic. We have seen also how the space of rites is consecrated and how it is connected to the origins of the community, if not of the cosmos, in the oral traditions transmitted through the chants. 'The oral traditions that enabled them to periodically renovate the world', in Eliade's words, are precisely the ones we analyzed in our investigation of Chaumos. We have found the 'ritual clash between two groups' of participants and the idea of the invisible presence of the gods during the celebrations, and of sacrifice as a meal enjoyed by gods and humans together, in which the god's share is burnt in the sacrificial fire. Furthermore, like the ancient Indo-Europeans, the Kalasha do not build temples for their gods (with the only exception, we have seen, of the temple of the goddess Jeshtak) and their holy places are open-air shrines in a consecrated space, sometimes delimited by an enclosure (as is the case with Praba's altar in Birir). The wealth of chants and songs we have recorded, finally, bears witness to the importance they attribute to the oral transmission of traditional knowledge.[16] Among the Kati of Bashgal, if not among the Kalasha, we have moreover data concerning the horse sacrifice (Edelberg 1972: 37) – celebrated once a year, probably for the New Year festival – which was the main ritual in Vedic times (*ashvameda*) and for Eliade ([1975] 1979: 240–1) is certainly a rite of Indo-European origin. For Sergent (2005: 388), lastly, and we touch here on a point most directly connected to our research, it is possible to detect a common Indo-European model at the

---

16 We have chosen to include in this volume mainly the texts of women's songs, because they are more directly connected to Chaumos. The task of transmitting traditional knowledge is entrusted instead to the songs generally (but not necessarily) sung by men – *d'ushak* and *drazha'ilak* – of which we have presented only two examples. But many other chants of this kind are present in our recorded materials.

core of the yearly ritual cycles of the Vedic world and of the pagan, Scandinavian world. Both were based on three festive nuclei that, in India, were staged in spring, in the summer rainy season, and in autumn – in Scandinavia in mid-October, mid-January and in spring. Correspondingly we have found, as seen, three great festive nuclei in the Kalasha annual ritual cycle. Apart from the variations that can be ascribed to climatic differences, the model outlined by Sergent seems to correspond quite closely to the one we have analyzed in this work.

Conclusions

By putting together the available data concerning the material culture, the social structure, the political organization, and the symbolic and religious system of the Proto-Indo-Europeans, we have therefore seen that an overall picture emerges of that ancient culture which appears to exhibit significant parallels with that of the Kalasha and of the pre-Islamic world of the Hindu Kush in general. Naturally, the work of reconstruction could outline nothing more than the mere skeleton of a cultural pattern. Next to nothing is known, we have seen, about the names of the divinities, the myths, the rituals and the festivals of the people who spoke the Proto-Indo-European language.

The correspondences we highlighted, have possibly some importance not so much for what concerns material culture – the Indo-Europeans, we can assume, were certainly not the only pastoralists/agriculturalists with that level of technology in Eurasia – as for the other spheres of social life, especially for the symbolic and ideological one.

The data from Peristan give full support, in the first place, to the idea that the ancient Indo-European society was not stratified, except in relation to the artisan group. This view, we have seen, does not exclude the possibility of the existence of kings, for such a role would have had merely sacral functions. At the level of the symbolic-ideological system our data are perhaps not incompatible with the last formulation of Dumézil theory (even if we may share Mallory's perplexities about its usefulness), though in the absence of a corresponding tripartite social structure and of any indication of its former existence, we have possibly spotted some faint traces of the tripartite ideology in Kalasha mythology. They appear, however, to be quite evanescent and, at any rate, certainly overridden by a dualistic ideology that would also belong, we have seen, to the symbolic patrimony of the Indo-European world.

On the strictly religious plane the parallels we discovered with the cultural reconstruction made by Campanile through the textual method, seem quite interesting. We found in the traditional Kalasha system the same lack of interest for the Afterlife that the Italian scholar considers typical of the Indo-European worldview, and a corresponding notion of immortality as survival of a person's name in the memory of his offspring in this world, rather than the idea of a soul-like entity perpetuating human life in a distant afterworld. On the same religious plane, we found also other parallels in the open-air design of the cult places and in the conception of sacrifice as a communal meal shared by gods and humans ideally seated together.

We can finally observe that the most significant contribution that Kalasha data can offer to Indo-European studies is probably in the field of ritual. As Sergent also remarks, this is a field in which, for lack of data, little progress has been made in the work of reconstruction. Next to nothing is known, we have seen, about the ritual systems of pre-Christian Europe, while information is scant even about the better documented realities, such as Greece and Rome. As for the East, the knowledge we have of the Vedic sacrifice is not enough, in its turn, to make up for the scarcity of data on the pre-Vedic Indian world or on the pre-Zoroastrian Iranian one. In this context, the knowledge of a ritual complex like the one documented in this work can offer some points of reference perhaps not devoid of significance.

Epilogue

Our search for intercultural connections has led us far. We have seen that, if in its pantheon and in its fundamental symbolic nucleus, the religion of the Kalasha belongs undoubtedly to the Indian world, in its ritual cycle it is closer to the pre Christian world of Europe.

In our comparative investigation of European folklore, we found parallelisms between the festive period from All Saints' to Carnival and the Kalasha winter sequence centred on Chaumos. Under the cover of the Christian feasts we found traces of a festive complex that seems to have many traits in common with the Kalasha one. The greatest affinities with Chaumos we found in Carnival, as a container hosting and preserving many 'ritemes' of former pre-Christian feasts, but we found also among the Kalasha the essential trait of Christmas, that of the divine Visitor. Comparison has showed that this belief in a divine being, the bringer of life, who descends among humans in the darkest time of the year, is a very ancient idea. Since we found it both in the pagan roots of Europe and in the pre-Vedic ones of Hinduism, we suggested – of course, only as a mere hypothesis – that it may have emerged in the context of the agro-pastoral societies of Indo-European speech.

As for the Indian universe, it is confirmed that, though Kalasha religious vocabulary frequently leads to the Vedic pantheon, we are dealing here with a connection that harks back to times preceding the Vedas. The roots of the Peristani complex seem to be located exactly where we would have expected to find them on the basis of linguistic data: very close to the undivided Indo-Iranian world, as Witzel believes, but on the Indian side of the divide.

Naturally, as we made clear from the beginning, we do not imagine we have found a living fossil that has preserved, after more than four millennia, a fragment of that ancient world. Yet, there are strong indications that the people of Peristan may be the descendants of some of the earliest waves of Indo-European (Indo-Iranian) speaking migrants to the Indian subcontinent who, until the advent of Islam, followed in their isolation largely autonomous lines of development. The parallels we found between the Peristani cultural model and the Proto-Indo-European one, as reconstructed on the basis of the compact vocabulary and textual analysis, seem interesting in this regard.

The fact that a complex today so marginal and peripheral like the Peristani one managed to maintain for so long its specificity despite the influences that – to different extents in different historical periods – must have reached it from the plains, should not surprise us. In the first place we must not forget that only in recent history has this complex become marginal. Not only did it cover a large part of the Hindu Kush/Karakorum chain until two centuries ago, but comparison also showed that in all likelihood it formerly reached even further, to include the Western Himalayas. This part of the great Asian range may once have been the cradle of a large cultural area wherein the Indo-European language prevailed, not as an area on the periphery of other worlds, but as a centre in its own right.

Apart from its extension and its being rooted in the fastness of a remote mountain area, one of the points of strength of the complex, which the Peristani data indicate, must have been its cult of the past based on a very sophisticated verbal art. An important role in preserving local identities must have been played by genealogical memory, which in Peristan is particularly deep. Jan Vansina, a world-wide authority on the issue of the historical value of oral traditions, which he investigated mainly in Africa, has written that he knows of no example of an uninterrupted series of recollections reaching back more than three centuries (Vansina [1961] 1976: 311–12). Among the Kalasha this limit can be exceeded and among the Kom Nuristani the case is documented of an oral tradition that could be traced back even more than five centuries.[1] These quite exceptional data appear to confirm Campanile's idea that the cultivation of genealogical memory, and therefore of collective memory, had a particularly prominent role among peoples of Indo-European language. Since the notion of a common descent and the memory of a shared history are among the founding elements of an *ethnos*,[2] i.e. of an ethnic identity, it is reasonable to think that they should have played an important role in preserving the identity of Peristani cultures, and in supporting their centuries-long resistance to outside influences and pressures.

But the real strength of the complex must have been the consistency of the

---

1 Comparing data collected at different times from informants who could not have been in contact, Morgenstierne (1973b: 312) could ascertain the historical character of genealogies thirty generations deep.

2 Smith [1986] 1998: 69–74; Tullio Altan 1995: 19–30.

model on which it was based. We are not faced, that is, with something un-accomplished, with a rough sketch of a system, as for example Propp – maybe erroneously – seemed to think was the case for the pre-Christian beliefs of Russia,[3] but with a true system, endowed with a unitary nexus that expresses consistent values to which correspond mental attitudes and behavioural models. A system based on a true cosmology, an ideal vision of relations between humans, humans and nature, humans and the supernatural: a set of cultural ideals expressed in the rites of Chaumos.

In the field of human relations we found the explicit statement of an *ethos* of solidarity, expressed by the principle of sharing within the group, which is one of the foundation stones of the whole system. As is generally the case in traditional societies, it is not a universal ethos, of course. It only applies to the members of the community, while against outsiders perceived as enemies any act of appropriation is permitted, from robbery to murder. Importantly, the political reflection of this *ethos* of internal solidarity is a stateless political organization that confines the hierarchical principle to the sphere of relations between genders and age groups.

On the plane of relations between humans and the natural environment, we have found among the Kalasha a vision according to which humans cannot dispose of the resources of nature at will, because these do not belong to them but to their supernatural guardians, the mountain spirits. Humans are not the lords of nature, but they are rather guests of it, together with the other living beings. If this is a model frequently found in traditional societies, the connection established between the plane of relations between humans and that of relations between humans and nature, appears as a peculiarity of the Kalasha system; the principle of sharing implies the rejection of the domination of man over man, which is homologous, we have seen, to the rejection of the dominion of man over nature. At the deepest level of the cosmology, that of the relations with the supernatural, we found the principle of the *coincidentia* (or *coniunctio*) *oppositorum*, which aims at overcoming the antinomy of the hierarchical relation between the poles that takes shape in gender relations, by symbolically proclaiming their substantial unity, impersonated by the androgynous Visitor god.

This model had certainly many variants in Peristan, but its basic structure, as we said from the beginning, was the same throughout the region. The consistency of the cosmology and the cult of collective memory, together with the protected geographical location, are the factors that perhaps can explain, in connection,

---

3 Propp [1963] 1978: 177–80; cf. Bruzzese in Propp ibid.: 22.

of course, with historical occurrences, the millenary resistance of the Peristani complex.

Chaumos is the ritual representation, or better the ritual enactment, of that Peristani cosmology. In its deeper nucleus, however, we have seen the expression of a universal aspiration, connected to the experience of the transience, the impermanence, of the human condition. At the core of the whole system of oppositions, expressed in the language of the pure and the impure, we found the fundamental opposition between birth-and-death and life-freed-from-death, that is, between mortal and immortal, limited and unlimited life, *bios* and *zoè*, which is overcome in the great ritual of collective regeneration. A great ritual in which – as Bakhtin ([1965] 1984: 256) writes about Carnival feasts – people experience materially and sensually their unity, their being a whole. This is not so much about concepts as it is about experience. The chants, the songs, the dances, the sacrifices, bring about a condition of participation of feelings[4] based on a direct involvement of the subjects in the reality that ritual symbols express: communion with fellow human beings, with nature, with the gods.

The experience of this communion from which solidarity arises and in which the anguish of death is overcome by making sense of the fugacity of human life, is in our view the deepest, and universal, meaning of Chaumos. A message that in its essential core, though in a great variety of manifestations, probably resonates in all New Year festivals in general, a message that we, dwellers in Western post-industrial societies, perhaps can still hear in our Christian winter feasts. But while in the ancient worlds, which we have been analysing, the battle of life against death had to be fought and won again every year through its ritual enactment, in Christianity, a salvific religion, the battle is won once and for all with the descent of the Saviour in human form.

Yet, the ancient symbols survive: in the Christian liturgic year Jesus has the traits of the Visitor god when he descends on Earth at the time of the winter solstice, and those of the Dying god when, at Easter, with his death and resurrection, he does not just ensure the rebirth of nature but – in the Christian view – opens the gates of eternal life to all human beings. Thus, the human aspiration to transcend the limits of *bios*, mortal life, and to enter the sphere of *zoé*, the realm of non-death once reserved to the gods, is given complete fulfilment.

---

4 For the Italian anthropologist Carlo Tullio Altan (1992: 85–6) this is 'one of the most characterizing modalities of symbolic experiencing'.

Appendix

Chronological Outline of Birir Winter Feasts

Preparations for Chaumos

Acharik and gandalikan – 10 December 2006
  - virgin boys make preparations and the shrine of the god Praba
  - girls meet with the shepherds in the forests and receive gifts of carved figurines
  - old baskets are burned and songs and dances of Chaumos are anticipated

Chaumos (14–20 December 2006)

Desh sucein – 14 December
  - purification sacrifice in a holy place up-valley from the inhabited area
  - purification of the inhabited territory with juniper smoke
  - backward dance of the bhut spirits: Bhutungushék (held every four years, not in 2006)
Ruzhias – 15 December 2006
  - cleaning of the houses
  - rites with juniper smoke for the bhut spirits
  - animal sacrifices for the first wine of the year
  - offerings to the dead
Goshtsaraz – 16 December 2006
  - purification rites at the goat sheds with juniper smoke
  - the initiates gather in groups that roam the valley shouting
  - torchlight processions, insults especially to elders
  - dances and songs in the temples until the early hours of the morning; lineages belonging to the same temple are reunited

Nongrat – 17 December 2006
- collecting rounds by virgin boys
- grinding of the grain collected to obtain the flour for the bread to be consumed in the days of separation
- sacrifices at the goat sheds in preparation of the initiation rites of the following day
- purification rites in the homes for the girls to be initiated
- evening fast
- rite with rice and juniper in the early hours of the morning

Istongas rat – 18 December 2006
- little girls take offerings to the dead
- dressing up of the initiates in the home with the assistance of the maternal uncle
- presentation and dance of the initiates in the temples
- sacrifices for male initiations at the goat sheds
- beginning of the separation period for the novices
- banquets in the goat sheds of the families of the male novices
- sacrifice at dawn at the shrine of the god Praba with the novices in the foreground
- dancing and singing in the temples
- nocturnal torchlight procession; the downstream half reunites in the Aspar temple, the upstream one in the temple of Biyu

Kot shatek – 19 December
- daytime singing and chanting in the open-air dancing ground; the two halves, upstream and downstream, are reunited
- dance of the novices in the area of the goat sheds close to the dancing-ground
- ritual of the storming of the fortress
- fox scaring ritual
- running race between the two halves and lightening of the fires
- brawl
- rite with mistletoe and secret prayer in the area of the goat sheds
- dancing and singing on the dancing ground
- the markhor dance signals the end of the celebration; a long human chain led by a man with a mistletoe bough extinguishes the fire by stepping on it

Dahu tattu – 20 December 2006
- open-air, daytime dancing and singing in front of Aspar's temple
- bean collecting round of the girls

- last ajhona baiak song (forbidden until the following autumn)
- rite with mistletoe marking the end of the separation of the novices
- adolescent girls monitor the cooking of the beans under the porch of the temple, where youngsters gather until late at night

Post-Chaumos period

Dahu pacein – 21 December 2006
- end of the cooking of the beans and distribution, consumption in the homes
- back and forth between temples and houses for provisioning

Shish kurr – six days later
- the heads and the paws of the animals sacrificed for the initiations are eaten

Lagaur – (3 9 January 2007)

Day 1 – 3 January 2007
- the *kaz'is* announce in the morning the beginning of the festival
- in the evening ritual meal with cheese

Day 2 – 4 January 2007
- ritual meal with beans cooked with their pods and walnuts

Day 3 – 5 January 2007
- children, male and female, walk in a body to a goat shed area downstream singing the song of the crow
- they gather green boughs to decorate the temples
- in the morning the women make bread figurines of goats in the homes
- in the evening the men mould bread figurines of markhors filled with walnut mush and prepare a large bread cake to take to the goat sheds in the morning

Day 4 – 6 January 2007
- two hours before dawn women gather in the temples and invoke the White Crow
- at dawn the men take the large bread cakes to the goat sheds
- dancing and singing in the villages for the children who imitate the rituals of Chaumos
- six more days of dancing for the children follow (reduced to two in 2007)

Last day – 9 January 2007
- game for children imitating the running race of the day of Kotshatek
- the boys take the bread figurines made by the men to a plateau above the village and give what is left to the crows
- the figurines made by the women are given to the goats

Jhanì

Day 1 – 23 January 2007
- collecting rounds (flour and red beans) of the girls through all the villages of the half they belong to
- cooking of the beans at the temples
- young boys and girls gather there

Day 2 – 24 January 2007
- end of the cooking of beans and distribution to the families (only for women)

Day 3 – 25 January 2007
- purification rite for the dolls

New Year celebrations

Salgherek – 31 January 2007
- morning sacrifice at the shrine of the god Mahandeo
- rite in the homes in honour of the goddess Jeshtak in the evening, inauguration of new crops

Benjishtem – 1 February 2007
- beginning of the new year: in the morning breakfast with pumpkin
- fertility rites at the goat sheds
- ritual meal with cheese and walnut mush at the goat sheds

Raistam – middle of February

- repetition first phase initiation rite for boys and for girls
- the families of the novices offer two walnut filled bread loaves to each family of their villages
- sacrifice of a lamb at the shrine of Raistam Praba
- sacrifice of a kid at the shrine of the god Mahandeo
- rite of the first sowing with millet seeds dipped in the blood of the sacrificial victim

Bibliography

Addobbati, A. (2002) *La festa e il gioco nella Toscana del Settecento*. Edizioni Plus. Università di Pisa.

Alder, G.J. (1963) *British India's Northern Frontier 1865–95. A Study in Imperial Policy*. Longmans. London.

Allen, N. (1991) 'Some gods of Pre-Islamic Nuristan'. *Revue de l'Histoire des Religions*. 208, 2, pp. 141–68.

Augé, M. (1980) 'Puro/impuro'. In: *Enciclopedia Einaudi*. Vol. 11. Einaudi. Turin.

Augé, M. (2002) *Il genio del paganesimo*. Bollati Boringhieri. Turin. Or. ed. Gallimard. Paris, 1982.

Babb, L.A. (1975) *The Divine Hierarchy: Popular Hinduism in Central India*. Columbia University Press. New York.

Backstrom, P.C. & C.F. Radloff (1992) *Languages of Northern Areas*. National Institute of Pakistan Studies, Quaid-i-Azam University & Summer Institute of Linguistics. Islamabad

Bakhtin, M. (1984) *Rabelais and His World*. Indiana University Press. Bloomington. Or. ed. Mosca, 1965.

Barozzi, G. (1982) 'La città e la festa. Mantova e il Carnevale tra Settecento e Ottocento'. *La Ricerca Folklorica*, 6, pp. 65–79.

Barth, F. (1956) 'Ecologic Relationships of Ethnic Groups in Swat, North Pakistan'. *American Anthropologist*. 58, pp. 1079–89.

Bashir, E. (1988) *Topics in Kalasha Syntax: An Areal and Typological Perspective*. Ph.D. Dissertation. University of Michigan. Ann Arbor. Unpublished.

Bashir, E. (2003) 'Dardic'. In: Cardona, G. & Dhanesh Jain (eds.), *The Indo-Aryan Languages*. Routledge. London.

Bashir, E. & Israr-ud-Din (1996) (eds.) *Proceedings of the Second International Hindukush Cultural Conference*. Oxford University Press. Karachi.

Basilov, V.N. (1999) Cosmos as Everyday Reality in Shamanism: An Attempt to formulate a More Precise Definition of Shamanism. In: Mastromattei, R. & A. Rigopoulos 1999, pp. 17–39.

Bateson, G. (1988) *Naven. Un rituale di travestimento in Nuova Guinea.* Einaudi. Turin. Or. ed. Stanford, 1958.

Bausinger, H. (1982) 'Dietro il Carnevale'. *La Ricerca folklorica*, 6, pp. 87–93.

Bell, C. (1997) *Ritual. Perspectives and Dimensions.* Oxford University Press. New York & Oxford.

Bellew, Henry W. (1973). *An Inquiry into the Ethnography of Afghanistan.* Repr. Graz: Akademische Druck. Or. Ed. London 1891.

Benveniste, E. (2001) *Il vocabolario delle istituzioni indoeuropee.* 2 vol. Einaudi. Turin. Or. ed. Paris, 1969.

Berger, H. (2008) Burushaski – 'Destinies of a Central Asian Language Remnant'. *Journal of Asian Civilizations*, XXXI, 1–2, pp. 147–67. Islamabad

Berreman, G. (1963) *Hindus of the Himalayas.* University of California Press. Berkeley.

Berreman, G. (1972) *Hindus of the Himalayas.* New extended edition. University of California Press. Berkeley.

Bianco, C. (1988) *Dall'evento al documento.* CISU. Rome.

Bhatt, R.P., H.W. Wessler & C.P. Zoller (2014) 'Fairy lore in the high mountains of South Asia and the hymn of the Garhwali fairy "Daughter of the Hills". *Acta Orientalia*, 75, pp. 79–166.

Biddulph, J. (1880) *Tribes of the Hindoo Koosh.* Calcutta. Repr. Peshawar, 1986.

Bloch, M. (1989) 'Symbols, Song, Dance and Features of Articulation'. In: Bloch, M., *Ritual, History and Power.* London. Or. ed. in: *Archives Européennes de Sociologie*, 15, 1974.

Bloch, M. (1992) *Prey into hunter.* Cambridge University Press. Cambridge.

Bogatyrev, P. (1982) *Semiotica della cultura popolare.* Giorgio Bertani Editore. Verona. Or. ed. Warsaw, 1975.

Branston, B. (1991) *Gli Dei del Nord.* Mondadori. Milan. Or. ed. London 1955.

Brelich, A. (2007) *Il politeismo.* Editori Riuniti. Rome.

Bremmer, J.N. (1994) 'Greek Religion'. *Greece & Rome*, n. 24. Oxford University Press.

Brugnoli, G. (1984) 'Il carnevale e i Saturnalia'. *La Ricerca folklorica*, 10, pp. 49–54.

Bruzzese (1978) Premessa del traduttore. In Propp [1963] 1978.

Buddruss, G. (1960) 'Zur Mythologie der Präsun-Kafiren'. *Paideuma.* 7, 4–6, pp. 200–9.

Buddruss, G. (1973) 'Archaisms in Some Modern Northwestern Indo-Aryan Languages'. In: Embassy of the Federal Republic of Germany (ed.), *German Scholars on India*. Vol. 1, pp. 31–49. Varanasi.

Buddruss, G. (1974) 'Some Reflections on a Kafir Myth'. In: Jettmar & Edelberg 1974, pp. 31–6.

Buddruss, G. (2008) 'Reflections of the Islamization of Kafiristan in Oral Tradition'. *Journal of Asian Civilizations*, XXXI, 1–2, pp. 16–35. Islamabad.

Buddruss, G. & P. Snoy (2008) 'The German Hindu Kush Expedition (DHE) 1955–56'. *Journal of Asian Civilizations*, XXXI, 1–2, pp 1–15. Islamabad.

Buddruss, G. & A. Degener (2015) *Materialen zur Prasun-sprache des Afghanischen Hindukusch*. Harvard University Press. Cambridge, Mass.

Burke, P. (1980) *Cultura popolare nell'Europa moderna*. Mondadori. Milan. Or. ed. 1978.

Bussagli, M (1955) 'The "Frontal" Representation of the Divine Chariot.' *East & West*, VI, 1, pp. 9–23.

Buttitta, A. (1989) 'Madre mediterranea. Radici e dispersione'. In: Buttitta, A. & S. Miceli 1989.

Buttitta, A. (1995) 'Ritorno dei morti e rifondazione della vita'. Introduction to Lévi-Strauss 1995.

Buttitta, A. (1996) *Dei segni e dei miti*. Sellerio. Palermo.

Buttitta, A. & S. Miceli (1989) *Percorsi simbolici*. Flaccovio. Palermo

Buttitta, I.E. (1999) *Le fiamme dei santi*. Meltemi. Rome.

Buttitta, I.E. (2006) *I morti e il grano*. Meltemi. Rome.

Cacopardo, A.M. (1974) *I Kalash dello Hindu Kush: economia e società*. Unpublished dissertation. School of Social and Political Sciences 'C. Alfieri'. University of Florence, Italy.

Cacopardo, A.M. (1985) 'Kalash, gli infedeli dello Hindu Kush'. *L'Universo*. 65, 6, pp. 700–3.

Cacopardo, A.M. (1991) 'The Other Kalasha. A Survey of Kalashamun-Speaking People in Southern Chitral. Part I: The Eastern Area'. *East & West*. 41, 1/4, pp. 273–310.

Cacopardo, A.M. (1996) 'The Kalasha in Southern Chitral. Part I: The Eastern Area.' In: Bashir & Israr-ud-Din 1996, pp. 247–69.

Cacopardo, A.M. (2006) Review of Brandstetters, A.M. & C. Lentz (2006). *East & West*. 56, 4, pp. 478–9.

Cacopardo, A.M. (2009) *Chi ha inventato la democrazia?* PhD dissertation. Università di Sassari. Published on line: http://eprints.uniss it/880/1/ Cacopardo_A_Tesi_Dottorato_2009_Chi.pdf

Cacopardo, A.M. (2011) 'L'estinzione della guerra e l'orizzonte dell'etica.' In *Nonviolenza e mondo possibile*. Edizioni Piagge. Florence.

Cacopardo, A.M. & A.S. Cacopardo (1977) 'Circuiti di scambio economico e cerimoniale presso i Kalash (Pakistan)'. *Uomo & Cultura*. 19/22, pp. 106–19.

Cacopardo, A.M. & A.S. Cacopardo (1989) 'The Kalasha (Pakistan) Winter Solstice Festival.' *Ethnology*. 28, 4, pp. 317–29.

Cacopardo, A.M. & A.S. Cacopardo (1992) 'The Other Kalasha. A Survey of Kalashamun-Speaking People in Southern Chitral. Part III: Jinjeret Kuh and the Problem of Kalasha Origins.' *East & West*. 42, 2/4, pp. 333–75.

Cacopardo A.M. & A.S. Cacopardo (1995) 'Unknown Peoples of Southern Chitral. Part I: The Dameli.' *East & West*. 45, 1–4, pp. 233–82.

Cacopardo, A.M. & A.S. Cacopardo (1996) 'The Kalasha in Southern Chitral. Part III: Jinjiret Kuh and the Problem of Kalasha Origins.' In: Bashir & Israr-ud-Din 1996, pp. 299–313.

Cacopardo, A.M. & A.S. Cacopardo (2001) *Gates of Peristan. History, Religion and Society in the Hindu Kush*. Is.I.A.O. Rome.

Cacopardo, A.M. & R. Laila Schmidt (2006) (eds.) *My Heartrendingly Tragic Story*. The Institute for Comparative Research in Human Culture. Oslo.

Cacopardo, A.S. (1974) *I Kalash dello Hindu Kush: Tradizioni religiose*. Unpublished dissertation. School of Social and Political Sciences 'C. Alfieri'. University of Florence, Italy.

Cacopardo, A.S. (1985) 'Chaumos: la festa del solstizio d'inverno.' *L'Universo*. 65, 6, pp. 724–53.

Cacopardo, A.S. (1991) 'The Other Kalasha. A Survey of Kalashamun-Speaking People in Southern Chitral. Part II: The Kalasha of Urtsun.' *East & West*. 41, 1/4, pp. 311–50.

Cacopardo, A.S. (1996) 'The Kalasha in Southern Chitral. Part II: The Pre-Islamic Culture of the Urtsun Valley.' In: Bashir & Israr-ud-Din 1996, pp. 271–98.

Cacopardo, A.S. (1999) 'Shamans and the Space of the Pure Among the Kalasha of the Hindu Kush (Pakistan).' In: Mastromattei, R. & A. Rigopoulos 1999, pp. 57–71.

Cacopardo, A.S. (2006) 'Anthropomorphic Representations of Divinities among the Kalasha of Chitral (Pakistan).' *Acta Orientalia*. 67, pp. 127–58. Oslo.

Cacopardo, A.S. (2008) 'The Winter Solstice Festival of the Kalasha of Birir: Some Comparative Suggestions.' *Acta Orientalia*. 69, pp. 77–120. Oslo.

Cacopardo, A.S. (2010) 'Texts from the Winter Feasts of the Kalasha of Birir.' *Acta Orientalia*, 71, pp. 187–242.

Cacopardo, A.S. (2011) 'Are the Kalasha Really of Greek Origin? The Legend of Alexander the Great and the Pre-Islamic World of the Hindu Kush.' *Acta Orientalia*, 72, pp. 47–92.

Cacopardo, A.S. (2016). A World In Between: the Hindu Kush before Islam. In: Pellò, S. (ed.) *Borders, Itineraries on the Edges of Iran*, pp. 243–70. Edizioni Ca' Foscari. Venice.

Caillois, R. (2001) *Man and the Sacred*. University of Illinois Press. Urbana and Chicago. Or. ed. Gallimard. Paris, 1939.

Campanile, E. (1990) *La ricostruzione della cultura indoeuropea*. Giardini. Pisa

Campanile, E. (1997) Antichità indoeuropee. In Ramat A.G. & P. Ramat. *Le lingue indoeuropee*. Il Mulino. Bologna. Or. ed. 1993.

Canali, L. (1983) (ed.) *Tacito. La Germania*. Editori Riuniti. Rome.

Cardini, F. (1995) *Il cerchio sacro dell'anno*. Il Cerchio. Rimini.

Caro Baroja, J. (1989) *Il Carnevale*. Il Melangolo. Genoa. Or. ed. 1979.

Cattabiani, A. (1988) *Calendario. Le feste, i miti, le leggende & i riti dell'anno*. Rusconi. Milan.

Cavalli-Sforza, L. L. (1996) *Geni, popoli & lingue*. Adelphi. Milan.

Chandra, R. (1992) *Highlanders of North Western Himalayas*. Inter-India Publications. New Delhi.

Charachidzé, G. (1987) *La mémoire indo-européenne du Caucase*. Hachette. Paris.

Clemens, J. & M. Nüsser (2008) 'Animal Husbandry and Utilization of Alpine Pastures in the Nanga Parbat Region of Northern Pakistan: Comparison of Raikot and Rupal Valleys.' In: Israr-ud-Din 2008.

Clemente, P. (1982) 'I canti di questua: riflessioni su una esperienza in Toscana.' *La Ricerca Folklorica*, 6, pp. 101–6.

Clifford, J. (1988) *The Predicament of Culture. Twentieth-Century Ethnography, Literature, and Art*. Harvard University Press. Cambridge.

Clifford J. & G. Marcus (1986) *Writing Culture*, University of California Press. Berkeley.

Connerton, P. (1999) *Come le società ricordano*. Armando. Rome. Or. ed. Cambridge, 1989.

Court, A. (non dated, ca. 1840) *Notice sur le Kafféristan dressée sur la demande qui m'en fut faite par la Societé asiatique de Paris. Mémoires*. Vol. 4, pp. 81 104. Unpublished manuscript. Musée Guimet. Paris.

Crapanzano, v. (1995) *Tuhami. Ritratto di un uomo del Marocco*. Meltemi. Rome. Or. Ed. Chicago 1980.

Cristoforetti, S. (2003) *Il Natale della luce in Iran*. Mimesis. Milan.

Crooke, W. (1894) *An Introduction to the Popular Religion and Folklore of Northern India*. Government Press. Allahbad.

Daniélou, A. (1980). *Shiva & Dioniso*. Ubaldini. Rome. Or. ed. Arthème Fayard. Paris, 1979.

D'Agostino, G. (2002) *Da vicino e da lontano. Uomini e cose di Sicilia*. Sellerio. Palermo.

D'Apremont, A. (2005) *La vera storia di Babbo Natale*. Edizioni L'età dell'Acquario. Turin. Or. ed. Pisseaux, 2000.

Darling, E.G. (1979) *Merit Feasting among the Kalash Kafirs of North Western Pakistan*. Tesi M.A. Vancouver.

Das, V. (1990) *Structure and Cognition. Aspects of Hindu Caste and Ritual*. Oxford University Press. Delhi. Or. ed. 1977.

Davidson, H.R.E. (1988) *Myths and Symbols in Pagan Europe. Early Scandinavian and Celtic Religions*. Syracuse University Press. Syracuse.

Decker, K.D. (1992) *Languages of Chitral. Sociolinguistic survey of northern Pakistan*. 5 vols., vol. 5. National Institute of Pakistan Studies and Summer Institute of Linguistics. Islamabad.

De Gubernatis, A. (1872) *Zoological Mythology*. 2 vols. Trübner & Co. London.

Descola, P. (2005) *Par-delà nature et culture*. Gallimard. Paris.

Detienne, M. (2007) *Dioniso e la pantera profumata*. Laterza. Rome-Bari. Ed or. Gallimard. Paris 1977.

Devoto, G. (1962) *Origini Indeuropee*. Sansoni. Florence.

Di Carlo, P. (2007) The Prun Festival of the Birir Valley, Northern Pakistan, in 2006. *East & West*. 57, 1–4, pp. 45–100.

Di Carlo, P. (2008) *Representations of lineage in the Prun festival of the Kalasha of the Birir Valley*. Paper presented at the '14th Himalayan Languages Symposium', Goteborg 21–23 August 2008.

Di Carlo, P. (2010a) 'Take Care of the Poets! Verbal Art Performances as Key Factors in the Preservation of KalashaLanguage and Culture.' *Anthropological Linguistics*, 52, 2, pp. 141–59.

Di Carlo, P. (2010b) *I Kalasha del Hindu Kush. Ricerche linguistiche e antropologiche*. Florence University Press. Florence.

Di Carlo, P. (2011) 'Two clues of a former Hindu Kush linguistic area?' In Everard & Mela-Athanasopoulou 2011.

Di Nola, A.M. (1974) *Antropologia religiosa*. Vallecchi. Florence.

Di Nola, A.M. (1993) *Lo specchio e l'olio. Le superstizioni degli italiani*. Laterza. Rome – Bari.

Dollfus, P. (1987) 'Lo-gsar, le nouvel an au Ladakh.' *L'Ethnographie*. LXXXIII, 100–101, pp. 63–96.

Dorian, N.C. (1999) 'Linguistic and Ethnographic Fieldwork.' In: Fishman, J.A. (ed.), *Handbook of Language and Ethnic Identity*. Oxford University Press. Oxford.

Douglas, M. (1968) 'Pollution.' In: Sills, D. (ed.), *The International Encyclopedia of the Social Sciences*. Vol. 12. Macmillan and Free Press. New York.

Douglas, M. (1975a) *Purezza e pericolo*. Il Mulino. Bologna. Or. ed. Hardmondsworth, 1966.

Douglas, M. (1975b) *Implicit meanings*. Routledge & Kegan Paul. London

Drew, F. (1875) *The Jummoo and Kashmir Territories, a Geographical Account*. London. Repr. Karachi, 1980.

Dughlat, Muhammad Haidar (Mirza) (1895) *Tarikh-i-Rashidi A History of the Moghuls of Central Asia. An English Version, Edited, with Commentary, Notes and Map by N. Elias, the Translation by E. Denison Ross*. London.

Dumézil, G. (1929) *Le problème des Centaures*. Librairie orientaliste Paul Geuthner. Paris.

Dumézil, G. (1949) *L'héritage indoeuropéen à Rome*. Gallimard. Paris.

Dumézil, G. (1958) *L'idéologie tripartie des Indo-Européens*. Collection Latomus, XXXI. Bruxelles.

Dumézil, G. (1974) *Gli dèi dei Germani*. Adelphi. Milan. Or. ed. Paris, 1959.

Dumézil, G. (1977) *La religione romana arcaica*. Rizzoli. Milan. Or. ed. Paris, 1974.

Dumézil, G. (1982) *Mito e Epopea*. Einaudi. Turin. Or. ed. Paris 1968.

Dumézil, G. (1985) *Gli dei sovrani degli indoeuropei*. Einaudi. Turin. Or. ed. Paris 1977.

Dumézil, G. (1996) *Il libro degli eroi*. Adelphi. Milan. Or. ed. Paris 1965.

Dumont, L. (1979) *Homo Hyerarchicus*. TEL Gallimard. Paris. Or. ed. 1966.

Dumont, L. & D.F. Pocock (1959) 'Pure and Impure.' *Contributions to Indian Sociology*, 3, pp. 9–39.

Duprée, L. (1971) 'Nuristan: the "Land of Light" seen darkly.' *The American Universities Field Staff. South Asia Series*. 15, 6, pp. 1–19.

Durand, A.G. (1899) *The Making of a Frontier*. London. Repr. Graz, 1974.

Duranti, A. (2000) *Antropologia del linguaggio*. Meltemi. Rome. Or. ed. Cambridge University Press, 1997.

Edelberg, L. (1960) 'Statues de bois rapportées du Kafiristan à Kabul après la conquète de cette province par l'émir Abdul Rahman en 1895–6.' *Arts Asiatiques*. 7, 4, pp. 243–86.

Edelberg, L. (1972) 'Some Paruni Myths and Hymns.' *Acta Orientalia*. 34, pp. 31–94.

Edelberg, L. & S. Jones (1979) *Nuristan*. Akademische Druck. Graz.

Edelman, D.I. (1983) *The Dardic and Nuristani Languages*. Nauka Publishing House. Moscow.

Eggert, P. (1990) *Die Frühere Sozialordnung Moolkhoos und Toorkhoos*. Franz Steiner. Wiesbaden.

Eliade, M. (1968) *Il mito dell'eterno ritorno*. Borla. Rome. Or. ed. Gallimard. Paris, 1949.

Eliade, M. (1971) *Mefistofele & l'androgine*. Edizioni Mediterranee. Rome. Or. ed. Gallimard. Paris, 1962.

Eliade, M. (1974) *Lo sciamanismo & le tecniche dell'estasi*. Edizioni Mediterranee. Rome. Or. ed. Payot. Paris, 1951.

Eliade, M. (1976) *Trattato di storia delle religioni*. Boringhieri. Turin. Or. ed. Payot. Paris, 1948.

Eliade, M. (1979) *Storia delle credenze & delle idee religiose*. Sansoni. Florence. Or. ed. Payot. Paris, 1975.

Evans-Pritchard, E.E. (1956) *Nuer Religion*. Oxford University Press. Oxford.

Everard C. & Mela Athanasopoulou (2011) *Selected Papers from the International Conference on Language Documentation and Tradition; with a special interest in the Kalash of the Hindu Kush valleys, Himalayas.* School of English, Department of Theoretical and Applied Linguistics. Aristotle University. Thessaloniki.

Fabietti, U. (1999) *Antropologia culturale. L'esperienza e l'interpretazione*. Laterza. Rome – Bari.

Fabietti, U. (1998) (ed.) *Etnografia e Culture. Antropologi, informatori e politiche dell'identità*. Carocci. Rome.

Fabietti, U. & V. Matera (1999) *Memorie e identità*. Meltemi. Rome.

Faizi, I. (2008a) 'Siege of Chitral: Socio-Political Impacts of the British Influence (1895 – 1995).' In: Israr-ud-Din 2008.

Faizi, I. (2008b) 'The Turbulent Periods – An Account of Mass Movements in Chitral (1917 – 1953).' In: Israr-ud-Din 2008.

Fentz, M. (2010) *The Kalasha. Mountain People of the Hindu Kush*. Rhodos. Humblebaek.

Foley, W.A. (1997) *Anthropological Linguistics*. Blackwell. Oxford.

Forsyth, T.D. (1875) *Report of a Mission to Yarkund in 1873, under command of Sir T.D. Forsyth..., with Historical and Geographical Information Regarding the Possessions of the Ameer of Yarkund*. Calcutta.

Frankfort, H. (1992) *Il dio che muore*. La Nuova Italia. Florence.

Frazer, J.G. (1987) *The Golden Bough*. Papermac. London. Or. Ed. Macmillan. London, 1922.

Frembgen, J. (1999) 'Indus Kohistan. An Historical and Ethnographic Outline.' *Central Asiatic Journal*. 43, 1, pp. 70–98.

Fussman, G. (1972) *Atlas Linguistique des parlers dardes et kafirs*. Vol. 1: Cartes. Vol. 2: Commentaire. Paris.

Fussman, G. (1977) 'Pour une problématique nouvelle des religions indiennes ancienne.' *Journal Asiatique*. 265, 1/2, pp. 21–70.

Fussman, G. (1983) 'Nouveau ouvrages sur les langues et civilisation de l'Hindou-Kouch (1980–82).' *Journal Asiatique*. 271, 1/2, pp. 191–206.

Fussman, G. (1988) 'La strada dimenticata tra l'India e la Cina.' In: AA.VV., *I viaggi della storia*. Dedalo. Bari.

Gardner, A. (1977) 'A Scetch [*sic*] on Kattiristan and the Kaffirs...' With an Introduction by S. Jones. *Afghanistan Journal*. 4, 2, pp. 47–53. Or. ed. 1869.

Geertz, C. (1987) *Interpretazione di culture*. Il Mulino. Bologna. Or. ed. 1973.

Gellner, E. (1995) *Anthropology and Politics.Revolution in the Sacred Grove*. Blackwell. Cambridge, Mass.

Giallombardo, F. (1990) *Festa orgia e società*. Flaccovio. Palermo.

Gianotti , G. & F. Quaccia (1986) *Il getto delle arance nel Carnevale di Ivrea*. Ivrea.

Ginzburg, C. (2008) *Storia notturna. Una decifrazione del sabba*. Einaudi. Turin. Ed or. 1989.

Glavind Sperber, B. (1995) 'Nature in the Kalasha Perception of Life.' In: Bruun, O. & A. Kalland (eds.), *Asian Perceptions of Nature. A Critical Approach*. Curzon Press. Richmond, pp. 126–47.

Glavind Sperber, B. (1996) 'Dresses, Body Decorations, Textile Techniques.' In: Bashir & Israr-ud-Din 1996, pp. 377–408.

Glavind Sperber, B. (2008) 'No People Are an Island.' In: Israr-ud-Din 2008.

Glavind Sperber, B. & Yasir Kalash (2007) *The sacred Goats of the Kalash in the Hindukush in NW Pakistan*. Ethnographic film (44').

Gluckman, M. (1965) *Politics, Law and Ritual in Tribal Society*. Basil Blackwell. Oxford.

Gnoli, G. (1980) *Zoroaster's Time and Homeland. A Study on the Origins of Mazdeism and Related Problems*. Istituto Universitario Orientale. Napoli.

Gonda, J. (1976) *Triads in the Veda*. North-Holland Publishing Company. Amsterdam.

Graf, F. (1995) 'Dionysos'. In: van der Toorn, K., B. Becking, P.W. van der Horst (eds) *Dictionary of Deities and Demons in the Bible*. E.J. Brill. Leiden, pp. 480–90.

Graziosi, P. (1961) 'The Wooden Statue of Dezalik, A Kalash Divinity, Chitral, Pakistan.' *Man*. 183, 1, pp. 49–151.

Graziosi, P. (1964) 'Prehistoric Research in Northwestern Punjab. Anthropological research in Chitral.' In: Desio, A. (ed.), *Italian Expeditions to the Karakorum (K2) and Hindu Kush. Scientific Reports* (V – Prehistory-Anthropology). Leiden.

Graziosi, P. (2004) *'Pakistan 1955'* – Appunti di viaggio di Paolo Graziosi. Ciruzzi, S., S. Mainardi & M.G. Roselli (eds.). *Archivio per l'antropologia e la etnologia*, CXXXIV.

Graziosi, P. (2007) *'Pakistan 1960'* – Appunti di viaggio di Paolo Graziosi. Ciruzzi, S., S. Mainardi & M.G. Roselli (eds.). *Archivio per l'antropologia e la etnologia*, CXXXVII.

Griaule, M. (1972) *Dio d'acqua*. Bompiani. Milan. Or. ed. Paris, 1966.

Grossato, A. (2008) 'Alessandro Magno e l'India. Storico intreccio di miti e di simboli.' In: Saccone, C. (ed.), *Quaderni di Studi Indo-Mediterranei, I, 'Alessandro/Dhû l-Qarnayn in viaggio tra i due mari'*. Edizioni dell'Orso. Alessandria.

Goody, J. (1990) *The Oriental, the Ancient and the Primitive. Systems of marriage and the family in the pre-industrail societies of Eurasia*. Cambridge University Press. Cambridge.

Grottanelli, C. (1999) *Il sacrificio*. Laterza. Bari.

Guillard J.M. (1974) *Seul chez les Kalash*. Carrefour des Lettres. Paris.

Hambly, G. (1970) *Asia Centrale*. Storia Universale Feltrinelli. Vol. 16. Milan.

Harper, E.B. (1964) 'Ritual Pollution as an Integrator of Caste and Religion.' In: Harper, E.B., *Religion in South Asia*.

Hasrat, G.M.K. (1996) 'Some Ancient Customs of Chitral.' In: Bashir & Israr-ud-Din 1996, pp. 181–92.

Hayward, G.S.W. & Mahomed Amin (1869) 'Route from Jellalabad to Yarkand through Chitral, Badakhshan and Pamir Steppe, given by Mahomed Amin of Yarkand, with Remarks by G.S.W. Hayward.' *Proceedings of the Royal Geographical Society*. 13, pp. 122–30.

Heegård, J. (1998) Variational Patterns in Vowel Length in Kalashamon.
In: Niemi, J., T. Odin & J. Heikkinen, *Language Contact, Variation, and Change*. University of Joensuu. Joensuu.

Heegård, J. (2006) *Local Case Marking in Kalasha*. PHD Dissertation.
University of Copenhagen. Unpublished.

Heegård, J. (2015) Kalasha Texts – With introductory grammar. *Acta Linguistica Hafniensia*. 47, S1, 1–275, http://dx.doi.org/10.1080/03740463.2015.10690
49 TCLC XXXV.

Heegård, J. e I.E. Mørch (2004) 'Retroflex vowels and other peculiarities in the Kalasha sound system.' In: Saxena, A. (ed.), *Himalayan Languages. Past and Present*. Mouton de Gruyter. Berlin and New York.

Heesterman, J.C. (1993) *The Broken World of Sacrifice*. The University of Chicago Press. Chicago & London.

Himmelmann, N. (2006) 'Language documentation: What is it and what is it good for?' In Gippert, J., N.P. Himmelmann & U. Mosel (eds..), *Essentials of Language Documentation*. Mouton de Gruyter. Berlin, pp. 1–30.

Hjelmslev, L. (1971) *Essais linguistiques*. Editions de Minuit. Paris.

Herzfeld, M. (2006) *Antropologia. Pratica della teoria nella cultura e nella società*. Seid. Florence. Or. ed. Blackwell. Oxford, 2001.

Holzwarth, W. (1994) Die Ismailiten in Nordpakistan. Zur Entwicklung einer Religiösen Minderhait im Kontext neuer Aussenbeziehungen. *Ethnizität und Gesellschaft: Occasional Papers*. 21. Berlin.

Holzwarth, W. (1996) 'Chitral History, 1540–1660: Comments on Sources and Historiography.' In: Bashir & Israr-ud-Din 1996, pp. 117–34.

Holzwarth, W. (1998) 'Change in Pre-Colonial Times: An Evaluation of Sources on the Karakorum and Eastern Hindukush Regions (from 1500 to 1800).' In: Stellrecht, I., *Karakorum-Hindukush-Himalaya: Dynamics of Change. Part II*. Rüdiger Köppe. Köln.

Holzwarth, W. (2006) Sources of Gilgit, Hunza and Nager History (1500–1800) and Comments on the Oral Roots of Local Historiography. In: Kreutzmann, H. 2006.

Hubert, H. & M. Mauss (1909) 'Essai sur la nature et la fonction du sacrifice.' In: *Mélanges d'histoire des religions Sacrifice*Félix Alcan. Paris, pp. 1–130.. Or. ed. Paris, 1899.

Hultkranz, Å (1961) (ed.) *The Supernatural Owners of Nature*. Almqvist & Wiksells. Uppsala.

Hussam-ul-Mulk (1974a) 'Kalash Mythology'. In: Jettmar, K. & L. Edelberg 1974, pp. 81–3.

Hussam-ul-Mulk (1974b) Chitral Folklore. In: Jettmar, K. & L. Edelberg 1974,
    pp. 95 – 115.
Hutton, R. (1996) *Stations of the Sun. A History of the Ritual Year in Britain.*
    Oxford University Press. Oxford.
Illi, D.W. (1991). *Das Hindukush-Haus. Zum symbolischen Prinzip der
    Sonderstellung von Raummitte und Raumhintergrund.* Stuttgart.
Ingold, T. (2001) *Ecologia della cultura.* Meltemi. Rome.
Ingold, T. (2004) 'Two Reflections on Ecological Knowledge.' In: Sanga, G. &
    G. Ortalli (eds.), *Nature Knowledge. Ethnoscience, Cognition, and Utility.*
    Istituto Veneto di Scienze, Lettere ed Arti. Berghahn Books. New York.
Israr-ud-Din (1969) 'The People of Chitral: A Survey of their Ethnic Diversity.'
    Pakistan Geographical Review. 24, 1, pp. 1–13.
Israr-ud-Din (2008) (ed.) *Proceedings of the 3rd International Hindukush
    Cultural Conference* (Chitral 1995). Oxford University Press. Karachi.
Ivanov, V.V. (1984) 'Carnival as Inversion of Opposites.' In: Eco, U., V.V.
    Ivanov & M. Rector, *Carnival!..* Mouton. Berlin.
Izard, M. & P. Smith (1988) (eds.) *La funzione simbolica.* Sellerio editore.
    Palermo. Or. ed. Gallimard. Paris, 1979.
Jarrige, J.F. (2007) 'Il tesoro di Fullol.' In: Cambon, P. (ed.), *Afghanistan. I
    tesori ritrovati*, pp. 25–32. Umberto Allemandi. Turin.
Jeanmaire, H. (1972) *Dioniso. Religione e cultura in Grecia.* Einaudi. Turin. Or.
    ed. Payot. Paris, 1951.
Jesi, F. (1972) Nuovi documenti e nuovi studi sulle origini di Dioniso. In:
    Jeanmaire, H. [1951] 1972.
Jettmar, K. (1974) 'Iranian Influence in the Culture of the Hindukush.' In:
    Jettmar, K. & L. Edelberg 1974, pp. 39 – 43.
Jettmar, K. (1975) *Die Religionen des Hindukush. Die Religionen der
    Menscheit.* 4 vols., vol. 1. Verlag W. Kohlhammer. Stuttgart.
Jettmar, K. (1982) *Rockcarvings and Inscriptions in the Northern Areas of
    Pakistan.* Institute of Folk Heritage. Islamabad.
Jettmar, K. (1986) *The Religions of the Hindu Kush. The Religion of the Kafirs.*
    Vol. 1. Aris & Phillips. Warminster.
Jettmar, K. & L. Edelberg (1974), *Cultures of the Hindu Kush. Selected Papers
    fromt the Hindukush Cultural conference held at Moesgard in 1970.* Franz
    Steiner. Wiesbaden.
Jones, S. (1966) An Annotated Bibliography of Nuristan (Kafiristan) and the
    Kalash Kafirs of Chitral. Part one. *Hist. Filosof. Medd. Dan. Vid. Selsk.* 41, n.
    3.

Jones, S. (1974) *Men of Influence in Nuristan*. Seminar Press. London.

Jones, S. & P. Parkes (1984) 'Ethnographic Notes on Clan/Lineage Houses in the Hindukush and "Clan Temples" & Descent Group Structure among the Kalasha ("Kalash Kafirs") of Chitral.' *Proceedings of the Sixth International Symposium on Asian Studies. Vol. 4: South and Southwest Asia*, pp. 1155–76. Hong Kong.

Kakar, Hasan (1981) 'International Significance of the Conquest of Former Kafiristan in 1896.' *Afghanistan*. 34, 2, pp. 47–54. København.

Karim Baig, R. (1994) *Hindu Kush Study Series*. Vol. 1. Peshawar.

Karim Baig, R. (1997) *Hindu Kush Study Series*. Vol. 2. Peshawar.

Karim Beg (=Baig), R. (1996) 'Defence Organization of the Former State of Chitral: Strategy of Collective Responsibility.' In: Bashir & Israr-ud-Din 1996, pp. 139–46.

Karim Baig, R. (2008) 'Prince Sher Afzal Khan: The Ill-Fated Adventurer of Chitral.' In: Israr-ud-Din 2008.

Keay, J. (1990) *The Gilgit Game*. Oxford University Press. Karachi.

Kerényi, K. (1993) *Diontso*. Adelphi. Milan. Or, ed Munich, 1976.

Kezich, G. (2015) *Carnevale, Re d'Europa. Viaggio antropologico nelle mascherate d'inverno*. Priuli &Verlucca. Scarmagno.

Khan Mir, A. (2008) 'Maulana Noor Shahidin (1887–1967): His Political Role in the History of Chitral.' In: Israr-ud-Din 2008.

Kirfel, W. (1953). 'Siva und Dionysos'. *Zeitschrift fur Ethnologie*. 78, pp. 83–90. Braunschweig.

Klimburg, M. (1999) *The Kafirs of the Hindu Kush*. 2 vols. Franz Steiner Verlag. Stuttgart.

Klimburg, M. (2008a) 'Status Culture of the Kalasha Kafirs in Chitral: Some Notes on Culture Change.' In Israr-ud-Din 2008.

Klimburg, M. (2008b) 'Status Culture of the Kalasha Kafirs.' *Journal of Asian Civilization*, XXXI, 1–2, pp. 168–94.

Klimburg, M. (2014) 'Viticulture in Kafiristan.' In: Fragner, B.G., Kauz, R. & F. Schwarz (eds.), *Wine Culture in Iran and Beyond*. Österreichische Akademie der Wissenschaften. Vienna

Kreutzmann, H. (2006) (ed.) *Karakorum in Transition*. Oxford University Press. Karachi.

Kuiper, F.B. (1970) 'Cosmogony and Conception: A Query.' *History of Religions*. 10, 2, pp. 91–138.

La Cecla, F. & M. Tosi (2000) *Bruce Chatwin: viaggio in Afghanistan*. Bruno Mondadori. Milan

Laila Schmidt, R. (2006) 'A Nāga-Prince Tale in Kohistan.' *Acta Orientalia*. 67, pp. 159–88. Oslo.

Lakoff, G. (1987) *Women, Fire and Dangerous Things. What Categories Reveal about the Mind*. University of Chicago Press. Chicago.

Lanternari, V. (1981) Spreco, ostentazione, competizione economica. Antropologia del comportamento festivo. In: Bianco, C. & M. De Ninno, *Festa. Antropologia e semiotica*, pp. 132–50. Nuova Guaraldi. Florence.

Lanternari, V. (1983a) *La grande festa*. Dedalo. Bari. 1st ed. 1976.

Lanternari, V. (1983b) *Festa, carisma, apocalisse*. Sellerio. Palermo.

Lanternari, V. (2003) *Ecoantropologia*. Dedalo. Bari.

Leach, E. R. (1969) (ed.) *Aspects of Caste in South India, Ceylon, and North-West Pakistan*. Cambridge.

Leach, E. R. (1971) *Rethinking Anthropology*. Athlone Press. London.

Leach, E. R. (1981) *Cultura e comunicazione*. Franco Angeli. Milan. Or. ed. Cambridge, 1976.

Leitner, G.W. (1895) 'The Future of Chitrál and Neighbouring Countries. Reprinted from the *Asiatic Quarterly Review*, July 1895, with the addition of an Appendix, Routes, etc.' In: Lasker, B., *Human Bondage in Southeast Asia*. Chapel Hill, 1950.

Lévi-Strauss, C. (1992) *Antropologia strutturale*. Mondadori. Milan. Or. ed. Paris, 1964.

Lévi-Strauss, C. (1995) *Babbo Natale giustiziato*. Sellerio. Palermo. Or. ed. in: *Les Temps modernes*, 1952.

Lévi-Strauss, C. (1998) *L'uomo nudo*. Il Saggiatore. Milan. Or. ed. Paris, 1971.

Levy, R.I. (1990) *Mesocosm. Hinduism and the Organization of a Traditional Newar City in Nepal*. University of California Press. Berkeley.

Lièvre, V. (1996) 'The Status of Kalasha Women in the Religious Sphere.' In: Bashir & Israr-ud-Din 1996, pp. 337–43.

Lièvre, V. & J.-Y. Loude (1990) *Le chamanisme des Kalash du Pakistan*. Presses Universitaires de Lyon. Lyon.

Lièvre, V. & J.-Y. Loude (1991) 'Le vin du ciel.' *L'univers du vivant*. 34, pp. 16–37.

Lines, M. (1988) *Beyond the North-West Frontier*. The Oxford Illustrated Press. Sparkford.

Lorimer, D.L.R. (1929) 'The Supernatural in the Popular Belief of the Gilgit Region.' *Journal of the Royal Asiatic Society of Great Britain and Ireland*. 1929, pp. 507–36.

Lorimer, D.L.R. (1935) *The Burushaski Language (3 vols). Vol. 2: Texts and Translations*. Instituttet for Sammenlignende Kulturforskning. Serie B. 29, 2. Oslo.

Loude, J.-Y. (1980) *Kalash*. Paris.

Loude, J.-Y. (1982) 'Les statues funeraires des Kalash-Kafirs du Chitral.' *Object et Monde*. 22, 1, pp. 7–18.

Loude, J.-Y (1996) 'The Kalasha Shamans' Practices of Exorcism.' In Bashir & Israr-ud-din 1996, pp. 329–35.

Loude, J.-Y. & V. Lièvre (1984) *Solstice païen*. Presses de la Renaissance. Paris.

Loude, J.-Y. & V. Lièvre (1987) 'Fêtes d'été chez les Kalash du Nord-Pakistan: cascades de lait, vin de jambes et berger géniteur'. *L'Ethnographie*. 83, 100/101, pp. 191–220.

Maggi, W. (2001) *Our Women are Free. Gender and Ethnicity in the Hindu Kush*. The University of Michigan Press. Ann Arbor.

Maggi, W. (2008) 'Don't Cry My Daughter: Lullabies as a Keyhole into Kalasha Culture.' In: Israr-ud-Din 2008.

Malamoud, C. (1976) 'Village et forêt dans l'idéologie de l'Inde brâhmanique.' *Archives Européennes de Sociologie*. XVII, 1, pp. 3–20.

Mallory, J.P. (1989) *In Search of the Indo-Europeans*. Thames and Hudson. London and New York.

Mallory, J.P. & D.Q. Adams (1997) *Encyclopedia of Indo-European Culture*. Fitzroy Dearborn. London and Chicago.

Maraini, F. (1997) *Gli ultimi pagani*. Red edizioni. Como.

Marcus, G.E. & M.J. Fischer (1986) *Anthropology as Cultural Critique. An Experimental Moment in the Human Sciences*. The University of Chicago Press. Chicago.

Maribelli, R. (1982) 'Zanni e danze armate nel Reatino tra Ottocento e Novecento.' *La Ricerca Folklorica*, 6, pp. 107–14.

Marsden, M. (2005) *Living Islam. Muslim Religious Experience in Pakistan's North-West Frontier*. Cambridge University Press. New Delhi.

Masica, C.F. (1991) *The Indo-Aryan Languages*. Cambridge University Press. Cambridge.

Masson, C. (1842) *Narrative of Various Journeys in Balochistan, Afghanistan, The Panjab and Kalat, During a Residence in Those Countries, to which is added an Account of the Insurrection at Kalat and a Memoir on Eastern Baluchistan*. 4 vols., vol. 1. London. Repr. Akademische Druck – u. Verlagsanstalt. Graz, 1975.

Mastromattei, R. & A. Rigopoulos (1999) (eds..) *Shamanic Cosmos*. Venice. Venetian Academy of Indian Studies. New Delhi. D.K. Printworld (P) Ltd.

Matera, V. (2004) *La scrittura etnografica*. Meltemi. Rome.

Mauss, M. (1965) 'Saggio sul dono.' In: *Teoria generale della magia e altri saggi*. Einaudi. Turin. Or. ed. *L'Année Sociologique*. 1923–4.

McGovern, P.E. (2004). *L'archeologo e l'uva*. Carocci. Rome. Or. ed. Princeton University Press, 2003.

Marriott, McK. (1968) 'The Feast of Love.' In: Milton Singer (ed.), *Krishna, Myths, Rites, and Attitudes*. The University of Chicago Press. Chicago & London. Or. Ed. University of Hawaii, 1966.

Merkelbach, R. (1991). *I Misteri di Dioniso*. ECIG. Genoa. Or. ed. Stuttgart, 1988.

Miceli, S. (1989) 'Rito. La forma e il potere.' In: Buttitta, A. & S. Miceli 1989.

Miles, C.A. (1976) *Christmas Customs and Traditions. Their History and Significance*. Dover. New York. Unabridged republication of *Christmas in Ritual and Tradition, Christian and Pagan*. T. Fisher Unwin 1912.

Mock, J. (1997) *Dards, Dardistan and Dardic: an Ethnographic, Geographic, and Linguistic Conundrum*. http://www.mockandoneil.com/dard.htm. Di prossima pubblicazione in: Allan, N.J.R. (ed.), *Northern Pakistan: Karakorum Conquered*. New York. St. Martin's Press.

Mock, J. (2011) 'Shrines Traditions of Wakhan Afghanistan.' *Journal of Persianate Studies*, 4, pp. 117–45.

Mørch, I.E. (2000) 'How fast will a language die when it is officially no longer spoken?' *Odense Working Papers in Language and Communication*. 19, II. University of Southern Denmark. Odense.

Mørch, I.E. & J. Heegård, (2008) 'Some Observation on the Variation in the Pronounciation of Kalashamon as Spoken Inside and Outside Present-day Kalasha Society.' In: Israr-ud-Din 2008.

Mohan Lal (1846) *Travels in the Panjab, Afghanistan and Turkistan, to Balkh, Bokhara, and Herat; and a Visit to Great Britain and Germany*. London.

Montgomerie, T.G. (1872) 'Report of a Havildar's Journey through Chitral to Faizabad in 1870.' *Journal of the Royal Geographical Society*. 42, pp. 180–201.

Morelli, R. (1982) 'Gli alberi nei rituali primaverili del Trentino.' *La Ricerca Folklorica*, 6, pp. 47–56.

Morgenstierne, G. (1932) 'Report on a Linguistic Mission to North-Western India.' *Instituttet for Sammenlignende Kulturforskning*. Serie C. 1, 3. Oslo.

Morgenstierne, G. (1942) 'Notes on Dameli, a Kafir-Dardic Language of Chitral.' *Norsk Tidsskrift for Sprogvidenskap.* 12, pp. 115–98.

Morgenstierne, G. (1947a) 'The Spring Festival of the Kalash Kafirs.' *India Antiqua, a volume of Oriental studies presented to J.P. Vogel*, pp. 240–8. Leyden.

Morgenstierne, G. (1947b) 'Some Features of Khowar Morphology'. *Norsk Tidsskrift for Sprogvidenskap.* 14, pp. 5–28.

Morgenstierne, G. (1951) 'Some Kati Myths and Hymns.' *Acta Orientalia.* 21, pp. 161–89.

Morgenstierne, G. (1965) 'Notes on Kalasha.' *Norsk Tidsskrift for Sprogvidenkap.* 20, pp. 183–238.

Morgenstierne, G. (1968) 'Mythological Texts from the Kates of Nuristan.' *Mélanges d'indianisme à la mémoire de Louis Renou*, pp. 529–38. Paris.

Morgenstierne, G. (1973a) *Indo-Iranian Frontier Languages. The Kalasha Language.* Vol. 4. Institute for Comparative Research in Human Culture. Oslo.

Morgenstierne, G. (1973b) *Genealogical Traditions Among the Kati Kafirs.* Irano-Dardica. Ludwig Reichart. Wiesbaden, pp. 307–16.

Morgenstierne, G. (1974) 'Languages of Nuristan and Surrounding Regions.' In: Jettmar & Edelberg 1974, pp. 1–10.

Motz, L. (1984) 'The Winter Goddess: Percht, Holda and Related Figures.' *Folklore*, 95:ii.

Müller-Stellrecht, I. (1973) *Feste in Dardistan. Darstellung und Kulturgeschichtliche Analyse.* Franz Steiner. Wiesbaden.

Müller-Stellrecht, I. (1981) 'Menschenhandeln und Machtpolitik im westlichen Himalaya. Ein Kapitel aus der Geschichte Dardistans (Nordpakistan).' *Zentralasiatische Studien.* 15, pp. 391–472.

Munphool Mir (1869) 'On Gilgit and Chitral.' *Proceedings of the Royal Geographical Society.* 13, pp. 130–3.

Murtaza, G. (1982) *New History of Chitral (Nai Tarikh Chitral).* Translated from the Urdu Version into English by Wazir Ali Shah. Manoscritto. Chitral.

Nawaz Khan, M. (2008) 'One Hundred Years After the Siege of Chitral: An Analysis of the Campaign.' In: Israr-ud-Din 2008.

Neelis, J. (2006) 'Hunza-Haldeikish Revisited: Epigraphical Evidence for Transregional History.' In: Kreutzmann, H. 2006, pp. 160–70.

Neubauer, H.F. (1974) 'Die Nuristanrebe, Herkunft der Edelrebe und Ursprung des Weinbaues.' *Afghanistan Journal.* 1, 2, pp. 32–6.

Nicholas, R.W. (1981) Shraddha, Impurity and Relations Between the Living and the Dead. *Contributions to Indian Sociology*. 15, 1–2. New Delhi.

Nicoletti, M. (2006) *The Ancestral Forest*. Vajra Publications & Ev-K2-CNR Publications. Kathmandu and Bergamo.

Olivier de Sardan, J.P. (1995) 'La politique du terrain. Sur la production des donneés en anthropologie.' *Enquête*. 1, pp. 71–112.

Olivieri, L.M. (2009) *Swat. Storia di una frontiera*. Is.I.A.O. Rome.

Olivieri, L.M. (2011) 'Behind the Buddhist Communities: Subalternity and Dominancy in Ancient Swat.' *Journal of Asian Civilizations*, 34, 1, pp. 123–51.

Olmo, H.P. (2000). 'The origin and domestication of the *Vinifera* grape'. In: McGovern, P.E., S.J. Fleming & S.H. Katz (eds..), *The origins and ancient history of wine*, pp. 31–44. Routledge.

Otto, W.F. (2006) *Dioniso. Il melangolo*. Genoa. Or. ed. Frankfurt, 1933.

Owen, G. R. (1996) *Rites and Religions of the Anglo Saxons*. Barnes & Noble Books. Or. ed. 1981.

Palwal, A.R. (1969) 'History of Former Kafiristan. Polytheism of the Kafirs.' *Afghanistan*. 21, 4, pp. 61–88.

Palwal, A.R. (1970) 'History of Former Kafiristan. The Images from Kafiristan.' *Afghanistan*. 23, 2, pp. 21–52.

Palwal, A.R. (1974) 'The Harvesting Festivals of the Kalash in the Birir valley.' In Jettmar & Edelberg 1974, pp. 73–4.

Parkes, P. (1975) *The Social Role of Historical Tradition Among the Kalash Kafirs of Chitral*. Bachelor of Letters thesis. Oxford University.

Parkes, P. (1983) *Alliance and Elopment: Economy, Social Order and Sexual Antagonism among the Kalasha (Kalash Kafirs) of Chitral*. PhD dissertation. Oxford University.

Parkes, P. (1986) 'Etymological Glossary of Kafiri Religious Vocabulary.' In: Jettmar, J. 1986, pp. 149–58.

Parkes, P. (1987) 'Livestock Symbolism and Pastoral Ideology among the Kafirs of the Hindu Kush.' *Man*. 22, pp. 637–60.

Parkes, P. (1991) 'Temple of Imra, Temple of Mahandeu: A Kafir sanctuary in Kalasha cosmology.' *Bulletin of the School of Oriental and African Studies*. 54, 1, pp. 75–103.

Parkes, P. (1992) 'Reciprocity and Redistribution in Kalasha Prestige Feasts.' *Anthropozoologica*. 16, pp. 37–46.

Parkes, P. (1994) 'Personal and Collective Identity in Kalasha Song Performance: The Significance of Music-Making in a Minority Enclave.' In:

Stokes, M. (ed.), *Ethnicity, Identity and Music*, pp. 157–87. Berg. Oxford/ Providence.

Parkes, P. (1996a) 'Kalasha Oral Literature and Praise Songs.' In: Bashir & Israr-ud-Din 1996.

Parkes, P. (1996b) 'Indigenous Polo and the Politics of Regional Identity in Northern Pakistan.' In: MacClancy, J. (ed.), *Sport, Identity and Ethnicity*, pp. 43–67. Oxford.

Parkes, P. (1997) 'Kalasha Domestic Society: Practice, Ceremony and Domain.' In: Donhan, H. & F. Selier (eds.), *Family and Gender in Pakistan: Domestic Organization in a Muslim Society*, pp. 25–63. New Delhi.

Parkes, P. (2008) 'A Minority Perspective on the History of Chitral: Katore Rule in Kalasha Tradition.' In: Israr-ud-Din 2008.

Parpola, A (2015) *The Roots of Hinduism. The Early Aryans and the Indus Civilization.* Oxford University Press. New Delhi.

Pensa, C. (1974) 'Considerazioni sul tema della bipolarità nelle religioni indiane.' *Gururajamanjarika, Studi in onore di Giuseppe Tucci*, vol. II. Istituto Universitario Orientale. Naples.

Perrot, M. (2001) *Etnologia del Natale*. Elèuthera. Grasset & Fasquelle. Or. ed. 2000.

Pettazzoni, R. (1957) *L'Essere Supremo nelle religioni primitive*. Einaudi. Turin.

Piasere, L. (2002) *L'etnografo imperfetto*. Laterza. Rome – Bari.

Pitrè, G. (1978) *Spettacoli e feste popolari siciliane*. Il Vespro. Palermo. Or. ed. 1870–1913.

Polo, M. (2005) *Il Milione*. Turin. Einaudi.

Poppi, C. (2006) 'La maschera dell'Europa: riti invernali e identità culturali.' In: Kezich & Poppi (eds.), *Demoni pastori e fantasmi contadini*. esaExpo. Civezzano (TN).

Pratt, M. L. (1986) 'Fieldwork in Common Places.' In Clifford & Marcus 1986.

Propp, V. (1978) *Feste agrarie russe*. Dedalo. Bari. Or. ed. Leningrad, 1963.

Quigley, D. (1993) *The Interpretation of Caste*. Oxford University Press. Oxford.

Rabinow, P. (1977) *Reflections on Fieldwork in Morocco*. University of California Press. Berkeley.

Rappaport, R.A. (1971) 'Ritual, Sanctity and Cybernetics.' *American Anthropologist*. New Series, 73, 1, pp. 59–76.

Rappaport, R.A. (1984) *Pigs for the Ancestors*. Yale University Press. New Haven. Or. ed. 1968.

Rappaport, R.A. (1999) *Ritual and Religion in the Making of Humanity.* Cambridge University Press. Cambridge.

Raverty, H.G. (1888) *Notes on Afghanistan and Part of Baluchistan, Geographical, Ethnographical and Historical, Extracted from the Writings of Little known Afghan and Tajik Historians.* London. Repr. Lahore, 1976.

Renfrew, C. (1987) *Archaeology and Language.* Cambridge University Press. Cambridge & New York.

Rennell, J. (1792) *Memoir of a Map of Hindoostan; or the Mogul Empire. The Second Edition. With very considerable additions, and many corrections.* London.

Rensch, C.R., S.J. Decker & D.G. Hallberg (1992) *Languages of Kohistan. Sociolinguistic Survey of Northern Pakistan.* 5 vols., vol. 1. Islamabad.

Robertson, G.S. (1896) *The Kafirs of the Hindu Kush.* Lawrence & Bullen. London. Repr. Oxford University Press. Karachi, 1974.

Robertson, G.S. (1898) *Chitral. The Story of a Minor Siege.* London.

Ruhlen, m. (2001) *L'origine delle lingue.* Adelphi. Milan. Or. Ed. 1994.

Sabatucci, D. (1998) *Il politeismo.* 2 vols. Bulzoni. Rome.

Sahlins, M. (1980) *L'economia dell'età della pietra.* Bompiani. Milan. Or. ed. 1972.

Saifullah Jan (1996) 'History and Development of the Kalasha.' In: Bashir & Israr-ud-Din 1996, pp. 239–45.

Sanga, G. (1982) 'Personata Libido.' *La Ricerca Folklorica*, 6, pp. 5–20.

Sanjek, R. (1990) (ed.) *Fieldnotes. The Makings of Anthropology.* Cornell University Press. Ithaca and London.

Scarcia, G. (1965) *Sifat-Nama-yi Darvis Muhammad Han-i Gazi.* Is.M.E.O. Rome.

Scarduelli, P. (2007) (ed.) *Antropologia del rito.* Boringhieri. Turin.

Schomberg, R.C.F. (1935) *Between the Oxus and the Indus.* London. Repr. Lahore, n.d.

Schomberg, R.C.F. (1938) *Kafirs and Glaciers, Travels in Chitral.* London.

Scialpi, F. (1989) 'La Grande Madre nella cultura induista.' In: Giani Gallino, T. (ed.), *Le Grandi Madri*, pp. 47–64. Feltrinelli. Milan.

Sen, A. (2006) *Identità e violenza.* Laterza. Bari. Or. ed. New York & London, 2006.

Seppilli, T. (1984) 'Trasgressioni rituali e controllo sociale.' In: *Il mondo alla rovescia ovvero la trasgressione controllata.* Catalogo della 2° Rassegna internazionale di documentari cinematografici e televisivi. Istituto Superiore Regionale Etnografico. Nuoro.

Sergent, B. (1996) *Homosexualité et initiation chez les peuples indo-européens*. Payot et Rivages. Paris.

Sergent, B. (1997) *Genèse de l'Inde*. Payot & Rivages. Paris.

Sergent, B. (2005) *Les Indo-Européens*. Payot & Rivages. Paris.

Shah, W.A. (1974) 'Notes on Kalash Folklore.' In: Jettmar & Edelberg 1974, pp. 69–80.

Siiger, H. (1956) 'Ethnological Field Research in Chitral, Sikkim and Assam.' *Det Kongelige Danske Videnskabernes Selskab*. 35, 2, pp. 5–35.

Siiger, H. (1963) 'Shamanism among the Kalash Kafirs of Chitral.' *Folk*. 5, pp. 295–303.

Siiger, H. (1967) 'Shamanistic Ecstasy and Supernatural Beings. A Study Based on Field-Work among the Kalash Kafirs of Chitral from the Third Danish Expedition to Central Asia 1947–54.' *Scripta Instituti Donneriani Aboensis*. 1, pp. 69–81.

Siiger, H. (1974) 'The Joshi of the Kalash. Main Traits of the Spring Festival at Balangru in 1948.' In Jettmar & Edelberg 1974.

Siiger H., S. Castenfeldt, M. Fentz (1991) 'Small Functional Items and Regeneration of Society. Dough Figurines from the Kalash People of Chitral, Northern Pakistan.' *Folk*, 33, pp. 37–66.

Smith, A. D. (1998) *Le origini etniche delle nazioni*. Il Mulino. Bologna. Or. Ed. 1986. Oxford.

Smith, P. (1988) 'Aspetti dell'organizzazione dei riti.' In: Izard, M. & P. Smith [1979] 1988, pp. 131–79.

Snoy, P. (1959) 'Last Pagans of the Hindu Kush.' *Natural History*. 68, 9, pp. 520–9.

Snoy, P. (1960) 'Kalasch – Nordwestpakistan (Chitral).' *Almauftrieb mit Opfern. Encyclopaedia Cinematografica*. 3, 12. Gottingen.

Snoy, P. (1965) 'Das Buch der Kalasch.' *'Ruperto-Carola'. Mitteilungen der Vereinigung der Freunde der Studentenschaft der Universität Heidelberg*. 38, pp. 158–62.

Snoy, P. (1974) 'Dizila Wat!' In: Jettmar, K. & L. Edelberg 1974, pp. 84–6.

Snoy, P. (1993) 'Alpwirtschaft im Hindukusch und Karakorum.' In: Schweinfurth, U. *Neue Forschungen im Himalaya*. Erdkundliches Wissen. Vol. 112., pp. 49–73. Stuttgart.

Snoy, P. (2008) The Rites of the Winter Solstice among the Kalash of Bumburet. In: *Journal of Asian Civilizations*, XXXI, 1–2, pp. 36–64. Islamabad.

Sordi, I. (1982) 'Dinamiche del carnevale.' *La ricerca folklorica*, 6, pp. 21–36.

Spineto, N. (2005). *Dioniso a teatro: il contesto festivo del dramma greco.* L'Erma di Bretschneider. Rome.

Staal, F. (1979) 'The Meaninglessness of Ritual.' *Numen.* 26, 1, pp. 2–22.

Staley, J. (1964) 'The Pool Festival of the Kalash of Birir.' *Folklore.* 74, pp. 197–202.

Staley, J. (1982) *Words for My Brother.* Oxford University Press. Karachi.

Stein, M.A. (1921) *Serindia. Detailed Report of Explorations in Central Asia and Westernmost China.* 4 vols., vol. 1. Oxford.

Strand, R.F. (1973) 'Notes on the Nuristani and Dardic Languages.' *Journal of the American Oriental Society.* 93, 3, pp. 297–305.

Strand, R.F. (2001) The Tongues of Peristan. In: Cacopardo, A.M. & A.S. Cacopardo 2001, pp. 251–9.

Strand, R.F. (1997–2008): *Nuristan. Hidden Land of the Hindu-Kush.* http:// users.sedona.net/~strand/index.html

Stutley, M. & J. Stutley (1980) *Dizionario dell'Induismo.* Ubaldini. Rome. Or. ed. Routledge & Kegan Paul. London, 1977.

Tacito Cornelio, see Canali, L.

Tambiah, S.J. (1995) *Rituali e cultura.* Il Mulino. Bologna. Or. ed. Cambridge (Mass.), 1985.

Tedlock, D. (2002) *Verba manent.* L'ancora. Naples. Or. Ed. Philadelphia 1983.

Thapar, R. (1966) *A History of India.* Vol. 1. Penguin Books. Harmondsworth.

Thornton, E. (1844) *A Gazetteer of the Countries Adjacent to India on the North-West.* Vol. 1. London.

Toschi, P. (1976) *Le origini del teatro italiano.* 2 vols. Bollati Boringhieri. Turin. Or. ed. 1955.

Trail, G. (1996) *Tsyam Revisited.* In: Bashir & Israr-ud-Din 1996.

Trail, R. (1996) 'Kalasha Case-Marking System'. In: Bashir & Israr-ud-Din 1996.

Trail, R.L. & G.R. Cooper (1999) *Kalasha Dictionary.* Summer Institute of Linguistics and National Institute of Pakistan Studies. Islamabad.

Tucci, G. (1956) *Preliminary Report on Two Scientific Expeditions in Nepal.* Is.M.E.O. Rome.

Tucci, G. (1963) 'Oriental Notes (II). An Image of a Devi discovered in Swat and Some Connected Problems.' *East & West.* 14, 3/4, pp. 146–82.

Tucci, G. (1977) 'On Swat. The Dards and Connected Problems.' *East & West.* 27, 1/4, pp. 9–104.

Tucci, G. (1977) *Nepal: alla scoperta del regno dei Malla.* Newton Compton. Rome.

Tucci, G. (1978) *La via dello Swat*. Newton Compton. Rome.

Tullio-Altan, C. (1992) *Soggetto, simbolo e valore*. Feltrinelli. Milan.

Tullio-Altan, C. (1995) *Ethnos e civiltà*. Feltrinelli. Milan.

Turner, R.L. (1966) *A Comparative Dictionary of Indo-Aryan Languages*. Oxford University Press. London.

Turner, V. (1967) *The Forest of Symbols*. Cornell University Press. Cornell.

Turner, V. (1986) *Dal rito al teatro*. Il Mulino. Bologna. Or. ed. New York, 1982.

Turner, V. (1990) *Le phénomène rituel*. Presses Universitaires de France. Paris. Or. ed. USA, 1969.

Turville-Petre, E.O.G. (1964) *Myth and Religion of the North*. Greenwood Press. Westport.

Van Gennep, A. (1981) *I riti di passaggio*. Boringhieri. Turin. Or. ed. Emile Nourry. Paris, 1909.

Van Gennep, A. (1958) *Manuel de folklore français contemporain. Cycle des douze jours: Noël*. Vol. 7, 1. Picard. Paris. Repr. 1987.

Van Gennep, A. (1988) *Manuel de folklore français contemporain. Cycle des douze jours: de Noël aux Rois*. Vol. 8, 1. Picard. Paris.

Van Gennep, A. (1998) *Le folklore français. Du berceau à la tombe. Cycle de Carnaval-Carême et Pâque*. Editions Robert Laffont. Paris. Or. ed. Picard, 1943.

Van Gennep, A. (1999) *Le folklore français. Cycle de mai, de la Saint-Jean, de l'été et de l'automne*. Editions Robert Laffont. Paris. Or. ed. Picard, 1949.

Vansina, J.C. (1976) *La tradizione orale. Saggio di metodologia storica*. Officina Edizioni. Rome. Or. ed. Musée Royal de l'Afrique Centrale, Tervuren 1961.

Vansina, J.C. (1985) *Oral Tradition as History*, James Curry. London. Heinemann Kenya. Nairobi.

van Skyhawk, H. (2003) *Burushaski-Texte aus Hispar*. Harrassowitz. Wiesbaden.

Viazzo, P.P. (1990) *Comunità alpine*. Il Mulino. Bologna. Or. ed. Cambridge University Press. Cambridge, 1989.

Watts, A. (1978) *The Two Hands of God*. Rider & Company. London. Or. ed. New York, 1963.

Wessels, C. (1997) *Early Jesuit Travellers in Central Asia, 1603–1721*. Asian Educational Services. New Delhi. Or. ed. Martinus Nijhoff. The Hague, 1924.

Wittgenstein (1975) *Note sul 'Ramo d'oro' di Frazer*. Milan. Or. ed. 1967.

Witzel, M. (2004) The Rgvedic Religious System. In: Griffiths, A. & J.E.M. Houben (eds..), *The Vedas, Texts, Language & Ritual. Proceedings of the Third International Vedic Workshop, Leiden 2002.* Egbert Forsten, Groningen.

Wolff, J. (1852) *Narrative of a Mission to Bokhara in the years 1843–45.* 7th ed. Repr. *A Mission to Bokhara. Edited and abridged with an introduction by G. Wint.* London, 1969. Or. Ed. 1845.

Wood, John (1872). *A Journey to the Sources of the River Oxus: New Edition, Edited by His Son, with an Essay on the Geography of the Valley of the Oxus by Colonel Henry Yule.* London: John Murray. Or. Ed. 1841.

Wutt, K. (1976) 'Über Zeichen und Ornamente der Kalash in Chitral.' *Archiv für Völkerkunde.* 30, pp. 137–73.

Wutt, K. (1983) 'Chaumos = "Vier Mal Fleisch": Notizen zum Winterlichen Festkalender der Kalash von Bumburet, Chitral.' *Archiv für Völkerkunde.* 37, pp. 107–48.

Younghusband, F.E. & G.J. Younghusband (1895) *The Relief of Chitral.* London. Repr. Islamabad, 1976.

Index

Note: *n* following a page number denotes a footnote with the relevant number.